{the art of charcuterie

the art of charcuterie

JOHN KOWALSKI

AND The Culinary Institute of America

WILEY

JOHN WILEY & SONS, INC.

The Culinary Institute of America

President	Dr. Tim Ryan '77
Vice-President, Dean of Culinary Education	Mark Erickson '77
Senior Director, Educational Enterprises	Susan Cussen
Director of Publishing	Nathalie Fischer
Editorial Project Manager	Lisa Lahey '00
Editorial Assistants	Shelly Malgee '08
	Erin Jeanne McDowell '08

Published by John Wiley & Sons, Inc., Hoboken, New Jersey

Published simultaneously in Canada

For general information on our other products and services or for technical support, please contact our Customer Care Department within the United States at (800) 762-2974, outside the United States at (317) 572-3993 or fax (317) 572-4002.

Wiley also publishes its books in a variety of electronic formats. Some content that appears in print may not be available in electronic books. For more information about Wiley products, visit our web site at www.wiley.com.

Library of Congress Cataloging-in-Publication Data:
Kowalski, John, 1954-
 The art of charcuterie / The Culinary Institute of America and John Kowalski.
  p. cm.
 Includes index.
 ISBN 978-0-470-19741-7 (cloth)
 1. Meat--Preservation. 2. Fishery products--Preservation 3. Cookery (Cold dishes) I. Culinary Institute of America. II. Title.
 TX612.M4K73 2010
 641.7'9--dc22
                        2009013399

Printed in the United States

10 9 8 7 6 5

I would like to dedicate this book to my parents in deep appreciation for the love and guidance they've shown over my lifetime. They taught me that the difference between the impossible and the possible lies in a person's determination. To my mother and father — Maria and Mieczyslaw "Mitch" Kowalski.

acknowledgments

I would like to offer my deeply felt thanks to the following people. Many individuals and organizations contributed generously to this work. Without them and their input, this book would never have been started, let alone completed.

The administration, faculty, staff, and students of The Culinary Institute of America all touched and influenced this work. Having the knowledge and abilities of all these individuals at my disposal was an invaluable asset.

My son Michael Kowalski deserves special credit for his countless hours spent editing drafts and giving focus to my writing, as well as providing occasional scientific insight. Without his help, I would never have undertaken and finished the project.

Many thanks to my colleagues in the Garde Manger Department for supporting my efforts and sharing their opinions and expertise.

The staff of the Food and Beverage Institute had a great deal to with the production of this volume and deserve my thanks. In particular, Lisa Lahey and Maggie Wheeler, who both gave me the final push to commit to writing this book.

Nathalie Fisher for donating her hard work and time in the production of this book.

My colleague Henry Rapp, for his friendship and professional advice, along with supplying the recipes for Chicken Sausage with Plums and Ginger (page 251), Chicken Sausage with Mushrooms and Asiago (page 246), and Buffalo Wing–Style Sausages (page 244).

The following people played key roles in assisting with formula development, photography, or both: Kate Chappell, Sarah Thompson, Paige Bodtke, Laura Alexander, and Paul Moncebo. I thank them for their patience and their ability to change midstream with the recipes.

The following individuals and companies outside The Culinary Institute of America also made important contributions to this work.

The stunning photography of Ben Fink graces the pages of this book and brings life to it.

For sharing their knowledge and enthusiasm, I thank Bruce Armstrong from Saratoga Food Specialties for his input on spices and flavorings and Robert Rust and Rust Associates for help with sausage making and casing information and the ideas for moisture-enhanced fresh pork, turkey, and beef. Robert was my sounding board and for that he deserves another thanks.

Doctor Roger Mandigo, University of Nebraska, for his input on sausage formulation, meat emulsions, and batter technology.

For their help in providing equipment for this project, I thank Ted Vaughn and World Pac International USA.

Dr. James Lamkey of Chris Hansen for his help with starter cultures and the white mold for salamis.

My greatest thanks, however, go to my family, for putting up with me during the frustrating and fruitful times I endured in this process and for their continuous support.

introduction

The art and practice of the production of charcuterie, involving the chemical preservation of meats as a means for the total utilization of various meat products, goes back to ancient times. Today the art of charcuterie can provide a chef with a means to provide the diner with uniquely flavorful options while utilizing the highest quality ingredients.

The trade of *charcutier* goes back at least as far as classical Rome. In such a large town, slaughterhouses, butchers, and cooked-meat shops were well organized to safeguard public health. This system was still being followed—after a fashion—in medieval Paris, although in the Middle Ages a great increase in cooked-meat purveyors put an intolerable strain on such control as there was. From this chaos, the charcutiers emerged and banded together, by edict of the king in 1476, for the sale of cooked-pork meat products and raw pork fat. But they did not have the right to slaughter the pigs they needed, which put them at the mercy of the general butchers until the next century. At the beginning of the seventh century, charcutiers gained the right to sell all cuts of uncooked pork, not just the fat. And since during Lenten time meat sales declined, charcutiers were allowed to sell salted herring and fish. Now the trade could develop in a logical manner.

By the eighteenth century, the charcutier was closely connected with two other cooked-meat sellers. The *tripier* bought the insides of all animals from both the butcher and charcutier and sold cooked tripe; the *traiteur* bought raw meat of all kinds and sold it cooked in sauce as ragoûts, either to be eaten at home or on his premises. At this time private kitchens in the city were in a poor state, and often nonexistent; people sent out to the cooked food shops for their prepared dishes. This was starting to become a big trade, and each set of tradesmen jealously guarded their growing businesses.

The art of charcuterie now falls in the domain of the *garde manger*, which includes the preparation of all cold items in the kitchen. Today, the resurgence in the popularity of these items is bringing about a change in the ingredients and manner of fabrication. There is a wider array of seasonings and herbs used to create fresher and lighter fare. Sausages are now made with seafood ingredients, or constructed in such a way as to reflect a healthier style of eating. Even when traditional techniques, flavor profiles, and recipes are still used, a change can be seen in the manner of presentation. Traditional charcuterie, while still flavorful and delicious today, is often presented as smaller, more refined bites.

equipment

chapter one

This chapter describes the equipment used in preparing charcuterie
products and tells how to use it safely.

Electric meat grinders, food processors, choppers, mixers, and sausage stuffers have all but replaced the hand tools once used to make sausages and other forcemeats. These tools are certainly great for saving time and labor, but even more important, they produce charcuterie of superior quality to those made by the laborious process the original charcutiers and garde manger chefs knew.

To maintain safe operation and food safety, use the following guidelines:

1. Make sure all equipment is in excellent condition. Evaluate any machinery you use in the kitchen and consider its functionality and safety as part of a standard checklist. Are the blades sharp? Are all the safety features fully functional? Are the cords and plugs in good repair?

2. Make sure the equipment is scrupulously clean before setting to work. Every part of the equipment must be thoroughly cleaned and sanitized between uses. Cross contamination is a serious problem, especially for foods as highly processed and handled as sausages.

3. Chill any part of the machine that comes into direct contact with the sausage ingredients. Place grinder parts in the freezer or refrigerator, or chill equipment rapidly by placing it in a clean sink or container of ice water. Remember that if your sausage mixture becomes warm during production, you may need to cool both the mixture and the equipment before continuing.

4. Choose the right tool for the job. Do not overload your equipment. If you do not have equipment large enough to handle bulk recipes, break the formula down into batches that your equipment can handle without straining.

5. Assemble equipment correctly. Novices often make the mistake of improperly setting up the grinder blade and die/plate assembly. Be certain that the blade is sitting flush against the die. This cuts the food neatly, rather than tearing or shredding it. Make sure the power is disconnected before assembling or disassembling the equipment.

6. Always turn off the power before assembling, cleaning, or servicing equipment.

7. Use the tamper, never your hands, to feed food into a grinder.

Before you begin grinding, chill the grinder parts in ice water.

Dice the meat and other required ingredients to a size that fits the feed tube, and chill or semifreeze before grinding.

Assembling the grinder correctly is key. Be sure that the die is sitting flush against the blade.

Grind to the desired texture.

Once the meat is properly ground, mix it long enough to distribute the fat and lean components evenly, and add any liquids slowly.

Mise en place for grinding: cubed
meat and fat, seasonings, and
marinade ingredients

MEAT GRINDER ASSEMBLY

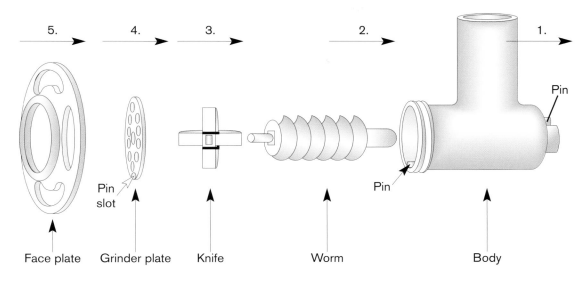

5. →   4. →   3. →   2. →   1. →

Pin

Pin
slot

Pin

Face plate   Grinder plate   Knife   Worm   Body

PROPER GRINDING PROCEDURE

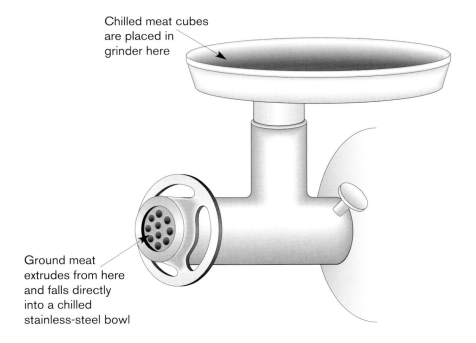

Chilled meat cubes
are placed in
grinder here

Ground meat
extrudes from here
and falls directly
into a chilled
stainless-steel bowl

grinders, cutters, and choppers

buffalo chopper

A buffalo chopper, also known as a food cutter or bowl cutter, is a high-speed bulk chopper and mixer. It is a large, typically cast-aluminum machine with a stainless-steel bowl and blades. It has a main body encasing an engine, as well as an inset bowl, bowl cover, knife shaft, and blades. The bowl of the buffalo chopper rotates and helps to carry the food under the machine's blades. The rotating bowl (20 to 24 rpm) and revolving knives (1,725 rpm) make short work of meats, vegetables, and other food items, reducing them to uniformly small pieces.

BUFFALO CHOPPER

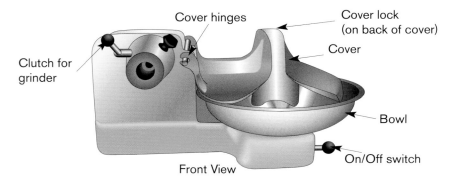

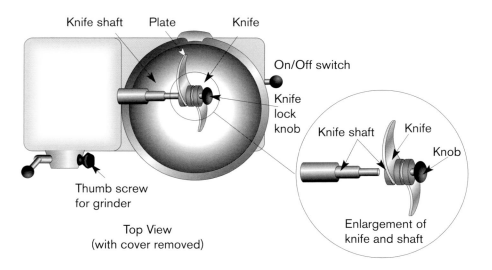

grinding plates and knives

The grinding plates (also sometimes referred to as dies) and knives are the most important parts of a grinding machine. Plates and knives require special care in a kitchen. They can be misplaced and can rust quickly if not properly taken care of. Cleaning the plates and knives is particularly important because cross contamination is a big problem, especially when dealing with meats. The plates and knives should be cleaned thoroughly and then dried in an oven for a few minutes.

It is important to chill the plate and blade before grinding.

After the grinder is set up and the grinding process begins, the knife cuts the meat and the meat forces itself out through the plate. The blades must always remain sharp. The meat must be cut into the plate instead of being squashed into the plate.

The parts of a meat grinder, from left to right: grinder housing or grinder body, worm, blade, different-size plates, and collar.

GRINDER PLATE AND SAUSAGE STUFFER NOZZLE SIZES

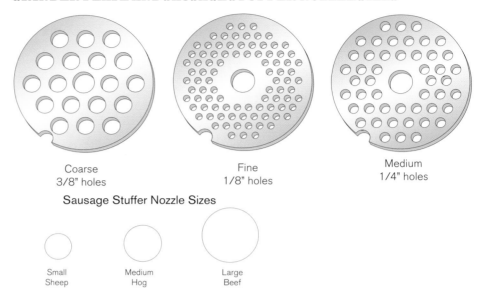

Coarse
3/8" holes

Fine
1/8" holes

Medium
1/4" holes

Sausage Stuffer Nozzle Sizes

Small
Sheep

Medium
Hog

Large
Beef

Actual Diameter of Nozzle Opening and Type

Robot Coupe

A Robot Coupe food processor houses the motor separately from the bowl, blades, and lid. Food processors can grind, purée, blend, emulsify, crush, knead, and, with special disks, slice, julienne, and shred foods. The R2 is a smaller machine than the R6, with less power that operates at one speed. The R6 is not only larger than the R2, but it also has more power and is able to operate at variable speewds.

Stephan cutter

A Stephan cutter, also known as a vertical bowl cutter mixer, consists of a stainless-steel bowl with a lockable lid pierced by a stirring arm, two blades, a timer, and a speed selector. It is used to fine-cut, mix, and emulsify, primarily in making a 5/4/3 emulsion (see "Emulsification and Binding," page 46).

mixers

These electric machines have large rotating bowls of varying capacities (5-, 10-, 20-, 40-quart/4.80-, 9.60-, 19.20-, 38.40-L). The bowl is locked in place and the beater, whip, paddle, or dough hook rotates through the contents.

standing mixer

Mixers in a butcher shop or charcuterie are usually tabletop units. Mixers are used to ensure ingredients are mixed homogenously. Although the tabletop 20-quart/19.20-L mixers are to be found in most of the kitchens, with bowls and grinding attachments, in larger operations, floor models or free-standing mixers specifically made for sausage mixing are used.

8

STEPHAN CUTTER: GENERAL ASSEMBLY

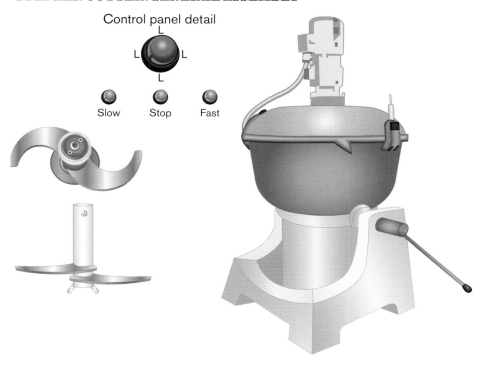

Control panel detail

L

L   L

L

Slow   Stop   Fast

stuffers and stuffing equipment

sausage stuffer (crank and pressure)

There are many sizes of sausage stuffers available. The smaller sausage stuffers are manually powered, while the larger stuffers are powered by electrohydraulics. Manual sausage stuffers can range from 5- to 20-lb/2.27- to 9.07-kg capacity.

stainless-steel table for sausage stuffing

Nearly as important as the active equipment used to grind and stuff the sausage links is the surface upon which this is taking place. A good sausage-stuffing surface must meet a few specific characteristics or else the charcuterie operation could be slowed, disrupted, or even dangerous. Any table to be used should be constructed of stainless steel. This type of material is nonabsorbent and extremely easy to clean. Raised edges around the table will help keep water on the table so that the sausages can slide easily as they come off the stuffer.

hog rings and casing clips

Hog rings and casing clips are the two kinds of closures available for crimping-sealing the ends of large sausages. Hog rings are used on the fill end of a casing at the stuffer and are used to seal the ends of the casings, keeping the juices in. A casing clip is applied to one end of a casing as it is being prepared for stuffing.

MANUAL SAUSAGE STUFFER

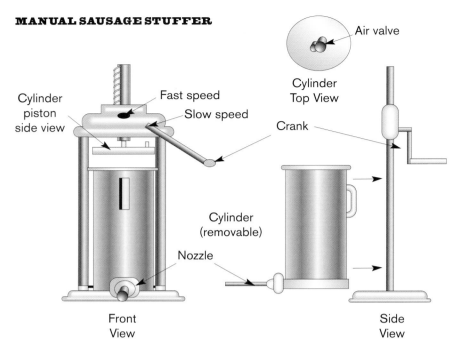

You will need hand tools to apply these closures.

Hog rings, which are versatile and attractive, come in packages of one hundred and are sized for various casings. They are often used in commercial settings when producing large amounts of sausages, such as summer sausage, where the rings are used as a reinforcement to keep the meat separated and sealed. To use hog rings, clamp the ends with hog ring pliers to seal the sausage casings.

measurement instruments

scales
Scales are used to weigh ingredients for preparation and portion control. There are different kinds of scales, such as spring, balance beam, and electronic scales.

hydrometer and hydrometer jar (salimeter)
The hydrometer measures the density or specific gravity of a liquid. It was invented by an English chemist named William Nicholson in the 1790s. When placed in liquid, the glass tube floats; the height at which it floats indicates the density of the liquid. This is useful when measuring the amount of salt or sugar in a brine. The hydrometer has the amounts labeled directly on it, given in either strengths of the brine or percentages of salinity.

pH meter and buffers
The pH meter is used to measure the acidity or alkalinity of a meat product. Meat with a higher pH reading (more alkalinity) has better water-retention properties. The pH meter is also used for dry sausage production to make sure that the meat is acidi-

fied and that it goes down below 5 percent pH level on the meter in a reasonable amount of time. This is to make sure that the meat is at a level of acidity that can prevent the growth of bacteria. The buffer is a solution that resists changes in pH, helping to create a more stable product.

For very precise work, the pH meter should be calibrated before and after each measurement. For normal use, calibration should be performed at the beginning of each day. The pH probe measures pH as the activity of hydrogen ions surrounding a thin-walled glass bulb at its tip. The probe produces a small voltage (about 0.06 volt per pH unit) that is measured and displayed as pH units by the meter. For more information about pH probes, see "glass electrode."

Calibration should be performed with at least two standard buffer solutions that span the range of pH values to be measured. For general purposes, buffers at pH 4 and pH 10 are acceptable. The pH meter has one control (calibrate) to set the meter reading equal to the value of the first standard buffer and a second control (slope), which is used to adjust the meter reading to the value of the second buffer. A third control allows the temperature to be set. Standard buffer sachets, which can be obtained from a variety of suppliers, usually state how the buffer value changes with temperature.

The calibration process correlates the voltage produced by the probe (approximately 0.06 volts per pH unit) with the pH scale. After each single measurement, the probe is rinsed with distilled water or deionized water to remove any traces of the solution being measured; blotted with a clean tissue to absorb any remaining water, which could dilute the sample and thus alter the reading; and then quickly immersed in another solution. When not in use, the probe tip must be kept wet at all times. It is typically kept immersed in an acidic solution of around pH 3.0. In an emergency, acidified tap water can be used, but distilled or deionized water must never be used for longer-term probe storage as the relatively ionless water "sucks" ions out of the probe through diffusion, which degrades it.

Occasionally (about once a month), the probe may be cleaned using pH-electrode cleaning solution; generally a 0.1 M solution of hydrochloric acid (HCl) is used(1), having a pH of about one.

relative humidity thermometer

The relative humidity thermometer is used in the charcuterie kitchen to ensure safe processing of meat, fish, and poultry. Relative humidity is a term used to describe the amount of water vapor that exists in a gaseous mixture of air and water. This is particularly important when you age sausage. You need to monitor the humidity in the area so they dry properly and do not develop case hardening. Relative humidity can be measured with the use of wet- and dry-bulb thermometers:

dry-bulb thermometer

A dry-bulb thermometer is a conventional mercury glass thermometer that measures ambient air temperature.

wet-bulb thermometer

A wet-bulb thermometer is a dry-bulb thermometer, but the bulb is kept moist by a thin cloth (e.g., muslin) bag connected by a wick to a bath of clean (preferably distilled) water. The thermometer's accuracy is dependent on making sure the thermometer is in constant contact with the pan of water.

As long as the air is not saturated, evaporation from the muslin keeps the wet-bulb thermometer at a lower temperature than the dry-bulb thermometer beside it, with which its readings are compared. The depression of the wet-bulb temperature gives a measure of the saturation deficit, from which the relative humidity and dew point can be calculated.

Thermometers

Thermometers are essential for charcuterie preparations; you need to have the correct temperature of the product whether it needs to be cold or hot. There are different types and styles of thermometers, each varying in technology and price, such as digital, dial, candy/deep-fry, oven-safe, and instant-read thermometers. Instant-read thermometers are used to test the internal temperature of food products.

thermocouples

Thermocouples are able to read and display the final temperature in two to five seconds. The temperature results will be displayed on a digital panel. A thermocouple thermometer measures temperature at the junction of two fine wires found at the tip of the probe. Thermocouples used in scientific laboratories have very thin probes, similar to hypodermic needles, while others may have a thickness of $^{1}/_{16}$ inch.

Since thermocouple thermometers are able to respond so quickly, the temperature can be checked faster in different parts of the food to ensure that it is thoroughly cooked. This is very useful for cooking large foods, such as turkeys or roasts, which require temperatures to be read in more than one place. The thin probe of the thermocouple also enables it to accurately read the temperature of thinner foods like hamburger patties, pork chops, and chicken breasts.

Thermocouple thermometers are not designed to remain in the food during cooking. They should be used during the end of the cooking time to get the final temperatures. Always check the temperature before the food is expected to finish cooking to prevent any overcooking.

water movement meter

measuring water activity (AW)

The water activity (aw) represents the ratio of the water vapor pressure of the food to the water vapor pressure of pure water under the same conditions, and it is expressed as a fraction.

The water activity scale extends from 0 (bone dry) to 1.0 (pure water), but most foods have a water activity level in the range of 0.2 for very dry foods to 0.99 for moist fresh foods. Water activity is in practice usually measured as equilibrium relative humidity (ERH).

If we multiply the ratio by 100, we obtain the equilibrium relative humidity (ERH) that the foodstuff would produce if enclosed with air in a sealed container at constant temperature. Thus, a food with an aw of 0.7 would produce an ERH of 70 percent.

predicting food spoilage

Water activity has its most useful application in predicting the growth of bacteria, yeasts, and molds. For a food to have a useful shelf life without relying on refrigerated storage, it is necessary to control either its acidity level (pH) or the level of water activity (aw), or a suitable combination of the two. This can effectively increase the product's stability and make it possible to predict its shelf life under known ambient storage conditions. Food can be made safe to store by lowering the water activity to a point that will not allow dangerous pathogens such as *Clostridium botulinum* and *Staphylococcus aureus* to grow in it. We also know that *Clostridium botulinum*, the most dangerous food-poisoning bacterium, is unable to grow at an aw of .93 and below.

The risk of food poisoning must be considered in low acid foods (pH > 4.5) with a water activity greater than 0.86 aw. *Staphylococcus aureus*, a common food-poisoning organism, can grow down to this relatively low water activity level. Foods that may support the growth of this bacterium include cheese and fermented sausages stored above correct refrigeration temperatures.

refrigeration

Maintaining adequate refrigerated storage is crucial to any food-service operation. It is especially important when processing meats because of the dangers of cross contamination and bacterial growth. All units should be maintained properly, which means regular and thorough cleaning

on-site refrigeration

Refrigerated drawers or under-the-counter reach-ins allow ingredients in the prep area to be held at the proper temperature.

portable refrigeration

A refrigerated cart can be placed as needed in the kitchen.

reach-in

A reach-in may be a single unit or part of a bank of units, available in many sizes. Units with pass-through doors are especially helpful for the pantry or prep area, where cold items can be retrieved as needed.

walk-in

This is the largest style of refrigeration unit and usually has shelves arranged along the interior walls. It is possible to zone a walk-in to maintain appropriate temperature and humidity levels for storing various foods. Some walk-ins are large enough to accommodate rolling carts for additional storage. Some units have pass-through or reach-in doors to facilitate access to frequently required items. Walk-ins may be situated in the kitchen or outside the facility.

other equipment

brine pump

The brine pump is one of the most-used tools for brining, to inject brine into the meat for more uniform distribution. A brine pump consists of a plunger, cylinder, strainer, hose, and needle. Brine pumps come in different volume sizes.

brine tubs

Brine tubs (also known as curing tubs) are large containers used to hold pieces of meat submerged in a brine. They come in a variety of sizes. Brine tubs should only be used for brining or salting items.

sausage sticks

Sausage sticks are stainless metal rods used for smoking and drying sausages. Sausage sticks may be used to suspend other items in the smoker as well.

bacon combs

Bacon combs are used to hang bacon and consist of about six or so pointy hooks attached to one hook. The six or so hooks penetrate the bacon and hold it up. The one hook attaches itself onto sausage sticks so the bacon can air-dry or be cold- or hot-smoked.

skin buckets

Skin buckets are used to store and transport sausage casings. Casings should be sorted by their size and type, and the buckets labeled clearly and covered. The only use for these buckets would then be for storing casings.

smokehouse

Several types of smokehouses are available for both at-home chefs and commercial settings. The basic features shared by all are a smoke source, a smoke chamber where the food is exposed, circulation, and ventilation. A commercial smokehouse will have fans inside to dry the product and have dampers to control the moisture in the smoker. A smoke chamber is usually outside of the smokehouse.

spray head and hose

This equipment is usually used at the end of the sausage-making process to spray cold water on sausages to cool them after smoking to bring them quickly to a food-safe temperature for storage. Other sausages might need a warm-water shower during processing to maintain the correct balance of relative humidity and water activity. Some sausages require a cool shower as they come out of the smoker, while others need a warm shower during the smoking phrase. To use, the spray head is attached to a hose and the hose is attached to the water faucet.

BRINING SYSTEMS

Commercial operations use a variety of high-production brining systems. In some, vacuum pressure is used to force brine into the meat. Another process, known as artery pumping, was introduced by a New Zealand undertaker named Kramlich in 1973. In this method, brine is injected through the arterial system. Stitch pumps inject brine via a single needle inserted into the meat at specific points. Multiple needle pumps rapidly inject meats through a large number of evenly spaced offset needles.

vacuum massage tumblers

Vacuum massage tumblers are used in the charcuterie kitchen to assist in marinating, adding cure, and adding flavor to meat products. The goal of massage tumbling is to bring salt-soluble proteins to the surface of the meat without damaging the tissue. Once these proteins have been brought to the surface, they can absorb water and dissolved seasonings into the meat for better-tasting products.

Pieces of meat to be treated are placed into a tumbling drum that rotates around a horizontal axis. The drum is sealed by a water- and airtight door that can be opened and closed as needed. This drum contains evenly spaced toothed rods parallel to the axis of rotation. Upon rotation of the drum, the teeth produce a mass of small cuts in the surface of the meat. The drum is sealed by a watertight door that can be readily opened and closed, as needed.

teasing needle

A teasing needle is a tapering needle mounted in a handle and used for teasing or letting the air out of the sausage (casing) when it has been filled so there are no air pockets. These needles come in different shapes; older kinds will have three needles attached or mounted in the handle.

spice grinder

A coffee grinder can be used as a spice grinder to grind dry spices into powder.

bar blender

Blenders have become a must-have item in every kitchen, bar, coffee shop, and many other food-service establishments. Whether you need a classic bar blender, a durable food blender, or a slick, trendy immersion blender, these work to make chickpea flour from chickpeas or to make paste from herbs to rub on products.

mortar and pestle

A mortar and pestle is a tool used to crush, grind, and mix substances. The pestle is a heavy stick whose end is used for pounding and grinding, and the mortar is a bowl. The substance is ground between the pestle and the mortar.

spices, herbs, & seasonings

{ chapter two

We will explore the seasonings most often used in sausages and meat products and the flavors commonly associated with certain processed meats.

commonly used spices and herbs

mustard

Mustard is one of the most common spices used in the meat industry. Mustard is considered an emulsifier and is used in just about every recipe. It is grown in Montana, North Dakota, and the adjoining Canadian provinces. Mustard has little flavor, but it is important because it contains 29 percent protein. The advantages of using mustard are this additional protein, which can be added to meat emulsions, and mustard's binding ability. There is, however, an active enzyme in mustard that creates acid that, in higher concentrations, will break down a meat emulsion. In order to use more mustard in an emulsion, the mustard needs to be "deheated." The mustard is heated to 150°F/66°C, which deactivates the enzyme and increases the binding ability. Adding mustard to a product helps save a small amount of money due to the binding ability and extra protein.

black pepper

Black pepper is picked earlier than white pepper. Black pepper is used for its spicy, pungent flavor. It is the most important spice because it is used in almost all sausage products. It is used at levels of 2 to 8 oz/57 to 227 g per 100 lb/45.36 kg meat, with 4 oz/113 g being the most common.

white pepper

White pepper is the ripe form of black pepper. It is used when dark specks of black pepper are not desired in a product. It is a mature berry with a mild, less-imposing flavor than black pepper. Its mature flavor is sometimes described as "musty."

red pepper

Red pepper is used for the sensations of heat and tickling in the throat. When used in smaller amounts, the product will have the tickling sensation without the burn. A small amount (½ to ¾ oz/14 to 21 g) per 100 lb/45.36 kg will give a seasoned product more heat sensation. Red pepper is commonly used in crushed (flake) form to aid visual appearance. If the heat of the red pepper is not desired, alcohol may be added to eliminate the heat while maintaining the appearance.

paprika

Though paprika has a sweet, aromatic, and pleasantly spicy flavor, it is used in the meat industry for its color as well as flavor. This pepper is very mild compared with cayenne and chile peppers.

nutmeg or mace

This is the flavor most commonly associated with hot dogs, bologna, and similar sausages. Mace and nutmeg come from the same tree. Mace is the lacy, bright aril (lace-like covering) that surrounds the nutmeg. Mace is used when the dark color of nutmeg is a disadvantage and when a more delicate flavor is desired. Both nutmeg and mace are highly fragrant. Mace has a rich smooth flavor while nutmeg has slightly bitter undertones.

The tongue is divided into four general regions of taste:

SWEETNESS: Tip of the tongue

SALTINESS: Front edge of the tongue

BITTERNESS: Rear edge of the tongue

SOUR: Across rear of tongue

UMAMI: Center of tongue

Everyone experiences these basic sensations; they are biologically built in. But spices and other flavors in meat products require training to recognize as these tastes. Some spices and herbs taste sweet, some taste bitter, some are pungent (strong or sharp flavor), and some are aromatic (distinctive, savory smell).

Most spices that are sweet are also aromatic, such as cinnamon and coriander. A few are sweet and pungent, such as nutmeg and mace. Some herbs, such as sage, are bitter as well as aromatic.

THE SENSE OF SMELL AS IT RELATES TO TASTE

As we experience the taste of something, in many instances up to 75 percent of that experience is actually the smell, or the aromatic properties of the food rather than the flavors picked up by the preceptors related through the tongue.

While taste buds allow us to perceive only bitter, salty, sweet, and sour, our sense of smell is much more refined and offers the brain more complex information.

coriander

Whole or ground seeds, coriander has a sweet, floral flavor. As fresh leaves, it is known as cilantro. It is the flavor of some hot dogs, bologna, and smoked sausages. Coriander complements nutmeg very well.

garlic

This is a bulb that has a strong flavor and is available fresh, granulated, and powdered. Garlic has been used throughout recorded history for both culinary and medicinal purposes. It is closely related to onions, shallots, and leeks, and has a strong and hearty flavor. Its pungent, spicy flavor mellows and sweetens considerably with cooking. The garlic bulb, the most commonly used part of the plant, is divided into numerous fleshy sections called cloves.

Garlic is most often used in beef sausages and products that are eaten cold. It is useful in avoiding the tallow flavor of beef.

garlic flakes

Garlic flakes are also known as dehydrated minced garlic. When the flakes are rehydrated in water, they provide much of the flavor and texture of fresh garlic. For substitutions, ½ tsp/2.50 mL garlic flakes is equivalent to one clove of garlic; ½ tsp/2.50 mL dry garlic flakes is equivalent to ⅛ tsp/0.625 mL garlic powder.

garlic powder

Garlic powder is ground dehydrated garlic. It provides some of the flavor of fresh garlic, but does not provide the texture that rehydrated garlic flakes do. Garlic powder disperses well in liquids, which makes it a good choice for marinades.

garlic salt

Garlic salt is a mixture of about half garlic powder and half table salt, with the addition of an anticaking agent to keep the mixture from clumping. When substituting garlic salt in a recipe, it is important to account for the extra salt, otherwise the product will be too salty.

granulated garlic

This is a convenient and reliable product from California. Its texture is a little coarse as it is not ground as fine as garlic powder. Like garlic powder, granulated garlic provides the flavor, but not the texture, of fresh garlic. It disperses well in liquids.

sage, dried

Sage leaves are highly aromatic and fragrant, characterized by a medicinal, piney-woody flavor. Sage is available as whole leaves, rubbed (leaves are crumbled), or in ground form. It is most often used in pork sausage, but is also used in sauces and stuffings for fatty meats such as goose, duck, pork, and sausage.

chili powder

Chili powder consists of ground red chile peppers with herbs and spices. Flavors and intensity of heat will vary.

ginger

Ginger is aromatic and pungent and has a warm flavor. It can be purchased whole, powdered, or crystallized.

fennel seed

Fennel is available whole, cracked, powdered, or pollen. It has a licorice-like flavor and is most commonly used in pepperoni and Italian sausage.

other charcuterie seasonings

The following herbs, spices, and flavoring agents are also used in charcuterie for terrines, marinades, brines, and sauces.

parsley, fresh

Parsley is probably the most well-known and used herb in the United States. It is used extensively in flavoring and garnishing foods, as well as flavoring sauces, stews, and stocks. Curly leaf parsley is best known for garnishing, while flat-leaf parsley is used in bouquets garnis and other flavoring applications.

tarragon, fresh

The slender, dark green leaves of tarragon have a pleasant, anise-like flavor. Tarragon blends well with other spices. It is used in many sauces, particularly béarnaise, and is used in making tarragon vinegar. In French cuisine, it is an integral part of fines herbes and Dijon mustard as well as marinades, terrines, sausages, and sauces.

basil, fresh

Basil, also known as sweet basil, is a member of the mint family. Basil is a small, bushy plant that grows to about 2 feet/61 cm tall. Its botanical name is derived from the Greek word meaning "to be fragrant." Pesto and basil oil are examples of products made from basil. It is also used in marinades, sausages, and sauces.

thyme, fresh

The thyme plant grows to about 18 in/46 cm tall and produces small flowers that are very attractive to honeybees. The leaves measure about $\frac{1}{4}$ in/6 mm in length and $\frac{1}{10}$ in/2.5 mm in width. This a versatile herb that can be used to season almost any meat, poultry, or fish, and usually will blend well with other herbs.

marjoram, fresh

Most scientists consider marjoram to be a species of oregano. Available whole or crushed, marjoram's light grayish-green leaves have a sweet flavor, more delicate than oregano. Its flavor is mild, sweet, complex, and inviting. Marjoram is used for seasoning fish, poultry, and meats, in marinades for pork, and in fresh or smoked Polish sausage.

bay (laurel) leaves

Whole bay leaves are elliptically shaped, light green in color, and brittle when dried and are also available ground. The leaves come from an evergreen tree and have a distinctively strong, aromatic, spicy flavor. Bay leaf is the approved term for this herb, but the name "laurel" is still frequently seen. It is used in marinades, terrines, and poaching liquid.

cloves

Cloves are the dried, unopened, nail-shaped flower buds of an evergreen tree. They are reddish-brown in color, can be whole or ground, have a strong aromatic flavor and spicy aroma, and are used in seasoning sausages.

celery seed

Celery seeds are the dried fruit of a plant that is related, but not identical, to the celery plant. The tiny brown seeds have a celery-like flavor and aroma and are available whole or ground.

caraway seed

Caraway seeds are the dried fruit of an herb related to both dill and carrots. The small, tannish brown seeds have a flavor similar to a blend of dill and anise, sweet but faintly sharp.

anise seed

Whole or ground, anise is the dried, ripe fruit of an herb. The crescent-shaped seeds are unmistakably identified by their distinctive licorice-like flavor. Anise is not related to the licorice plant, whose roots are the source of true licorice. It is used in pepperoni and other sausages.

allspice

Whole or ground, allspice is a dried, unripened fruit of a small evergreen tree. The fruit is a pea-sized berry that is sun-dried to a reddish-brown color. It is called allspice because its flavor suggests a blend of cloves, cinnamon, and nutmeg. It is used in blood sausages and pepperoni.

juniper

The juniper is a small shrub, 4 to 6 feet high. It is the berry that is used dried either whole or ground. It has a slightly bitter flavor.

onion

Used fresh or cooked, onion is also available and commonly used dehydrated, chopped, or powdered. Flavor ranges from sweet and heavy to strong and hot. It is used in terrines, sausages, and marinades.

pickling spice

A mixture of whole leaves, berries, and pods, pickling spice contains a range of flavors from sweet to spicy and tangy. It is used for pickling, canning, pickles, bread, butter, tomatoes, peppers, eggs, and onions.

truffles

Truffles are one of the most expensive of the fungi, but they are packed with flavor. Raw truffles can be grated into salads or they can be chopped, sautéed, and used to flavor sauces. The flavor of truffles is complex, so they work best in delicately flavored dishes like cream sauces. Truffles are highly perishable, so you should plan to use them within a few days after buying them. To preserve them, cut the truffles into slices and add to bourbon, then use the bourbon and truffle pieces to flavor sauce. Fresh truffles are often sold in containers filled with rice. The rice absorbs some of the truffle's exquisite flavor and should be reserved for use. Morels or porcini can be substituted if truffles are not available.

herb and spice chart

NAME	TYPE	AVAILABLE FORM(S)	USAGE (SAUSAGE)
ANISE	Seed	Whole, ground, oil	Italian
BASIL	Leaf	Crushed, ground (dried)	Italian
CARDAMOM	Pod	Whole, ground	Cooked salami
CLOVE	Bud	Whole, ground	Braunschweiger
CHIVES	Leaf/Stem	Chopped (fresh, dried)	Seafood sausage
CORIANDER	Seed	Whole, ground	Frankfurter
FENNEL	Seed	Whole, ground	Italian
MACE	Membrane (covers nutmeg)	Ground	Wieners and wursts
MARJORAM	Leaf	Crushed, ground (dried)	Polish sausage
MUSTARD	Seed	Whole, ground (dry)	Summer sausage
NUTMEG	Nut	Whole, ground	Frankfurter
OREGANO	Leaf	Crushed, ground (dried)	Italian
PAPRIKA	Pod/Seed	Ground	Italian
PARSLEY	Leaf	Whole, chopped (fresh, dry)	Italian
PEPPER, CAYENNE	Pod/Seed	Ground	Cajun sausage
PEPPER, WHITE	Berry	Whole, ground	Weisswurst
PEPPERCORNS, BLACK	Berry	Whole, ground	Italian
PEPPERCORNS, GREEN	Berry	Whole (dried; in brine)	Terrine
SAGE	Leaf	Whole, rubbed, ground	Breakfast

Sweeteners
TOP ROW: Corn syrup, honey, molasses
MIDDLE ROW: Granulated sugar, maple sugar, dextrose, turbinado sugar
BOTTOM ROW: Palm sugar, jaggery, brown sugar

sugar and other sweeteners

Sweeteners, including dextrose, granulated or brown sugar, corn syrup solids, honey, and maple sugar or syrup, can be used interchangeably in most recipes. If you want to make a substitution, remember that 1 oz/28 g of dextrose is the equivalent of ²/₃ oz/21 g granulated sugar. Some sweeteners have very distinct flavors, so be certain the one you choose will add the taste you intend.

maple syrup and maple sugar

Maple syrup is made by boiling down the sap of the sugar maple tree. Once almost all the water has been boiled off, all that is left is a solid maple sugar. By composition, the sugar in the syrup and the sugar itself are about 90 percent sucrose, the remainder consisting of variable amounts of glucose and fructose. Maple sugar is about twice as sweet as standard granulated sugar. Maple sugar is difficult to make because the sugar easily burns if boiled at too high of a temperature. It is often used as an alternative to granulated sugar.

brown sugar

Brown sugar is a mixture of superfine sugar and molasses. It contains from 3.5 percent molasses (light brown sugar) to 6.5 percent molasses (dark brown sugar). It is naturally moist since molasses retains a lot of water, and is often referred to as "soft." The particles are generally smaller than granulated white sugar. When a recipe here calls for brown sugar, it refers to dark brown sugar; light brown sugar should only be used when specified.

Brown sugar can be made by mixing superfine sugar with molasses, using 1 tbsp/15 mL molasses to 1 cup/240 mL superfine sugar (¹/₁₆ or 6.25 percent of the total volume). The resulting product after mixing will be dark brown sugar. To make light brown sugar, use 1 to 2 tsp/5 to 10 mL molasses for every cup of superfine sugar.

sucrose

Sucrose is common table sugar and is processed from two main sources: sugarcane and sugar beets. It is 100 percent relative sweetness. In addition to adding flavor, it also acts as and may be used as a preservative as it will hedge against pathogens.

dextrose

As glucose, dextrose is 70 percent on the sweetness scale. It is the best choice for encouraging fermentation as it provides the best source of energy for growth.

corn syrup and corn syrup solids

These consist of a mixture of carbohydrates. Corn syrup is the best choice for promoting browning during cooking. Also, corn syrup works to increase water retention.

seasonings in specific meat products

Most sausages in the United States have a European base. New sausage products include Mexican, Cajun, Caribbean, and Asian products. The use of different ingredients, along with new seasonings, can give them new flavor profiles. This can increase the marketability of these products, allow creation of more upscale products, and form a basis of ingredients in gourmet cooking. There are also many possibilities to create a healthier product that can be menued as appetizers or even featured as an entrée on fine-dining menus.

Cured products, such as ham, bacon, Canadian bacon, and so on, use little or no spices. Seasonings, such as allspice, cloves, cinnamon, and garlic and their extractives, are not used often in the curing of these products and if they are used, they are only used in small amounts, since the spices will impart a very strong flavor to the cured products. Milder seasonings such as salt, pepper, mustard, and sweeteners are used instead.

The following common European-based sausages use fairly standard seasonings. Recipes for many appear in Chapter 8.

frankfurters/hot dogs

The flavor of most frankfurters comes from black pepper and nutmeg. Sometimes coriander may be used for a lighter, sweeter flavor. Beef frankfurters have a distinct garlic flavor, and onion is a popular flavor in chicken hot dogs.

Regardless of the type of frankfurter, smoke is an important flavoring agent in frankfurters. It is not a spice, but it can be confusing when tasting two products for flavor comparison and it is the only difference. Mustard is another common spice used in making frankfurters. Frankfurters are eaten warm in order to bring out more flavors in the product.

what is in a frankfurter's seasoning?

Much of what is in a frankfurter is detailed on the product's label. The label must show the ingredients in order of predominance. For example:

> Pork, water, beef, salt, corn syrup solids, dextrose, spices, sodium erythorbate, and sodium nitrite.

The amounts of some of the additives are regulated by the U.S. Food and Drug Administration. Corn syrup solids, sodium phosphate, sodium erythorbate, and sodium nitrite are regular ingredients found in frankfurter seasonings. Corn syrup solids are used to bind the meat, as well as sweeten it, and are regulated to a maximum of 2 percent of the finished product. Sodium erythorbate is allowed up to $7/8$ oz/24.5 g per 100 lb/45.36 kg meat, or 550 ppm (parts per million). Sodium nitrite is regulated to $1/4$ oz/7 g per 100 lb/45.36 kg meat, or 156 ppm.

If used, sodium phosphates are regulated to 0.5 percent of the finished product. Protein content of the product will determine mustard usage. Mustard can be used to about 3 percent of the finished product. If using more than 1.5 percent, the correct mustard to use is deheated mustard, so that the emulsion does not break down.

SOME EXAMPLES OF THE FLAVORS OF SEASONINGS THAT STIMULATE THE MOUTH

BLACK PEPPER: Tip of the tongue

NUTMEG: Pungent, sweet flavor on the tongue

CORIANDER: Sweet floral note along the roof of the mouth

RED PEPPER: Delayed tickle or heat in throat

GARLIC: Hearty flavor on tongue

ONION: Complements and sweetens garlic

HYDROLYZED PROTEIN (SOY, CORN, OR WHEAT): A protein obtained from various foods (like soybeans, corn or wheat), which are then broken down into amino acids by a chemical process called acid hydrolysis. Hydrolyzed plant or vegetable protein is used as a flavor enhancer in numerous processed foods like soups, chilis, sauces, stews, and some meat products like frankfurters.

bologna

Bologna has the same type of flavor as frankfurters. The common difference between the two is that bologna usually has garlic in addition to the other spices. Because bologna is served cold, the garlic increases the overall flavor.

smoked sausage

There are two types of smoked sausage: Wisconsin and hot link. The flavor of a Wisconsin smoked sausage comes from coriander, black pepper, and high levels of dextrose. The flavor of hot link smoked sausages comes from a good amount of sage and red pepper. Both products earn their name from the heavy smoke application they undergo. The smoke and dextrose blend to create a desirable flavor.

kielbasa/Polish sausage

Polish sausage and kielbasa are similar to smoked sausage. The flavor of Polish sausage comes from black pepper, coriander, nutmeg, and garlic. Marjoram is usually added to kielbasa to give it a unique flavor.

fresh pork sausage

Black pepper and sage are the typical flavors in pork sausage. Red pepper can be added to create hot varieties. Dextrose is added to help the browning characteristics of the sausage.

bratwurst

Black pepper and nutmeg are typical flavors in bratwurst. Corn syrup and dextrose are used in bratwurst for added browning.

Italian sausage

Black pepper and fennel are the typical flavors in Italian sausage. Mild Italian sausages have garlic added for flavor. Red pepper and paprika are added to hot Italian sausages for flavor and color.

liverwurst/braunschweiger

White pepper, nutmeg, and onion are the typical flavors in liverwurst. Bacon is added to create braunschweiger, which can be smoked. These products benefit from the sweet flavor of nonfat dry milk.

cotto (cooked) salami

Black pepper, nutmeg, and garlic are typical flavors of salami. Whole or cracked black pepper aids the visual impact of this sausage.

pepperoni

Black pepper, red pepper, paprika, and garlic are typical seasonings used in pepperoni. In addition, a significant flavor is the "tang" produced by a lactic acid starter culture.

summer sausage

Black pepper and nutmeg are the typical flavors of summer sausage. Garlic is sometimes added, particularly to beef summer sausage. The "tang" produced by a lactic acid starter culture is an important flavor of summer sausage. Summer sausages are not as dry as pepperoni.

dry sausage

Dry sausages are sausages that have not been cooked. Drying over long periods of time gives them a distinct flavor and firmness. Black pepper, nutmeg, garlic, and wines give them their typical and unique flavors.

flavor combinations used in meat processing

MEAT	FLAVORINGS
BEEF (GENERAL)	Basil, dill, marjoram, mustard seeds, peppercorns, rosemary, sage, thyme
BEEF (BRAISED)	Bay leaves, marjoram, summer savory, tarragon
CORNED BEEF	Dill seed, dill, peppercorns
GROUND MEAT	Celery seed, chervil, cumin (ground), curry powder, oregano, summer savory
HAM	Cloves, mustard (dry), rosemary
HAM GLAZE	Allspice, cinnamon, cloves, ginger, mustard, nutmeg (all should be ground)
KIDNEYS	Basil, caraway seed, rosemary, summer savory, thyme
LAMB	Basil, cumin, dill seed, dill, lemon, mint, sage, summer savory, oregano, rosemary, tarragon
LIVER	Basil, caraway seed, fennel seed, marjoram, nutmeg (ground), oregano, thyme
PORK	Anise seed, basil, caraway seed, coriander seed, fennel seed, dill weed, marjoram, rosemary, sage, tarragon, thyme
SHISH KEBAB	Bay leaves, marjoram
SPARERIBS	Celery seed, mustard (dry), oregano, summer savory
STEWS	Anise seed, bay leaves, celery seed, chervil, oregano, rosemary, sage, tarragon
SWEETBREADS	Dill, tarragon
TONGUE	Bay leaves, thyme
TRIPE	Bay leaves, cumin, thyme
VEAL	Basil, dill, marjoram, mint, oregano, parsley, rosemary, saffron, summer savory, tarragon, thyme

As well as removing moisture from the meat, nitrates and nitrites decompose to nitric oxide (NO) over time. This chemical slows the formation of rancid and sour flavors, and creates a sharp flavoring in meat. Nitric oxide also binds with myoglobin in the muscle fibers to maintain color and create the characteristic bright pink associated with cured meats. Nitrates break down to nitric oxide much slower than nitrites, as nitrates must first be broken down into nitrites by naturally occurring bacteria in the meat. Thus, nitrates are typically used on foods that have a long curing and drying process. Sodium nitrate and nitrite have replaced potassium nitrate in the preserving process, and sodium nitrite is currently the primary salt used.

CONCERNS OVER THE USE OF NITRATE AND NITRITES

There are several concerns related to the use of nitrates and nitrites. The most prominent concern is the formation of nitrosamines via the binding of nitrates to amino acids, which are a by-product of the degradation of proteins. A study done in the 1970s showed that rats that were exposed to nitrosamines developed malignant tumors. As a result, the USDA and FDA placed restrictions on the amount of residual nitrates and nitrites on food to 200 parts per million (0.02 percent) or lower. However, it becomes exceptionally hard to deal with such small amounts of the ingredient. Thus, premade mixtures are available for purchase: Insta Cure No. 1 and Insta Cure No. 2.

Insta Cure No. 1 is a blend of 6 percent sodium nitrite and 94 percent sodium chloride (table salt). It has a distinctive pink color, which is why it is also known as Tinted Cure Mix (TCM). Insta Cure No. 2 is much like its counterpart, but contains sodium nitrate instead of nitrite. As a further precaution, the FDA requires meat packers to use antioxidants such as ascorbic acid (vitamin C), citric acid, or a vitamin C derivative (sodium ascorbate or sodium erythorbate) to further prevent the formation of nitrosamines.

The USDA recommends the following ratios of meat to nitrate/nitrite:

TYPE OF MEAT	NITRITE LEVEL (PPM)	NITRATE LEVEL (PPM)
Bacon, pumped (injected with the brine 10%)	120 (with 550 ppm ascorbate or erythorbate)	None
Bacon, immersion-cured (immersed in the brine)	200 (2 lb/907 g to 100 gal/384 L brine)	None
Cooked sausage	156 (¼ oz/7 g to 100 lb/45.36 kg meat)	None
Dry and semidry sausage	625 (1 oz/28 g to 100 lb/45.36 kg meat, dry-cured)	1,719 (2¾ oz/76 g to 100 lb/45.36 kg meat)
Dry-cured meats	156 (¼ oz/7 g to 100 lb/45.36 kg meat)	2,188 (2 lb/907 g to 100 gal/384 L brine at 10 % pump (10% in brine of the total weight is injected into product)

other ingredients used in charcuterie

sodium caseinate

Sodium caseinate is a derivative of the protein casein found in milk. The casein is extracted from milk curd after it is dried to 45 percent of its original water weight, at which point it has a pH level between 6.5 and 7. Once extracted, the casein is treated with sodium hydroxide, which results in the end product, sodium caseinate. This protein derivative is a very versatile substance, as it can be used as a fat emulsifier, a stabilizer, a thickener, and it can also be used to add texture. Furthermore, being a protein derivative, it also has nutritional value and is water soluble, making it much more versatile than other ingredients used for the same reasons.

potassium nitrate/sodium nitrate/sodium nitrite

Potassium nitrate (KNO_3), sodium nitrate ($NaNO_3$), and sodium nitrite ($NaNO_2$) are all salts that are or have been used in the preservation of meat. They help preserve meat by drawing internal moisture from the meat fibers, making the meat uninhabitable by undesirable bacteria. This allows for foods to be smoked for long periods of time at temperatures below 100°F/38°C without fear of bacteria, such as *Clostridium botulinum* (the bacterium that causes botulism), growing on the product.

As well as removing moisture from the meat, nitrates and nitrites decompose to nitric oxide (NO) over time. This chemical slows the formation of rancid and sour flavors, and creates a sharp flavoring in meat. Nitric oxide also binds with myoglobin in the muscle fibers to maintain color and create the characteristic bright pink associated with cured meats. Nitrates break down to nitric oxide much slower than nitrites, as nitrates must first be broken down into nitrites by naturally occurring bacteria in the meat. Thus, nitrates are typically used on foods that have a long curing and drying process. Sodium nitrate and nitrite have replaced potassium nitrate in the preserving process, and sodium nitrite is currently the primary salt used.

ascorbic acid/sodium ascorbate

Ascorbates—sodium erythorbate (sodium iso-ascorbate) and citric acid—reduce oxidation and subsequent off-flavor and off-color that would result from oxidation. They speed the curing reaction by the rapid reduction of nitrates and nitrites to nitrous acid and ultimately nitric oxide that combines with myoglobin in the muscle tissues to fix the cured color, about 0.01 percent for citric acid and 0.05 percent for erythorbate.

Ascorbic acid, otherwise known as vitamin C, prevents the oxidation of fats and proteins, which in turn prevents spoiling. They prevent the fats and proteins from oxidizing by allowing themselves to be oxidized before other substances.

sodium erythorbate/erythorbic acid

Erythorbic acid and sodium erythorbate are stereoisomers of ascorbic acid and sodium ascorbate; that is, their chemical structures are the same, but the orientation of the atoms in the molecule is slightly different. These chemicals are isolated and created in a much easier and less expensive fashion than their counterpart, ascorbic acid. Thus, these are much more commonly used.

SPICES, HERBS, & SEASONINGS

citric acid

Citric acid has many uses in food. It can be used in combination with ascorbic or erythorbic acid as a preservative, as well as a substitute for lemon juice. Citric acid can be added to keep fat globules separate, which is why citric acid can be utilized as an emulsifier. It helps to keep fats dissolved and distributed evenly throughout a product. Its purpose is to break down large clumps of fat into smaller pockets of fat that are more easily dissolved.

ascorbic acid, sodium ascorbate, and sodium erythorbate

These additives speed up the chemical conversion of nitrite to nitric oxide, which in turn will react with meat myoglobin to create a pink color. They also deplete levels of meat oxygen and prevent the fading of the cured meat color.

Sodium erythorbate (C_6H7NaO_6) is a food additive used predominantly in meats, poultry, and soft drinks. Chemically, it is the sodium salt of erythorbic acid. When used in processed meat such as hot dogs and beef sticks, it reduces the rate at which nitrate reduces to nitric oxide, thus retaining the pink coloring. As an antioxidant structurally related to vitamin C, it helps improve flavor stability and prevents the formation of carcinogenic nitrosamines.

sodium tripolyphosphate

Phosphates are used to improve the water-binding capacity of the meat, solubilize proteins, act as antioxidants, and stabilize the flavor and color of the product. Their maximum benefit to the processor is to reduce purge, or water that is cooked out of product. Phosphates also help to increase shelf life of a product. The maximum amount of phosphates approved for sausage products is limited to 0.5 percent of the finished product weight. If used, they must be food-grade.

INGREDIENT	MAXIMUM AMOUNT
Ascorbic acid	¾ oz/21 g per 100 lb/45.36 kg of meat
Erythorbic acid	¾ oz/21 g per 100 lb/45.36 kg of meat
Sodium erythorbate	⅞ oz/25 g per 100 lb/45.36 kg of meat
Citric acid	May replace up to 50 percent of above listed ingredients
Sodium citrate	May replace up to 50 percent of above listed ingredients
Sodium acid pyrophosphate	Alone or in combination with others may not exceed 8 oz (0.5%)
Glucono delta lactone (GDL)	8 oz/227 g per 100 lb/45.36 kg of meat

other ingredients used in charcuterie

ITEM	USE/FUNCTION(S)	NOTE(S)
SALT	Preservative; flavor enhancer; improves binding (emulsion)	Kills trichina over a period of time
TCM (TINTED CURE MIX)/ CURING SALT/PRAGUE POWDER I/INSTA CURE NO. 1	Brings out the rich red color in cured meats; kills botulism	Composed of 94% salt, 6% sodium nitrite; not used in fresh sausage
SALTPETER (POTASSIUM NITRATE)	Use in sausage production; greatly limited after 1975 by USDA	Not currently used
DEXTROSE	Counteracts bitterness in liver; counteracts harshness of salt; helps stabilize color when using TCM; aids in fermentation of salami-type products	
SODIUM ERYTHORBATE/ SODIUM ASCORBATE/ ASCORBIC ACID/CITRIC ACID	Helps retain color; slows down nitrite reaction; antioxidant: reduces molecular oxygen levels, inhibiting decomposition	First three are basically the same; citric acid is similar to sodium ascorbate; expensive
SODIUM CASEINATE	Secondary binder; helps prevent shrinkage	Very slight but pleasing taste
NONFAT DRY MILK	Secondary binder; prevents shrinkage of sausages	Very slight but pleasing taste
SODIUM PHOSPHATE	Secondary binder; improves binding and makes the emulsion creamier; improves product yield	Phosphates are widely used in the meat industry. Phosphates used include: sodium tripolyphosphate, tetrasodium pyrophosphate, sodium hexametaphosphate, sodium acid pyrophosphate, disodium phosphate, etc.

other ingredients used in charcuterie (continued)

ITEM	USE/FUNCTION(S)	NOTE(S)
SODIUM TRIPOLYPHOSPHATE	Alkaline phosphate salts (sodium tripolyphosphate and tetrasodium pyrophosphate) elevate the pH of meat, thus improving its water-holding power.	The acid reacting phosphates (alkali-metal salts or ortophosphoric acid and pyrophosphoric acid), on the contrary, lower the pH. Although both sodium tripolyphosphate and tetrasodium pyrophosphate are superior to all other phosphates, sodium tripolyphosphates have a higher solubility and are less prone to form insoluble precipitates. Sodium acid pyrophosphate in particular is often utilized in sausages. The permissible maximum concentration of residual phosphates in meat products is set at 0.5%. Phosphates also retard development of oxidative rancidity in meat products.
SOY PROTEIN/SOY CONCENTRATE/SOY PROTEIN ISOLATE	Improves binding	Soy protein is made from hulled, flaked, and de-oiled soybeans. Soy protein concentrates have a bland taste. An isolate is achieved by extracting the proteins with water at high pH of approximately 10. Soy protein concentrate, often called SPC, is basically soybean without the water-soluble carbohydrates. Soy protein concentrate contains about 70% protein. Will absorb as much as 70% of its weight in water. Soy protein isolate, often called SPI, is the most refined form of soy protein and is mainly used in meat products to improve texture and mouthfeel. Soy protein isolate contains about 90% protein and will absorb as much as 90% of its weight in water.
WATER	Dispersing medium for salts, nitrites, phosphates, and other curing ingredients; assists in maintaining moist, juicy end product; compensates for moisture loss during hot smoking (thermal processing)	

starter cultures, fermentation, and drying

There is an acceptable range of temperatures that correspond to each particular process. When starter cultures are used, the fermentation temperature can vary from the minimum to the maximum recommended by the manufacturer's setting,

BACTOFERM T-SPX: Slow-fermented culture for traditional fermentation profiles applying fermentation temperatures not higher than 75°F/24°C; $^{7}/_{8}$ oz/25 g of culture ferments 441 lb/200 kg of meat.

BACTOFERM F-LC: Bio-protective culture capable of acidification as well as preventing growth of *Listeria monocytogenes*. This can be added for production of fermented sausage with a short production type. The culture works in a wide temperature range. Low fermentation temperatures 77°F/25°C result in traditional acidification profile, whereas high fermentation temperatures 95° to 115°F/35° to 46°C give a product that is sought for in the United States. Seventh-eighths ounce/25 g of culture ferments 220 lb/100 kg of meats.

FERMENTO: A dairy-based powdered product that is added to sausages during production to eliminate the necessary curing times that allow for fermentation.

pâté spice mix #1

MAKES 13 OZ/369 G

3 oz/85 g ground cloves

3 oz/85 g ground coriander

1¾ oz/50 g dried thyme

1½ oz/43 g white peppercorns

1½ oz/43 g ground nutmeg

1 oz/28 g dried cèpes

¾ oz/21 g ground mace

½ oz/14 g bay leaves

Combine all ingredients and grind them using a mortar and pestle, spice grinder, or blender. Store in an airtight container in a cool, dry place.

four-spice mix

MAKES 6 OZ/170 G

4 oz/113 g ground white pepper

1 oz/28 g ground ginger

1 oz/28 g ground nutmeg

2 tsp/10 mL ground cloves

Combine and mix all ingredients together. Store in an airtight container in a cool, dry place.

pâté spice mix #2

MAKES 10 TBSP/150 ML

7 tbsp/105 mL white
peppercorns

1 tbsp/15 mL
ground nutmeg

1 tbsp/15 mL cloves

1 tbsp/15 mL ground
cinnamon

Combine all ingredients and grind them using a mortar and pestle, spice grinder, or blender. Store in an airtight container in a cool, dry place.

dry-cured capacolla spice mix

MAKES 2½ TBSP/37.5 ML

1½ tsp/7.5 mL sweet
or hot paprika

1½ tsp/7.5 mL cayenne

1½ tsp/7.5 mL ground
fennel seeds

1 tbsp/15 mL ground
black pepper

Combine and mix together the ingredients. Store in an airtight container in a cool, dry place.

coppa spice mixes

HOT SPICE MIX

¼ cup/32 g hot paprika

1 tbsp/9 g cayenne

SWEET MIX

3 tbsp/40 g granu-
lated sugar

2 tbsp/20 g ground
black pepper

1 tbsp/8 g ground coriander

2 tsp/12 g minced garlic

1 tsp/4 g ground mace

1 tsp/4 g allspice berries

¾ tsp/3 g juniper berries

Combine the ingredients of the desired mix and mix together. If making the Sweet Mix, grind them using a mortar and pestle or a blender. Store in an airtight container in a cool, dry place.

Note: Gram weight is more precise for obtaining the flavors of the coppa, but volume measurements are provided if a digital scale is unavailable.

bratwurst seasoning mix

2 lb/907 g kosher salt

6 oz/170 g ground
white pepper

1 oz/14 g rubbed sage

½ oz/14 g ground
celery seed

½ oz/14 g ground mace

Combine and mix all ingredients together. Store in an airtight container in a cool, dry place.

meats, poultry, & seafood

{ chapter three

We will explore raw meats and seafood that are used in the charcuterie kitchen.

using meats and seafood in the charcuterie kitchen

All meat intended for human consumption must be inspected in accordance with established programs of federal, state, and/or local governments.

Charcuterie is an art of meat transformation. All type of meats are used to create numerous items. Scraps from previous fabrication that would have otherwise been wasted can be used. The charcuterie kitchen is a great way to effectively use up any extra ingredients. All the usual cooking methods are practiced, such as poaching, roasting, and baking, as well as brining, curing, and smoking. Arrays of items can be made using different combination of choices from all preparation methods.

Another factor in the variety of charcuterie items that can be produced is the selection of meats available. Pork, beef, lamb, game meats, poultry, fish, and seafood can all be used. Every animal used for consumption has a similar muscle construction, but the characteristics and muscle science of meats are so complex that the finished product will be affected greatly by the difference in the meats used. Fish and seafood, of course, have the biggest difference. The protein structure is what holds the meat together and affects the texture of every product. Every aspect of meat has an influence on the products made in the charcuterie kitchen.

Cleaning items used for charcuterie will be different for each specific use. When I refer to clean meat, I mean that pork, beef, lamb, and veal should be handled in the following manner: the item is trimmed of excess fat and sinew, and cartilage is removed. Then the meat is cubed $\frac{1}{2}$ to 1 inch. When I use these products for sausages, I separate the fat from meat and from all the sinew. The fat I will not use but replace with fat back, jowl fat, or pork bellies. If the pork recipe calls for a product with the ratio of 80 percent meat and 20 percent fat, you can use the straight pork or an item that is similar in the fat:meat ratio.

the science of meat

Basic meat science is mostly the same for all species of meats. Muscle organization is the general formation of a solid muscle mass. To understand the different textures of meats, an understanding of the parts of the muscle that make up the meat is needed. The chemical and physical characteristics of the muscle are a function of its parts, the composition, and what makes up the entire muscle. The composition refers to the ratio of water to fat to proteins within the body. The chemical structure of the proteins in the muscle give it its unique texture and is the main reason meat is edible.

The progression of life and advancement of millions of species on Earth can be observed by looking deep and understanding the composition and complexity of muscle. All animals have strands of cells that come together as very strong protein-rich organs. Ironically, these muscles that allow animals to strive are the fuel for humanity. Rarely do we look at our steak dinner and understand what has happened scientifically to allow that piece of meat to be on our table.

Muscle makes up 40 percent of total body weight of an animal and has three general types: skeletal, cardiac, and smooth muscle. They all have very distinct differences in purpose, complexity, and shape. What all do have in common, though, is that they all contain many types of proteins, carbohydrates, fats, and essential trace elements. The collaboration of these elements coming together creates a product that provides strength for movement for one organism and edible nutrition for another.

structure of meat

In analyzing meat, it is easy to realize its importance in our consumption and capability to thrive. Meat has many different proteins and carbohydrates, and is put together in a very complex structure to form a gracefully productive organ. The protein that meat contains contributes to our body's protein, which constitutes 54 percent of our body mass. The trace elements such as iron and different sulfites are used in our own body for the same process as in any animal. We cannot survive without consuming protein. It is possible to find it and other nutrients in plants, but meat gives it to us in an abundant source. We know to look for meat with bright red color, tender nature, and good marbling. Little do we know that we analyzed the entire chemical background of a piece of meat by those visual elements of quality.

COMPOSITION OF LEAN RED MEAT

- 75 PERCENT WATER

- 20 PERCENT PROTEIN
    Sarcoplasmic: soluble in low-strength salt solutions
    Myofibrillar: structural type, soluble in concentrated salt solutions
    Connective: insoluble in salt solution at low temperatures
- 3 PERCENT FAT

- 2 PERCENT NONNITROGENOUS SOLUBLE SUBSTANCES
    (carbohydrates, minerals, lactic acid)

muscle structure and composition

Muscle has a very interesting composition. The cell structure is much different from any other type of cell. The single muscle fiber has an outer coating called the sarcoplasmic reticulum, or sarcolemma. This contains individual threads called fibrils that are roped and woven together to form a casing for the muscles, surrounding them and keeping them together in a tight bundle. Woven into the sarcolemma are mitochondria, known as "the powerhouses of the cell." They are organelles in the cell that take in nutrients and convert them into energy for the cell. On the outer edge of this bundle, just under the sarcolemma, is the nucleus of the fibers. Each fiber contains myofibrillar, a structure similar to fibrils that holds protein gel together (the substance that allows contraction) and makes up 80 percent of the fiber's volume. These muscle fibers work together in clusters that are attached to bone via a tendon unless the muscle is a cardiac muscle, which has more of a crosshatched or webbed nature and is used for the repetitive motion of circulating blood to the rest of the body. In smooth muscle cells, this alignment is absent; hence, there are no apparent striations and so the muscle looks smooth.

muscle composition: proteins

When muscles are observed on a molecular and chemical level, many interesting aspects are noticed. Protein is the driving force of all muscle fiber. There are a plethora of different types of protein that join together to make muscles work. The three main groups of proteins are myofibrillar, sarcoplasmic, and stromal. Each type of protein holds its own purpose in the muscle composition.

Myofibrillar proteins are the converters of chemical energy into a reaction between the proteins in muscle fibers. The reaction between the proteins is what makes the muscles stretch or contract. The main proteins within myofibrillars are myosin (54 percent), actin (21 percent), and tropomyosin (15 percent), with other less significant proteins making up the last 10 percent. These protein strands are laid next to and between each other. There are thick and thin strands, the thick made of the protein myosin and the thin of mainly actin and tropomyosin. These thick and thin strands are interconnected, with six thin strands surrounding each thick strand. Chemical energy from carbohydrates is converted by the mitochondria and makes the thick strands pull the thin strands closer together or lets them stretch out. This process is what gives muscles movement. One segment of these thick and thin strands is called a *sarcomere* (Greek for "part of muscle"). These segments connect together to form the long strands of muscle fiber, which, in bundles, constitute muscle. Muscle contraction is initiated by release of small amounts of calcium ions. This process is also seen after death, when animals' muscles stiffen due to the release of these calcium ions. The release, along with other factors, decreases the length of sarcomeres. This is called rigor mortis. In a nutshell, the myofibrillar proteins are the contractile or action proteins.

Proteins that do not necessarily have anything to do with the movement or contractile traits of muscle are sarcoplasmic proteins, representing other functionality and mechanics behind the movement of muscles. The duties of these proteins include transporting electrons, functions of metabolism, and carrying pigment. Myoglobin is the protein that stores oxygen in the cells and gives fresh meat its red color. The color we see in cut meat in stores is also affected by hemoglobin, another sarcoplasmic protein. When meat is bled out postmortem (following death), some hemoglobin and blood plasma are left behind. These proteins are responsible for transporting oxygen and brighten when exposed to air postmortem. If there is too much hemoglobin left after bleeding due to improper procedure, the meat can take on the darker color sometimes seen in the center of ground meat. This color is due to the proteins not being able to breathe in enough oxygen to give the meat fresh color; other aspects of quality can also be affected. More minor sarcoplasmic proteins include other enzymes and proteases. These contribute to other aspects of functionality, such as changing the structure of carbohydrates.

Stromal protein gives structure like myofibrillar protein and does not act in the transport of nutrients or enzymatic activity like sarcoplasmic proteins. The two main proteins in the category of stromal protein are the connective tissues of collagen and elastin. These proteins are mostly insoluble. When meat is cooked, these are the proteins that do not change and are not digestible by humans. As animals age, more connective tissue is formed, which makes meat tougher. But the overall percentage of stromal protein is lower over time as a percentage of total muscle protein. This means that more muscle has been formed than connective tissue, but the connective tissue has become more dispersed and supportive of the muscle. This growth does not contribute to the quality of edible meat. Other adverse effects stromal proteins have on meat quality are that they decrease emulsifying capabilities of meat, lower the water-holding capabilities, and lower the nutritional value. Basically, an old animal with lots of connective tissue is nearly worthless in comparison to a young animal.

muscle composition: carbohydrates

Even considering all types of protein, one compound in the bodies of animals, carbohydrates, is more responsible for their proper functioning than any other. Carbohydrates are long chains of different kinds of sugars. These chains are made of simple sugars like glucose or fructose (called monosaccharides) and complex sugars like sucrose and lactose (polysaccharides). The exact name of each type of carbohydrate depends on its length and what sugars it is made up of. Their names also correspond with their function in different processes in the body. The levels of carbohydrates present at the point of slaughter will affect the meat color, firmness, emulsifying ability, shelf life, and overall texture. As a result, the carbohydrate levels in certain meats will change the quality of that meat. Also, the Maillard reaction that develops appealing flavor in cooked meats includes some carbonyl groups of carbohydrates as vital elements to interact with protein.

muscle composition: lipids and fats

Lipids, along with protein and carbohydrates, constitute the three principal structural components of living cells. They are not miscible with water and include fats, waxes, phosphates, and related compounds. Lipids are created and stored by animals and plants as a concentrated form of energy with twice the calories as the same weight of either sugar or starch. They tenderize many foods by permeating and weakening the structure, provide flavor, and add smoothness. There are two main types of fatty acids: saturated and unsaturated. Saturated fatty acids are long chains of hydrocarbons, or chains of carbon-carbon bonds with branches. These branches are full of, or saturated with, hydrogen atoms. Unsaturated fatty acids are hydrocarbon chains that have branches that, instead of being full with hydrogen, are bonded with one another.

Fatty acid composition is affected by the following:

- DIET—Especially in pigs and chickens

- ANATOMICAL LOCATION—Interior (leaf fat) is more saturated than subcutaneous

- TYPE OF LIPID—Phospholipids are more unsaturated than triglycerides

Fatty acid composition affects:

- MELTING POINT—Impacts sausage manufacture and the temperature of fermentation.

- TEXTURE—Unsaturated fats are softer than saturated fats.

- FLAVOR STABILITY—Unsaturated fats are vulnerable to oxidation, leading to rancidity. Beef is more stable than pork, and pork is more stable than chicken.

Saturated fatty acids primarily come from animal products such as meat and dairy. In general, animal fats are solid at room temperature. Saturated fats are more stable than unsaturated fats, making them less vulnerable to rancidity. Animal fats are about half saturated and half unsaturated and solid at room temperature. Beef and lamb fats are harder than pork or poultry fats because more of the fatty acids in the meat are saturated.

Unsaturated fatty acids are not fully saturated with hydrogen atoms because of the presence of carbon-carbon double bonds (the branches on the chain bind with each other and strengthen the bond between adjacent carbon bonds). The double bond leaves an open space unprotected by hydrogen atoms on one side of the chain, making them more susceptible for rancidity. Most vegetable fats are about 85 percent unsaturated fats. They are much healthier than saturated fats, and are liquid at room temperature. They can be saturated by using a process called hydrogenation, which breaks apart the branches and adds hydrogen atoms back to them.

Most fatty acids in meats are found bound to a molecule called glycerol. Glycerol is a three-carbon chain with each of the three carbons branched with a hydrogen and an alcohol (oxygen bound to hydrogen). Fatty acids bind to the alcohols on the glycerol to create fats. The composition of these fats are affected by the number of fatty acids that bind to the glycerol, whether it be one, two, or three. Fatty acids can be transformed by heat and oxygen into molecules that smell fruity or floral. They give different meats their distinctive flavors. For example, compounds from foraged plants give beef its "cowy" flavor; in pigs and ducks, the flavor comes from intestinal microbes and their fat-soluble products of amino acid metabolism. The sweetness in pork also comes from lactones, the molecule that gives peaches and coconuts their character.

Fats are susceptible to being changed by oxygen. Exposure to oxygen over time causes a chain reaction in the fats, changing the composition and degrading them. This is called lipid oxidation. Lipid oxidation cannot be prevented, but it can be delayed with careful handling: wrap meat tightly in plastic wrap, keep it in the dark, store it in the coldest corner of the freezer, and use it as soon as possible. Salt encourages the lipid oxidation, so the less salt you use, the slower the meat will spoil after being cooked. Also, herbs like rosemary can prevent oxidation. Browning the meat surface in a pan, as in searing, also delays lipid oxidation.

color in meat

Color is the first impression we have when choosing meat. The color could range from bright red to gray or even green, in extremes. Meat colors come from the muscle pigment myoglobin. Myoglobin stores oxygen for the muscles in animals; it has a high affinity for oxygen. This means that exposure to air will quickly lead to the attachment of oxygen molecules to myoglobin, forming oxymyoglobin. Oxymyoglobin is bright red in color in fresh meat. Both myoglobin and oxymyoglobin can become oxidized. The resulting pigment, memyoglobin, is brown-gray in color. This develops when meat is aged, spoiled, or improperly handled, and is hard to reverse. Fresh meat color tends to change in a fairly short time and curing methods have been developed partly because they help meat retain its color longer under proper storage conditions.

Meat color depends on:

- MYOGLOBINS—how much

- IRON AND PROTEIN STRUCTURE—whether the protein is raw or cooked

chemical and physical characteristics of meat

The chemical and physical characteristics of meats are the qualities that make it an edible product. Chemical characteristics involve the chemical structure of the muscle tissues. The tissue components vary with species, maturity, harvesting location, nutritional intake, genetics, and the different cuts of the carcass. The chemical composition of the muscle is approximately 75 percent water, 19 percent protein, 2.5 percent fats, 1.5 percent non-protein compounds, 1 percent carbohydrates, and 1 percent inorganic matter.

general physical characteristics

The physical characteristics are aspects such as texture forming, water-holding capacity, fiber swelling, solubility, gelation, color, emulsification, binding, and palatability.

water retention

Water in the meat exists in a bound form, attached in some way to proteins or fats, or as a free liquid. Water affects the overall juiciness and tenderness of cooked meat. Bound water is held throughout the proteins; free-flowing water is held in different compartments. Salt and phosphates added to meat improve water retention once it is cooked. Water-holding capacity is the ability of meat to retain its own or added moisture. It can be increased by the use of salt or sodium phosphate. It is the most important factor in the evaluation of meat quality. Water in meat is primarily contained in the myofibrillar lattice (the casing around the muscle strands) and as the pH drops closer to the isoelectric point (5.0 to 5.1) of myosin and actin, water-binding capacity is at a minimum. The isoelectric point refers to the pH at which there is no net charge on a compound. Higher pH values result in greater net charges on muscle protein and greater percentages of bound and immobilized water, keeping natural juices bound in the cells and reducing drip loss.

solubility

Solubility is the percentage of original protein that dissolves under specific conditions. Heat, pH, and other factors contribute to the solubility of proteins. Ions, phosphates, and the amount of muscle fiber have an effect on the extractability.

gelation

Gelation is the ability to form a gel once meat is cooked and cooled. Once the meat has heat applied to it, many of the proteins unfold and change structure, strands are formed, and the muscle fibers contract, entrapping water that together forms a gel. This gel acts as an adhesive to bind most meat particles, stabilizes fat globules, entraps flavor, and immobilizes water. This affects the texture of the meat or the product made with gel. Foods that are processed or made with a large amount of water usually need a form of gelatin added to them.

color

Color, or pigment, is an important physical characteristic. A good color depends on the freshness of the meat. Fresh raw meat is known to have a bright color, and fresh cooked meat should have a gray or tan color. Myoglobins are the primary meat pigment, and color depends on the amount that is present in the meat.

emulsification and binding

Emulsification has to do with the amount of fat globules being dispersed and stabilized evenly throughout the muscle fibers and proteins. This influences the texture and helps with the binding process of meat. When we take ground meat that has salt added, we pool the myosins out to help bind everything, and we add water to it to disperse the proteins so that they can absorb a certain amount of fat. We then mix in fat by mixing with a paddle or mixing with a high-speed cutter to form a homogenous and almost spongy mixture. The mixture can be chunky or a smooth paste, as in bologna. We need to mix the protein with the water that it has in it or any extra that has been added, then we mix in the fat. This process is like what happens when you make Hollandaise sauce. You add liquid to the protein to thin it or disperse it so that it can accept the fat that you are going to mix into it.

Bind-in sausages and forcemeat are products that, when cooked, will hold together without losing a lot of water, fat, and texture.

palatability

Palatability is the most important characteristic. The taste of the meat depends on all the other characteristics put together. For a meat to be palatable, it must be juicy, tender, and flavorful. This is all affected by the fat content, moisture content, and muscle fibers with good marbling.

muscle organization

The muscle organization of meat used in charcuterie is a lot like human muscle. Live cells join together and lead to the formation of organs and tissues. There are three types of muscles in the body: striated voluntary or skeletal muscle, striated involuntary or cardiac muscle, and the smooth or involuntary muscle. Muscle also may contain fat and connective tissue.

Skeletal muscle helps the animal to adjust to its external environment. It makes up to 35 to 65 percent of all muscle in an animal. The fibers can range from 0.00196 to 0.00393 inches to 50 to 100 micrometers in diameter and can be extremely long. The fibers constitute 75 to 92 percent of the muscle, while the rest is nerve fibers, blood vessels, and connective tissues. Cardiac muscle is the heart. The fibers have a diameter of 0.00059 inches/15 micrometers. Smooth muscle helps maintain the body's internal environment. It is found in the arteries and in the lymph, digestive, and reproductive systems. Smooth muscle has long spindle-shaped fibers, 0.000236 inches/6 micrometers in diameter.

There can also be fat, called intramuscular fat, deposited within the muscle. If it is between muscles, it is then known as intermuscular fat. Connective tissue is what holds the fibers together in the muscle. The epimysium is the sheath surrounding the entire muscle. The perimysium is the layer beneath that, dividing the fibers into small groups. The endomysium is the layer under the perimysium that surrounds each muscle fiber. Each layer is thinner than the one before.

Muscles engaged in lighter activities have a finer texture; heavily worked muscles will have a coarse texture. The finer textured meats will be more tender and moist. These nonmotion muscles are located more toward the center of the body. Motion muscles are the legs and arms in humans.

Fish muscles are made up of myotomes and myocammata. The anatomy of fish muscle is simple. Basically, there are two bundles of muscles on each side of the vertebral column, and each of these bundles is further separated into upper mass above the horizontal axis. A septum, ventral mass below this septum, and the muscle cells run in a longitudinal direction, separated perpendicularly by sheets of connective tissue (myocommato). The muscle segments lying in between the sheets of connective tissue are called myotomes. The longest muscle cells are found in the twelfth myotome counting from the head. The length of the cells as well as the thickness of the myocommato will increase with age.

MARKET FORMS OF MEAT

After slaughtering, inspection, and grading, the animal carcass is cut into manageable pieces. Sides are prepared by making a cut down the length of a backbone. Each side is cut into two pieces to make quarters, dividing the sides between specific vertebrae. Saddles are made by cutting the animal across the belly, again at a specified point. The exact standards for individual animal types govern where the carcass is to be divided.

The next step is to cut the animal into what are referred to as primal cuts. There are uniform standards for beef, veal, pork, and lamb primals. These large cuts are then further broken down into subprimals. Subprimals are generally trimmed and packed as food service, value added, or HRI (hotel, restaurant, and institution) cuts. There may be even more fabrication or butchering done to prepare steaks, chops, roasts, or ground meat. These cuts are referred to as portion control cuts.

BEEF CARCASS BREAKDOWN

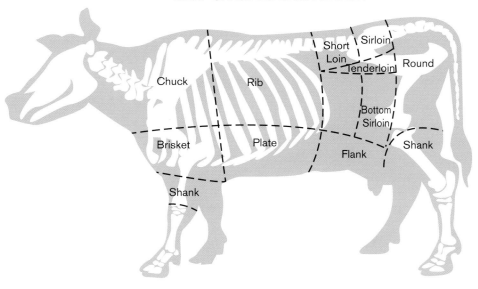

VEAL CARCASS BREAKDOWN

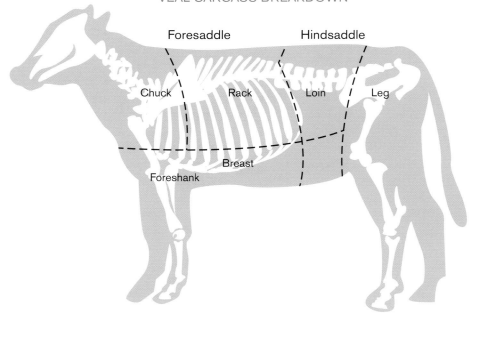

PORK CARCASS BREAKDOWN

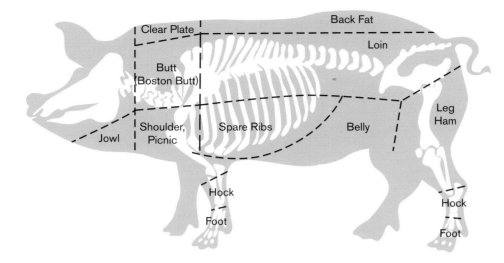

Clear Plate

Back Fat

Loin

Butt
(Boston Butt)

Leg
Ham

Jowl

Shoulder,
Picnic

Spare Ribs

Belly

Hock

Hock

Foot

Foot

LAMB CARCASS BREAKDOWN

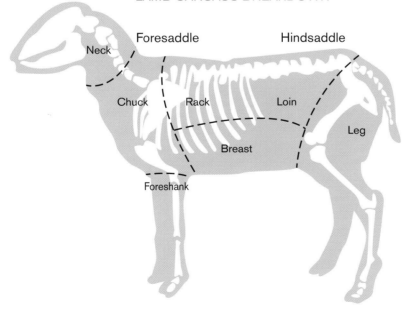

Foresaddle

Hindsaddle

Neck

Chuck

Rack

Loin

Leg

Breast

Foreshank

fish and seafood

The difference between meat and fish muscle tissue is that in fish there is no tough connective tissue between the muscles and bones.

As discussed earlier, fish muscles are quite different from those in mammals. Fish float in water and so don't need muscle to support their weight. Their muscle fibers, which are very short, are called myotomes and are held together by connective tissue called myocammata, which is much more delicate than collagen and breaks down much more easily when cooked. The only muscles that most fish use extensively are around the tail and fins (areas that aren't eaten as often by humans), which are used for constant cruising around in the water. Once caught, (dead) fish are stored in an ice room with standing temperature of 30° to 38°F/1° to 3°C.

Fish muscles come in three different types: red, pink, and white. Most fish have a mixture of two or all three types of muscle, but keep the types in discrete groupings; however, in the salmonid fishes, the red and white muscle types are mixed to form a mosaic type of muscle. The colors these muscles show are related to the amount of hemoglobin present in the muscles, with red muscle having plenty of hemoglobin present and white very little, if any. When looking at fish muscles, be aware that some fish, particularly salmonids, that feed on crustaceans develop a pink color to their muscles as a result of a carotenoid pigment they acquire from their food, in the same way that flamingos get their pink color from the crustaceans they eat.

Red muscle, also known as slow muscle, is red because it has a high number of capillaries present in it and thus has a high hemoglobin content. Being well supplied with oxygen, red muscle is used for steady, constant-effort swimming and is found in active fish, particularly those that live in the open waters of seas and oceans; nevertheless, red muscle seldom makes up even as much as 20 percent of a fish's total muscle mass. White muscle, or fast muscle, has thicker fibers than red muscle and possesses significantly fewer capillaries, and so it has a much reduced blood flow, and therefore, a reduced oxygen availability. Most white muscle activity is anaerobic (glycogen is converted to lactate). White muscle fibers can produce tensions that are up to 2.7 times greater than those of red muscle, but they are more energetically wasteful, and therefore, the cost to the animal is higher. Finally, white muscles can only work for short periods of time: a couple of minutes maximum is not unusual before they exhaust their supply of glycogen and need to rest. All this means white muscles are convenient for short quick bursts of movement, in which capacity they outcompete red muscle easily, but they are no good for prolonged swimming. Pink muscle is intermediate between the two and is good for continued swimming efforts lasting a few tens of minutes at a relatively high speed. Of course, like all animals, fish use all their muscles in concert as they go about their daily lives.

People who practice a regular diet of fish generally avoid suffering from such ailments as heart disease, prostate cancer, high blood pressure, arthritis, bronchial asthma, psoriasis, as well as many other chronic and acute ailments due to the unique nutrients found in seafood. This observation of seafood's impact on human health was first identified in a paper published in 1970 that observed how the Greenland Eskimo traditional way of life resulted in virtually no heart disease. The Greenland Eskimos were observed to consume large amounts of fat, protein, and cholesterol, but did not contract atherosclerosis. This condition was at that time the leading cause of death for many European-Americans consuming a similar fatty diet. However, upon further observation, it was discovered that the Eskimos' fatty diet consisted primarily of sea animals and fish.

In addition to iodine and calcium, fish and shellfish are excellent sources of protein, B vitamins, and various other nutrients. The fat contained in fish and seafood that we consume is unsaturated omega-3 fatty acids, a polyunsaturated fat that cannot be manufactured by the human body and can only be obtained through dietary means. Saturated fat resulting from the consumption of meat can be harmful to the body if consumed regularly, resulting in heart disease or other chronic illnesses.

DIRECT AND INDIRECT BENEFITS OF THE CONSUMPTION OF OMEGA-3 FATTY ACIDS

- Aids in development and function of the brain and retina
- Ensures the health of the central nervous system in infancy and through life
- Helps limit inflammatory response
- Lowers the incidence of heart disease and cancer
- Lowers LDL ("bad") cholesterol

It is important to understand that omega-3 fatty acids can only be obtained by the consumption of fish that have themselves consumed ocean plants called phytoplankton. Fish that eat phytoplankton in turn might be consumed by other fish, thus providing larger fish with this fatty acid. It should be noted that freshwater fish do not consume phytoplankton, so they have negligible amounts of omega-3 fatty acids. Farmed saltwater fish also have negligible amounts of omega-3 fatty acids due to the limited amount of phytoplankton in their measured diets.

seafood safety concerns

As much as fish and shellfish contribute to the consumption of important vitamins and minerals, they are also capable of introducing very infectious toxin-producing microbes that can result in severe sickness and even death.

As a general rule, infectious bacteria and parasites can be mitigated by cooking seafood to 140°F/60°C. The highest potential risk of infection from bacteria or parasites is in seafood that is served raw or uncooked. This is particularly true for some bivalves and mollusks that are filter feeders, trapping viruses as they filter water for food. When we, in turn, eat the raw shellfish, the virus is attached to their digestive track.

fin fish structure

Physically, the structure of most, if not all, fin fish is similar.

market forms of fish

Fish can be purchased fresh in one of the market forms described below, as well as in frozen, smoked, pickled, or salted forms.

whole fish This is the fish as it was caught, completely intact.

erawn fish The viscera (guts) are removed, but head, fins, and scales are still intact.

h&g (headed and gutted or head-off drawn) The viscera and head are removed, but scales and fins are still intact.

dressed fish The viscera, gills, scales, and fins are removed. The head may or may not be removed. Also known as pan-dressed, these fish are usually appropriate for a single serving.

steak This is a portion-sized, cross-section cut from a dressed fish. Portion cuts from the fillets of large fish, such as tuna and swordfish, are also commonly called steaks.

fillet This is a boneless piece of fish, removed from either side of the backbone. The skin may or may not be removed before cooking. Purveyors often sell fillets "pin-bone in," so it is important to specify "pin-bone out" when ordering.

tranche A portion-sized slice of a fillet is cut at a 45-degree angle to expose a greater surface area. A tranche is generally cut from a large fillet—for example, from salmon or halibut.

pavé This is a portion-sized, square cut from a fillet. A pavé is generally cut from a large fillet—for example, salmon, halibut, mahi mahi, or tuna.

freshness checks for finfish

To ensure that fish are of the best quality, the chef should carefully inspect the fish, checking for as many of the following signs of freshness and quality as possible:

Fish should be received at a temperature of 40°F/4°C or less.

The fish should have a good overall appearance (clear slime, no cuts or bruising, pliable fins, etc.).

The scales should tightly adhere to the fish.

The flesh should respond to light pressure and not feel soft.

The eyes should be clear, bright, and bulging.

The gills should be bright pink to maroon in color, and if mucous is present, it should be clear.

There should be no belly burn—evidence that the viscera were left in the fish too long.

The fish should have a clean, sweet, sea-like smell.

storage

Under correct storage conditions, fish and shellfish can be held for several days without losing any appreciable quality. Ideally, however, the chef should purchase only the amount of fish needed for a day or two and should store it properly, as described below.

1. Always keep fish at a proper storage temperature and handle it as little as possible: Fin fish: 28° to 32°F/−2° to 0°C; live mollusk: 35° to 40°F/2° to 4°C; live crustacean: 39° to 45°F/4° to 7°C; caviar: 28° to 32°F/−2° to 0°C; smoked fish: 32°F/0°C.

2. Check the fish carefully for freshness and quality. The fish may be rinsed at this point; scaling and fabricating should be delayed until close to service time.

3. Place the fish on a bed of shaved or flaked ice in a perforated container (such as a hotel pan with a draining pan), preferably stainless steel. The fish should be belly down, and the belly cavity should be filled with shaved ice as well.

4. Cover with additional ice; the fish may be layered, if necessary, with shaved or flaked ice. Cubed ice can bruise the fish's flesh. It also will not conform as closely to the fish. Shaved or flaked ice makes a tighter seal around the entire fish. This prevents undue contact with the air, slowing loss of quality and helping to extend safe storage life.

5. Set the perforated container in a second container. In this way, as the ice melts, the water will drain away. If the fish is allowed to sit in a pool of water, flavor and texture loss will occur. The longer it sits, the greater the loss of quality.

6. Re-ice the fish daily. Even when properly iced, the fish will gradually lose some quality. To slow this loss, skim the top layer of ice from the storage container and replace it with fresh ice. Fish purchased as fillets should be stored in stainless-steel containers set on ice. They should not be in direct contact with the ice, however, because as the ice melts, much of the flavor and texture of the fish will be lost.

common fish types

The skeletal structure of fish is a useful means of separating fin fish into smaller groupings. The three basic types of fin fish are round, flat, and nonbony. Roundfish have a middle backbone with one fillet on either side and one eye on each side of the head. Flatfish have a backbone that runs through the center of the fish, two upper and two lower fillets, and both eyes on the same side of the head. Nonbony fish have cartilage rather than bones.

Fish may also be categorized by their activity level: low, medium, or high. The more a fish swims, the darker its flesh will be. Darker-fleshed fish have a higher oil content and, therefore, a stronger flavor. When choosing the best cooking technique for a given fish, consider the oil content of the flesh. Low- and high-activity fish have limited cooking methods, while medium-activity fish are quite versatile.

sanitation

chapter four

Good care at all stages of preparation determines both the quality and the safety of the product later on.

charcuterie production and sanitation

Because you are making a product that is typically handled multiple times and may not necessarily be eaten the day it is made, it is extremely important to follow proper sanitation procedures. Prior to slaughter, the edible meat of a healthy animal is sterile, protected from contamination by skin on the outside. Once the animal is slaughtered and cut up, contamination starts through the skinning and dressing operations.

Sausage production relies on fermentation, certain chemicals, and the growth of beneficial microorganisms for both flavor and preservation. Unfortunately, not all microorganisms are beneficial to sausage; some can cause sickness and even death to consumers. There are many opportunities for harmful organisms to grow, first simply because the meat must be out of refrigeration while being ground and stuffed, putting it in the temperature danger zone (41° to 140°F/5° to 60°C); and also due to the anaerobic (lacking in oxygen) environment of a smokehouse and long-term aging. For this reason, it is of the utmost importance to handle every step and ingredient with care while making sausages.

Microorganisms include bacteria, viruses, some parasites, and fungi (yeasts and molds); they are invisible to the naked human eye, yet they are living and can multiply at very fast rates given the right conditions. Many microorganisms can be found all around us. They live on our skin and in our bodies, on dirty countertops and utensils, and in food. While we rely on certain types of bacteria in order to function, such as those that help us digest food, and mold-based drugs that fight infections (such as an-

SANITATION PROCEDURES FOR SAUSAGE PRODUCTION

PRACTICE THE 3 **C**'s: KEEP IT COLD–KEEP IT CLEAN–KEEP IT COVERED

- Chill all metal equipment that will come in contact with the meat, in an ice-water bath in a clean sink or hotel pan, or under refrigeration.

- Keep all perishable products and meat at proper chilled temperature, below 41°F/5°C.

- Wash hands before beginning any preparation; use gloves if product will not be cooked later.

- Clean and sanitize all surfaces that will be in contact with the meat: tabletop, grinder parts, pans, cutting boards, etc.

- Keep all items covered after and during processing; this will help eliminate

    Cross contamination
    Contamination from pathogens
    Physical contamination from foreign matter, such as hair

tibiotics), other types can be harmful. The key to sausage production is encouraging the beneficial organisms while deterring the harmful ones.

The main techniques of charcuterie include poaching, baking, salting or dry-curing, brining, air-drying, and smoking, either with or without heat. There are several food safety issues that are introduced through room-temperature treatments involved in air-drying and cold smoking. In order to help avoid these issues, curing salts are often used to prevent the growth of pathogens (disease-causing bacteria), particularly *Clostridium botulinum*, the bacterium that causes botulism (see page 61).

Sausage products require a wide array of control measures in their processing. Cured meats and most sausage products utilize additives such as salt, nitrates, nitrites, and sugars in processing procedures such as cooking and smoking. Salt may limit bacterial flora to salt-tolerant species. Smoking and/or cooking will destroy many vegetative cells (active, metabolizing cells). Applying heat is one of the simplest ways to kill microbes, at least for controlling vegetative cells and viruses. High temperatures do their damage by destroying organic molecules such as proteins, carbohydrates, lipids, and nucleic acids. These molecules have important roles for proper function-ing of cells and viruses. Although salting, smoking, and/or cooking can aid in the prevention of bacterial growth, the processing environment, product handling, and product packaging still have the opportunity to introduce microorganisms, including pathogens, into the packaged product. There is a particular concern when these types of pathogens are present since they can grow in cooked products without effort.

In addition to biological contamination (by pathogenic bacteria, parasites, viruses, and mold), charcuterie may also be contaminated by excess chemicals and unwanted physical items. We will discuss those later in this chapter.

water activity and microorganisms

Water activity (signified as "aw") is defined as the amount of water available for microbial growth. Water activity is based on a scale of aw 0.00 to aw 1.00, with pure water having a water activity of 1.00. Typically, products that contain a lower mois-ture percentage have lower water activities. Foods with lower water activities are quite shelf-stable in that they contain very little water available for microorganisms to use for growth. When microorganisms grow, they make the food impure, causing spoilage as well as health dangers for the consumer.

Protein, such as meat, that is high in water content (70 to 80 percent) is more open to the growth of unwanted microorganisms, so it is very important to handle and store meat properly in order to prevent these microorganisms from growing.

Even though there can be an association between the total moisture content of a food and its water activity, the correlation does not occur at all times. Food products can exist with high moisture content and still have very little water activity. Many nat-ural ingredients can be added to a product to "bind" the water or absorb the moisture so that it is unavailable for microorganisms to grow in. Several common ingredients that can be used to bind water are sugar, salt (which has six times the capacity of sugar to bind water), pectin, and glycerol.

Meat products where water activity is important as a means to increase shelf stability include cured meats such as ham, fermented meats such as sausage and pepperoni, and dried meats such as jerky. Most meat products with lower water activity levels use salt to bind water, as well as drying techniques to lower the total moisture content of the product, which in turn lowers the water activity.

biological hazards in sausage production

Sausage makers must ensure that their products are not contaminated by pathogens. Manufacturers cook products to enhance the flavor and color, produce the desired final product, and inhibit the bacteria responsible for spoilage. In order to produce a safe product, products should be cooked to destroy pathogenic bacteria, parasites, viruses, and fungi. Sausages can be cooked in a variety of ways: through immersion in a heated water bath, smoking, on the stovetop, or in the oven. The cooking process must be carefully controlled to ensure that the product reaches an exact desired temperature for a definite period of time. Thermocouples are used to monitor the temperature during the cooking progression.

The cooling process must also be carefully monitored and controlled; the cooked product must be lowered from 140° to 70°F/60° to 21°C within a two-hour period, and then from 70° to 41°F/21° to 5°C or less within a four-hour period. For food safety requirements concerning the growth of *Clostridium perfringens* (see page 60), uncured products can be cooled from 130° to 80°F/54° to 27°C within 1½ hours and 80° to 40°F/54° to 4°C within a five-hour period.

Dry sausages are almost always smoked and cooked before they are left to dry. However, some dry sausages, such as pepperoni, are rarely smoked and can be consumed either cooked or uncooked. Today, some establishments choose to treat dry sausages with heat as a critical step designed to reduce *E. coli* (see page 60). The drying process for sausages is a critical step in ensuring product safety; it requires that these products undergo a carefully controlled and monitored air-drying process that cures the manufactured goods by removing moisture from the product.

A moist heat process can be used as well for some products. This process utilizes a sealed oven or steam injection to raise the heat and relative humidity to meet a specific temperature and time requirements sufficient to eliminate pathogens.

Manufacturers are required to control the ratio of moisture to protein in the final product. The Moisture/Protein Ratio (MPR) is controlled by stabilizing the amount of added water based on the overall product formulation and, above all, by the drying procedure. In some products, the MPR can affect the final microbiological stability of the product; in other products, the MPR is important to ensure elements of the overall product quality, such as the texture. The prescribed treatments used have proved to be insufficiently lethal for some bacterial pathogens; as a result, most of the industry has volunteered to execute a more rigorous treatment. To ensure that the fermenta-

BACTERIA CAN SURVIVE IN MEAT UNDER THE RIGHT CONDITIONS

- Exposure to air (incorrectly wrapped)

- Exposure to incorrect temperatures (danger zone)

- Prolonged holding time in the fresh state

tion and drying procedure is sufficient to reduce or eliminate any pathogens present in the product, the procedures must be legalized to prove that they achieve a specific reduction in organisms.

Products containing pork must be treated to destroy trichinae; sausages made without pork have no such requirement.

microorganisms in meats

A number of product characteristics influence the growth of microorganisms. Each of these characteristics must be controlled to create an environment that is hostile to microbial growth. Microbial growth also results from defects in the product production process and/or during product handling. Microorganisms can survive the heating process due to insufficient heating time and temperatures. Contamination can occur after processing, and during handling and packaging. Spoilage can occur during the retail sale phase, if the product is stored for a long period of time or at temperatures in excess of 41°F/5°C.

harmful bacteria in sausages

salmonella enteritidis

This bacterium, usually referred to simply as salmonella, is a leading cause of foodborne illness in the United States. About 1,800 different types of salmonella are known to exist, and each is considered to be pathogenic to humans. Warm-blooded animals serve as hosts to these microorganisms. They are found in the intestinal tract of poultry and large meat animals without causing any ill effects in the animal. Salmonella results from animals ingesting feces.

Salt content and acidity of prepared meat products help keep the growth rate of salmonella down in foods. Salmonella organisms can be eliminated from cooked sausages in the same way that *E. coli* is eliminated: by proper cooking processes. In dry sausages, the manufacturer must follow a combination of processes to control the pathogen; use of a fermentation starter culture, expended product temperatures during fermentation, and careful control of the product pH, cure, and salt content all need to be followed and monitored by the manufacturer. Product handling procedures are designed and monitored to guarantee and ensure that cross contamination of the finished products with raw materials does not occur.

PRECAUTIONS FOR PREVENTING SALMONELLOSIS INFECTION

- Wash and sanitize surfaces for food production.

- Keep fresh meats and meat products out of the danger zone; store properly wrapped.

- Prevent cross contamination by washing and sanitizing all cutting boards and food contact surfaces between handling of different foods.

- Cook products to 165°F/74°C.

Escherichia coli 0157:H7 is a very serious pathogen found in the intestinal tract of cattle, which can be transferred through raw ground beef. To prevent the proliferation of *E. coli* in other foods and to destroy it at its source, we must avoid cross contamination and cook all ground beef products thoroughly.

Escherichia coli (*E. coli*) are members of a large group of bacterial germs that inhabit the intestinal tracts of humans and other warm-blooded animals (mammals, birds). Newborns have a sterile alimentary tract that becomes colonized with *E. coli* within two days of birth.

It is important to remember that most kinds of *E. coli* bacteria do not cause disease in humans.

E. COLI O157:H7

Shiga toxin is one of the most potent toxins known to man. Although *E. coli* O157:H7 is responsible for the majority of human illnesses attributed to *E. coli,* there are additional Stx-producing *E. coli* that can cause severe illness.

Stx-producing *E. coli* organisms have several characteristics that make them so dangerous. They can survive several weeks on surfaces such as countertops and up to a year in some materials like compost. They have a very low infectious dose, meaning that only a relatively small number of bacteria are needed to cause infection.

The Centers for Disease Control and Prevention (CDC) estimates that every year at least two thousand Americans are hospitalized and about sixty die as a direct result of *E. coli.*

staphylococcus aureus

This is the most common cause of food-borne illness. Most often known as "staph," this bacterium produces a poison/toxin that causes food-borne illness. *Staphylococcus aureus* bacteria can be found in processed meat products, such as ham and sausage, poultry, eggs, milk, and dairy products. Foods that require a lot of handling, preparation work, and reheating are also very susceptible to *Staphylococcus aureus* contamination.

Although food handlers are the main source of staphylococcal food poisoning, equipment and surfaces are also common media for the staph bacteria. The toxin produced by staph bacteria is very heat stable; it cannot be destroyed easily by heat at normal cooking temperatures. The bacteria themselves may be killed, but the toxin remains. It is important to ensure careful handling of food that is prepared ahead of time. Quick cooling and refrigeration, or holding at or above 140°F/60°C, can help guarantee that the toxin does not have a chance to form. Foods that require significant handling during preparation and that are kept at slightly elevated temperatures after preparation are frequently involved in staphylococcal food poisoning.

clostridium perfringens

Clostridium perfringens are spore-forming bacteria found in soil, feces, and the intestines of healthy people and animals; they are also often found in raw meat and poultry. Spores can survive normal cooking temperatures. After cooking, small numbers of the organism may still be present. The spores grow when cooked food is kept in the temperature danger zone, between 40° and 140°F/4° and 60°C. They only grow when exposed to little or no oxygen (anaerobic environment).

C. perfringens food poisoning is most common with meat products and gravies. The bacteria can be found in uncooked meat and poultry; they can also be found in many other foods, particularly in high-protein or high-starch foods. They can be transferred to food from human feces if proper hand-washing procedures are not practiced. Cooling foods slowly can also allow *C. perfringens* spores to grow.

PRECAUTIONS FOR PREVENTING CLOSTRIDIUM PERFRINGENS ENTERITIS

- The best way to reduce the bacteria is to store foods properly.

- Do not leave food out on the table or countertop, or warming in the oven, for more than two hours.

- All leftovers should be frozen or discarded after four days.

- Serve hot foods immediately or keep them above 140°F/60°C.

- Leftovers should be put into small, shallow containers so they will cool rapidly and, if they are reheated, they should be heated to 165°F/74°C.

clostridium botulinum

Clostridium botulinum is widespread in the environment, occurring in soil, water, and animals. As a result, various foods may naturally contain these bacteria, which form cells known as spores that can survive many cooking processes due to their high heat resistance. Even though *C. botulinum* is common, foods only become dangerous when *C. botulinum* grows and produces its toxin in the food. These bacteria are anaerobic, meaning they only grow where there is little or no oxygen. They are also sensitive to acid and cold, and usually cannot grow and produce toxin in acidic foods or in the refrigerator. Foods that have been associated with outbreaks of botulism include improperly canned foods (both homemade and commercially canned), flavored oils containing garlic and herbs, smoked and salted fish, and potatoes that have been baked in aluminum foil and then kept (still wrapped in foil) at room temperature for several hours. All of these are low-acid foods that may be stored in a room-temperature environment in the absence of oxygen. Another environment where *C. botulinum* can grow is on the surface of fresh vegetables wrapped tightly in plastic, which keeps out oxygen. Botulism can be prevented by practicing safe food handling techniques and looking for warning signs in food packaging. Visible indicators, such as bulging or dented cans, clear liquids that have turned milky, and cracked jars, can suggest that *C. botulinum* could be present. Today botulism is prevented in sausage and other cured meats by the use of nitrites and nitrates in cures.

listeria monocytogenes

Listeria infection, also known as listeriosis, is caused by the bacterium *Listeria monocytogenes*. Listeriosis, a serious infection caused by eating food contaminated with the bacterium, has recently been recognized as an important public health problem in the

COLD-SMOKING:
Items that are cold
smoked for any period
of time and will not be
cooked immediately;
should contain nitrites

VACUUM PACKING:
Cryovac-packaged
foods that would be
held for any period of
time and not cooked or
heated properly before
consuming

United States. Infection is rare, but when it does occur it most frequently affects pregnant women in their last trimester, newborns, and children and adults whose immunity is not yet fully developed or destabilized by disease such as cancer or AIDS. People who have had various types of transplants are also more at risk for listeriosis. Listeria bacteria can be transmitted through soil and water. A person can ingest listeria by eating foods such as deli meats and cold cuts, soft-ripened cheese, milk, undercooked chicken, uncooked hot dogs, shellfish, and coleslaw made from contaminated cabbage. Many cases of infection, however, have no identified source. Listeria infections may create symptoms such as fever, vomiting, diarrhea, lethargy, difficulty breathing, and loss of appetite. Pregnant women who develop listeriosis may experience only mild flu-like symptoms, although they are at risk for premature delivery, miscarriage, and stillbirth. People who have weakened immune systems are at particular risk for developing other more serious illnesses from listeriosis, including pneumonia, meningitis, encephalitis, and sepsis. Cases of listeriosis are relatively rare. In 2004, only 120 cases were reported in the United States. In all cases, the earlier listeriosis is detected and treated, the better. If you are pregnant or in one of the other high-risk groups, avoiding certain foods and beverages can help reduce your risk of contracting this infection. Reheat precooked, prepackaged foods, such as deli meats or hot dogs, to steaming-hot temperatures.

parasites in sausages

trichinella spiralis

Trichinosis, a disease that can be deadly at times, is caused by the consumption of the trichina parasite, *Trichinella spiralis*. Trichinosis is a major concern for sausage producers. Trichinae larvae commonly infest pork muscle, so most cases occur in people who have consumed improperly treated or prepared pork products. Infections from consumption of sausage products typically occur when a fresh sausage product has not been sufficiently cooked by the consumer, or the sausage product has not been properly treated by the producer. Since the microscopic size of the trichina larva (0.00393-inch/0.1 mm) makes it difficult to identify in a typical packinghouse operation, it is required that all pork be treated to destroy the parasite through heating, refrigeration, or curing. Heating is the most common treatment method in the sausage-processing industry. A temperature of 140°F/60°C is considered fatal to all trichinae organisms. This temperature is typically exceeded during the cooking process; however, products that are partially cooked at lower temperatures, such as smoked pork sausage, require additional treatment. These products typically undergo a formulation and curing process designed to eliminate trichinae. The process includes controlling the size of the chopped meat in the product, ensuring a specific salt content, and specifying the length of time in a drying room at a specific temperature. Another form of treatment to eliminate trichina is freezing.

PRECAUTIONS FOR PREVENTING TRICHINA CONTAMINATION

- Cook fresh pork properly. Trichinae are killed by exposing them to a temperature of at least 138°F/59°C for 10 seconds The U.S. Code of Federal Regulations for processed pork products reflects experimental data and requires pork to be cooked for 2 hours at 126°F/52.2°C, for 15 minutes at 132°F/55.6°C, and for 1 minute at 140°F/60°C.

- Irradiation treatment of fresh pork with 30 krad (0.3kGy) of cesium-137 has been proven to render trichinae completely non-infective. Irradiation with cobalt-60 or high-energy x-rays at this same level should also be effective for inactivating trichinae.

- If you are producing a fermented dry sausage or other pork item that will not be subject to the above temperatures, there are two options to follow:
  - The sausage must contain 3.5 percent or more salt and be held in a drying chamber 14 days for a 1-in-/2.5-cm-diameter product and up to 50 days for a 6-in/15-cm-diameter product.
  - If the product is only about ¾ in/2 cm thick or less, make the product using pork that has been certified free of trichinae by freezing according to the following table. The U.S. Department of Agriculture's Code of Federal Regulations requires that pork intended for use in processed products be frozen; it states pork meat, but jowl fat has some meat in it.

- Store pork in containers with no more than a 6-in/15-cm depth to the pork product.

certifying pork via freezing

MINIMUM TEMPERATURE	MINIMUM FREEZING AND HOLDING TIME
5°F/−15°C	20 days
−10°F/−23°C	12 days
−20°F/−34°C	6 days

harmful molds in sausages

Visible molds are actually a colony made up of multiple types of cells that require oxygen for growth. Under suitable conditions of moisture, air, and temperature, molds will grow on almost any food. Some molds cause allergic reactions and respiratory problems, and a few molds, under the right conditions, produce mycotoxins that are poisonous substances that can make people sick. Mold growth can even occur in refrigerators, because molds are much more tolerant to cold than to heat. Molds can grow at reduced water activities and can be a problem in improperly processed dry and semidry fermented products. Mold is a commonly encountered problem in the production of dry sausages. The common technique for inhibiting the growth of mold is to dip the sausage in a mold-inhibitor solution, typically 2.5 percent solution of potassium sorbate or a 3.5 percent solution of propylparaben.

pathogens in fish products

The following microbes are among the most important for fish and shellfish.

MICROBE	SOURCE	SYMPTOMS
VIBRIO CHOLERAE (01 AND NON-01)	Naturally occurring in estuaries, bays, and brackish water	01: Watery diarrhea, vomiting, abdominal cramps; non-01: diarrhea, abdominal cramps, fever
VIBRIO PARAHAEMOLYTICUS	Naturally occurring in estuaries and other coastal areas throughout the world	Diarrhea, abdominal cramps, nausea, vomiting, headache
VIBRIO VULNIFICUS	Naturally occurring marine bacterium	Skin lesions, septic shock, fever, chills, nausea
CLOSTRIDIUM BOTULINUM	Heat-resistant spores found throughout the environment	Diarrhea; vomiting; abdominal pain; nausea; weakness; double, blurred vision; dilated, fixed pupils; respiratory paralysis
NORWALK VIRUS	Contaminated coastal water	Nausea, vomiting, diarrhea, abdominal cramps, fever
HEPATITIS A VIRUS	Contaminated coastal waters	Weakness, fever, abdominal pain, jaundice

TRANSMISSION	CONTROL
Cross contamination from raw to cooked seafood; consumption of raw seafood	Proper cooking of seafood, preventing cross contamination of cooked seafood
Cross contamination from raw to cooked seafood; consumption of raw seafood	Proper cooking of seafood; preventing cross contamination of cooked seafood
Cross contamination from raw to cooked seafood; consumption of raw seafood	Proper cooking of seafood; preventing cross contamination of cooked seafood
Semipreserved seafood (lightly preserved fish products), improperly canned foods	Proper canning; aw <0.93, pH <4.7 This group includes fish products with low salt content (Water Phase Salt (WPS) <6 percent) and low acid content (pH >5.0). Preservatives (sorbate, benzoate, NO_2, smoke) may or may not be added. The products may be prepared from raw or cooked raw material, but are normally consumed without any prior heating. Product examples are salted, marinated, cold-smoked, or gravad fish. These products have a limited shelf life and are typically stored at temperature 41°F/5°C. The presence in these products of low numbers of pathogenic bacteria normally found in the aquatic and the general environment (*Clostridiums botulinum*, pathogenic *Vibrio* sp., *Listeria monocytogenes*) is a potential hazard. Due to their low numbers, the mere presence is not a significant hazard. However, if these organisms are allowed to grow to high numbers, they are very likely to cause a serious disease, and are therefore representing a significant hazard. It should be remembered that growth and toxin production can take place in the raw material as well as in the final product.
Cross contamination from raw to cooked seafood; consumption of raw seafood	Proper cooking of seafood; preventing cross contamination of cooked seafood
Cross contamination from raw to cooked seafood; consumption of raw seafood	Proper cooking of seafood; preventing cross contamination of cooked seafood.

chemical hazards in sausage production

nitrites and nitrates

Curing agents such as nitrites and nitrates have traditionally been used in sausage formulations. Nitrites inhibit the growth of bacteria, provide antioxidant properties, and improve the taste and color of the sausage. Although nitrates and nitrites may be helpful in preventing bacterial growth, consuming large amounts is very harmful. Since nitrites and nitrates can be toxic to humans, the use of these ingredients in sausage formulations is carefully controlled. They are sometimes referred to as "restricted ingredients." Supplies of sodium nitrite, potassium nitrite, and mixtures containing them must be kept securely under the care of a responsible employee of the establishment. The specific nitrite content of such supplies must be known and clearly marked accordingly. The acceptable maximum level of these additives is spelled out in the USDA Food Safety and Inspection Service (FSIS) regulations, as indicated in the following table.

SUBSTANCE	AMOUNT
Sodium or potassium nitrate	2¾ oz to 100 lb/78 g to 45.36 kg chopped meat
Sodium or potassium nitrite	¼ oz to 100 lb/7 g to 45.36 kg chopped meat

The amount of nitrite added to the product needs to be less than 200 parts per million based on the total amount of meat and meat by-products. Nitrites dissipate quickly in the finished product, and the parts per million in the finished product does not necessarily reflect the amount that was used in formulation. This makes sampling the finished product for nitrite an impractical control measure.

other chemical contaminants

- To prevent growth of bacteria during storage, natural casings should be salted or kept in brine at 40°F/4°C or lower (but not frozen) in covered containers. To avoid mold growth after opening, collagen and fibrous casings should not be kept in warm humid areas but rather in sealed bags or containers in a dry cooler. Meat ingredients should be stored covered at 40°F/4°C or lower and if shop generated materials are used, ensure they are labeled with the production date.

- Spices and seasonings should be stored covered and be protected from humidity, pests, and cleaning chemicals. Whenever possible place smaller quantities in spice and seasoning bins to avoid opened product from remaining unused for long periods where bacteria or other contaminants may increase.

- Inspect natural casings to ensure they are relatively free of patches of spongy tissue on their lining, which can result in shortened shelf life. If ice is used in sausage production, ensure that the ice box is cleaned regularly and that only clean scoops, never hands, are used to remove it. Inspect meat for off odor, bone chips, cartilage, glands, foreign materials, or any other condition that would make it unsatisfactory for use. Select all meat ingredients in accordance with a first in–first out system, and whenever possible, avoid the use of rework. Use of whole muscle cuts for grinding will enhance shelf life.

- Before the start of production, all equipment should be inspected to ensure that it is free of visible meat residues or pooled water and that all parts and fasteners are accounted for and properly secured. A written procedure for disassembly and sanitation of the grinder, mixer, stuffer, and all other equipment should be followed each production day, or more often if needed. If sausage is being produced from a different species than a previous batch, then a cleanup should be performed. When equipment is cleaned, it should also be inspected for rust, excessive wear, or any other condition that could produce contamination or make cleaning difficult. Individuals involved with sausage production must ensure that their hands and garments are clean.

- Sausage production areas should be kept at no more than 50°F/10°C and whenever possible 39.2°F/4°C or colder. During production, the meat block should be sufficiently cold to ensure that the finished product leaving the stuffer is 39.2°F/4°C or less. When moisture addition is required, use ice or cold potable liquids dispensed using cleaned and sanitized containers. Following stuffing, finished product should be packaged using clean trays and placed in a refrigerated display case or cooler as quickly as possible.

- If potential allergens are used in the production of sausage, ensure that they are declared in applicable labeling or ingredient lists and that equipment is cleaned before other products are made. Always follow sausage recipes and do not substitute ingredients that would require labeling or ingredient list changes.

physical hazards in sausage production

Set up a chart stating standard operating procedures and the standards for each stage of the process.

A simple chart would include:

1. Receiving and storing of raw materials
2. Receiving and storing of nonmeat ingredients
3. Formulation
4. Grinding and mixing
5. Cooking
6. Chilling and holding
7. Packaging
8. Storage
9. Distribution

The main types of physical hazards in food include:

- **GLASS:** Common sources found in food-processing facilities are light bulbs, glass containers, and glass food containers.

- **METAL:** Common sources of metal include metal from equipment, such as splinters, blades, broken needles, fragments from worn utensils, and staples.

- **PLASTICS:** Common sources of soft and hard plastics include material used for packaging, gloves worn by food handlers, utensils used for cleaning equipment, and tools used to remove processed food from equipment.

- **STONES:** Field crops, such as peas and beans, are most likely to contain small stones picked up during harvesting. Concrete structures and floors in food-processing facilities can also be a source of small stones.

- **WOOD:** Common sources of wood come from wood structures and wooden pallets used to store or transport ingredients or food products.

There are many ways food processors can prevent physical hazards in food products, including:

- Inspect raw materials and food ingredients for field contaminants (for example, stones in cereals) that were not found during the initial receiving process.

- Follow good storage practices and evaluate potential risks in storage areas (for example, sources of breakable glass such as light bulbs, staples from cartons, etc.) and use protective acrylic bulbs or lamp covers.

- Develop specifications and controls for all ingredients and components, including raw materials and packaging materials. Specifications should contain standards for evaluating acceptability of ingredients or packaging materials. (For example, recycled cardboard used for packaging sometimes contains traces of metals that can be detected by metal detectors. A limit for metal detection should be established to avoid false positive detection of metal in food.)

- Set up an effective detection and elimination system for physical hazards in your facility (for example, metal detectors or magnets to detect metal fragments in the production line and filters or screens to remove foreign objects at the receiving point). Properly and regularly maintain the equipment in your facility to avoid sources of physical hazards, such as foreign materials that can come from worn-out equipment.

- Periodic employee training on shipping, receiving, storing, handling, equipment maintenance, and calibration will also help prevent physical hazards from being introduced into food products.

microorganisms to be encouraged in sausage production

We have been growing beneficial bacteria during the curing process for centuries, and although we knew nothing of bacteria, we had observed that cured meats developed nicer color, tasted better, and lasted longer.

Without beneficial bacteria, it would not be possible to make fermented sausage. They are naturally occurring in the meat, but in many cases, they are added to meat in the form of starter culture.

There are two classes of beneficial (friendly) bacteria.

1. Lactic acid–producing bacteria, *Lactobacillus, Pediococcus*

2. Color- and flavor-forming bacteria, *Staphylococcus, Kocuria* (previously known as *Micrococcus*)

beneficial bacteria in sausage production

lactic acid bacteria

Lactic acid bacteria are a group of related bacteria that produce lactic acid as a result of carbohydrate fermentation. These microorganisms are generally used in the production of fermented food products, such as yogurt, cheeses, sauerkraut, and sausage.

Lactic acid bacteria cause rapid acidification of meat by metabolizing sugar. They produce not only lactic acid but also acetic acid, ethanol, different aromas, bacteriocins, and other enzymes. By increasing the acidity of the meat, they influence not only safety and shelf life of the product but also its flavor.

Lactic acid bacteria are used in the food industry for several reasons. Their growth lowers both the carbohydrate content of the foods that they ferment and the pH due to lactic acid production. It is this acidification process that is one of the most desirable side effects of their growth. The pH may drop to as low as 4.0, low enough to inhibit the growth of most other bacteria including the most common human pathogens, thus allowing these foods extended shelf life.

Producers of dry sausages and semidry sausages must use controlled, bacterially induced fermentation in order maintain the meat and impart flavor. Bacterial fermentation is used to produce the lower pH (a range of 4.7 to 5.4) that results in the tangy flavor associated with this type of sausage. When the pH is lowered it causes the proteins to give up water, resulting in a drying effect that creates an environment that is unfavorable to spoilage organisms, which helps to maintain the product.

white mycelium

White mycelium is a heavy growth of molds on the surface of European-type sausages such as Italian salami, as well as country-cured hams. White mycelium helps in the preservation of these food products by inhibiting the activities of pathogenic and food-spoilage bacteria, and may also enhance flavor development.

curing & brining

chapter five

The two primary reasons to cure or brine meats, poultry, and seafood are preservation and flavor.

Curing and brining—and salting in general—are historically among the most popular methods of preserving meats, poultry, and fish. At one time hard-curing was the only method used to preserve meat. The meat was placed (packed) in a container with just salt. Over a period of a few days, the salt would draw moisture out of the meat, producing a brine. The liquid was drained off. More salt was added, and the process was repeated several times until the meat was hard and dry. The final product would keep indefinitely but had to be soaked in fresh water several times to get rid of the salt before it was edible.

They still are popular for preserving to an extent, but due to our better refrigeration and freezing, they are more often used to add flavor and texture to meat.

Curing, a dry process, can take from hours to many weeks or months. Curing is done before smoking most products (see Chapter 6). The quest to add flavor when curing has us using items like maple sugar and molasses along with many different herbs, spices, and seasonings such as five-spice powder, miso, garlic, basil, thyme, or rosemary. All of these items add depth to the flavor of the product, not just a salty effect. We tend to create our own flavor profiles based on what we like.

Brining is a wet process, in which we basically take a cure and add water to it to create a saline solution (sometimes also known as a pickle or curing solution). The product needs to be immersed in brine; when you brine items, they usually will take a shorter period of time to cure as opposed to dry-curing items. A portion of the brine may also be injected into the product. For injection, 10 percent of the total weight in brine solution should be used, and it should be injected into a few of the thickest areas of the product at the same time. Introducing a portion of the brine by injection will also reduce brining time by about one-half, as the injection process hastens the absorption and therefore the rate of curing.

Seasoning meats is more complicated than just mixing salt and pepper with some herbs and spices. Flavor is introduced through various means, such as marinades, injection solutions, seasoning rubs, and glazes that affect both taste and texture.

Flavors that are often lost during processing can be added by injecting and/or tumbling meats with marinade solutions under cold conditions before cooking and/or by applying seasonings topically either through a glaze or a rub to highlight the appearance of the outer surface.

main ingredients and their function in curing and brining

salt

For centuries, meat has been preserved with salt. At certain levels, salt prevents growth of some types of bacteria that are responsible for meat spoilage. Salt prevents bacterial growth either because of its direct inhibitory effects or because of the drying effects it has on meats (most bacteria require substantial amounts of moisture to live and grow).

Salt should be food grade, have no anti-caking agents added to it, and should not be iodized. The size of the crystal of table salt is smaller than kosher salt, and it is usually cubic in shape. Table salt contains additives to keep the small crystals from caking and clumping.

Unrefined salt, such as sea salt, fleur de sel, or all natural salts, contain different minerals giving each a unique flavor. All four cationic electrolytes (sodium, potassium, magnesium, and calcium) are available in unrefined salt along with other vital minerals.

After raw salt is obtained, it is refined to purify it and improve its storage and handling.

Table salt is a refined salt that can have as little as 60 percent or as much as 90 percent sodium chloride and usually will contain a substance that makes it free flowing, like an anti-caking agent.

Kosher salt, the type of salt called for in the recipes in this book, usually has no additives, and it has big crystals with large surface areas. This size and shape allows it to absorb more moisture than other forms of salt, and this makes kosher salt excellent for curing meats. That is essentially where the name comes from. The salt itself is not kosher, meaning it doesn't conform to Jewish food laws, but this salt is used to make meat kosher. The Jewish holy book, the Torah, prohibits consumption of any blood, which is why kosher meat must be slaughtered and prepared in a specific manner. A common way of removing the final traces of blood from meat is to soak and salt it.

PRESERVING WITH SALT

Salt draws water out of microbial cells through a process known as osmosis. This process draws water out of the cell in order to maintain the same salt concentration inside and outside of the cell. The combination of the lack of moisture and high salt content inhibits the growth of microorganisms that cause the food to spoil. A salt concentration of about 20 percent is required to kill most species of bacteria.

As the unwanted bacterial population decreases, the beneficial bacteria, primarily of the *Lactobacillus* genus (commonly found in yogurt), comes to the foreground and generates an acidic environment of about 4.5 pH. The process of curing is, in fact, a form of fermentation, and in addition to reducing further the ability of spoilage bacteria to grow, accounts for the tangy flavor of some cured products. In order to fuel the lactobacilli to complete the fermentation process, sugar is included in the cure. Dextrose, a form of glucose, is generally preferred over sucrose (granulated sugar). This is because glucose is a simple sugar, while sucrose is a complex sugar, made of glucose and fructose. The bacteria use glucose as their food source. If sucrose is used, the bacteria will break down the sucrose into its two parts and leave the fructose behind, sweetening the product.

sweetener

The sweetener you use depends on the relative sweetness and the overall flavor of the product. Whiter sugars (for example, glucose, fructose, sucrose, etc.), brown sugar, maple sugar, and other sugars all have their own unique tastes.

relative sweetness

Sweetness is universally regarded as pleasurable. "Perception" is not the same thing as "liking," though the two are related. It is common knowledge that not all sweeteners taste equally sweet.

The perception of sweetness we get from items is different from one another; each item brings with it a perception we think of as sweet with a good flavor and also a point where it is too much and overpowering. This will drive us to use certain types and different amounts of sweeteners.

relative sweetness scale

COMPOUND	RATING
Sucrose (granulated sugar)	100
Fructose	140
High-Fructose Corn Syrup	120–160
Glucose (dextrose)	70–80
Galactose	35
Maltose	30–50
Lactose	20

Relative Sweetness Scale – Sucrose = 100

In charcuterie, the relative sweetness of 1 lb/454 g dextrose is equal to ⅔ lb/303 g granulated sugar, which is also equivalent to 8 oz/227 g honey. You would need ⅔ lb/303 g sugar and only 8 oz/227 g honey to achieve the same taste of sweetness you get from 1 lb/454 g dextrose.

nitrites and nitrates

As the use of salt as a meat preservative spread, a preference developed for certain salts that produced a pink color and special flavor in meat. The reddening effect on meats was first mentioned during the latter part of the Roman Empire. Nitrate was probably present in the crude form of salt that was used: in many cases it was the result of evaporated sea water. In the early 1900s, it was discovered that salt (NaCl) did not produce the red color, but that sodium and potassium nitrates present in impure salt did. It was also discovered that sodium nitrate was converted into sodium nitrite by bacteria found in meat, and then into nitric oxide. The amount of color change is dependent on the amount of myoglobin present in meat (the more myoglobin, the darker reddish-pink the cured color). Chicken has the lowest myoglobin content, whereas beef has the highest content. Seafood contains no myoglobin.

More important than for color enhancement, nitrites have been the only acceptable substance to prevent botulism in cured and smoked products, even though more than 700 substances have been tested as possible replacements.

Today the nitrite used in meat curing is produced commercially as sodium nitrite. There is a movement to use natural nitrates from vegetable products, such as beet powder and celery juice.

COMMERCIAL PRODUCTS CONTAINING NITRITES AND/OR NITRATES:
INSTA CURE NO. 1 (TINTED CURE MIX [TCM]/PRAGUE POWDER NO. I)
This product is used to develop and stabilize the pink "cured color" in lean muscle tissue of meat and comprise 94 percent sodium chloride (salt) and 6 percent sodium nitrite. It inhibits the growth of a number of food poisoning and spoilage organisms, in particular the *Clostridium botulinum* organism. To prevent botulism, 4 oz/113 g of TCM is needed to cure 100 lb/45.36 kg of meat. TCM contributes to the characteristic flavor of cured meats, and retards lipid fat oxidation—also known as rancidity—in product, preventing stale taste.

INSTA CURE NO. 2
This is a combination of salt, sodium nitrite, sodium nitrate, and pink coloring. It is used for dry and dry-fermented products, particularly products with longer curing and drying periods.

saltpeter (potassium nitrate)

Use of saltpeter has been limited by the USDA since 1975. It is not allowed in the production of smoked or cooked meat or sausages. This restriction is primarily related to the fact that the exact level of residual nitrites in products treated with potassium nitrate is hard to determine in advance.

NITRITES AND CANCER

A controversy during the late 1970s came about when it was suggested that nitrite consumption led to the development of cancer. Tests found that when nitrite and nitrite-cured products were exposed to certain conditions, the nitrite changed into nitrosamine, which was believed to cause cancer of the pancreas and alimentary tract. The tests were done with laboratory animals, feeding them large quantities of nitrosamines. Nitrosamines develop when bacon is cooked brown. Nitrosamines also develop when pepper and paprika were mixed with nitrite in dry form and stored for a few months.

As a result of these tests, there is stricter control of the use of nitrite in food processing. Less nitrite is used to cure meats, and residual nitrites must be less than 200 ppm (parts per million) in finished processed meats. Today bacon contains erythorbate or some other vitamin C compound to prevent nitrosamine formation. Also, nitrite cannot be premixed with paprika and pepper in spice blends; they are packaged separately and should be mixed and then used right away.

seasonings

Here your creativity comes into play. Depending on what kind of flavor you want to have in the finished product, you can add herbs, spices, and other flavorings to cures so that those flavors will develop in the product brining. You can also infuse them into brines by heating the flavors (sage, rosemary, garlic, and ginger) as an example. To infuse the items into the brine, you would bring the brine up to a simmer with the flavorings to release the flavors into the brine. You can also use dry spices or even toasted spices. There are also flavors that you can purchase like liquid smoke, and flavors developed by chemists that can be added to the brine to create certain tastes such as autolyzed yeast extracts, salt, and phosphates, and they may also include sweeteners, starches, and hydrocolloids, often called gums, soy proteins, or other ingredients. Starches from a variety of natural sources, such as corn and potato, remain the leading hydrocolloids, followed closely by gelatin. Most important among these properties are viscosity (including thickening and gelling) and water binding but also significant are many others including emulsion stabilization. The degree with which the hydrocolloid solutions mix with saliva can determine the flavor perception you have. Selecting and blending these ingredients pose challenges, even to "seasoned" chefs. Flavoring meat and poultry is still a trial-and-error process; you need to mix and remix seasonings many times to reach the flavor profile you want to achieve.

Over the last few years, there has been an explosion in the types of flavors that meat processors are prepared to look at and consumers are willing to accept. The industry has gone from simple to very complex flavor profiles. Ethnic foods are definitely in, and the meat industry is no exception. Authentic ethnicity is key today. For example, although there is still a market for Tex-Mex food, consumers now want to see true Mexican cuisine rather than an Americanized version. Ethnic flavor trends include Thai, Caribbean, Latin American, Middle Eastern, Greek, and even Egyptian. Other popular flavors include teriyaki, honey, tropical orange, lime, coconut, ginger, garlic, and specific chiles. Sophisticated consumers are looking for high-quality, value-added meat and poultry products, eye appeal, and good taste. In food stores there is a variety of meats that are marinated and Cryovac-ed, so they develop flavor as they are waiting to be sold to customers. But many chefs and customers will still prefer the basic flavors developed with salt and pepper and basic seasonings.

water

Water is essential if you are going to use a brine. Water helps dissolve all the ingredients and flavorings, making the ingredients easier to be injected or to penetrate the mass by absorption.

curing methods

There are two basic methods for curing meats: dry curing and wet curing, the latter also known as brining. Dry curing can be used for many different products, such as bacon, salmon, and pancetta, to name a few. Brining can be used for a variety of products as well, but this type of curing is the most beneficial when applied to large items such as whole turkeys, briskets, or bone-in hams.

To use these processes, large containers, mixing bowls, and a decent amount of storage space are necessary. The processes can take anywhere from 1 to 2 hours to 40 to 45 days, depending on the item (fish or meats) being cured and the ingredients used in the specific cures or brines. Curing items usually takes longer than brining. The item being cured will determine the amount of time, the texture of the protein, the thickness of the product, and if there is skin.

USES AND RESULTS OF DIFFERENT CURING METHODS

DRY CURE: Used for products where a lower water content and drier texture are required. The product has a longer shelf life due to its lower moisture content.

BRINE (WET CURE): Used for items that will be cooked. The final product can have moisture content equal to or higher than the original item. This method is used primarily for larger pieces of meat and for whole poultry.

dry curing

The use of salt was very important before our current method of refrigeration was invented. In colonial America, almost all foods were salted in order to preserve them, especially before winter. Salted meat was particularly common; little fresh meat was eaten except right after an animal was killed, because there was no means of keeping the meat fresh afterward.

Curing refers to a specific preservation and flavoring process, especially of meat or fish, through the addition of a combination of salt, sugar, and either nitrate or nitrite. Curing with salt and sugar may be called salting, salt curing, sugar curing, or honey curing. The application of pellets of salt, called corns, is often called corning.

Dry curing can be as simple as salt alone, but more often the cure is a mixture of salt, a sweetener of some sort, flavorings, and, if indicated or desired, a commercially or individually prepared curing blend. Preserving foods by curing lets the food take on a saltier, sharper flavor, with a much drier texture. Foods to be cured must be in direct contact with the cure to help ensure an evenly preserved product. Some may be wrapped in cheesecloth or food-grade paper; others may be packed in bins or brine tubs with cure scattered around them and in between layers. They should be turned or rotated periodically as they cure. This process is known as overhauling. Larger items such as hams may be rubbed repeatedly with additional cure mixture over a period of days. If there is an exposed bone in the item, it is important to rub the cure around and over the exposed area to cure it properly.

ratios for basic dry cure

The basic ratio of salt to sweetener in a dry cure is 2 parts salt to 1 part sugar (by weight). The other seasonings will depend on the item being cured and the depth of flavor you want to develop.

If using a gravlax-style cure (page 101), the ratio of salt to sugar will differ. The ratio will only be 1 to 1½ parts salt to 1 part sugar (by weight), which will be mixed with the seasonings. Also, the length of time to cure will differ: if using standard cure on fish, it will take 6 to 12 hours; gravlax-style will take 3 days, or 72 hours, to cure. This is 1½ parts salt to 1 part sugar.

dry cure method for meats

The basic steps taken in curing of meat items are:

1. Fabricate the product.

2. Prepare the dry cure.

3. Calculate the amount of dry cure you will use according to weight of product (8 oz/227 g of cure mix for every 10 lb/4.54 kg of product).

4. Rub the measured amount of dry cure into the product. Place it in a covered nonreactive container, with the items in the container covered.

5. Overhaul the product every other day.

6. Wait the required amount of time for your product to complete the curing process.

7. Rinse or soak the product in lukewarm water.

8. Air-dry the product to form a pellicle, a tacky film formed on the top of the item that has been cured or brined and rinsed and then air-dried. This process will form the film that will help hold the smoke on the product.

9. Hot- or cold-smoke the product. Cool until 40°F/4°C, then wrap and store in a refrigerator.

meat curing times using the dry cure method

ITEM	APPROXIMATE TIME
Meat, approx. ¼ in/6 mm thick	1–2 hours
Meat, approx. 1 in/2.54 cm thick	3–8 hours
Pork belly (1½ in/4 cm thick)	7–10 days
Ham, bone-in (15–18 lb/6.80–8.16 kg)	40–45 days

dry cure method for seafood

The process used in curing fish varies slightly from the one used to cure meat. The ingredients and techniques are the same, except you do not overhaul the seafood, you use all of the cure, and the time span is shorter. (See Gravlax, page 101.)

1. Trim the item (remove fins, fat; pull out pin bones; but leave skin on fillet).

2. Prepare the cure.

3. Score the skin of the fish.

4. Pack dry cure on the fish.

5. Wait the required amount of time for your product to complete the curing process.

6. Rinse or soak the product in lukewarm water.

7. Place on a rack and air-dry to form the pellicle.

8. Hot- or cold-smoke, if desired.

seafood curing times using the dry cure method

ITEM	APPROXIMATE TIME
Shrimp, scallops	½–1 hour
Trout fillets	2 hours
Whole trout	4–6 hours
Salmon fillets[*]	6–12 hours

*A normal fillet of 2½ lb/1.13 kg will take 6 hours.

brining (wet curing)

Curing in a salt-and-water solution or brine is known as wet curing, pickling, or brining. The curing of fish is sometimes called kippering. Historically, brining has been used as a method to preserve meat. Brine is basically a solution of water and salt. Thus, to brine means to treat with or steep in a solution of water and salt. Sweeteners and other seasonings may also be added to a brine.

There are one of two ways to dissolve your sugar, salt, and spices in a liquid. You may use warm water to dissolve the dry cure, or you can bring to a simmer to infuse it with spices or aromatics. The saline solution should be heated so that the salt and sugars get dissolved; then it needs to be cooled so the meat or fish does not get cooked. Either way, the brine must be thoroughly chilled before being used to cure foods. Both the brine alone and the product being brined need to be kept refrigerated under 40°F/4°C.

The length of time you leave the product in the brine depends on:

- Thickness of the item
- Thickness of fat and/or skin cover
- Density of the meat
- Temperature of the brine

For safety, discard the brine solution after use. Do not reuse a brine.

submersion method for brining

Traditionally, in this method, meat is soaked for many days in a very strong saltwater solution with addition of sugar, spices, and other ingredients. This curing process binds the water in the meat or removes it altogether so it is not available for the growth of food-spoiling microorganisms. This method is normally used for items such as ham hocks, Cornish hens, hams, and Canadian bacon.

More recently, brining has become more popular and is sometimes called flavor brining. Flavor brining is achieved by soaking the product in a moderately salty solution for a few hours to a few days. The sort of brining we use today is meant to improve flavor, texture, and moisture content while infusing new flavors into lean meat, poultry, and seafood. This form of brining does not have to contain any nitrates or nitrites. The main ingredients in a flavor brine are water and salt. Other ingredients may be brown sugar, honey, maple syrup, fruit juices, beer, liquor, molasses, bay leaves, pickling spices, cloves, garlic, onion, chiles, citrus fruits, peppercorns, as well as herbs and spices.

When brining, the items must be immersed completely in the brine. Brining time varies according to:

- Thickness of item overall
- Thickness of fat and/or skin cover
- Density of meat
- Brine temperature (40°F/4°C for good results and to keep the product out of the danger zone)

brine pumping

The most popular method being used today for meats to be barbecued or smoked, or for flavor development, is brine pumping. Brine pumping results in a more rapid and uniform distribution of the brine throughout the item, curing from the center to the surface, as well as from the surface to the center. Once injected, the items must also be immersed in a brine and held under refrigeration until the brine is distributed evenly throughout the flesh of the product.

Here are some ways that a brine is injected into the product.

STITCH PUMPING is done by inserting a needle with multiple holes into the meat and injecting the brine into the thickest part of the flesh, as close to the bone as possible.

ARTERY INJECTION involves the use of a needle with a single hole and injecting the brine through a main artery. The artery in the early days was left slightly exposed, and the brine was pumped into it to the arterial system. It traveled through the arteries and worked its way out through the walls and into the meat; needless to say, that was not the best way, but it worked.

MULTINEEDLE INJECTION is a commercial process used today for curing meat. A machine that contains multiple needles automatically injects the meat with the proper amount of brining solution.

The most current process in the industry for bacon production is brining the pork bellies by injecting them with brine. This is a very even process that is not only fast but efficient as well.

brine enhancing

Enhanced meat is injected by the producer with a solution of water, salt, and other ingredients to enhance the moisture content and flavor of the meat and some cases tenderize the product. The use of phosphates along with the water-salt solution will retain more water in the product. The product does not have to be immersed. The phosphates retain water, keeping the product moist, creating the juice ham water that is found in supermarkets.

For larger items such as turkeys, use a continuous-feed brine pump to inject the brine into the meat.

After the brine is injected, completely submerge the meat in a brine bath.

Finished brined and smoked turkey breast

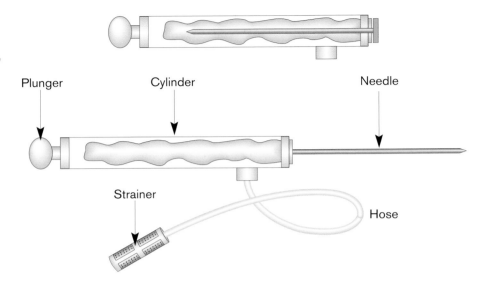

RIGHT: Brine pump with needle
properly stored

BELOW RIGHT: Continuous-feed brine
pump

Plunger   Cylinder   Needle

Strainer

Hose

meat curing times using the brine method

ITEM	TIME, NOT PUMPED	TIME, PUMPED
Chicken or duck breast	1–2 hours	not recommended
Chicken whole	24–36 hours	12–16 hours
Pork butt or loin, boneless	5–6 days	2½–3 days
Turkey, whole (10–12 lb/ 4.54–5.44 kg)	5–6 days	3 days
Beef brisket (corned beef)	7–8 days	3–5 days
Ham, boneless	6 days	4 days
Ham, bone-in	20–24 days	6–7 days

what can go wrong with brines and cures?

GRAY SPOTS: If you notice gray spots in the center of the product, this means that either the product was not cured long enough, or that the cure was too cold so the salt did not penetrate the center. In order to prevent gray spots from forming, be sure to cure the product for the correct length of time indicated in the recipe. Make sure to check the temperature of the brine before using it to ensure that it is not too cold. If both of these guidelines are followed, the salt should thoroughly penetrate the item being cured and there should be no occurrence of gray spots in the item.

SPOILAGE: Spoilage can occur when there is an insufficient amount of salt, when the area that the curing product was stored in was too warm, or when the curing time for that particular item was too short. To avoid spoilage, make sure that the cure has been packed evenly onto the product, and that the product being cured is stored under proper refrigeration for the indicated length of time. In order to ensure safety, be sure to keep the product cold at all times, keep all equipment very clean, and keep the product covered and correctly dated.

tenderizing and flavoring

marinades

The verb "to marinate" means to steep food in a savory acidic sauce (a marinade) to enrich its flavor, tenderize it, and, in many cases, preserve it. Today, a marinade usually consists of a cooking oil (infused oils can also be used) plus an acid (vinegar, citrus juice, wine), with herbs, spices, seasonings, and aromatics.

The role of acid in a marinade is to break down long protein strands—the part of the meat that causes it to be tough. For tenderizing tough cuts of meat it's the acid base that counts. Start with an acidic base like vinegar, wine, or buttermilk. Fruit juice or milk may also serve as a marinade's base. A vinaigrette penetrates meat fibers particularly well, since the addition of oil to a marinade aids the penetration of the acid. If you use prepared vinaigrettes with emulsifiers in the ingredients, these appear to penetrate deeper into the meat, making a better marinade. Emulsifiers may be listed as monoglyceride, diglyceride, or polysorbate 80. These are natural substances and not considered harmful additives.

In marinades, herbs and spices are combined with tenderizing ingredients such as lemon juice to give marinades their hearty flavor. Marinades really begin to blossom with fruit-based flavors, herbs, wines, and liqueurs. The range runs from sweet to spicy, piquant to fruity, with lots of zesty flavors in between. You'll find that most recipes are designed for versatility. What tastes great with chicken wings is a surefire winner for marinating spareribs. A passion-fruit marinade that complements chicken breast can cross over to shrimp.

For the most part, the list of ingredients should be easy to follow. It starts with acids, followed by oils and fresh and dry aromatics. Lemon juice is a good substitute for lime juice, while an equal amount of vinegar may be too sharp. When in doubt, use a neutral flavor. Don't double up on other aromatics to compensate for leaving out a portion of one of them. The aromatics are there as support flavors. Doubling up on a strong spice like cumin may throw the marinade out of balance. If you have qualms about substituting an herb or a spice, put a little bit of your marinade aside, sprinkle in a pinch, and taste.

As the food stands in the mixture, the acid and/or oil impart the savory flavors of the spices to the food. The acid also causes tissues to break down, which has a tenderizing effect. The breaking down of the tissues also causes the item to hold more liquid, making it juicier. However, too much vinegar or hot sauce in a marinade can have the opposite effect, causing the meat to be stringy and tough.

For naturally tender cuts, marinades usually take a short time to preserve. For example, in a steak house, steaks may be placed in a hotel pan or container and marinated in some herbs, rosemary, garlic, sage, and oil and stored in a refrigerator to hold until they are ready to be grilled. Also, the oil can be infused with items and then used to marinate and hold the product. The oil coats the product, gives it some flavor, and seals it by not allowing the air to get to it as fast, and therefore, slowing down the spoilage process.

TYPE OF MARINADE	USES
Oil and spice	For naturally tender cuts; usually short time bases (can infuse seasonings for a longer shelf life)
Acid and oil	Typically a vinaigrette; slight tenderization and preservation
Acid and spice	Heavy tenderization (e.g., sauerbraten); preservation (ceviche)

amount of marinade to use

Ideally, the marinade should cover the food in order to flavor it evenly. In a baking dish, the wider the dish, the shallower the depth of the marinade. In that case you'll find that you need to turn the food more frequently. Use 1 cup/240 mL of marinade to 1 lb/454 g of meat if you're using resealable plastic bags, or 2 cups/480 mL of marinade if you are submerging the meat in a small, flat baking dish.

marinating times

Fish needs the shortest marinating time, followed by chicken, then meat with the longest. The firmer the texture, the longer the soak. You can marinate fish or chicken in the refrigerator overnight or up to a couple of days by adding the acid portion of your recipe during the last few hours. The acid level for seafood should be lower than for chicken. If the acidic level is more than 25 percent—when the vinegar or citrus exceeds 25 percent of the total liquid volume—reduce the marinating time. Lean foods absorb marinades faster due to low fat content. More fat requires more time.

You can start marinating food immediately after mixing the marinade together, or you can leave a marinade refrigerated overnight for the flavors to meld. Marinades can last for four to five days before they start to break down and the aromatics lose their strength. You may need to refresh the marinade's flavor with additional aromatics and citrus the day you start marinating your food. Like brines, marinades should not be reused.

ACIDS AND ENZYMES IN MARINADES

The two most popular types of marinades are acidic (made with citrus, vinegar, or wine) and enzymatic (made with ingredients such as pineapple and papaya). Although both types work primarily on the surface of the food, they lead to different results: highly acidic marinades can actually toughen food, while enzymatic marinades can turn the surface of the food to mush. For true tenderizing, the most effective marinades are those that contain dairy products.

ACIDS

Acidic marinades denature proteins. Imagine the protein in raw meat, chicken, or fish as individual units of coiled ribbon, with bonds holding each coil in a tight bundle. When these proteins are exposed to an acidic marinade, the bonds break and the proteins unwind. Almost immediately, one unwound protein runs into another unwound protein and they bond together into a loose mesh. (This is the same thing that happens when proteins are exposed to heat.)

At first, water molecules are trapped within this protein mesh, so the tissue remains juicy and tender. But after a short time, if the protein is in a very acidic marinade, the protein bonds tighten, water is squeezed out, and the tissue becomes tough.

In limited cases, mildly acidic marinades can add wonderful flavor to fish and meat, especially if you enhance the mixture with fresh herbs, spices, or perhaps another liquid such as Worcestershire sauce. The key is to use the correct strength acid for the food you're marinating.

ENZYMES MAKE MEAT MUSHY

Enzymatic marinades work by breaking down muscle fiber and collagen (connective tissue), cutting proteins instead of denaturing them. Raw pineapple, figs, papaya, honeydew melon, ginger, and kiwi all contain such enzymes, known collectively as proteases (protein enzymes). Unfortunately, these enzymes work almost too well, turning tough meat muscle into mush without passing through any intermediate stage of tenderness. The longer the meat marinates, the greater the breakdown of proteins and the mushier the texture. When you place product in an acidic environment that is under 5 on the pH scale, it will denature the product but also act to preserve it, as bacteria do not survive well in an acidic environment.

Most commercial meat tenderizers rely on enzymes to do their "tenderizing;" a papaya enzyme, papain, is a common ingredient in these products.

FOR TRUE TENDERIZING, USE BUTTERMILK OR YOGURT

Dairy products are, in my opinion, the only marinades that truly tenderize. Hunters have long known to marinate tough game in milk; Indian recipes use yogurt marinades for mutton and tough goat meat; and some Southern cooks soak chicken in buttermilk before frying. Buttermilk and yogurt are only mildly acidic, so they don't toughen the way strongly acidic marinades do. It's not quite clear how the tenderizing occurs, but it seems that calcium in dairy products activates enzymes in meat that break down proteins, a process similar to the way that aging tenderizes meat.

In deciding how long to marinate, consider the texture of the meat or fish. In general, open-textured flesh like fish fillets needs only a few minutes of soaking. Food with a tighter texture, such as chicken or lamb, can tolerate several hours in a marinade, even one that's mildly acidic.

rubs and dry marinades

Rubs are mixtures of ground herbs, spices, and similar dry ingredients that are massaged into the surface of food (most often meat) to add flavor. A rub is not a true marinade because it neither preserves nor tenderizes. The ingredients can be as simple as salt and pepper rubbed on chicken before roasting. They may encompass traditional spice mixes such as India's masala, Malaysia's rempahs, North Africa's berbere, and Thailand's curry pastes. Rubs blacken redfish in Louisiana; mint and lemon is pressed into lamb dishes of Greece; and a mixed peppercorn crust is placed on grilled steak.

Generally, highly spiced dry rubs tend to work better on meat and poultry, while wet rubs or pastes are better with seafood. Rubs can be prepared entirely from dried herbs and spices. Spices should be bought whole and ground as needed. Stale spices will taste bitter or medicinal. For the best flavor, toast whole spices that you plan on using and grind them. This accentuates the flavors in the spices. When a recipe calls for pepper, avoid the preground type. Once pepper is ground and in a glass shaker, its oils are exposed to air and light, with flavor fading quickly.

The only equipment needed to prepare rubs is a blender or spice grinder, although the time-honored tradition of mortar and pestle is still preferred by some cooks. A rub need not be pulverized to a fine powder to release flavor. If using a spice grinder or blender, avoid grinding to the point that some of the oils are released into the rub from the heat of processing. This causes the rub to become somewhat pasty. If this happens, the rub will need to be used fairly quickly, as the oil will turn rancid. (To clean your spice grinder, run a couple of spoonfuls of raw rice through the grinder, then throw out the rice. Dry rice collects all the spice particles of the previous mix.)

Only a small amount of rub is needed. Less than a tablespoon will flavor a whole chicken breast or dust a 6- to 8-oz/170- to 227-g fillet of fish. A quarter cup (60 mL) will easily cover a side of spareribs, or a whole breast of turkey. The rub can be applied under the breast skin of poultry. The natural juices mix with the rub to provide a savory baste when it hits a hot grill or broiler.

No spice mix will store indefinitely. Nor do all the ingredients age evenly. Storing a dry rub in a cool airtight environment will maintain its flavor for two to three months, but the flavor will not be as intense.

When you use a rub, take small handfuls (using your hands is the most effective) and coat the entire surface of the food. Use a bit of pressure to rub the spices in, mixing the spices slightly with some of the liquid from the flesh so they adhere. When cooking, expect the rub to turn dark brown; this is what happens as the spices cook. However, if the rub begins to smoke, heat adjustments need to be made.

dry marinades and rubs

Dry marinades and rubs add flavor without excess moisture. Some chefs prefer rubs to marinades because the rubs provide better flavor penetration. The basic difference between a rub and paste is that a rub is dry and a paste has a bit of moisture to bind it. Like marinades, rubs grew out of the need for food preservation. Today the jerk joints of the Caribbean and the barbecue pits of Texas still use traditional dry rubs.

To use a dry rub, spread thickly over the meat and rub into the surface. The dry rub then creates a crust on the surface of a food that is grilled or broiled. Dry rubs can be prepared from any combination of ingredients, depending on the flavoring that is required.

wet rubs and pastes

Wet rubs or pastes are literally dry rubs that are bound by liquid, usually oil. Because they cannot be applied as thickly, they are milder in flavor than the dry versions, which make them good on fish or poultry. Besides adding flavor, wet rubs also help keep the meat moist during long cooking periods. Meat is also usually treated with a rub or paste before it is smoked; in some cases, rubs assist in tenderizing the meat.

Pastes have moisture. The moisture can come from fresh herbs or aromatics such as onions, shallots, or garlic. Pastes can be bound together with wine, citrus juices, or oils. Since most pastes are generally mixed from fresh ingredients, their shelf life is short. Pastes tend to be less piquant than rubs; they work well with seafood without overpowering it. To get deeper flavor penetration with pastes before cooking, rub the fish or meat with a paste, and then tightly wrap it with lightly oiled plastic wrap. The liquid and seasonings will be absorbed into the food's surface.

common types of cured meats

MEAT	DESCRIPTION
Bacon	Cured, smoked pork belly
Canadian Bacon	Cured, smoked, fully cooked boneless pork loin
Smoked Pork Butt	Cured, smoked, fully cooked cottage butt
Corned Beef	Cured beef brisket
Ham, cooked	Cured, molded, fully cooked ham (boiled ham)
Ham, smoked	Cured, smoked, fully cooked ham
Pastrami	Cured beef brisket or plate, rubbed with spices and smoked
Prosciutto	Dry cured, flattened ham—e.g., Parma ham from the Po Valley in Italy
Smithfield Ham	Dry-cured ham from peanut-fed hogs, from Smithfield, Virginia

asian-style rub

MAKES 1½ CUPS/360 ML

4 oz/113 g brown miso

3 tbsp/45 mL liquid yellow
food coloring (optional)

3 tbsp/45 mL soy sauce

3 tbsp/45 mL sherry

2 tbsp/30 ml kosher salt

1 tbsp/15 mL liquid red
food coloring (optional)

¼ tsp/1.25 mL garlic powder

¼ tsp/1.25 mL ground
white pepper

1. Combine all of the ingredients. Place in a tightly sealed container and refrigerate or use as needed.

2. To use, spread the rub over the protein and wrap it in cheesecloth. Allow the protein to marinate for 24 to 48 hours under refrigeration. Remove the cheesecloth and rinse the protein with warm water. Dry the protein under refrigeration to form a pellicle (see page 78).

rosemary-pepper dry rub

MAKES 1 CUP/240 ML

4 oz/113 g rosemary,
chopped

2 tbsp/30 mL black
peppercorns

2 tsp/10 mL Colman's
dry mustard

2 tsp/10 mL dried oregano

2 tsp/10 mL garlic powder

1 tsp/5 mL kosher salt

1 tsp/5 mL white
peppercorns

1 tsp/5 mL cayenne

Combine all of the ingredients in a spice mill or blender and grind to a coarse powder. Store in an airtight container in a cool, dry place.

chipotle rub

MAKES APPROXIMATELY 1 CUP/240 ML

½ cup/120 mL
Madeira wine

½ cup/120 mL chipotles
in adobo, chopped

¼ cup/60 mL
low-sodium soy sauce

3 tbsp/45 mL grated
orange zest

2 tbsp/30 mL
Worcestershire sauce

6 garlic cloves, minced

Combine all ingredients in a blender or food processor. Process until smooth. Store in an airtight container under refrigeration.

tandoori rub

MAKES 1 CUP/240 ML

5 tbsp/75 mL sweet paprika

2½ tbsp/37.50 mL
ground coriander

2½ tbsp/37.50 mL
kosher salt

2 tbsp/30 mL ground cumin

1 tbsp/15 mL ground
black pepper

1 tbsp/15 mL
granulated sugar

1 tbsp/15 mL ground ginger

1 tsp/5 mL ground cinnamon

1 tsp/5 mL saffron threads

½ tsp/2.50 mL cayenne

Combine all ingredients together. Store in an airtight container in a cool, dry place.

bacon

Basic bacon is an example of a fully cooked smoked item which first undergoes a conventional dry-curing method, based on a standard ratio of 2 parts salt to 1 part sugar (by weight).

For the most accurate results, weigh the fresh pork bellies and then determine how much of the cure mixture you will need. The ratio we have found most useful is 8 oz/227 g of dry cure for every 10 lb/4.54 kg of fresh belly.

A cured belly will lose 7 to 8 percent of its water volume throughout curing and smoking.

MAKES 4-5 LB/20.41 KG

5 pork bellies, skin on
(10 lb/4.54 kg each)

CURE MIX

1 lb 8 oz/680 g kosher salt

12 oz/340 g brown or
granulated sugar

2½ oz/71 g Insta Cure No. 1

1. Wash and dry the bellies. Pierce the skin side with either the tip of a paring knife or a 6-prong ice chipper. This allows the cure to penetrate the pork a little faster.

2. Mix the salt, sugar, and Insta Cure thoroughly to make the cure mix.

3. Rub the bellies with the cure mix, making sure to cover all areas. Stack the bellies skin side down in covered plastic or stainless-steel tubs.

4. Refrigerate the pork for 7 to 10 days to cure. Overhaul them every other day by re-rubbing them with the liquid that has collected in the tub and also rotating the product, top to bottom, and so on.

5. Rinse the bellies in slightly warm water. Soak in fresh warm water for 30 minutes and blot dry. Hang the bellies on a bacon comb and refrigerate them for 18 hours to air-dry and form a pellicle.

6. Hot-smoke them at 185°F/85°C to an internal temperature of 155°F/68°C, then cool. (See Chapter 6 for full information on smoking.) Maple, cherry, birch, and apple work well on pork products. Use about a medium smoke on the product.

7. Remove the rind. Slice or cut the bacon as required for baking, sautéing, or grilling. The bacon may be wrapped and refrigerated for up to 2 weeks.

After rinsing, hang the bellies on hooks to air-dry.

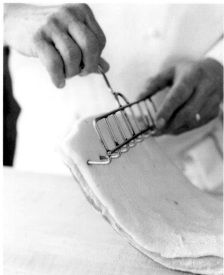

After curing and fully cooking, use a sharp knife to slice the bacon into thick strips.

maple-cured bacon

MAKES 9 LB 4 OZ /4.19 KG

10 lb/4.54 kg pork
belly, skin on

CURE MIX

5 oz/142 g kosher salt

2¾ oz/78 g maple sugar

⅘ oz/22 g Insta Cure No. 1

1. Wash and dry the belly. Pierce the skin side with either the tip of a paring knife or an ice chipper. This allows the cure to penetrate the pork a little faster.

2. Mix the salt, sugar, and Insta Cure thoroughly to make the cure mix. Rub the belly with the cure mix, making sure to cover all areas. Put the belly skin side down in a covered plastic or stainless-steel tub.

3. Refrigerate the pork for 7 to 10 days to cure. Overhaul it every other day.

4. Rinse the belly in slightly warm water. Soak in fresh warm water for 30 minutes and blot dry. Hang the belly on a bacon comb (hooks) and refrigerate it for 18 hours to air-dry and form a pellicle.

5. Hot-smoke the belly at 185°F/85°C to an internal temperature of 155°F/68°C, then cool. (See Chapter 6 for full information on smoking.) Maple, cherry, birch, and apple work well on pork products. Use about a medium smoke on the product.

6. Remove the skin. Slice or cut the bacon as required for baking, sautéing, or grilling. The bacon may be wrapped and refrigerated for up to 2 weeks.

dry-rub barbecued bacon

MAKES 18 LB/8.16 KG

MARINADE

10 oz/284 g ketchup

2 tbsp/30 mL
Tabasco sauce

2 tbsp/30 mL
Worcestershire sauce

6 oz/170 g molasses

⅔ cup/160 mL malt vinegar

2 pork bellies, skin on
(10 lb/4.54 kg each)

DRY CURE

1 lb/454 g smoked
salt (see Note)

14 oz/397 g brown sugar

4 oz/113 g Insta Cure No. 1

1 cup/240 mL smoked
Spanish paprika

1 cup/240 mL Colman's
dry mustard

⅓ cup/80 mL ground
black pepper

¼ cup/60 mL onion powder

3 tbsp/45 mL garlic powder

1. Combine the ketchup, Tabasco and Worcestershire sauces, molasses, and vinegar. Coat the bacon slabs with the marinade.

2. Combine the salt, sugar, Insta Cure, paprika, mustard, pepper, and onion and garlic powders to make the dry cure. Rub the dry cure over the bellies, making sure to cover all areas. Place in a large covered plastic tub.

3. Refrigerate the pork bellies for 7 days to cure. Overhaul them every other day.

4. After 7 days, rinse the bacon with warm water and place on bacon combs. Air-dry the bacon overnight under refrigeration.

5. Cold-smoke the bacon for 3 hours. (See Chapter 6 for full information on smoking.) Maple, cherry, birch, and apple work well on pork products. Use about a medium smoke on the product.

6. Turn the smokehouse to 185°F/85°C and smoke the bacon to an internal temperature of 155°F/68°C.

7. Remove the bacon from the smokehouse. Cool the bacon to room temperature, then transfer to a refrigerator to cool overnight. The bacon is ready to be used or it may be wrapped and refrigerated for up to 2 weeks. Remove skin before use.

Note: Smoked salt is salt that has been cold-smoked to impart flavor to salt. Place salt on foil on a rack and cold-smoke until the desired smoke flavor is achieved.

dry-cured pancetta

MAKES 9 LB 4 OZ/4.19 KG

10 lb/4.54 kg pork belly, skin on

DRY CURE

9 oz/255 g kosher salt

2 oz/57 g brown sugar

½ oz/14 g Insta Cure No. 1

1 oz/28 g juniper berries, crushed

6 bay leaves, crushed

1 tsp/5 mL ground nutmeg

2 tsp/10 mL thyme leaves (about 6 sprigs)

4 garlic cloves, mashed

2 tbsp/30 mL coarsely ground black pepper

1. Trim the pork belly and square off the sides. Trim off the skin.

2. Place the pork belly in a nonreactive container. In a mixing bowl, combine the salt, sugar, Insta Cure, juniper berries, bay leaves, nutmeg, thyme, garlic, and pepper to make the dry cure. Rub the cure mix over the belly, making sure to cover all areas evenly. Cover the pork with plastic wrap and cover its container with a lid or top.

3. Refrigerate the pork for 7 to 8 days to cure. Overhaul it every other day.

4. After 7 days, check the belly for firmness. If it is firm at the thickest point, it is cured. If it is a little soft, refrigerate the pork for 1 or 2 more days.

5. Remove the belly from the container and rinse it in warm water to wash off the cure mix. Place the belly on a rack in a sheet pan. Refrigerate for 4 to 6 hours to air-dry and form a pellicle.

6. Starting with the long side, roll the pork belly into a tight cylinder, making sure that there are no air pockets inside the roll. Tie it securely with string.

7. Place the pancetta in a tight net or wrap it in cheesecloth. Hang the pancetta for 7 days in a cool area (50° to 60°F/10° to 16°C), with 60 to 65 percent humidity.

8. After 7 days, the pancetta should be firm, but slightly pliable. It is ready to use or may be wrapped well and refrigerated for up to 3 weeks.

Remove the pork belly from the curing tub, rinse in warm water. Skin is taken off before curing. It is rinsed in warm water.

Roll the pancetta into a cylinder.

Secure the cylinder tightly with string.

bresaola

1 oz/28 g kosher salt

1 oz/28 g granulated sugar

2 lb 8 oz/1.13 kg beef
eye round, cleaned
of fat and sinews

1 tbsp/15 mL black
peppercorns

1½ tsp/7.50 mL
chopped rosemary

8 juniper berries, chopped

1. Mix the salt and sugar together. Rub the beef with this mixture and let stand in a refrigerator for 2 hours.

2. Grind the peppercorns, rosemary, and juniper berries together in a spice grinder or blender.

3. Remove the beef and rub the spices over the beef, making sure to cover all areas.

4. Wrap the beef in cheesecloth and hang in a refrigerator for 5 weeks at 60° to 65°F/16° to 18°C with 55 to 60 percent humidity. When the beef is done, unwrap it from the cheesecloth, wrap in plastic, and store in refrigerator or freeze for up to 4 weeks.

Note: If desired, the beef may be soaked in enough gin to cover for 12 hours before placing the cure and seasoning on it. You also will need to dry the beef before placing the cure and seasonings on top.

dry-cured capacolla

5 lb/2.27 kg pork shoulder, trimmed, boneless (see Notes)

CURE MIX

5 tbsp/75 mL kosher salt

5 tbsp/75 mL granulated sugar

1½ tbsp/22.50 mL ground black pepper

1 tsp/5 mL Insta Cure No. 2

2 tsp/10 mL garlic powder

10 juniper berries

½ tsp/2.50 mL ground mace

½ cup/120 mL powdered glucose

¼ cup/60 mL corn syrup solids

1 tbsp/15 mL Dry-Cured Capacolla Spice Mix (page 36)

10 in/25 cm beef bung (see page 218)

1. Treat the pork shoulder for trichinae by storing it at 5°F/−15°C for 20 days. (See "Precautions for Preventing Trichina Contamination," page 62 in Chapter 4.)

2. Bring the meat to 34° to 36°F/1° to 2°C.

3. Mix the salt, sugar, pepper, Insta Cure, garlic powder, juniper berries, mace, glucose, corn syrup solids, and spice mix, and grind in a spice grinder or blender to make the cure mix.

4. Rub the pork on all sides with half of the cure mix. Reserve the remaining cure mix.

5. Place the pork in a single layer in a plastic container. Cure in the refrigerator for 9 days at 36° to 38°F/2° to 3°C, keeping the container covered with plastic wrap so that the air is kept out and the meat will not become dry.

6. After 9 days, overhaul the pork. Keep it in the refrigerator for an additional 9 days.

7. Remove the pork from the refrigerator and rinse off any remaining cure with warm water. Place the pork on a rack and air-dry in the refrigerator to form a pellicle.

8. Coat the capacolla with the reserved cure mix; rub well, making sure to cover all areas.

9. Stuff the capacolla tightly into the beef bung, making sure to get all air pockets out; it should look like one solid piece. Hold at 70° to 80°F/21° to 27°C for about 12 hours to dry out the bung.

10. Hold at 60°F/16°C for 27 more days at 70 to 80 percent relative humidity.

11. The capacolla is now ready. It may be wrapped and refrigerated for up to 1 month or may be wrapped and frozen and held for later use.

Notes: The pork will lose 20 to 30 percent of its weight.

The product should be in separate pieces not exceeding 6 in/15 cm in thickness.

Make sure that the pork is trimmed of excess fat.

duck-breast bacon

2 oz/57 g kosher salt

1¾ oz/50 g brown sugar

Pinch of Insta Cure No. 1

1 Moulard duck breast, skin on (approx. 1 lb/454 g)

1. Combine the salt, sugar, and Insta Cure in a stainless-steel mixing bowl to make the cure mix.

2. Rub the cure mix over the duck breast and wrap it in cheesecloth. Cure the duck breast under refrigeration for about 8 hours, hung up in cheesecloth at 40°F/4°C.

3. Rinse the duck breast in warm water to stop the curing process and to wash off any remaining salt.

4. Let the duck breast air-dry on a rack under refrigeration to form a pellicle.

5. Hot-smoke the duck breast at 185°F/85°C to an internal temperature of 152°F/67°C. (See Chapter 6 for full information on smoking.) Hickory, mesquite, and birch work well with duck products. Use a medium smoke intensity.

6. Cool, wrap, and refrigerate the duck breast. The duck breast may be refrigerated for up to 2 weeks and used as needed, or frozen for up to 4 weeks.

Note: Duck breast bacon may be served on its own or used in sandwiches.

coffee-cured duck breast

4 Moulard duck breasts, skin on

1 cup/240 mL fresh ground coffee

¾ cup/180 mL kosher salt

½ cup/120 mL granulated sugar

3 tbsp/45 mL grated orange zest

1. Trim the duck breasts. Separate the breasts, trim the cartilage between the breasts, trim excess fat from around the breasts, and trim about ¼ in/6 mm fat from breast.

2. Mix the coffee, salt, sugar, and zest to make the cure mix. Spread half of the cure mix in a half hotel pan.

3. Score the fat of the duck breasts. Place the breasts skin side down in the hotel pan. Rub the breasts with the remaining cure mix. Cover with plastic wrap and refrigerate for 12 hours.

4. Rinse with warm water. Dry in a refrigerator for about 12 hours to create a pellicle

5. Hot-smoke at 185°F/85°C to an internal temperature of 150°F/66°C. (See Chapter 6 for full information on smoking.) Hickory, mesquite, and birch work well with duck products. Use a medium smoke intensity.

6. Cool and hold for service, or chill completely and serve cold. Slice thinly to serve.

7. If not using right away, the duck can be wrapped and refrigerated for up to 2 weeks.

duck-breast prosciutto

1 Moulard duck breast (approx. 1 lb/454 g), trimmed

6 oz/170 g kosher salt

1 cup/240 mL water

¼ cup/60 mL distilled white vinegar

1 tbsp/15 mL black peppercorns

1 tbsp/15 mL fennel seeds

2 tbsp/30 mL coriander seeds

1. Cover the duck breast with the salt and cure for 48 hours under refrigeration at 40°F/4°C in a noncorrosive container with plastic wrap on top. Cover the container with a lid.

2. Combine the water and vinegar. Rinse the duck breast with this solution. Blot the duck breast dry with paper towels.

3. Mix the peppercorns, fennel, and coriander seeds, and grind in a spice grinder.

4. Cover the duck breast with the seasonings. Wrap the duck breast in cheesecloth and tie the ends of the cheesecloth with twine.

5. Hang the duck breast to dry in a 58°F/14°C and about 70 percent humidity with good air circulation for 14 days.

6. Unwrap the duck breast and slice thinly to serve.

7. It may be wrapped well and refrigerated for up to 3 weeks.

gravlax

1 salmon fillet (approx. 3 lb/1.36 kg), skin on

1 cup/240 mL granulated sugar

¾ cup/180 mL kosher salt

1 tbsp/15 mL cracked black pepper

2 bunch dill, chopped

½ lemon

1. Remove the pin bones from the salmon and score the skin.

2. In a bowl, mix the sugar, salt, and pepper to make the cure mix.

3. Place a large piece of cheesecloth on a sheet pan. Place half of the chopped dill on top. Sprinkle half of the cure mix over the chopped dill. (The layer should be slightly thinner where the fillet tapers to the tail.)

4. Place the salmon skin side down on top of the cure mix. Squeeze the lemon juice over the salmon flesh and sprinkle with the remaining cure mix and dill.

5. Wrap the salmon in the cheesecloth.

6. Place the salmon in a solid hotel pan. Top the salmon with a second hotel pan. Press down with a 6- to 8-lb/2.72- to 3.63-kg weight.

7. After 3 days, unwrap and gently scrape off the cure; you can rinse the salt off with warm water. Sprinkle some chopped dill on top and let dry for about 2 to 3 hours The gravlax is now ready to use or it may be wrapped and refrigerated for up to 5 days.

Procedure photos continue on next page.

On a piece of cheesecloth, lay down an even layer of the cure mixture, then place the salmon on top.

Cover the remainder of the salmon with an even layer of the cure mix and begin wrapping with the cheesecloth.

Wrap the salmon completely in the cheesecloth, making sure that all sides are secure but loose around the fish.

Place the wrapped salmon in a pan and place a second pan on top to keep the salmon in direct contact with the cure.

Weight the top pan to ensure an even, well-preserved product.

Once the salmon has cured under refrigeration, unwrap the cheesecloth.

Scrape or rinse off the cure, dry with a paper towel, and sprinkle the chopped dill on top. Use a slicing knife to cut the salmon into paper-thin slices.

prosciutto hudson valley

25 to 28 lb/11.34 to 12.70 kg trimmed whole pork leg, bone-in (see Notes)

1 lb 2½ oz/525 g kosher salt

1⅕ oz/34 g Insta Cure No. 2

4 oz/113 g pork leaf fat (kidney fat), ground

½ oz/15 g rice flour

1. Trim the leg (see notes). Remove the foot just below the lower knuckle.

2. Tie a string just below the bulge in the leg where it was cut, you need to secure the shank in two places so that it is secured very well. When tying with string, tie it twice around the bone in two places so that it will hold.

3. Weigh the leg and record the green (uncured) weight.

4. Place the leg on a cutting board. Cut away excess flesh; trim any silver skin and any soft fat.

5. Mix the salt and Insta Cure to make the cure mix. Spread half of the cure mix on the leg and massage it in well; reserve the remaining mix.

6. Place the leg in a deep perforated hotel pan on top of a small cutting board to create a 45-degree angle so gravity will help pull some of the moisture out. Place a 7- to 8-lb/3.18- to 3.63-kg wooden cutting board on top to weight the leg down and give it the traditional shape.

7. Place the pressed leg in a refrigerator at 40°F/4°C at 60 to 70 percent relative humidity for 20 days.

8. On the twentieth day, spread with the second half of the cure mix and massage it in well. Weigh to see loss and document. Put it back in the refrigerator for 20 days more.

9. After 40 days, the ham should feel firm all over and have taken in almost all the salt. (At this point, about 15 percent of its initial weight should be lost.)

10. Rinse the leg with warm water and hang it in the refrigerator to begin the drying process. (Store at 38° to 40°F/3° to 4°C at around 70 to 75 percent relative humidity with slow air movement for 5 to 6 months.) Periodically wipe off any mold or dust that collects on the ham. At the end of this stage, the ham should have lost up to 25 percent of its initial raw weight.

11. Seal the prosciutto with a mixture of the pork leaf fat and rice flour. Smear the mixture evenly on the rump knucklebone and the entire cut surface of the ham. Hang at 50°F/10°C and 50 to 75 percent relative humidity for about 6 months.

12. Ham should have lost about one third of its original trimmed weight. It is now ready to eat. Slice very thinly. Wrap in plastic and hold in the refrigerator or can freeze for up to 4 weeks.

Notes: Pork legs for prosciutto weigh in at 30 to 35 lb/13.61 to 15.88 kg before trimming and are cut free from the carcass perpendicular to its length at a point 3½ in/9 cm above the tip of the aitchbone.

Make sure the aitchbone is taken off but do not make a big hole when you take it out. Removal of the trotter, tail bone, pelvic bone, sirloin, and flank-side fat yield a leg ready for salting in the ideal range of 25 to 28 lb/11.34 to 12.70 kg.

The leg should have ample fat cover, about 1½ in/4 cm, and all the skin.

The leg should be as fresh as possible and kept cold prior to trimming and salting.

Weight the leg down with a cutting board to create the traditional prosciutto shape.	Cover the exposed flesh evenly with the leaf fat–rice flour mixture to help keep it from overdrying.	Cut the finished prosciutto into paper-thin slices for serving.

fully cooked capacolla

MAKES 12 LB 8 OZ/5.67 KG

2½ qt/2.16 L cold water

½ cup/120 mL dextrose

2 tbsp/30 mL Insta
Cure No. 1

⅓ cup/80 mL kosher salt

3 to 4 (12 lb 8 oz/5.67
kg) boneless pork
butts, lean, trimmed

½ cup/120 mL hot
Spanish paprika,

½ cup/120 mL cayenne

10 in/25 cm beef bung

1. Combine the water, dextrose, Insta Cure No. 1, and salt to prepare the brine.

2. Chill the pork butts to 38°F/3°C. Inject the pork butts with brine equal to 10 percent of the total weight. (A 4-lb/1.81-kg pork butt should be pumped with 6 to 7 oz/180 to 210 mL of brine.) Submerge the pork butts in the remaining brine solution in a covered brine tub.

3. Brine the pork butts under refrigeration for 3 days.

4. Rinse or soak the pork butts in warm water for about an hour to wash the salt off, then let dry. Place a on rack or hang.

5. Rub the pork butts with the paprika and cayenne.

6. Stuff the pork butts into the bung casings, making sure to pack the pork very tightly. Prick the casings with a teasing needle to let the air escape. You want this to be one piece, so you need to get rid of all the air pockets and pack firmly.

7. Hang the pork butts in a refrigerator, ideally overnight, at least 6 to 8 hours in a walk-in, at 40°F/4°C. Air-dry to form a pellicle.

8. Hot-smoke at 130°F/54°C for 3 hours. (See Chapter 6 for full information on smoking.) Maple, cherry, birch, and apple work well on pork products. Use about a medium smoke on the product.

9. Increase the temperature to 150°F/66°C for 2 hours. Apply light smoke for the last 2 hours. The smoke should be constant but not heavy.

10. Raise the temperature to 160° to 165°F/71° to 74°C and smoke the pork butts until they reach an internal temperature of 152°F/67°C.

11. Remove the pork from the smokehouse. Dip the pork butts into boiling water momentarily to shrink the casing.

12. Place in an ice-water bath for 10 minutes.

13. Hang at room temperature until an internal temperature of 110°F/43°C is reached.

14. Cool overnight in a refrigerator.

15. Slice thinly to serve, wrap, and hold in the refrigerator up to 2 weeks or freeze up to 3 weeks.

sweet or hot coppa

MAKES 5 LB/2.27 KG

CURE MIX

5 tbsp/75 mL kosher salt

5 tbsp/75 mL granulated sugar

1½ tbsp/22.50 mL coarsely ground black pepper

1 tsp/5 mL Insta Cure No. 2

2 tsp/10 mL garlic powder

10 juniper berries

½ tsp/2.50 mL ground mace

5 lb/2.27 kg boneless pork shoulder certified (see Note)

3½ cups/840 mL powdered glucose

1¾ cups/420 mL light corn syrup solids

½ cup/120 mL Coppa Spice Mixes (page 37)

10 in/25 cm beef bung

1. Mix the salt, sugar, pepper, Insta Cure, garlic powder, juniper berries, and mace in a spice grinder or blender to make the cure mix.

2. Rub half of the cure mix on the meat and place in a covered plastic container for 9 days at 36° to 38°F/2° to 3°C, overhauling every other day.

3. Rub the remaining cure mix on the meat and cure for 9 more days. Overhaul every other day.

4. Rinse the meat in warm water and dry for 3 hours, on a rack or hang.

5. Season with glucose, corn syrup solids, and Coppa Spice Mix.

6. Stuff the pork shoulder into the beef bung, packing it in very well, getting all the air pockets out; this should be like one piece (see page 218).

7. Hang the coppa at 65° to 75°F/18° to 24°C for about 12 hours to air-dry.

8. Place in an area at 60°F/16°C at about 70 percent relative humidity, holding the coppa for 20 to 35 days.

9. The coppa may be wrapped and stored in the refrigerator for up to 2 weeks.

Note: See the table on "Certifying Pork via Freezing" on page 63 in Chapter 4.

duck confit (preserved duck)

MAKES 3 LB/1.36 KG

12 medium shallots, peeled

3 medium yellow onions

1 bunch parsley,
leaves and stems

CURE MIX

3 oz/85 g kosher salt

1 tsp/5 mL Insta Cure No. 1

¼ cup/60 mL brown sugar

2 garlic cloves, crushed

10 black pepper-
corns, crushed

½ tsp/2.50 mL
ground bay leaf

1 tsp/5 mL thyme leaves

1 tbsp/15 mL Four-
Spice Mix (page 35)

4 lb/1.81 kg whole
Moulard duck legs

2 qt/2 L rendered duck fat

1. Purée the shallots, onions, and parsley in a food processor until a paste forms.

2. In a mixing bowl, combine the onion mixture, salt, Insta Cure, sugar, garlic, peppercorns, bay leaf, thyme, and Four-Spice Mix to make the cure mix.

3. Disjoint the duck and trim the excess fat from the legs. Rub the duck well with the cure mix. Place the duck pieces in a nonreactive container. Place a second container on top. Place a weight, such as a brick, on top and allow the duck pieces to sit overnight under refrigeration to cure.

4. On day 2, overhaul the duck and let stand again under weight overnight.

5. On day 3, rinse off the cure and blot the duck pieces dry with paper towels. In a saucepan, place 2 cups water and all of the duck fat and cook over medium heat until the duck fat renders. The fat will become clear, so you can see the bottom of the pan, but make sure you do not burn the fat. Strain and hold until needed.

6. In a sauce pot, bring the duck fat to a simmer; add the duck pieces and simmer slowly for 2½ to 3 hours, until fork-tender.

7. Remove the duck pieces and chill.

8. Cool the duck fat to room temperature. Strain the duck fat, and store the duck pieces by immersing them in the cooled duck fat. Cover the duck and fat and refrigerate. The duck will last several weeks under refrigeration; store for at least a week before using, as this will allow the duck legs to develop flavor.

9. When ready to use, remove the duck pieces and reserve the duck fat for storing the next confit. Fat can be reused as long as it is not burned.

Note: You may elect to cold-smoke the meat between steps 5 and 6. Hickory, mesquite, and birch work well with duck products. Use hot smoke at 185°F/85°C at a medium smoke intensity. If meat is smoked, do not reuse the duck fat again unless you are cooking more smoked duck legs.

Disjoint and trim the duck legs, reserving any trim as it will be rendered down.

Rinse any remaining cure from the duck pieces and blot dry.

Remove the finished duck pieces from the fat as needed and wipe off any excess fat with your fingers.

Aging in the fat softens the meat's proteins, allowing the tender duck to be pulled off the bone easily.

spicy duck capacolla

5 lb 8 oz/2.50 kg duck legs and thighs, skin and bones removed and cleaned of fat, cartilage, and sinews

1 tsp/5 mL Insta Cure No. 2

2 tbsp/30 mL light corn syrup

2¼ oz/64 g kosher salt

8 oz/227 g fatback, cut into ¼-in/6-mm cubes, frozen

2 tsp/10 mL very coarsely ground black pepper

1 tbsp/15 mL red pepper flakes, crushed medium-fine

1 tsp/5 mL garlic powder

1 tbsp/15 mL hot paprika

1 tsp/5 mL cayenne

½ cup/120 mL ice-cold grappa

2 tsp/10 mL anise seeds, crushed

54 in/137 mm beef round casings

1. Trim the meat of fat and sinew. Cut into ½- to 1-in/1- to 3-cm cubes.

2. Combine and mix the meat, Insta Cure, corn syrup, and salt. Freeze until slightly frozen.

3. Grind the meat using a ½-in/1-cm grinder plate, passing the meat through the grinder twice. Divide the meat and grind half of the mixture through the ¼-in/6-mm grinder plate. (Remember to chill thoroughly between grindings.)

4. Grind the fatback using a ¼-in/6-mm grinder plate.

5. Once the meat and fat have been ground, place all of the meat and fat into a 20-qt/19.20-L mixer bowl with a paddle attachment.

6. Add the black pepper, red pepper flakes, garlic powder, paprika, cayenne, grappa, and anise seeds to the meat and fat. Mix on speed #1 for 60 seconds, then speed #2 for 15 to 30 seconds, until a sticky mass forms.

7. Make a taste tester (see page 154). Adjust the seasoning as needed.

8. Stuff into the prepared casings and tie the ends with a bubble knot (see page 222).

9. Hang the meat for 4 days in a 50°F/10°C area with low humidity (about 50 to 60 percent) and lots of air movement.

10. Hold the meat in a 60°F/16°C area with about 70 percent relative humidity for about 4 weeks. The capacolla will lose 20 to 30 percent of its moisture during this time and will become firm.

11. The capacolla is now ready for use. Wrap in plastic, hold under refrigeration for up to 3 weeks, or freeze for later use.

fennel-cured salmon

1 salmon fillet (approx. 3 lb/1.36 kg), skin on

2 cups/480 mL granulated sugar

13¼ oz/376 g La Baleine fine sea salt

1½ tsp/2.50 mL coriander seeds, toasted and cracked

1½ tsp/7.50 mL black peppercorns, toasted and cracked

1 tsp/5 mL grated lime zest

2½ tsp/12.50 mL grated lemon zest

1½ tbsp/22.50 mL grated orange zest

2 cups/480 mL chopped fennel fronds

1½-in/4-cm piece ginger, finely chopped

1½-in/4-cm piece lemongrass, finely chopped

½ cup/120 mL gin

1. Remove the pin bones from the salmon and score the skin.

2. In a bowl, mix the sugar, salt, coriander, pepper, and lime, lemon, and orange zests to make the cure mix. In a separate bowl, mix the fennel fronds, ginger, and lemongrass.

3. Brush the flesh side of the salmon fillet with a little bit of gin, pour the remainder of the gin into the cure mixture, and mix well. Place a large piece of cheesecloth on a sheet pan. Sprinkle some of the cure down on the cheesecloth. Center the salmon fillet on top of the cheesecloth and cure mixture. Sprinkle half of the cure mix evenly over the salmon fillet. (The layer should be slightly thinner where the fillet tapers to the tail.)

4. Pack the fennel frond mixture evenly over the salmon.

5. Sprinkle the remaining cure mix on top of the fillet.

6. Wrap the fillet in the cheesecloth and cure for 12 hours under refrigeration, at 40°F/4°C.

7. Rinse off the cure in warm water. Air-dry on a rack on a sheet pan, placed where there is a lot of air movement, for 6 to 8 hours under refrigeration to form a pellicle. Wrap and store for up to 1 week under refrigeration.

8. The salmon may be served as is, sliced thinly on a bias.

Note: The salmon may be cold-smoked for 2 hours following air-drying. Cold-smoke under 70°F/21°C, for about 2 hours at a medium smoke intensity. If you can cold-smoke at a temperature under 40°F/4°C, this would be ideal. Cool, wrap, and store in the refrigerator for up to 1 week, following air-drying. (See Chapter 6 for full information on smoking.)

balsamic herbal marinade

½ cup/120 mL balsamic vinegar

¼ cup/60 mL lemon juice

1 tbsp/15 mL grated lemon zest

⅔ cup/160 mL extra-virgin olive oil

2 garlic cloves, minced or pressed

¼ cup/60 mL chopped flat-leaf parsley

¼ cup/60 mL shredded basil

1 tsp/5 mL dried oregano

½ tsp/2.50 mL kosher salt

¼ tsp/1.25 mL cracked black pepper

Combine the vinegar, lemon juice, and zest in a nonreactive mixing bowl. Whisk in the oil gradually. Whisk in the garlic, parsley, basil, oregano, salt, and pepper. Place in a tightly sealed container and refrigerate or use as needed.

basil marinade

3 tbsp/45 mL
balsamic vinegar

¼ cup/60 mL fresh
lemon juice

1 tbsp/15 mL grat-
ed lemon zest

1 tbsp/15 mL Sambuca
or other licorice or
anise liqueur

½ cup/120 mL olive oil

⅓ cup/80 mL finely
chopped basil leaves,
tightly packed

3 garlic cloves,
minced or pressed

1 tbsp/15 mL
chopped shallot

½ tsp/2.50 mL kosher salt

8 black peppercorns

Combine the vinegar, lemon juice and zest, and Sambuca in a nonreactive mixing bowl. Whisk in the oil gradually. Whisk in the basil, garlic, shallot, salt, and
peppercorns. Place in a tightly sealed container and refrigerate or use as needed.

Note: This easy marinade is perfect for grilling fish in the summer. You also may drizzle it
over mozzarella cheese and fresh tomatoes. The Sambuca in the recipe adds a hint of licorice that really perks up the basil and lemon.

lemon-caper marinade

⅓ cup/80 mL lemon juice

1½ tbsp/22.50 mL grated lemon zest

1 tsp/5 mL Dijon mustard

½ cup/120 mL olive oil

3 tbsp/45 mL medium capers, rinsed

3 garlic cloves, minced or pressed

2 tbsp/30 mL chopped shallot

1 tbsp/15 mL chopped parsley

½ tsp/2.50 mL kosher salt

¼ tsp/1.25 mL ground black pepper

1½ cups/360 mL olive oil

Brine for Fish (below)

Combine the lemon juice, zest, and mustard in a nonreactive mixing bowl. Whisk in the olive oil gradually. Whisk in the capers, garlic, shallot, parsley, salt, and pepper. Place in a tightly sealed container and refrigerate or use as needed.

brine for fish

2 gal/7.68 L water

1 lb 8 oz/680 g kosher salt

1 lb/454 g granulated sugar

⅓ cup/80 mL lemon juice

½ cup/120 mL pickling spice

1 garlic clove, minced

Combine all of the ingredients in a stockpot. Bring the brine to a boil. Cool the brine to room temperature.

lemon and herb marinade

1½ cups/360 mL olive oil

1 cup/240 mL lemon juice

1 tbsp/15 mL chopped basil

1 tbsp/15 mL
Worcestershire sauce

2 garlic cloves, minced

½ tsp/2.50 mL
Tabasco sauce

¼ tsp/1.25 mL
granulated sugar

Pork and Beef Brine (below)

Combine all ingredients thoroughly. Place in a tightly sealed container and refrigerate or use as needed.

pork and beef brine

3 gal/11.52 L water

2 lb/907 g kosher salt

1 lb 8 oz/680 g
dextrose (see Note)

7 oz/198 g Insta Cure No. 1

2 tbsp/30 mL onion
powder (optional)

2 tbsp/30 mL garlic
powder (optional)

In a stockpot, combine all of the ingredients. Bring the brine to a boil. Cool the brine to room temperature. The brine is now ready to use.

Note: The amount of sweetener will depend on the type of sweetener used, due to the degree of sweetness. White or brown sugar, maple sugar, honey, and molasses are just a few types of sweeteners that can be used; you should taste the brine to determine the amount of sweetener you would like to have in the brine.

shrimp marinade

2 medium oranges, thinly sliced

1 medium lemon, thinly sliced

1 medium yellow onion, thinly sliced

1½ cups/360 mL vegetable oil

½ cup/120 mL white wine vinegar

1½ tsp/7.50 mL chopped dill

¼ tsp/1.25 mL garlic powder

Kosher salt, as needed

Ground black pepper, as needed

Granulated sugar, as needed

Brine for Scallops or Shrimp (below)

Combine all ingredients thoroughly. Place in a tightly sealed container and refrigerate or use as needed.

brine for scallops or shrimp

2 cups/480 mL water

4 oz/113 g kosher salt

2 oz/57 g granulated sugar

¼ cup/60 mL lemon juice

1 tsp/5 mL garlic powder

1 tsp/5 mL onion powder

3 cups/720 mL crushed ice

In a sauce pot, combine and mix all of the ingredients except for the ice. Bring the brine to a boil. Remove from the heat. Add the ice to cool the brine down. The brine is now ready to use.

poultry brine

MAKES 3 GAL/11.52 L

3 gal/11.52 L water

1 lb 8 oz/680 g kosher salt

1 lb 8 oz/680 g brown
sugar (see Note)

7 oz/198 g Insta Cure No. 1

9 garlic cloves, crushed

6 tbsp/90 mL pickling spice

¼ bunch sage

In a stockpot, combine all of the ingredients. Bring the brine to a boil. Cool the brine to room temperature. The brine is now ready to use.

Note: The amount of sweetener will depend on the type of sweetener used, due to the degree of sweetness. Honey and maple sugar are some types of sweeteners that can be used to replace the brown sugar.

maple brine for poultry

MAKES 3½ QT/3.36 L

2½ qt/2.16 L water

3 cups/720 mL
dry vermouth

1½ cups/360 mL
kosher salt

1 cup/240 mL maple syrup

1 yellow onion,
medium, sliced

½ lemon

6 garlic cloves, crushed

3 tbsp/45 mL ground
black pepper

1 tbsp/15 mL celery
seeds, crushed

6 sage leaves

3 bay leaves, crumbled

In a sauce pot, combine all of the ingredients. Bring the brine to a boil. Cool the brine to room temperature. The brine is now ready to use.

Pastrami sandwich

pastrami (brined, spiced, smoked beef)

MAKES 1 BRISKET, 10 TO 12 LB/4.54 TO 5.44 KG

1 beef brisket, 10 to 12
lb/4.54 to 5.44 kg
(see Note)

BRINE

1½ gal/5.76 L water

1 lb to 1 lb 4 oz/454
to 567 g kosher salt

5 oz/142 g
granulated sugar

3½ oz/99 g Insta Cure No. 1

3 garlic cloves

1 tbsp/15 mL pickling spice

2 oz/57 g coriander
seeds, toasted

2 oz/57 g black pepper-
corns, toasted, cracked

1. Trim the external fat on the brisket to $^1/_{16}$ in/1.50 mm thick.

2. In a brining tub, combine the water, salt, sugar, and Insta Cure. Mash the garlic cloves and crush the pickling spice and add to the brine solution.

3. Weigh the brisket and inject the brisket with brine equal to about 10 percent of its weight.

4. Place the brisket in the brining tub and use a plate or rack to keep it completely below the surface.

5. Brine the brisket for 3 days.

6. After 3 days, remove the brisket from the brine and soak it in warm water for 30 minutes. Drain and dry the brisket.

7. Grind the coriander and peppercorns to medium-fine in a spice grinder. Rub the spices over the surface of the brisket on all sides.

8. Cold-smoke the brisket for 2 hours. (See Chapter 6 for full information on smoking.)

9. Hot-smoke the brisket at 185°F/85°C to an internal temperature of 155° to 160°F/68° to 71°C. The smoke intensity should be about medium; you do not want it to be too strong. Cherry, mesquite, and hickory are woods that go well with beef products.

10. To finish the pastrami, simmer in water until tender, about 2 hours. It may also be cooled, wrapped, and refrigerated for up to 2 weeks. To reheat the brisket, place it in water or stock and reheat to an internal temperature of 165°F/74°C.

Note: Beef plate can also be used in place of brisket.

corned beef

1½ gal/5.76 L water

1 lb to 1 lb 4 oz/454 to 567 g kosher salt

5 oz/142 g granulated sugar

3½ oz/99 g Insta Cure No. 1

3 garlic cloves, mashed

1 tbsp/15 mL pickling spice, crushed

1 beef brisket, 10 to 12 lb/4.54 to 5.44 kg (see Note)

1. In a stockpot, combine the water, salt, sugar, and Insta Cure. Purée the garlic and pickling spice in a blender with about 1 cup/240 mL of the brine. Combine the puréed mixture with the brine.

2. Bring the brine to a boil. Remove from the heat and cool to room temperature.

3. Weigh the brisket and inject the brisket with brine equal to about 10 percent of its weight.

4. Place the brisket in a brining tub and add enough brine to submerge it. Use a plate or plastic wrap to keep it completely below the surface. Brine the brisket for 3 days under refrigeration.

5. After 3 days, drain the brisket. Place it in a stockpot.

6. Add enough water to cover the brisket. Simmer for 3 hours, or until tender.

7. Remove the brisket, split it in half, following the natural separation between the two pieces of meat (cap and brisket), and trim off the excess fat. The brisket is ready to serve. It may also be cooled, wrapped, and refrigerated for up to 2 weeks. Reheat by slicing the meat thinly and sautéing. You can also reheat it whole by placing the product in water or stock and slowly reheating to 165°F/74°C, then slice and use as required.

Note: You can use a bottom round of beef and cure like corned beef; this will give you a larger piece of meat and less fat.

honey-brined duck

MAKES 1 GAL/3.84 L BRINE/1 DUCK

2 sprigs thyme

1 bay leaf

8 black peppercorns

9 juniper berries

6 sage leaves

1 gal/3.84 L water

8 oz/227 g kosher salt

1 cup/240 mL honey

1 oz/28 g Insta Cure No. 1

½ cup/120 mL
Madeira wine

1 whole Moulard
duck, trimmed

1. Wrap the thyme, bay leaf, peppercorns, juniper berries, and sage in cheese-cloth and tie with string to make a sachet. In a stockpot, combine the sachet, water, salt, honey, Insta Cure, and Madeira to make a brine. Bring the brine to a boil.

2. Cool the brine to room temperature. The brine is now ready to be used.

3. A whole duck should be brined for 48 hours. If the duck is injected with brine equal to 10 percent of its weight beforehand, it will need to be brined only for 10 to 12 hours. Place the duck in a deep plastic or stainless-steel container and add enough brine to submerge it. Use a plate or plastic wrap to keep it completely below the surface.

4. Drain the duck and then rinse it with warm water. Pat the duck dry.

5. The duck may be finished by roasting as usual or by smoking.

6. If smoking the duck, place the duck on a sheet tray on a rack and air-dry under refrigeration at 40°F/4°C for 6 to 8 hours to form a pellicle.

7. Cold-smoke the duck for 2 to 4 hours. (See Chapter 6 for full information on smoking.) Hickory, mesquite, and birch woods go well with duck. Use a medium smoke intensity. During the cold-smoking, prick the breast many times with the tip of a paring knife to release the excess fat.

8. Finish the duck by hot-smoking it at 185°F/85°C to an internal temperature of 155°F/68°C. The duck may be served immediately or cooled, wrapped, and stored for up to 2 weeks under refrigeration.

soft brined roasted pork loin

MAKES 2 QT/2 L BRINE, 1 LB/454 G PORK LOIN

BRINE

2 qt/2 L water

5 oz/142 g kosher salt

3 oz/85 g brown sugar

1 lb/454 g pork loin, boned, trimmed, and tied to hold shape

1 oz/28 g Dijon mustard

SPICE RUB

¼ oz/7 g cardamom seeds

¼ oz/7 g fennel seeds

¼ oz/7 g black peppercorns

1 oz/28 g chili powder

½ oz/14 g kosher salt

1. In a sauce pot, combine the water, salt, and brown sugar to make the brine. Bring the brine to a boil, then cool to room temperature.

2. Brine the pork for 12 hours under refrigeration.

3. Rinse the pork with warm water and dry well. Spread the mustard evenly over the pork loin.

4. Lightly toast the cardamom, fennel, and peppercorns for the spice rub. Cool.

5. Grind the toasted spices, chili powder, and salt in a spice grinder or blender. Season the pork loin on all sides with the spice rub.

6. Roast the pork loin to an internal temperature of 145°F/63°C. The pork loin may be served hot with a sauce, or chilled and served thinly sliced with pickles and mustard. The pork may be held under refrigeration for up 2 weeks.

pickled swedish herring

1 large salt herring

1 medium red onion, sliced

6 allspice berries, crushed

¾ cup/180 mL
distilled white vinegar

¼ cup/60 mL water

5 tbsp/75 mL
granulated sugar

5 white peppercorns

5 allspice berries

2 bay leaves

2 tbsp/30 mL chopped dill

1. Clean the fish, remove the head, and soak in cold water overnight.

2. Remove the bones and cut the fish into fillets. Cut the fillets into small slices, about ½-in/1-cm tranches.

3. Place the fish in a covered plastic container. (If desired, arrange the slices in a glass bowl for a more elegant presentation.) Cover the fish with the onion slices and sprinkle with the crushed allspice. Cover and hold under refrigeration.

4. In a nonreactive sauce pot, combine the vinegar, water, sugar, peppercorns, allspice, and bay leaves. Bring to a boil and remove from the heat.

5. Chill, then strain out the solids.

6. Pour the strained liquid over the fish. Cover and let stand overnight in a refrigerator.

7. Garnish with chopped dill before servicing. Stored in a covered plastic container; this can be held for up to 1 week.

smoking

chapter six

Smoking foods is a chemical process achieved by burning whole hardwoods, sawdust, or herbs, spices, or even such material as grapevine clippings that create a vapor of smoke. There are many types of homemade and commercial smokehouses/smokers. They range in price from $200 to $4,000; capacity varies from 20 lb/9.07 kg to 50—100 lb/22.68—45.36 or more. When working with a smokehouse/smoker, make sure you open the damper wide to allow the moisture to escape (you can adjust the damper as needed) and keep items from sweating. When items are wet inside, the smoke will not stick to the wet surface.

When we think of smoked meats, poultry, and fish, we usually think of flavor first, then preservation. The moister, more lightly salted smoked foods produced today are more palatable than the heavily salted and very dry foods of the past. Remember, however, that heavily salted and dried foods are preserved; today's lightly salted and less dry foods need to be treated as perishable.

There are a number of reasons people choose to smoke foods. Doing it yourself is far less costly than buying the finished product. When you smoke product at home, for your own consumption, you have a lot more control over the outcome and the amount of smoke and salt used. When you produce an item for use in a restaurant, you need to follow your local health department's recommendations. You will need a HACCP procedure whereby you document the process followed and record the times and temperatures of the product during processing to ensure safe handling.

The smokehouse unit is the most important factor in successful processing. The smoke must circulate evenly around the food. Time, temperature, and moisture are the three elements that must be regulated properly for good results. Precise temperature regulation is essential for the quality and safety of both hot-smoke and cold-smoke products. Use professional equipment obtained from an established supplier. A restaurant already has many of the items needed for smoking. The bigger investment would be the smoker, which will need to be under a hood so the smoke can be vented. Determine the size of the smoker based on the volume you will be producing, Each individual establishment will have to determine the cost effectiveness of producing in-house or purchasing the product. Smoking is a simple, easy process that produces wonderful results. And you can control the salt, sugar, and fat content of your own smoked foods, as well as experiment with herbs and other flavorings.

Smoked foods may be treated as menu items on their own or used as a seasoning in other dishes.

properties of smoke

Smoke is the complex production of very complicated compounds that occur during the thermal decomposition of wood (chips or sawdust). This process primarily occurs in a temperature range of 390° to 750°F/199° to 399°C. Although at the point of generation, smoke is a gas, it rapidly separates into a vapor and a particle state. It is the vapor phase that contains the components largely responsible for the flavor and aroma that smoke imparts to foods. More than 300 different compounds have been isolated from wood smoke, but not all of these compounds occur in smoked meat products. The components most commonly found are phenols, organic acids, alcohols, carbonyls, hydrocarbons, and some gaseous components such as carbon dioxide, carbon monoxide, oxygen, nitrogen, and nitrous oxide.

Smoke is applied to meat for the following reasons:

PRESERVATION: Phenolic compounds and formaldehyde have antimicrobial action; this affects only the surface of the meat, as smoke does not penetrate deeply into items.

Smoke produces a number of acids that cling to the meat and form an outside layer or skin. The acids help the coagulation of the proteins on the surface of the meat and also help preserve the meat by preventing the growth of surface mold and bacteria.

COLOR: The bacterial action of smoking meat is due to the combined effects of heating, drying, and chemical components in the smoke. When present on the surface of the meat, smoke components such as acetic acid, formaldehyde, and creosote prevent microbial growth.

The phenols are known to possess strong bacteriostatis that contributes to preservation. Phenols also act as antioxidants. They contribute to the color and flavor of smoke products as well.

AROMA AND FLAVOR: Phenols, carbonyl compounds, and organic acids contribute to the smoky taste. Excessive smoke flavor can become bitter.

Color development is caused by the interaction of the carbonyls in the vapor phase of the smoke with amino groups on the surface of the foods. Maximum color formation is directly related to smoke concentration, temperature, and the moisture content of the surface of the products, with 12 to 15 percent of moisture at the exterior surface of meat resulting in maximum color development. Therefore, some surface drying is necessary for good color formation during the smoking of meats. When added with the reddish color of the cooked cured meat, you see a reddish brown color that is characteristic of smoked products.

PROTECTION FROM OXIDATION: Components in smoke prevent or slow down lipid oxidation that contributes to a stale-fat taste.

pellicle formation

Before cured foods are smoked, they should be allowed to air-dry long enough to form a tacky skin, known as the pellicle. The pellicle plays a key role in producing excellent smoked items. It acts as a kind of protective barrier for the food, and also helps to capture the smoke's flavor and color. Most foods can be properly dried by placing them on racks or by hanging them on hooks or sticks in the refrigerator or a cool room. They should be air-dried uncovered. It is important that air be able to flow around all sides. To encourage pellicle formation, place the foods so that a fan blows air over them. The exterior of the item must be sufficiently dry if the smoke is to adhere.

To form a pellicle, or tacky protective skin, on a food that will be smoked, air-dry the item on a rack that allows air to flow around all sides.

A properly formed pellicle enables the product to capture the smoke's flavor and color.

basic safety considerations

Raw material must be fresh with no signs of detectable spoilage, and must be maintained at 33°F/1°C or less prior to smoking.

Completely thaw meat or poultry before smoking. Thawing of frozen food must be done at a temperature no higher than 45°F/7°C. Because smoking may use low temperatures to process or cook the food, the item will take too long to thaw in the smokehouse, allowing it to linger in the temperature danger zone where harmful bacteria can multiply. Thawed meat also cooks more evenly.

Be sure to refrigerate and store smoked items properly when finished.

FIVE STEPS IN PREPARING SMOKED FOODS

1. Prepare item.
    -   Trim excess fat.
    -   Truss poultry.
    -   Bone large pieces of meat.
    -   Clean gills, guts, and blood from fish.
    -   Remove rind from cheese.
2. Cure or brine item (optional).
    -   Insta Cure No. 1 prevents growth of *Clostridium botulinum* in the anaerobic environment of cold-smoking.
    -   Add flavor.
    -   Enhance color.
3. Rinse the item to be smoked.
    -   Stop the curing process.
    -   Remove excess salt.
    -   Prevent salt crystallization on the surface.
4. Dry item well.
    -   Essential for pellicle formation
    -   A wet surface will not absorb smoke.
    -   You might use alcohol to brush on the outside of the product to give some flavor but more importantly the alcohol will help to dry the surface. To help in development of the pellicle. before foods can be smoked they need to air-dry to form a pellicle or tacky outer skin. The formation of this skin helps protect the interior of the food and allows the outer surface to better absorb the flavors and color from the smoke.
    -   Hanging foods from hooks or sticks or placing them on racks that allow them to come in full contact with the air is the best way to aid the pellicle formation. Foods should be allowed to dry uncovered in the refrigerator or in a cool room with a fan blowing air over them.
5. Smoke the item.

smoking methods

There are two basic types of smoking that can be applied to food products: cold-smoking or hot-smoking. Cold-smoking can be used as a flavor enhancer for items such as pork chops, beef steaks, chicken breasts, or scallops. They may then be finished to order by grilling, sautéing, baking, or roasting. (Proteins are not set by cold-smoking, so many foods need to be cooked before serving.)

Hot-smoking differs from cold-smoking in that once the foods have been hot-smoked, they are typically safe to eat without any further cooking. However, we generally reheat or further cook foods that have been hot-smoked.

IMPORTANT TEMPERATURES TO REMEMBER

103°F/39°C: Proteins begin to set or denature.

145°F/63°C: Seafood forcemeat is cooked.

145°F/63°C: Federal requirement for cooking pork.

160°F/71°C: All proteins are coagulated.

165°F/74°C: Federal requirement for cooking all poultry.

cold-smoking

The temperature of the smokehouse is set from 70° to 100°F/21° to 38°C, with 80°F/27°C as the average temperature. The closer you can keep the temperature to 40°F/4°C, the better it will be for the product. This is to keep it out of the temperature danger zone. The smoke is created from the smoldering of sawdust that is heated. To create the smoke without throwing off a lot of heat, the sawdust is heated by (1) hot coals and (2) a heat source—hot plates or a rod that heats up. In this temperature range, foods take on a rich smoky flavor, develop a deep mahogany color, and tend to retain a relatively moist texture. They are not cooked as a result of the smoking process, however. The time that it takes to cold-smoke an item may vary depending on the product and the intensity of the smoky flavor that is desired. The time may range from 1 to 18 hours.

Common products that are cold-smoked are salmon, chicken breasts, and seafood. Some uncooked smoked sausages such as chorizo are cold-smoked. The process also enhances flavor through the addition of smoke to an item that will be finished by some other cooking method, such as shrimp that may be finished by grilling or stewing.

A slight dehydration of overall texture occurs during cold-smoking; consider the texture of smoked salmon versus raw salmon. The outer layer of the product will dry out, creating a dryer surface, and the entire product will be less moist with a dry and/or slightly tacky texture.

PREPARATION FOR COLD-SMOKING

- Trim item and truss, net, or tie as necessary.

- Cure or brine item by desired method (optional).

- When cure is done, rinse the item or soak it in warm water to remove excess salt. Form a pellicle by placing the item on a rack over a sheet pan or hanging it in an area where there is a lot of air movement.

hot-smoking

The temperature of the smokehouse should be 160°F/71°C for all sausages in casings and 185°F/85°C for all solid meats. Sausages in casings are slowly worked up in steps starting with 120°F/49°C for about 2 hours, then 130°F/54°C for about 2 hours, then

Smokehouses should maintain temperatures below 100°F/38°C for cold-smoking to prevent the protein structure of meats, fish, or poultry from denaturing.

Hot-smoking occurs at 185° to 250°F/85° to 121°C. Hot-smoked foods are fully cooked, moist, and flavorful.

a final temperature of 180°F/82°C for the remainder of the time, until the sausages come up to the temperature they need to be cooked to. At these temperatures, foods are fully cooked, moist, and flavorful. If the smokehouse is allowed to get hotter than 185°F/85°C, smoked foods will shrink, buckle, or even split. The length of smoking time depends on the individual product being hot-smoked. All foods should be smoked to their minimum temperatures to kill bacteria. Common products that are hot-smoked are ham, turkey, and duck. Sausages in the smoked-cooked category include Kielbasa Krakowska (page 236).

As well as becoming imbued with the flavor of the smoke, during the hot-smoking process the product is cooked. The final internal temperatures of cured, hot-smoked products should be 165°F/74°C for poultry and 155°F/68°C for meats. The final internal temperature of uncured hot-smoked items, such as suitable cuts of beef, is 135°F to 139°F/57° to 59°C for rare. Shellfish is cooked to an internal temperature of 145°F/63°C. Fish is cooked to an internal temperature of 135° to 140°F/57° to 63°C.

PREPARATION FOR HOT-SMOKING

- Trim, truss, net, or tie item as necessary.

- Cure or brine the item by the desired method (optional).

- If the item has been cured, rinse or soak it in warm water to remove excess salt.

other hot-smoking methods

CONVECTION SMOKING

In this method, the item does not need to be dried before going into the smokehouse, as the smokehouse has a drying cycle with a fan to create a pellicle quickly. Some smokehouses will run using a program that you can develop for each different item.

PAN SMOKING

This may be done on the stovetop or in the oven with improvised equipment or a special "stovetop" smoking pan. Even though the process is short term, it can impart a heavy smoke flavor. A drawback of this method is the possibility of uneven flavor or doneness.

SMOKE ROASTING

"Pit roasting" or "barbecue" are other names for this method, which uses temperatures of 250°F/121°C and above. Items brown and become fully cooked while undergoing this process. Equipment may be improvised by placing wood chips on the heating element of a barbecue or grill, or by producing smoke in the bottom of an oven. In addition to smoldering hardwood logs, chips, or dust, dried herb stems and/or leaves, dried citrus peel, or tea leaves may be used to produce smoke, alone or in combination with sugar. Peanut shells are used to produce the unique flavor of Smithfield ham.

Requiring only two disposable aluminum pans, a rack, saw-dust, and a heat source, pan smoking is a simple way to give a smoky flavor to foods without an expensive smokehouse.

When pan smoking, you must carefully control the smoke to give the final product a complex, smoke-enhanced flavor that is not too bitter.

Smoke Roasting (Foil Pan Method)
Setup for Smoke Roasting

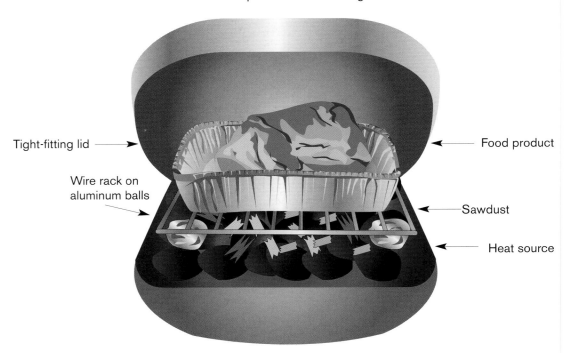

Tight-fitting lid →

Food product →

Wire rack on aluminum balls →

Sawdust →

Heat source →

smokehouse preparation

how a smokehouse works

Below is a simplified diagram of how a smokehouse works for both cold- and hot-smoking. Many of the larger smokehouses are computer programmed as to time and temperature.

woods for smoking

Most hardwood produces a good smoke flavor, but soft woods give off a pitch that coats foods with a thick sticky film. Soft or resinous woods should never be used; they will either flare up and burn—and produce no smoke—or add too much color to the product and impart a bitter taste. They are also high in creosote resin, which may cause cancer. Thus, hard fruit or nut woods are preferred.

Each wood imparts a slightly different flavor of its own. Although much is according to your personal taste, instruction manuals and recipe books for smokehouses will offer a guide to which wood works the best with a variety of meats, poultry, fish, and vegetables. Hickory is the most common wood used to achieve a good color and flavor. Apple, cherry, mesquite, and alder wood are other popular woods used. Other items commonly used for smoking are dry herbs and spices. Peanut shells and jasmine and a variety of other teas are used in Asian cooking.

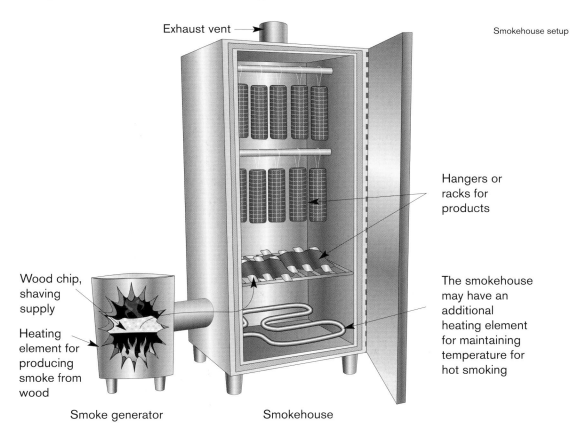

Exhaust vent

Smokehouse setup

Hangers or racks for products

Wood chip, shaving supply

Heating element for producing smoke from wood

The smokehouse may have an additional heating element for maintaining temperature for hot smoking

Smoke generator

Smokehouse

Wood is available in sawdust, chip or nugget, and chunk form; use the form recommended by the manufacturer of the smokehouse. Woods should be purchased from a reputable purveyor to ensure they are free of contaminants such as oil or chemicals. Never use pressure-treated wood because it may contain arsenic or other toxic compounds.

creating the smoke

Smoky fires are created by controlling oxygen: a decrease in oxygen causes wood to smolder and smoke. The addition of moisture through the use of damp products will cause them to smolder rather than burn.

smoking the food

It is recommended to cure all items that are to be cold-smoked because of the possibility of botulism. Items that are hot-smoked may be left uncured if desired. The product can be air-dried further if a drier product is desired. An example of an item that may be air-dried longer is beef jerky in order to give it its texture.

The type of item will dictate how to place it in the smokehouse. For example, large cuts of salmon or other items that cannot bear their own weight are placed on racks, while items such as sausages and bacon should be hung on a sausage stick or on hooks.

Smoke food until the desired color and flavor are achieved. Be sure to refrigerate and store everything properly afterward.

special considerations for smoking fish

In addition to the basic safety considerations discussed on page 128, fish to be smoked requires some special handling.

evisceration

Fish must be eviscerated in a separate area (from produce or poultry); it should have its own sink and be washed thoroughly.

brining

Fish species should not be brined together, to avoid any cross contamination. Brining or dry salting in excess of 4 hours must take place at a temperature of 38°F/3°C or less. Salt concentration and period of time must be adequate to ensure salt penetration to give a water phase salt (WPS) of 2.5 percent. The determination of water phase salt must be done on the thickest piece of fish.

FOUR STEPS IN PREVENTING FOOD-BORNE ILLNESS THROUGHOUT THE SMOKING PROCEDURE

1. CLEAN: Wash hands and surface often.

2. SEPARATE: Don't cross contaminate.

3. COOK: Cook to proper temperatures.

4. CHILL: Refrigerate promptly.

characteristics of woods and the foods they match

WOOD	CHARACTERISTICS	FOOD MATCH	NOTES
HICKORY	Pungent, smoky, bacon-like flavor	Pork; chicken; beef; wild game; cheese	Most widely used product
PECAN	Rich; more subtle than hickory but similar in taste	Pork; chicken; lamb; fish; cheese	Burns cool, so ideal for very low-heat smoking
MESQUITE	Sweeter, more delicate flavor than hickory	Beef; most vegetables	Tends to burn hot, so use carefully
ALDER	Delicate flavor that enhances lighter meats	Salmon, swordfish, sturgeon, other fish; chicken; pork	
OAK	Forthright but pleasant flavor	Beef items like brisket; poultry; pork	Blends well with a variety of toughness/tenderness and juiciness and has medium flavor
MAPLE	Mildly smoky, somewhat sweet flavor	Ham, bacon; poultry; vegetables	Try mixing with corncobs
CHERRY	Slightly sweet, fruity flavor	Poultry; game birds; pork	This is mild and fruity.
APPLE	Slightly sweet but denser fruity flavor	Beef; poultry; game birds; pork such as ham	
PEACH OR PEAR	Slightly sweet, woodsy flavor	Poultry; game birds; pork	
GRAPEVINES	Aromatic, similar to fruit woods	Turkey, chicken; beef	
WINE BARREL CHIPS	Wine and oak flavors	Beef; turkey; cheese	A flavorful novelty that smells wonderful, too
SEAWEED	Tangy and smoky flavors	Lobster, crab, shrimp, mussels, clams	Wash and dry in sun before use
HERBS, SPICES, AROMATICS (bay leaves, rosemary, mint, oregano, whole nutmeg, cinnamon sticks, or lemon peels, garlic; jasmine, other teas; peanut shells)	Vegetables; cheese; small pieces of meat (lighter and thin-cut meats; fish steaks and fillets; kebabs)		

the smoking process

hot-smoking

The fish should be arranged to facilitate complete smoking of all product surfaces. The internal temperature of the fish in the smokehouse must reach a minimum of 145°F/63°C and be held for at least 30 minutes. Temperature probes should be inserted in the thickest portion of at least three fish, and the lowest temperature reading recorded on the process record (see "Record Keeping," below). The temperature should be recorded at least three times during smoking.

cold-smoking

The fish should be arranged to facilitate complete smoking of all product surfaces. The smokehouse temperature should be maintained at a temperature no higher than 50°F/10°C for a period not exceeding 24 hours, or no higher than 90°F/32°C for a period not exceeding 20 hours. The smokehouse temperature should be recorded at least three times during smoking (see "Record Keeping," below).

cooling

Following smoking, fish must be cooled to 50°F/10°C within 5 hours and to 33°F/1°C within 12 hours, and maintained at that temperature until sold.

packaging

Smoked fish can only be sold air or vacuum packaged and must be labeled in bold print "Keep Refrigerated at 38°F [3°C]or Below."

record keeping

Production records must be kept on each batch of fish, showing the name of the product, date processed, and container size and number of containers, if applicable. A record must be kept in ink on the temperature of thawing, brining, smoking, cooling, and storage of each batch of fish processed. The record must also show the duration of smoking. Records must also show the name(s), address(es), and lot code(s) of initial sale.

beef jerky

Once a necessary provision, especially for those who needed lightweight, nutritious "road food," beef jerky is now enjoyed primarily for its intense, robust flavor. It makes a great snack food, and is wonderful pub or bar food. This version of beef jerky is tender enough to cut into a garnish or flavoring ingredient for sauces, pasta dishes, and salads.

MAKES APPROXIMATELY 12 OZ/340 G

3 lb/1.36 kg beef top round (see Note)

1 cup/240 mL strong brewed black coffee

1 cup/240 mL Worcestershire sauce

1 cup/240 mL ketchup

6 oz/170 g brown sugar

5 oz/142 g honey

½ cup/120 mL cider vinegar

2 tbsp/30 mL chili powder

1 tbsp/15 mL kosher salt

2 tsp/10 mL sweet paprika

2 tsp/10 mL onion powder

2 tsp/10 mL red pepper flakes

1 tsp/5 mL medium-ground black pepper

1 tsp/5 mL garlic powder

½ tsp/2.50 mL Insta Cure No. 1

1. Cut the beef across the grain into thin strips about 2 by 8 by ¼ in/5 by 20 cm by 6 mm.

2. Combine and mix all of the ingredients in a large mixing bowl. Transfer to resealable plastic bags and marinate the sliced meat for 24 hours.

3. Drain the meat well and place in a single layer on a wire rack over a sheet pan.

4. Place the meat in a 200°F/93°C oven. Turn the meat over after ½ hour.

5. Check the meat at the end of 2 hours. It should be 90 percent done (see Note). If using an oven, you want the meat to be dry but have a little moisture left.

6. Place the meat on racks and cold-smoke at 90°F/32°C for approximately 15 minutes. Hickory wood or saw dust is a good choice, but any type of hardwood will do depending on the flavor you wish to attain. Smoke should be a medium intensity; if there is too much smoke, the jerky could develop a bitter flavor. Each person will determine the amount of smoke flavor they prefer on the product. If you want to have a more smoky flavor, then simply keep the jerky longer in the smokehouse.

7. Remove the meat from the racks, cool, and store in a plastic container with a tight-fitting lid. The beef jerky may be stored for up to 2 to 4 weeks in a refrigerator or frozen for later use.

Note: Buffalo, venison, or other red game meat can be used instead of the beef. Most lean cuts, such as leg, are appropriate.

The meat can be done in a dehydrator.

Variations

The meat can be placed in the marinade (step 2) and frozen right away. Later, thaw it overnight under refrigeration, and it will be ready for cooking. This is a good method if the process has caught you over the weekend.

The beef jerky may also be dried in a food dryer after draining (step 3). Follow the manufacturer's directions.

dry-cured beef jerky

MAKES 1 LB 8 OZ/680 G

3 lb/1.36 kg beef top round (see Notes)

1¼ cups/300 mL kosher salt

½ cup/120 mL brown sugar

2 tsp/10 mL pickling spice, ground

1 tsp/5 mL celery seeds, crushed

1 tsp/5 mL coarsely ground black pepper

1 tsp/5 mL yellow mustard seeds

1 tsp/5 mL onion powder

1 tsp/5 mL garlic powder

½ tsp/2.50 mL cayenne

⅓ cup/80 mL soy sauce

⅓ cup/80 mL Worcestershire sauce

1. Cut the beef across the grain into thin strips about 2 by 8 by ¼ in/5 by 20 cm by 6 mm.

2. In a mixing bowl, combine the salt, sugar, pickling spice, celery seeds, pepper, mustard seeds, onion and garlic powders, and cayenne to make the cure mix.

3. Rub the cure mix well into both sides of the meat strips. Place the meat on a rack and let cure for 3 hours under refrigeration.

4. Rinse the meat strips and lightly blot them dry with paper towels.

5. In a mixing bowl, combine the soy sauce and Worcestershire sauce. Add the meat strips and coat with the sauce mixture.

6. Place the meat in a single layer on lightly oiled racks over sheet pans and air-dry in a refrigerator where there is a lot of air movement. Dry the meat overnight, or until a pellicle forms.

7. Place the meat in a 200°F/93°C oven for about 1 hour. It should be 90 percent done. Take a piece of meat and break it or taste it. It should be dry with a slight amount of moisture. You want to avoid its being very dry.

8. Cold-smoke the meat for 2 hours at 100°F/38°C or lower. Hickory wood or sawdust is a good choice, but any type of hard wood will do, depending on the flavor you wish to attain. Smoke intensity should be about medium, so you get a light smoke flavor on the product. If a stronger flavor of smoke is desired, then keep the meat in the smoker longer.

9. Place the meat in a well-ventilated area at room temperature to dry for 4 to 5 hours.

10. Remove the meat from the racks and store in a plastic container with a tight-fitting lid. The beef jerky may be stored for 2 to 4 weeks in a refrigerator or frozen for later use.

Notes: Buffalo, venison, or other red game meat can be used instead of the beef. Most lean cuts, such as leg, are appropriate.

The length of time needed to dry depends on the amount of jerky being made and the size of the strips, as well as variables such as temperature, humidity, and air movement.

Variations

The meat can also be placed in the sauce mixture (step 5) and frozen right away. Later, thaw it overnight under refrigeration, and it will be ready for drying (step 6). This is a good method if the process has caught you over the weekend.

The beef jerky may also be dried in a food dryer following air-drying (step 6). Follow the manufacturer's directions.

smoked dry-cured fish

MAKES 1 LB/454 G

FISH

2½ to 3lb/1.13 kg to 1.36 kg salmon

or

2½ lb/1.13 kg bluefish

or

4 to 5 ea trout (see Variation)

CURE MIX

2 lb/907 g kosher salt

1 lb/454 g brown sugar

2 tbsp/30 mL garlic powder

2 tbsp/30 mL onion powder

2 tbsp/30 mL crushed bay leaves

2 tbsp/30 mL crushed allspice

2 tbsp/30 mL ground mace

2 tbsp/30 mL ground cloves

1. Clean and trim the fish of choice. Score the skin.

2. In a stainless steel bowl, combine and mix all of the ingredients for the cure mix.

3. Place a large piece of cheesecloth on a sheet pan and spread a small amount of cure mix on the cheesecloth.

4. Place the fish skin side down on the cure and pack the remainder of the cure on top of fish. (The layer should be slightly thinner where the fillet tapers to the tail.)

5. Wrap the fish tightly in the cheesecloth and cure for 6 hours under refrigeration.

6. Rinse the fish under warm water to wash off the cure. Blot the fish dry with paper towels.

7. Dry the fish on a rack over a sheet pan, uncovered, in the refrigerator for a minimum of 6 hours for the pellicle to form.

8. Cold-smoke the fish for 2 to 3 hours. Apple and cherry are good woods to use to achieve a mild flavor. For the correct temperature refer to the cold smoking process discussed on page 130. The range of time will depend on how strong of a smoke flavor you want o achieve. Smoke intensity should be around medium to medium high; just be careful not to get too strong of smoke flavor or it will leave a bitter taste in the meat product.

9. The fish may now be chilled, wrapped, and stored under refrigeration for up to 2 weeks.

Variation

1. If smoking whole trout, pack the cure inside the trout as well as outside, and cure for 3½ hours.

2. Rinse the trout under warm water. Blot the fish dry with paper towel.

3. Dry the trout, uncovered, on a rack in the refrigerator until a pellicle forms.

4. Cold-smoke the trout for 4 to 6 hours. For the correct temperature refer to the cold-smoking process discussed on page 130. The range of time will depend on how strong of a smoke flavor you want o achieve. Smoke intensity should be around medium to medium high; just be careful not to get too strong of smoke flavor or it will leave a bitter taste in the meat product.

5. Finish the trout by hot-smoking at 185°F/85°C until the flesh is firm and an internal temperature of 135°F/57°C is reached.

6. The trout may be chilled, wrapped, and stored under refrigeration for up to 2 weeks.

smoked maple-brined poultry

POULTRY

5 to 6 lb/2.27 to 2.72 kg duck

or

3 to 4 lb/1.36 to 1.81 kg chicken

or

4 to 5 each/.81 to 2.26 kg Cornish hen

or

2 to 3 lb/.91 to 1.36 kg pheasant

3½ qt/3.36 L Maple Brine for Poultry (page 117)

1. Place the poultry of choice in the brine and brine overnight in a covered container under refrigeration.

2. Rinse the poultry with warm water and blot it dry with paper towels.

3. Place the poultry on a rack over a sheet pan. Refrigerate and air-dry for about 3 hours, until a pellicle is formed.

4. Hot-smoke the poultry to an internal temperature of 165°F/74°C. The smoke intensity should be medium to medium high, depending on how strong of a flavor you are looking to achieve. Cherry, apple, and maple woods can be used for smoking these products.

5. Serve immediately or cool, wrap, and refrigerate for up to 1 week. The poultry may also be frozen for later use.

Note: All poultry should be washed, with excess fat discarded, and trussed to hold shape. The wing should be locked behind the back. For the larger items like the duck, you might inject about 10 percent of the total weight in brine solution into the thickest area of the product and still submerged in the brine solution.

smoked dry-cured oily fish

MAKES 1 QT/960 ML CURE MIX/ONE 2 TO 3 LB/907 TO 1 KG 360 G FISH

3 lb/1.36 kg salmon, sturgeon, whitefish, or bluefish

CURE MIX

2½ cups/600 mL kosher salt

1¼ cups/300 mL brown sugar

6 tbsp/90 mL cracked black pepper

8 tsp/40 mL ground allspice

¼ cup/60 mL lemon juice

1. Trim the fish of all fat. Make sure that all of the pin bones have been removed and that the fins are trimmed off. Score the skin.

2. Combine the salt, sugar, pepper, and allspice to make the cure mix.

3. Place a large piece of cheesecloth on a sheet pan and spread half of the cure mix on top of the cheesecloth. Place the fish skin side down on top of the cure mix.

4. Brush the fish with the lemon juice and sprinkle the remainder of the cure on the fish. (The layer should be slightly thinner where the fillet tapers to the tail.)

5. Dry-cure the fish for 6 to 10 hours under refrigeration. The amount of time is determined by how dry the product should be. It needs to be cured for at least 6 hours to lose moisture so bacteria will not survive.

6. Rinse the fish under warm water to wash off the cure mix. Blot the fish dry with paper towels.

7. Dry the fish in a single layer on a rack, uncovered, under refrigeration for 6 hours to form the pellicle.

8. If using salmon, cold-smoke for 2 hours under a light to medium smoke intensity to finish it. For the correct temperature to use, refer to the cold smoking process discussed on page 130.

9. If using sturgeon, whitefish, or bluefish, hot-smoke at 160° to 165°F/71° to 74°C for about 1 hour, until it reaches an internal temperature of 135°F/57°C. Smoke intensity should be about medium.

smoked shrimp or scallops

MAKES 3 LB 8 OZ/1.59 KG

5 lb/2.27 kg shrimp
or scallops

6 cups/1.44 L Brine
for Scallops or
Shrimp (page 116)

1. Peel and devein the shrimp. If using scallops, remove the tough muscle tabs. Place the shrimp or scallops in a nonreactive container.

2. Pour enough brine over the shrimp or scallops to completely submerge them.

3a. If using large shrimp or sea scallops, brine for 1 hour under refrigeration, covered.

3b. Remove the shrimp or scallops from the brine, rinse, and spread on a rack over a sheet pan in one layer. Air-dry under refrigeration to form a pellicle.

3c. Cold-smoke for 3 to 4 hours. Apple and cherry are good woods to use to achieve a mild flavor. Smoke intensity should be about medium. For the correct temperature to use, refer to the cold smoking process discussed on page 130.

4a. If using bay scallops or small shrimp, brine for 20 minutes under refrigeration, covered.

4b. Remove the shrimp or scallops from the brine, rinse, and spread on a fine-mesh rack over a sheet pan in one layer. Air-dry under refrigeration to form a pellicle.

4c. Cold-smoke the shrimp or scallops for 1½ hours. Smoke intensity should be about medium. For the correct temperature to use, refer to the cold smoking process discussed on page 130.

5. Cook the shrimp or scallops by roasting, sautéing, or grilling until slightly opaque in the center, 5 to 10 minutes.

6. The shrimp or scallops are now ready to be used immediately. They may also be cooled, wrapped, and refrigerated for up to 1 week.

Presentation idea: Grill, sauté, poach, stew in a sauce, or prepare the shrimp/scallops according to other needs.

forcemeats

chapter seven

We will consider the classical methods of production of these products and explore more modern styles and items.

Terrine molds, left to right: three-pound enameled cast iron, two-pound enameled cast iron, pâté en croûte mold, triangular mold, half-cylinder mold, trapezoidal mold, cylindrical mold

terrine molds

Terrines are traditionally understood to be forcemeat mixtures baked in an earthenware mold with a tight-fitting lid. This preparation gets its name from its association with the material used to make the mold, once exclusively earthenware of unglazed clay or terra-cotta. Today, terrine molds are produced from materials such as stainless steel, aluminum, ceramics, enameled cast iron, ovenproof plastic, or glazed earthenware. These materials are more durable and more sanitary than the unglazed earthenware once favored by charcutiers.

Terrine molds come in any number of shapes, including triangle, half circle, and trapezoidal. These materials and shapes offer the garde manger chef an effective way to impress the guest.

forcemeat preparations

Forcemeat is a mixture of meat, poultry, or fish, ground or puréed with some form of fat along with seasonings and optional binders. One of the most significant garde manger preparations, forcemeat or *farce* (French for "stuffing") is used as the base for pâtés, terrines, galantines, and sausages.

Forcemeats historically were time-consuming preparations requiring laborious grinding and straining of meat, seasonings, and fat through metal sieves in a chilled atmosphere. Modern kitchen equipment today permits these preparations to be done in a fraction of the time.

The first three styles of forcemeats (country-style, straight, and gratin) we talk about, starting on page 157 are the primary forcemeats. These three products are made using the classical method, which produces delicious forcemeat that is heavy and fatty. These products are made using equal amounts of fat and meat (a ratio of 1 part meat to 1 part fat), yielding a product with great taste and a lot of flavor, as much of the flavor comes from fat. Recently, forcemeats have undergone a change more fitting to the cuisine of today, making them lighter; the fat content was reduced, making the new basic ratio 2 parts meat to 1 part fat. This creates a healthier, lighter product. In doing so, however, the charcutier needs to work that much harder to develop flavor through the addition of aromatics, herbs, seasonings, and spices. With this new ratio, it also becomes of paramount importance to use the freshest possible products. They will yield the most flavor and have a high moisture content, which is needed to develop the same mouthfeel without the fat, to which people are accustomed. Mousseline is the fourth forcemeat and its preparation method and classical use of lean meats, such as poultry breast and fish, naturally make it a lighter forcemeat. The use of eggs and cream as the binder in this forcemeat further acts to create a lean product. The final style, 543 emulsion, is used mostly for sausages and formed forcemeats like olive loaf. See Emulsion Forcemeats, page 223, in Chapter 8. With any of these four forcemeat preparations, simply by changing the flavors that are added through the selection of the main protein, the aromatics, herbs, and spices, you can create a forcemeat than can be used in a variety of different preparations.

To ensure the creation of forcemeat with a smooth texture and mouthfeel, both the ingredients and equipment must be kept chilled, around 28° to 30°F/−2° to −1°C. To chill the equipment, submerge it in ice water. Cold equipment will prevent the meat from getting too warm during processing.

All the blades for the grinder and all the blades for the food processor need to be very sharp so the meat can be cut quickly and neatly. Furthermore, the grinder equipment needs to be assembled correctly or it will not cut the meat properly.

If you cook the product too long, or the cooking temperature is too high, your forcemeat will come out improperly.

Finally, you have to have the correct ratio of lean meat to fat for the forcemeat (see "Lean-to-Fat Ratios," page 151, and "Forcemeat Ratios," page 155).

SIGNS OF A BROKEN FORCEMEAT

You can see problem signs in the forcemeat when you make a taste tester. When you look and see:

- a lot of fat coming out from the forcemeat, or

- a lot of moisture coming out from the forcemeat,

you will lose the consistency, along with the volume and flavor in the forcemeat.

four basic components of a classical forcemeat

1. PREDOMINANT MEAT: The predominant meat used in the forcemeat is typically a tougher, less tender meat that has more cartilage and more flavor. The predominant meat determines what the forcemeat will taste like.

2. SECONDARY MEAT: The secondary meat is most often lean pork, chicken, or veal. It should meet the following criteria:

   - Neutral in flavor

   - High in protein and moisture

   - Binds well

   - Has a low cost and a high availability

3. FAT: Use only fresh pork fatback without skin. Pork fat is used for flavoring; it has a neutral flavor, but it blends well with other flavors. Make sure the consistency of the fat is buttery and smooth. Pork fat is used over other possible alternatives because of its availability and low cost. The three forcemeat preparations use some cream in the panada to add moisture and mouthfeel. Cream in the mousseline forcemeat is used as fat instead of pork fat.

   Fat such as bacon, fatback, and caul fat is also used to line the terrine molds before baking, although in more modern terrines, you will see more thinly sliced ham, thinly sliced prosciutto, or just plastic wrap to line the mold. Lining the molds not only gives the forcemeat a nice look on the outside but also helps the forcemeat to come out of the mold much easier.

4. SEASONINGS: Seasonings such as salt will help draw out the moisture and protein from the meat and ensure a good "bind." Carefully measured herbs and ground spices create the flavor in the product. Seasonings should complement the main flavor of the meat used without overpowering it. In some cases we sauté items like onions, shallots, and garlic to further develop the flavor; in doing so we need to make sure the cooked product is cold before placing in the forcemeats. Items like wine, brandy, or grain-based spirits can be used to enhance flavor and aroma. Colorful garnishes allow the chef to add eye appeal and develop additional texture and flavor.

LEAN-TO-FAT RATIOS

Most contemporary recipes will call for pork fat (jowl fat or fatback) or heavy cream. Numbers appearing after meats in recipes refer to the ratio of lean to fat by weight. For example, 70/30 would be an approximate ratio of 70 percent meat to 30 percent fat, by weight. A usual mix of jowl fat or fatback with lean meat, indicated as 50/50, is half lean and half fat by weight. This is used in the sausage forcemeat and not in terrines, galantines, and pâtés.

additional elements for successful forcemeats

In addition to these four basic components, other processes and ingredients are important to the success of a forcemeat.

primary binding

Primary binding is the cold processing of meat, fat, and water by grinding, mixing, and taming. Salt is also added to bring out the myosin to help it bind.

secondary binders

Secondary binders are not always needed. The most common one is eggs.

Secondary binders from left to right: eggs, heavy cream, bread crumbs

panadas

A panada is a starch product used to absorb and hold moisture and ensure that the product is not dry. All panadas have a farinaceous base to stabilize the fat of the forcemeat by absorbing the natural juices when cooked, thus causing a swelling without separation. If a panada is needed, it should never comprise more than 20 percent of the total volume of the finished product, garnish included.

The four types of panadas used in forcemeats are:

- Bread crumbs soaked in milk

- Flour or pâte à choux dough

- Riced cooked potato

- Puréed cooked rice

progressive grinding

In progressive grinding, chunks of meat are ground by passing first through a coarse plate, then a medium plate, and finally a fine plate.

This process involves grinding meat through a chilled meat grinder, starting with the largest plate first, then progressing to smaller and smaller holed plates. When performing this task, it is very important to chill the meat between grindings.

garnishes for forcemeats

Different types of food products are used as garnish for forcemeats; they must be compatible with the types of meat used. Pistachio nuts, dried fruit, diced ham, tongue, and truffles are some examples.

There are two types of garnishes used in the forcemeats: random and inlay.

- Random garnish means that a product or products uniform in size are mixed into the forcemeat and wherever they end up, that is where they will be in the finished product.

- Inlay garnish simply means a garnish is placed in a specific spot in the terrine or pâté.

Laying garnishes into a terrine as it is being filled produces a centered dispersion, also known as inlay (left), while folding or stirring garnishes into a forcemeat produces a random dispersion (right).

temperature

To maintain the water-bath temperature at 160° to 170°F/71° to 77°C, when cooking forcemeat you should cook it at 300°F/149°C in a conventional oven so that it will hold at that constant temperature. When cooking a terrine, you can avoid hot spots by using multiple layers of paper towels under the mold.

testing forcemeats

Cook a taste tester of the forcemeat to check the bind, moisture, and flavor. Wrap a small amount of forcemeat in plastic wrap, secure the ends, make sure it is tight so it holds together, and poach in a 170°F/77°C water bath for about 10 minutes, or until it reaches the proper internal temperature for the product.

Wrap the test portion in plastic wrap and tie the ends securely with string.

Poach the test portion to the appropriate internal temperature, then allow it to cool to servicing temperature (cold).

The test portion will not taste or feel exactly like the finished product, but you can train your palate to evaluate quality, seasoning, and texture.

developing a forcemeat recipe

The process for developing a forcemeat recipe is relatively simple. First, select and trim the meats. Next, determine the ratio of predominant meat, secondary meat, pork fat, and (if necessary) panada. After that, select the internal garnish and seasonings you will use. Finally, select the mold you wish to use, as well as the yield you want, to determine the size and form of the final product—for example, galantine, terrine, or pâté.

The table below shows different ratios that can be used in making galantines, terrines, or pâtés. The ratios depend on the strength (flavor) of the predominant meat. The stronger the flavor, the lower the percentage used for the predominant meat. If the predominant meat is very mild, use a larger percentage of it. This chart will give you a good starting point in developing a forcemeat recipe.

forcemeat ratios

PREDOMINANT MEAT	SECONDARY MEAT	PORK FAT	PANADA*	GARNISH
33%	33%	33%	10–15%	10–15%
40%	30%	30%	10–15%	10–15%
50%	25%	25%	10–15%	10–15%
60%	20%	20%	10–15%	10–15%

*If a panada is needed, it should never comprise more than 20 percent of the total volume of the finished product, garnish included.

1. Figure out the volume in weight of the terrine mold by filling it with water and then weighing the water. "A pint's a pound the world around" is the saying; 1 pint of water (2 cups/960 mL) will weigh 1 lb/454 g.

2. Subtract the percentage of panada and garnish you wish to use from the total volume of the finished product.

3. Divide the remainder of the weight by the ratios for predominant meat, secondary meat, and fat.

4. Add seasonings and spices, depending on the flavor you wish to achieve.

5. Follow your method for the particular pâté or terrine you are making.

styles of forcemeat

There are five major styles of forcemeat:

- Country-style or campagne
- Straight method
- Gratin style
- Mousseline style
- 5/4/3 emulsion (used for sausage production)

Country-style forcemeats are hearty
in flavor and coarse in texture.

country-style or campagne forcemeat

This is probably the oldest type of forcemeat and is basically coarse sausage meat cooked in a terrine mold lined with thin slices of fatback, bacon, or caul fat.

1 part pork (lean)

1 part predominant meat (lean)

1 part pork fat

½ part liver (usually from the predominant meat)

½ part mirepoix (lightly caramelized, cooled)

¼ tsp/1.25 mL Insta Cure No. 1 (per 2 lb/907 g forcemeat; optional)

Panada, up to 20%, as needed

1 medium egg (per 2 lb/907 g forcemeat)

Pork fatback, sliced thinly, for lining terrine mold, as needed

Aspic, as needed

1. Cube all meats and fat, about 1-in/3-cm cubes.

2. Mix the meats with the mirepoix and Insta Cure (if using). Marinate for 6 hours under refrigeration.

3. Grind the mixture twice through a chilled grinder using a coarse plate (³⁄₈ in/9 mm).

4. Weigh the mixture and determine the amount of panada and eggs to add.

5. Remove one third of the meat mixture, combine with the egg, and purée in a food processor, keeping the product cold over a water and ice bath.

6. Recombine the meat, add the panada, and mix well. Chill in a water and ice bath or in refrigerator.

7. Test the forcemeat for flavor and consistency. Adjust as needed.

8. Fill desired fatback-lined mold with mixture and bake in a water bath to an internal temperature of 145°F/63°C, depending on the meat; if using poultry, the product will need to be cooked to 160°F/71°C, and it will carry over to 165°F/74°C to meet health regulations.

9. Pour off the excess fat and replace with aspic. Chill.

Procedure photos continue on next page.

Mise en place for a country-style forcemeat, including meats, panada, seasonings, and garnishes

Add the panada to the ground meat to help hold the finished product together after cooking.

straight-method forcemeat

This forcemeat combines pork and pork fat with a predominant meat in equal parts through a process of progressive grinding (see page 152) and emulsification.

1 part pork (lean)

1 part predominant meat (lean)

1 part pork fat

½ part shallots (sweated, cooled)

Seasonings and herbs, as needed

¼ tsp/1.25 mL Insta Cure No. 1 (per 2 lb/907 g forcemeat; optional)

1 medium egg (per 2 lb/907g forcemeat)

2 to 4 oz/60 to 120 mL heavy cream (optional)

Garnish, as needed

1. Cube the meats and fat, about 1 in/3 cm in size, and add the shallots, seasonings, and Insta Cure (if using).

2. Mix and let marinate 6 hours under refrigeration.

3. Grind through a chilled grinder using first a coarse plate (³⁄₈ in/9 mm), then a medium plate (¼ in/6 mm).

4. Chill the ground meat mixture.

5. Combine the meat mixture with the egg(s) and cream (if using), and purée in a food processor.

6. Test for flavor and consistency.

7. Use for terrines, galantines, pâtés en croûte, or other preparations, adding garnish as desired.

Procedure photos continue on next page.

straight-forcement method,
continued

RIGHT: Mise en place for straight forcemeat, including meat, panada, seasonings, and garnishes

Adding heavy cream to a straight forcemeat results in a smoother texture and a richer flavor.

Once thoroughly processed, the mixture should have a homogenous texture and a slightly tacky feel.

Straight forcement finished product

Finished gratin forcemeat

gratin forcemeat

1 part predominant meat (lean)

1 part pork fatback

1 part pork (lean)

2 medium eggs (per 1 lb/454 g forcemeat)

Seasonings and herbs, as needed

¼ tsp/1.25 mL Insta Cure No. 1 (per 2 lb/907 g forcemeat; optional)

Garnish, as needed

1. Sauté the predominant meat quickly. This will give it some color, but do not cook it completely.

2. Blanch the fatback for 30 seconds in boiling water. Cool it. When cool, mix it with the meats and chill.

3. Cube all the meats and fat. Chill.

4. Grind through a chilled grinder using a coarse plate (³/₈ in/9 mm), then a medium plate (¹/₄ in/6 mm).

5. Chill the ground meat mixture.

6. Combine meat mixture with the eggs, seasonings, and Insta Cure (if using) and purée in a food processor.

7. Test for flavor and consistency.

8. Use for terrines, galantines, pâtés en croûte, or other preparations, adding garnish as desired.

Mise en place for gratin forcemeat, including seared meat, panada, seasonings, and garnishes

Prepared gratin forcemeat will have a homogenous texture and feel slightly tacky.

mousseline-style forcemeat

This is the quickest forcemeat to make. It is typically used for lean, light meats or fish. Usually only one variety of meat is used (although mixtures work well) and unwhipped heavy cream is used as the source of fat. The cream is used to adjust the consistency as required by the type of meat or fish used. This forcemeat is quite stable during cooking since the fat is already emulsified in the cream. The area of caution comes in making sure you don't overwork the forcemeat in the food processor once the cream has been added.

1 lb/454 g lean white meat or fish

1 tsp/5 mL kosher salt

1 large egg (per 1 lb/454 g meat)

Seasonings, as needed

1 cup/240 mL heavy cream (approx.)

1. Cube the meat or fish. Chill.

2. Grind through a chilled grinder using a coarse plate ($^3/_8$ in/9 mm), then a medium plate ($^1/_4$ in/6 mm). Chill.

3. Combine the chilled ground meat mixture with the salt, egg(s), and seasonings. Purée in a food processor. until smooth.

4. Add the cream slowly and pulse in. An alternative way to do this is to remove the mixture from the food processor and place it in a mixing bowl over an ice bath, slowly working the cream into the meat with a rubber spatula or spoon.

5. Test the mixture for seasoning and consistency; adjust as necessary.

6. Use for the desired preparations.

FAT Fat contributes greatly to the eating quality of forcemeats. It enhances the flavor and the juiciness. Pork fat is preferred because it is softer, it melts at lower temperature, and it is easier to chop or grind, and the preferred pork fat is jowl fat. Fatback is used for forcemeat for terrines, galantines, and pâtés; jowl fat is used predominantly for sausage making. U.S. government regulations limit cooked sausage to 30 percent fat.

WATER Water, in the form of ice, is used to regulate heat generated by machine friction. This helps keep meat and fat from warming excessively during processing.

SALT Salt makes proteins soluble; that is, it draws the water-soluble protein, myosin, from meat to act as the primary binder. In addition, it adds flavor and retards the growth of bacteria. (See "Preserving with Salt," page 73.)

Procedure photos continue on page 166.

Mousseline forcemeat around a tenderloin, mousseline pinwheel with chicken breast, and mousseline piped into a boneless chicken leg

mousseline-style forcemeat,
continued

The formula for mousseline forcemeat is 1 lb/454 g lean white meat or seafood, 1 tsp/5 mL kosher salt, 1 large egg (or egg white for mild-flavored products like fillet of sole or flounder), 1 cup/240 mL heavy cream, and ground pepper as needed.

Slowly add the cream to the mixture and continue processing.

A mousseline should be pressed through a tamis to ensure that it is completely smooth.

To blend the mousseline properly, it is vital to scrape down the bowl periodically as you process.

emulsified meat method

Chill all metal equipment that will touch meat/fat products: Temperature control is important. If possible, chill the meat between grinding and chopping steps to compensate for the heat generated by grinding.

5 lb/2.27 kg meat

4 lb/1.81 kg fat

3 lb/1.36 kg ice or cold water

1. Trim the meat and cut into 1-in/3-cm cubes. Chill or partially freeze.

2. Cut the jowl fat into 1-in/3-cm cubes. Chill or partially freeze.

3. Progressively grind the fat from the coarse plate ($^3/_8$ in/9 mm) through the fine plate ($^1/_8$ in/3 mm).

4. Mix salt, Insta Cure (see Note), dextrose (if used) and other seasonings with the meat. Progressively grind the meat from the coarse plate ($^3/_8$ in/9 mm) through the fine plate ($^1/_8$ in/3 mm).

5. Place the meat in a Stephan cutter or other suitable food chopper. Place the ice on top of the meat.

6. Process the meat in the chopper to a temperature of 30°F/−1°C or lower. Continue processing until the temperature of the meat rises to 40°F/4°C.

7. At 40°F/4°C, add the fat and continue processing until the temperature of the meat is between 45°and 50°F/7°and 10°C.

8. Add the nonfat dry milk and continue processing until the temperature of the meat is 58°F/14°C.

9. Cook a small amount of the forcemeat, taste and check the binding, and adjust seasoning if necessary.

10. Process into the desired sausage product.

Note: Not all emulsified forcemeats require Insta Cure No. 1.

Procedure photos continue on next page.

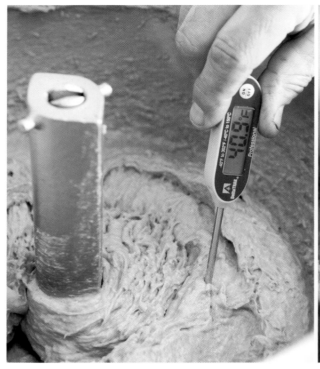

When the mixture reaches 40°F/4°C, add the ground fat to the meat.

Continue processing until the mixture forms a stable emulsion of the lean meat and fat, and the temperature is 45°F/7°C.

When the temperature reaches 45°F/7°C, add the nonfat dry milk, scraping down the bowl periodically as you continue mixing.

galantines

The term *galantine* derives from an Old French word, *galin*, meaning "chicken." Originally, galantines were made exclusively from boned poultry and game birds, and were stuffed with a forcemeat, tied in the bird's natural shape, and often lavishly decorated. Since deboning poultry is difficult and time consuming, this is a rather elaborate dish. Today, however, galantines are made from a wide range of products, including fish, shellfish, and meats. The skin, if available, is used as a casing to hold the forcemeat. Galantines are often pressed into a cylindrical shape.

cooking and assembly method for galantines

1. Cut the knuckle bone from the legs and cut the wing at the second joint to allow the skin to be removed without ripping it. Remove the skin, keeping it as intact as possible. Make an incision through the skin down the middle of the back and pull the entire skin away from the bird. Use a small knife to help loosen it, if necessary, working it carefully not to rip or cut, working the skin loose and peeling like an old pair of long johns, going around the wing joint and the legs. You then will need to remove the extra fat and sinew from the skin to ensure it will be flat.

2. Bone the predominant meat, reserving intact any pieces that will be used for garnish. All other meat should be cut into dice or strips of the appropriate size to prepare the forcemeat. The bones and any unusable trim should be used to prepare a rich stock and reduced to glace to add to forcemeat to give more flavor.

3. Trim the skin to form a large rectangle. Lay out the skin or other casing for the galantine on a large cheesecloth or plastic-wrap square. Mound the forcemeat lengthwise down the rectangle's center and position any garnish (for example, the tenderloin or marinated diced breast meat) as desired. Make into a cylinder with help from the cheesecloth, then wrap the skin-encased forcemeat tightly in cheesecloth to form a roulade or cylinder.

4. Tie the ends with butcher's twine and use a strip of cheesecloth to secure it at even intervals in order to maintain the shape of the cylinder.

5. Place the galantine on a perforated rack and submerge it in simmering stock. Be sure that the galantine is completely submerged. Maintain the liquid at an even simmer throughout the cooking time, generally 1 to 1½ hours, until an internal temperature of 150°F/66°C for meats, 140°F/60°C for fish, or 165°F/74°C for poultry has been reached.

6. Let the galantine cool overnight in the cooking liquid. The next day, rewrap the galantine in cheesecloth or plastic wrap. This will hold it in a cylindrical shape for storage. If cheesecloth or plastic wrap has been used, remove the casing. Rewrap the galantine in fresh plastic wrap, reroll it to form a tight cylinder, and refrigerate.

Make an incision along the backbone and carefully pull and cut
away the skin from the meat, keeping the skin intact.

Lay the skin out on cheesecloth or
plastic wrap.

Layer a garnish on the skin, then
pipe on the prepared forcemeat
filling.

Roll the galantine carefully around
the forcemeat. The skin should just
overlap itself, forming a seam.

After rolling, secure the galantine
by tying each end with butcher's
twine and secure the middle by
tying two bands of cheesecloth.

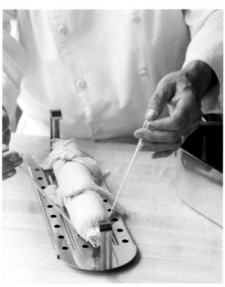

To keep the galantine submerged
during poaching, weight it with
a small plate and lower into the
poissonier.

Fill the poissonier with stock, cover, and poach the galantine to the appropriate internal temperature.

Remove the cheesecloth or plastic wrap, then tightly rewrap the galantine to produce an even density after it has cooked.

Slice the galantine to serve.

pâté

Pâté is a form of spreadable paste, usually made from meat and served with toast as a starter. *Pâté* is a French word that designates a mixture of minced meat and fat. It is generally made from finely ground or a chunky mixture of meats such as the liver of chicken, pigs, ducks, geese, or calves; and flavored with herbs, spices, wild mushrooms, wine, brandy, and often additional fat, vegetables, and in some cases, black truffles from Périgord, France. Pâté may be cooked in a crust as a pie or in a loaf, in which case it is called *pâté en croûte*. The most famous pâté is probably *pâté de foie gras*, which is made with fattened livers from force-fed geese.

Pâtés have been the staple of French chefs. They provide an opportunity to display the imagination and skill of an ambitious chef. Pâtés are delicate, fine, exquisite specialties that require great culinary skill and passion to create.

working with foie gras

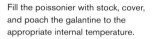

Upon receiving the foie gras, it is important to inspect it. This is an expensive product, whatever grade you buy. So take the time to be certain that you are getting the quality you are paying for. First, check that the packaging is still intact. Any rips or punctures may have damaged the foie gras. Weigh the foie gras yourself, and inspect it carefully for any unexpected imperfections.

Prepare the foie gras for refrigerated storage. Set the wrapped foie gras on a bed of crushed ice in a perforated hotel pan, set inside a standard hotel pan. Pack more ice around the liver and keep this assembly in the refrigerator until you are ready to prepare the foie gras.

Terrines from left to right: Terrine of Foie Gras and Butternut Squash, Smoked Chicken and Roasted Fennel Terrine, Chicken Pâté en Croûte, Gran Mere (gratin-style forcemeat), Chilled Emincé of Chicken and Vegetables

Temper the foie gras before cleaning by leaving out at room temperature for a few hours, so it becomes very soft and pliable. Ot you may place the foie gras in the packaging into water that is around 70° to 80°F/21° to 27°C for about 1 hour, or until soft to work with. for at least 2 hours. Separate the foie gras into lobes and remove the veins. Starting from the top of the lobe, where the veins are the thickest, pull out the veins, using tweezers, the tip of a knife, and/or your fingertips. When the foie gras has been cleaned, it is then soaked in salted ice water and/or milk. Marinate the foie gras according to the specific recipe and proceed with the recipe instructions to complete the foie gras terrine.

healthy terrines and pâtés

A popular trend is making terrines that do not contain forcemeat, but instead, use the natural juices from the meat product along with herbs to help hold the terrine together. For example, take chicken breasts, season them with salt, place them in a bag, toss them around, and let them sit for a time. As the chicken breasts sit, keep tossing or tumbling them around to extract the protein that is being denatured by salt. Once done, layer the breasts in a terrine mold, along with the extracted protein, and bake the product at a lower temperature (approximately 300°F/149°C) until the proper internal temperature is reached, and then cool the terrine to 100°F/38°C. As the terrine cools, press it with a light weight and let it cool thoroughly overnight. The following day, keep the product cold, rewrap it with new plastic wrap, and slice to serve. The resulting terrine is not only flavorful and tender but also contains no more fat than the initial product.

Another method is using a braised product such as oxtails. This would be done by braising in a short liquid until done. Once braised, strain the liquid into another container, and, keeping the meat as hot as possible, pick the meat over, breaking it into pieces and removing the fat. You can then season the braise using tart items, such as gherkins or other herbs. In the meantime, reduce the liquid to half, being sure not to burn it, and skim off the fat. Add just enough liquid back to the meat to make it moist, mixing the product throughout the addition of the liquid. Place the meat in a small mold, keeping it slightly pressed in the mold overnight. The product will be ready to slice and serve the next day.

Another trend with terrines is using flavorful aspic, or even vinaigrette that is bound with gelatin, to bind the terrine. An example of this would be using roasted vegetables, which are already flavored well, and layering them in a terrine mold while brushing each piece with the vinaigrette fortified with the gelatin. Arrange the different layers of vegetables, let the product sit for around 10 to 15 minutes in the refrigerator, then press it with a weight overnight.

There are a number of other items like activa that can be used to glue pieces together, bake them, and serve the glued pieces as a whole piece if desired. Activa is an enzyme that is frequently used to bind meats together.

People are always looking to cut down on the time that is required to produce terrines without the loss of binding and flavor. The usage of activa and aspic gelées may aid in the production of terrines without sacrificing time.

jellied and pressed meats

These are good examples of products that are easily made lighter and healthfully, to fit a more contemporary event or menu. The different preparation techniques make the food less heavy and a skillful chef can make them just as flavorful.

Jellied meats consist of cooked meats, garnish, and flavorings, cut attractively and set in a flavored stock that is high in gelatin content (and therefore able to set to a firm gel). Pressed meats are similar to the jellied meats except no additional liquid is used—only the natural gelatin from the meat. The item is cooked until tender and seasoned, and a garnish may be added. The meat is then pressed together, wrapped in plastic, or put in a plastic wrap–lined mold and cooled under pressure.

basics of jellied and pressed meats

MEAT: Any type of fresh or cured meat, poultry, or seafood can be used.

GARNISH: A garnish of various vegetables, meats, fruits, nuts, and so on can be used. All garnish should complement the meat item, be attractive, uniformly cut, and fully cooked.

LIQUID: The liquid should complement the meat item and garnish, be well seasoned, and, if possible, contain some natural gelatin—for example, a good strong stock.

SEASONINGS: Spices, herbs, onions, garlic, wines, or prepared seasoning preparations such as soy sauce may be added.

GELATIN CONTENT: Since gelatin is what will bind the item, meats that contain natural gelatin (collagen) are used; in some cases the gelatin content will have to be fortified with additional sheet gelatin.

cooking and assembly method for jellied and pressed meats

1. The meat item is cooked, usually by simmering in a flavored liquid; other methods are smoking and roasting. Bone and skin are removed if necessary and the meat is cut or broken into pieces.

2. The garnish and other flavorings are prepared and precooked if necessary, then mixed with the meat.

3. The liquid is reduced if necessary, degreased, seasoned, checked for gelatin strength, and adjusted if necessary.

4. All items are combined, checked for final seasoning and placed in a plastic wrap–lined mold, refrigerated for 24 hours, then sliced and served.

pâté dough

MAKES 2¾ LB/1 KG 247 G

1 lb 4 oz/567 g bread flour, sifted

1½ oz/43 g nonfat dry milk

¼ oz/7 g baking powder

½ oz/14 g kosher salt

3½ oz/99 g shortening

2½ oz/71 g unsalted butter

2 medium eggs

1 tbsp/15 mL white vinegar

1 to 1¼ cups/240 to 300 mL milk, or as needed

1. Place the flour, dry milk, baking powder, salt, shortening, and butter in a food processor and pulse until the dough is a fine meal.

2. Place the dough in a 20-qt. mixer with a paddle attachment.

3. Add the eggs, vinegar, and 4 to 5 oz/120 to 150 mL of milk. Mix on speed 1 just to form it into a ball. Here you determine the amount of milk if it needs more. The dough should be moist yet dry; if it does not hold together and is not moist enough, then add more milk. If the ball is formed and moist but dry, then mix on speed 2 for 3 to 4 minutes to develop the gluten.

4. Remove the dough from the mixer and knead by hand until smooth, tucking in all the end under as you would to shape a ball of bread. Square it off.

5. Wrap in plastic wrap and rest for a minimum 30 minutes (for best results, overnight) in the refrigerator. before rolling and cutting the dough to line the terrine molds.

terrine of duck confit

2 whole ducks

Cure Mix

3 oz/85 g kosher salt

1 tsp/5 mL Insta Cure No. 1

¼ cup/60 mL brown sugar

2 garlic cloves, crushed

10 black peppercorns, crushed

½ tsp/2.50 mL ground bay leaf

1 tsp/5 mL thyme leaves

1 tbsp/15 mL Four-Spice Mix (page 35)

1 lb/454 g boneless pork butt, trimmed of fat

1 lb/454 g pork fatback

½ cup/120 mL water

1 medium yellow onion, split

2 celery stalks, cut into 3-in/8-cm chunks

2 garlic cloves, smashed

2 tsp/10 mL grated orange zest

2 to 3 oz/57 g to 85 g garnish (see Note)

1. Disjoint the ducks. Trim and reserve the excess skin and fat. Use leg, thigh, and breast meat. Any excess trim can be reserved for stock.

2. Combine the salt, Insta Cure, sugar, garlic, peppercorns, bay leaf, thyme, and Four-Spice Mix for the cure mix. Rub the duck and pork butt well with the cure mix, using all the cure mixture on the meat. Cure both overnight under refrigeration.

3. Dice the fatback and grind with the reserved duck fat and skin through the fine plate (⅛ in/3 mm) of a meat grinder. Render the fat in a saucepan with the water. Strain the rendered fat. Rinse the meat under warm water to melt the salt. Wipe dry.

4. Combine the duck, pork, onion, celery, garlic, and rendered fat in a roasting pan or Dutch oven and cover. Braise in a 300°F/149°C conventional oven, turning occasionally, for 2½ hours, or until the meats are very tender.

5. Remove the meats from the fat and cool until you can handle them. Strain the fat and reserve. Discard the vegetables.

6. Remove the meat from the bones, making sure no bones and duck fat are left in and on the meat. Combine in a mixer bowl with the orange zest and 1¼ cups/300 mL of the strained fat.

7. Mix slowly with a paddle to coarsely shred the meats and evenly distribute the fat. Add any desired garnish once the meat is shredded, and mix briefly to distribute the garnish.

8. Line a terrine mold with plastic wrap, leaving an overhang. Pack the meat into the mold. Fold over the liner to cover, then cover with a press plate, weight with a 1-lb/454-g weight, and refrigerate overnight.

9. Carefully unmold and remove the plastic wrap from the finished terrine. The colder the terrine is before you slice it the better. Slice and serve or wrap and refrigerate for up to 1 week.

Note: Possible garnishes to include in this terrine may be braised kale, blanched pistachios, or dried cherries that have been rehydrated in a small amount of alcohol.

duck terrine with pistachios

1 duck (5 to 6 lb/2.27 to 2.72 kg)

1 qt/960 mL water

1 cup/240 mL red wine

1 sachet d'épices

4 oz/113 g mirepoix

¼ cup/60 mL orange juice

¼ cup/60 mL brandy

Oil, as needed

2 oz/57 g minced yellow onions

1 garlic clove, minced

1 lb/454 g pork butt, cleaned of fat, cubed

4 oz/113 g pork belly, skinned, cubed

1 medium egg

1 tsp/5 mL Pâté Spice Mix #1 (page 35)

⅛ tsp/0.625 mL thyme leaves

1½ tbsp/22.50 mL grated orange zest

½ oz/14 g kosher salt

2 oz/57 g shelled pistachios, blanched, roughly chopped

12 pork fatback slices (¹⁄₁₆ in/1.50 mm thick), or as needed

1 to 2 cups/240 to 480 mL aspic gelée (see page 280)

1. Debone the duck; reserve the breasts, leg/thighs, and liver. Trim the breasts of all fat. Remove the fat and sinews from the legs and thighs and reserve the meat and liver under refrigeration.

2. Chop the carcass and wings. Combine the duck bones, water, wine, sachet, and mirepoix in a stockpot. Simmer for 1½ hours.

3. Strain and degrease the stock. Reduce the stock to 1 cup. Chill.

4. Marinate the duck breasts in the orange juice and brandy overnight under refrigeration.

5. Remove the breasts from the marinade and blot dry. Reserve the marinade. In a sauté pan, sear the duck breasts in a small amount of oil. Remove the breasts from the pan and reserve.

6. Sauté the onion and garlic in the sauté pan until translucent; use about medium heat so they do not burn. Add the reserved marinade and reduce to a syrup.

7. Cool the onion mixture to room temperature.

8. In a mixing bowl, combine the onion mixture, pork butt, pork belly, duck leg/thigh meat, and liver. Progressively grind the meat from the coarse plate (³⁄₈ in/9 mm) through the fine plate (⅛ in/3 mm) into a mixing bowl over an ice bath.

9. Add the egg, reduced duck stock (slightly warmed to be liquid but cool), pâté spice, thyme, orange zest, and salt. Mix thoroughly. Test the forcemeat and adjust the seasoning if needed.

10. Fold the pistachio nuts into the forcemeat.

11. Lightly brush the terrine mold with oil. Line a terrine mold with plastic wrap, leaving an overhang. Line the plastic wrap with the thinly sliced fatback, letting it hang over by about ½ in to 1 in/1 cm to 3 cm on all sides. Pack half of the forcemeat into the mold, making sure there are no air pockets and that it is packed in very firmly. Place the duck breasts in the center (the duck breast might have to be trimmed so it fits into the mold, duck breast should be the length of the terrine), and top with the remaining forcemeat. Cover with slices of fatback and fold over the liner to cover. Cover the mold.

12. Bake in a hot water bath in a 300°F/149°C conventional oven to an internal temperature of 150°F/66°C.

13. Cool the terrine to 100°F/38°C.

14. Pour off the excess fat and fill with aspic heated to 100°F/38°C. Re-cover with plastic wrap and let sit in the refrigerator for 1 hour, and then press with a 2-lb/907-g press plate overnight under refrigeration. You could also use a Plexiglas (or even two) that is slightly narrower and shorter than the terrine press overnight.

15. Carefully unmold and remove the plastic wrap from the finished terrine. Slice and serve or wrap and refrigerate for up to 1 week.

After lining a terrine mold with plastic wrap that has been lined with the fat back slices, fill it halfway with the prepared forcemeat, smoothing over the top.

Lay the garnish into the terrine as it is being filled to produce a centered dispersion.

If desired, a pastry bag may be used to work the forcemeat into the corners and around the garnish.

Procedure photos continue on next page.

Fold the fatback slices first, then the plastic wrap over the fatback to completely encase it and cover the mold with a lid.

Set a press plate on the cooled terrine and place a weight on the press plate. You can make your own press plate by cutting Styrofoam, Plexiglas, or wood to size slightly smaller than the mold and covering it with plastic wrap.

Carefully unmold and remove the plastic wrap from the finished terrine.

Rewrap the terrine in plastic wrap to maintain the shape.

Cut the finished terrine into slices for serving.

pâté de foie (liver pâté)

MAKES ONE 3 LB/1.36 KG TERRINE

1 lb/907 g pork liver

Milk (optional), as needed

3 lb/1.36 kg pork belly, skinned

4 oz/113 g yellow onions, diced

3 medium shallots, diced

2 tbsp/30 mL butter

Seasoning

¼ oz/7 g kosher salt

Pinch of Insta Cure No. 1

⅓ tsp/1.67 mL ground black pepper

¼ tsp/1.25 mL Pâté Spice Mix #1 (page 35)

4 oz/113 g all-purpose flour

1 cup/240 mL heavy cream

4 medium eggs, beaten

12 slices pork fatback, thinly sliced

1. Clean the pork liver, soak in milk for 1 hour if desired, drain dry, and cube.

2. Cut pork belly into about 1-in/3-cm cubes.

3. Sauté the onions and shallots in the butter until translucent. Chill well.

4. Combine the pork liver, pork belly, and onion mixture with the seasoning ingredients.

5. Grind through a ¼-in/6-mm grinding plate, then through a ⅛-in/3-mm grinding plate into a mixer bowl over an ice bath.

6. Combine the flour, cream, and eggs in a mixing bowl; whisk together until smooth.

7. Place the bowl of ground meat in a mixer with a paddle attachment. On speed #1, stir in the flour mixture and mix well.

8. Line the terrine mold with plastic wrap, leaving an overhang, then line with the fatback so that it overhangs by about 1 in/3 cm on all sides. Pack the meat into the mold. Fold over the fatback and liner to cover.

9. Bake in a 300°F/149°C conventional oven in a hot-water bath to an internal temperature of 155°F/68°C.

10. Cool the terrine to 100°F/38°C.

11. Cover with a press plate and weight with a 2-lb/907-g weight. Refrigerate overnight.

12. Carefully unmold and remove the plastic wrap from the finished terrine. Slice and serve or wrap and refrigerate for up to 1 week.

Presentation idea: This pâté is excellent for sandwiches or canapés.

chicken galantine

MAKES 1 GALANTINE, APPROXIMATELY 4 LB/1.81 KG

1 chicken (about
3 lb/1.36 kg), boned,
wing tips removed,
skin removed intact

7 fl oz/210 mL sherry

2 medium shallots, sliced

2 garlic cloves, minced

1 tbsp/15 mL butter

⅛ tsp/0.625 mL
Insta Cure No. 1

5 tsp/25 mL kosher salt

4 oz/113 g pork
fatback, cubed

1 tbsp/15 mL glace
de volaille

1 medium egg

1 tbsp/15 mL chopped
fresh parsley

1 tbsp/15 mL chopped
sage or chervil

1 tsp/5 mL poultry
seasoning

1 tsp/5 mL ground
black pepper

2 oz/57 g heavy cream

Garnish

4 oz/113 g smoked tongue
(⅛-in/3-mm dice)

3 oz/85 g truffle peelings

4 oz/113 g pork fatback
(⅛-in/3-mm dice)

5 oz/142 g pistachios,
shelled, blanched, halved

Poaching liquid, as needed
to cover the galantine

1. Weigh 8 oz/227 g of the chicken leg and thigh meat and cube it, about 1-in/3-cm pieces. Set aside under refrigeration.

2. Cut the chicken breasts into ¼-in/6-mm cubes. Combine 1 cup/240 mL of the diced chicken breast with ½ cup/120 mL of the sherry and reserve under refrigeration for garnish.

3. Sweat the shallots and garlic in the butter. Deglaze with the remaining sherry. Reduce by half and cool to room temperature.

4. Combine the shallot mixture, Insta Cure, and 2 tsp/10 mL of the salt with the cubed chicken leg and thigh meat and cubed fatback. Cover and refrigerate for 4 hours.

5. Progressively grind the chicken meat and fatback from the coarse plate (⅜ in/9 mm) through the fine plate (⅛ in/3 mm) into a mixer bowl over an ice bath. Transfer to a mixer fitted with a paddle attachment.

6. Add the glace de volaille, egg, parsley, sage, poultry seasoning, remaining salt, and the pepper to the forcemeat; mix until just blended. Fold the cream into the forcemeat over an ice bath. Mix well and hold over the ice bath.

7. Make a taste test and adjust the seasoning as needed.

8. Fold the reserved chicken breast and garnish ingredients into the forcemeat.

9. Wrap the forcemeat in plastic wrap and roll into a tight round cylinder. Freeze for 1 hour.

10. Lay out the reserved skin on plastic wrap, skin side down and trimmed into a rectangle. Lay the forcemeat on top.

11. Roll the skin carefully around the forcemeat. The skin should just overlap itself by about 1 in/3 cm, forming a seam. Roll up the plastic wrap to cover tightly. Tie off both ends with butcher's twine.

12. Poach the galantine in enough water to cover the galantine totally to an internal temperature of 155°F/68°C.

13. Turn off the heat and let the galantine carry over to 165°F/74°C in the poaching liquid.

14. Let the galantine cool down to 100°F/38°C.

15. Remove the galantine from the poaching liquid. Remove the plastic wrap and rewrap the galantine tightly to produce an even, appealing texture. Store for up to 1 week. This can be served with Cumberland Sauce (page 301).

pâté de campagne (country-style terrine)

MAKES ONE 3 LB/1.36 KG TERRINE

2 lb 8 oz/1.13 g pork butt, 75/25, boned, cut into 1-in/3-cm cubes

8 oz/227 g pork liver or chicken livers, chicken livers cleaned of sinew

1½ garlic cloves, minced

4 oz/113 g yellow onions, finely chopped

5 parsley sprigs, finely chopped

2½ oz/71 g all-purpose flour

2 medium eggs

2 tbsp/30 mL brandy

½ cup/120 mL heavy cream

Seasoning

¾ tsp/3.75 mL Insta Cure No. 1

1½ tbsp/22.50 mL kosher salt

¼ tsp/1.25 mL ground white pepper

½ tsp/2.50 mL Pâté Spice Mix #1 (page 35)

12 slices pork fatback, or as needed, sliced paper thin

1 cup/240 mL aspic gelée (see page 280), or as needed

Cumberland Sauce (page 301), as needed

1. Progressively grind 1 lb/454 g of the pork, the liver, garlic, onions, and parsley from the coarse plate (³⁄₈ in/9 mm) through the fine plate (¹⁄₈ in/3 mm) into a mixing bowl over an ice bath. Place in large bowl.

2. Grind the remaining pork through the coarse plate (³⁄₈ in/9 mm). Add to the meat mixture. Reserve under refrigeration.

3. Combine the flour, eggs, brandy, and cream in a mixing bowl; whisk together until smooth.

4. Add the flour mixture and seasoning ingredients to the meat mixture. Mix on speed #1 for 1 minute, then mix on speed #2 until the mixture feels sticky to the touch. Make a taste test and adjust the seasoning if necessary.

5. Line the terrine mold with plastic wrap, if desired, leaving an overhang. Line the mold with the fatback. Pack the forcemeat into the mold. Fold over the fatback and liner (if using) to cover.

6. Bake in a 300°F/149°C conventional oven in a hot-water bath to an internal temperature of 150°F/66°C.

7. Cool to 100°F/38°C. Pour off the excess fat and fill with aspic heated to 100°F/38°C.

8. Cool slightly and refrigerate for 24 hours.

9. Carefully unmold and remove the plastic wrap from the finished terrine. Slice and serve with Cumberland Sauce, or wrap and refrigerate for up to 1 week.

Variations:

Chicken, rabbit, or turkey may be substituted for the pork.

Before grinding in step 1, sauté the onion and garlic in a small amount of oil until translucent. Chill the onion mixture. Add the onion mixture and ¼ cup/60 mL melted glace de viande when adding the seasoning.

chicken pâté en croûte

MAKES ONE 3 LB/1.36 KG TERRINE

1 half chicken breast, medium dice

½ cup/120 mL sherry

2 tbsp/30 mL allspice berries

2 medium shallots, sliced

2 garlic cloves, minced

1 tbsp/15 mL butter

5 tsp/25 mL kosher salt

1 tsp/5 mL ground black pepper

¼ tsp/1.25 mL Insta Cure No. 1

2 lb/907 g chicken legs and thighs, cleaned, cubed

8 oz/227 g pork fatback, cubed

1 tbsp/15 mL glace de volaille

1 medium egg

¼ cup/60 mL heavy cream

1 lb/454 g Pâté Dough (page 174)

¼ cup/60 mL egg wash (1 whole egg beaten with 1 tbsp/15 mL milk)

Garnish

14 to 16 thin slices ham

3 oz/85 g smoked ham, small dice

3 oz/85 g dried apricots, brunoise, plumped in sherry

1. Combine the chicken breast with 3 fl oz/90 mL of the sherry and 1 tbsp/15 ml of the allspice in a nonreactive mixing bowl. Reserve under refrigeration for garnish.

2. Sweat the shallots and garlic in butter; deglaze with the remaining sherry.

3. Combine the shallot mixture, 2 tsp/10 mL of the salt, the pepper, Insta Cure, and the remaining allspice with the chicken leg and thigh meat and fatback in a mixing bowl. Cover and marinate overnight under refrigeration.

4. Progressively grind the marinated meat and fat from the coarse plate (⅜ in/9 mm) through the fine plate (⅛ in/3 mm) into a mixing bowl over an ice bath. Transfer to a mixer fitted with a paddle attachment.

5. Drain the chicken breast, reserving the sherry; return the chicken meat to the refrigerator. Add the sherry, glace de volaille, egg, the remaining salt, and the heavy cream to the forcemeat. Mix well.

6. Make a taste tester and adjust the seasoning as needed.

7. Fold the diced chicken breast and garnish ingredients into the forcemeat, working over an ice bath.

8. Roll out the dough to a thickness of approximately ⅛ to¼ in/3 to 6 mm. Line a hinged mold with the dough. When the rolled dough is set in the mold, smooth the dough against the mold and seal the seams with egg wash and a piece of reserved trim dough. Leave an overhang on one side, enough to completely cover the top of the mold, and extend down into the mold on the opposite side at least ½ in/1 cm. Line the dough with thin ham slices on all sides, letting the ham overhang by½ in/1 cm on each side. Pack the forcemeat into the lined mold. Fold the dough over the forcemeat, cutting away any excess. Trim away any excess and tuck the edges down into the mold. Cut a hole in the top to permit steam to escape. Reinforce the vent hole by gluing a ring of dough around the hole into place with some egg wash and insert a chimney. Brush the surface with egg wash.

9. Bake at 450°F/232°C for 15 to 20 minutes. Reduce the heat to 350°F/177°C and finish baking to an internal temperature of 165°F/74°C, about 10 to 15 minutes.

3 oz/85 g pistachios, blanched or toasted

3 tbsp/45 mL chopped fines herbes

¾ to 1 cup/180 to 240 mL aspic gelée (see page 280), melted

10. Remove the pâté from the oven and cool to 90° to 100°F/32° to 38°C.

11. Ladle the aspic through a funnel into the pâté. When it fills up, let the aspic distribute evenly and top off with more if needed. You will see the aspic through the chimney. Refrigerate the pâté for at least 24 hours. Refrigerate in the mold; when ready to slice, unmold, scrape, or brush any aspic that might be formed on the outside.

12. Slice and serve immediately, or wrap and refrigerate for up to 5 days.

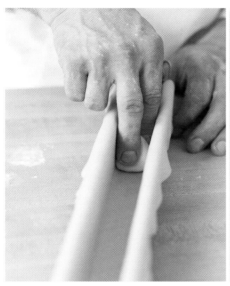

When the rolled dough is set in the mold, smooth the dough against the mold and seal the seams with egg wash and a piece of reserved trim dough.

If desired, a second liner of thinly sliced cooked meat can be added; the liner of ham or other product is usually used to protect the dough from the moisture of the forcemeat. Then evenly spread the forcemeat in the mold.

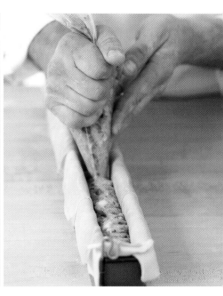

The forcemeat may be piped into the terrine mold to work into the corners more easily.

Procedure photos continue on next page.

Enclose the forcemeat by overlapping the overhanging sections of the liner.

Using a piping tip, cut a small hole in the top of the dough to allow steam to escape during baking.

Use a paring knife to carefully remove the cut dough from the hole.

Insert a chimney, a cylinder designed to keep the hole from closing as the pâté bakes, and use egg wash to adhere decorations made from dough scraps.

Carefully free the pâté en croûte from the mold after cooking.

terrine of foie gras and butternut squash

MAKES ONE 3 LB/1.36 KG TERRINE

3 lb/1.36 kg foie
gras, grade A

1 tbsp/15 mL
granulated sugar

2 tbsp/30 mL sea salt

2 tsp/10 mL ground
white pepper

¼ tsp/1.25 mL Insta
Cure No. 1

1 cup/240 mL Cognac
or Sauternes

2 lb/907 g butternut squash
(about 2 small squashes)

Honey, as needed

1 tsp/5 mL ground
cinnamon

1½ tsp/7.50 mL
ground nutmeg

2 tsp/10 mL ground ginger

Kosher salt, as needed

Ground black pepper,
as needed

30 flat-leaf parsley
leaves, blanched for 5
seconds and shocked

1. Temper the foie gras to around 70° to 80°F/21° to 27°C, so it becomes very soft and pliable. Clean the foie gras lobes by removing the veins (see page 171).

2. Place the lobes in a parchment paper–lined half hotel pan. Sprinkle the foie gras with the sugar, sea salt, white pepper, and Insta Cure and lightly rub to adhere them.

3. Sprinkle the foie gras liberally with Cognac or Sauternes and cover with a sheet of parchment paper. Place in refrigerator to marinate for 3 hours. Gently turn over the foie gras, rub with the accumulated marinade, and marinate for an additional 3 hours.

4. Line a terrine mold with plastic wrap, leaving an overhang. Place the lobes smooth side down in the mold; season as needed. Fill the mold to the inner lip and press down tightly to remove any air pockets. Fold over the liner and cover the terrine mold.

5. Bake the terrine in a hot water bath, maintaining the bath at a constant 160°F/71°C, to an internal temperature of 100°F/38°C. The oven temperature may need to be adjusted to keep the water at a constant 160° temperature. If it gets too hot, add cold water immediately to lower the temperature. Foie gras has the best texture and flavor when cooked to an internal temperature of around 100°F/38°C (be sure to check with your local and state authorities, however).

6. Remove the terrine from the water bath and allow it to rest for 2 hours at room temperature, then pour off the excess fat. Hold at room temperature.

7. Quarter the squash and scrape out the seeds using a spoon. Lay the squash skin side down in a hotel pan and lightly drizzle with honey. Season the squash with the cinnamon, nutmeg, ginger, and salt and black pepper.

8. Roast at 350°F/177°C, until cooked through but not browned. (Light browning on the edges of the squash is acceptable.)

9. Set aside the squash to cool to room temperature. Once cooled, separate the neck of the squash from the bulb-like lower section. Remove the skin with a knife and lightly flatten the pieces of squash with the palm of your hand.

10. To assemble the terrine, spray the terrine mold with vegaline spray and then line terrine mold with plastic wrap, leaving an overhang. Place one third of the foie gras smooth side down in the mold to create the bottom layer. Pack each

piece of foie gras into the mold using the back of your hands to push out any air bubbles. Place a few leaves of parsley over the foie gras, keeping the squash away from the edge of the terrine (1in/3 cm), then place two or three pieces of squash over the parsley. Lightly drizzle with additional honey and repeat the layering procedure. Once the second layer of squash is complete, finish it off with a third layer of foie gras.

11. Once the terrine is full, gently fold over the plastic wrap. Cover the terrine with a press plate and top with a 2- to 3-lb/907- to 1360-g weight, tied down with string.

12. Refrigerate the terrine for 6 hours. Unmold the terrine gently and rewrap it tightly with plastic wrap.

13. Slice the terrine with a heated knife and serve immediately, or refrigerate and store for up to 1 week for later use.

Carefully remove the vein network from the interior of each lobe of foie gras.

Soak the foie gras in salted ice water and dry well.

Press the foie gras into a pan lined with parchment.

Cognac is a classic marinade ingredient, which is poured liberally over the foie gras.

Place the marinated foie gras into the terrine mold.

When the cooked terrine cools to 90°F/32°C, place a press plate on top, tie on a weight, and refrigerate.

bierschinken

MAKES 24 LB/10.88 KG

10 lb/4.54 kg boneless fresh ham

Pork and Beef Brine (page 115), as needed

Cure Mix

2 tsp/10 mL Insta Cure No. 1

3¼ oz/92 g kosher salt

¾ oz/21 g dextrose

Spice Blend

½ oz/14 g ground white pepper

¼ oz/7 g Colman's dry mustard

½ oz/14 g onion powder

1 tsp/5 mL ground ginger

1½ tsp/7.50 mL ground mace

2 lb 8 oz/1.13 kg boneless beef, cleaned and cubed

2 lb 8 oz/1.13 kg boneless pork, cleaned and cubed

4 lb/1.81 kg pork, 50/50 (pork belly or jowl fat), cubed

3 lb/1.36 kg crushed ice

5¾ oz/177 g nonfat dry milk

1. Cube the ham into about ½-in/1-cm pieces and place in a deep plastic container with enough beef brine to cover. Cover and cure for 24 hours under refrigeration.

2. Combine the Insta Cure, salt, and dextrose to make the cure mix. In another mixing bowl, combine the pepper, mustard, onion powder, ginger, and mace to make the spice blend.

3. Toss the beef and boneless pork cubes with the cure mix and spice blend. Chill well, until nearly frozen.

4. Progressively grind the chilled meat from the coarse plate (⅜ in/9 mm) through the fine plate (⅛ in/3 mm) into a mixing bowl over an ice bath. Reserve under refrigeration.

5. Progressively grind the 50/50 mixture (pork bellies or jowl fat) from the coarse plate (⅜ in/9 mm) through the fine plate (⅛ in/3 mm) into a mixing bowl over an ice bath. Reserve under refrigeration.

6. Transfer the ground meat to a Stephan cutter. Place the ice on top of the ground meat. Process until the mixture reaches a temperature of 30°F/−1°C.

7. Continue processing until the temperature reaches 40°F/4°C.

8. Add the ground (50/50 mixture) fat and process until the temperature reaches 45°F/7°C.

9. Add the nonfat dry milk and process until the temperature reaches 58°F/14°C.

10. Make a taste test and adjust the seasoning as needed.

11. Drain the cubed ham and rinse under warm water for about 2 to 3 minutes. Dry on paper towels.

12. Add the ham to the emulsion and mix well. The emulsion should be kept cold in an ice-water bath.

13. Pack the mixture into well-greased loaf pans, smoothing the top. The size of the mold can vary, but a 2- to 3-lb/907- to 1360-g terrine mold can be a good mold to cook in. Let the bierschinken cure overnight under refrigeration.

14. Bake in a 300°F/149°C conventional oven in a hot-water bath to an internal temperature of 155°F/68°C. Cool at room temperature until 100°F/38°C, then store in a refrigerator up to 1 week. This can be frozen also and held up to 2 to 3 weeks.

leberkäse (bavarian loaf)

MAKES 12 LB 8 OZ/5.67 KG

Cure Mix

2 tsp/10 g Insta Cure No. 1

3¼ oz/92 g kosher salt

¾ oz/21 g dextrose

Spice Blend

½ oz/14 g ground white pepper

¼ oz/7 g Colman's dry mustard

½ oz/14 g onion powder

1 tsp/5 mL ground ginger

1½ tsp/7.50 mL ground mace

5 lb/2.27 kg boneless beef shoulder, cleaned, cut into 1-in/3-cm cubes

4 lb/1.81 kg pork jowl fat, cut into 1-in/3-cm cubes

3 lb/1.36 kg crushed ice

5¾ oz/177 g nonfat dry milk

1. Combine all the ingredients for the cure mix. In a separate mixing bowl, combine the ingredients for the spice blend. Toss the beef with the cure mix and spice blend. Place in resealable plastic bags and chill well, until nearly frozen.

2. Progressively grind the beef from the coarse plate (³⁄₈ in/9 mm) through the fine plate (¹⁄₈ in/3 mm) into a mixing bowl over an ice bath. Reserve under refrigeration.

3. Progressively grind the jowl fat from the coarse plate (³⁄₈ in/9 mm) through the fine plate (¹⁄₈ in/3 mm) into a mixing bowl over an ice bath. Reserve under refrigeration.

4. Transfer the ground beef to a Stephan cutter. Place the ice on top of the ground meat. Process until the mixture reaches a temperature of 30°F/−1°C.

5. Continue processing until the temperature reaches 40°F/4°C.

6. Add the fat and process until the temperature reaches 45°F/7°C.

7. Add the nonfat dry milk and process until the temperature reaches 58°F/14°C.

8. Make a taste tester and adjust the seasoning as needed.

9. Place the mixture into well-greased loaf pans. You can use leberkäse loaf pans or a 2- to 3-lb/907- to 1360-g terrine mold. Mound the top. Using a knife, score a diamond pattern on top. Let the leberkäse cure overnight or for up to 2 days under refrigeration.

10. Bake uncovered in a 350°F/177°C conventional oven in a hot-water bath to an internal temperature of 155°F/68°C. Take out and let cool at room temperature to 100°F/38°C, then store and hold in a refrigerator for 1 to 2 weeks. This can also be frozen for 2 to 3 weeks.

black and green olive loaf

MAKES 17 LB/7.71 KG

Cure Mix

2 tsp/10 mL Insta Cure No. 1

3¼ oz/92 g kosher salt

¾ oz/21 g dextrose

Spice Blend

½ oz/14 g ground white pepper

¼ oz/7 g Colman's dry mustard

½ oz/14 g onion powder

1 tsp/5 mL ground ginger

1½ tsp/7.50 mL ground mace

2 lb 8 oz/1.13 kg boneless beef, cleaned and cut into 1-in/3-cm cubes

2 lb 8 oz/1.13 kg boneless pork, cleaned and cut into 1-in/3-cm cubes

3 lb/1.36 kg crushed ice

4 lb/1.81 kg pork, 50/50 (jowl fat or pork belly), cut into 1-in/3-cm cubes

5¾ oz/177 g nonfat dry milk

1 lb 8 oz/680 g green olives with pimientos

1 lb 8 oz/680 g black olives, pitted

1. Combine the Insta Cure, salt, and dextrose for the cure mix. In a separate mixing bowl, combine the ingredients for the spice blend. Toss the cubed meat with the cure mix and spice blend. Place in resealable plastic bags and chill well, until nearly frozen.

2. Progressively grind the meat from the coarse plate (³⁄₈ in/9 mm) through the fine plate (¹⁄₈ in/3 mm) into a mixing bowl over an ice bath.

3. Transfer the ground meat to a Stephan cutter. Add the ice. Process until the mixture reaches a temperature of 30°F–1°C.

4. Continue processing until the temperature reaches 40°F/4°C.

5. Add the fat and process until the temperature reaches 45°F/7°C.

6. Add the nonfat dry milk and process until the temperature reaches 58°F/14°C.

7. Make a taste tester and adjust the seasoning as needed.

8. Rinse the green and black olives with hot water. Drain and dry on paper towels.

9. Add the olives to the emulsion and mix well, making sure that it is mixed really well. Mix the product over an ice-water bath.

10. Place the mixture into well-greased loaf pans (2- to 3-lb/907- to 1360-g terrine molds work well), smoothing the top. Let the olive loaves cure covered overnight under refrigeration.

11. Bake covered or uncovered (if you get too much color, then cover) in a 350°F/177°C conventional oven in a hot-water bath to an internal temperature of 155°F/68°C. Cool at room temperature until 100°F/38°C, then store in a refrigerator, up to 1 week. This can also be frozen and held up to 2 to 3 weeks.

green peppercorn loaf

Cure Mix

2 tsp/10 mL Insta Cure No. 1

3¼ oz/92 g kosher salt

¾ oz/21 g dextrose

Spice Blend

½ oz/14 g ground white pepper

½ oz/14 g Colman's dry mustard

½ oz/14 g onion powder

1 tsp/5 mL ground ginger

1½ tsp/7.50 mL ground mace

2 lb 8 oz/1.13 kg boneless beef, cleaned and cut into 1-in/3-cm cubes

2 lb 8 oz/1.13 kg boneless pork, cleaned and cut into 1-in/3-cm cubes

4 lb/1.81 kg pork 50/50 (jowl fat or pork belly), cut into 1-in/3-cm cubes

3 lb/1.36 kg crushed ice

5¾ oz/177 g nonfat dry milk

¾ oz/21 g green peppercorns, drained

1. Combine all the ingredients for the cure mix. In a separate mixing bowl, combine the ingredients for the spice blend. Toss the cubed beef and pork with the cure mix and spice blend. Place in resealable plastic bags and semifreeze.

2. Progressively grind the beef and pork from the coarse plate (³⁄₈ in/9 mm) through the fine plate (¹⁄₈ in/3 mm) into a mixing bowl over an ice bath. Reserve under refrigeration.

3. Place 50/50 (jowl fat or pork bellies) in a resealable plastic bag and semifreeze. Progressively grind the 50/50 mixture from the coarse plate (³⁄₈ in/9 mm) through the fine plate (¹⁄₈ in/3 mm) into a mixing bowl over an ice bath. Reserve under refrigeration.

4. Transfer the ground beef and pork to a Stephan cutter. Place the ice on top of the ground meat. Process until the mixture reaches a temperature of 30°F/−1°C.

5. Continue processing until the temperature reaches 40°F/4°C.

6. Add the fat and process until the temperature reaches 45°F/7°C.

7. Add the nonfat dry milk and process until the temperature reaches 58°F/14°C.

8. Make a taste tester and adjust the seasoning as needed.

9. Rinse the green peppercorns under hot water and drain on paper towels.

10. Add the green peppercorns to the emulsion and mix well, holding the emulsion over an ice-water bath.

11. Place the mixture into well-greased loaf pans or 2- to 3 -lb/907- to 1360-g terrine molds, smoothing over the top. Let the loaves cure covered overnight.

12. Bake in a 350°F/177°C conventional oven in a hot-water bath to an internal temperature of 155°F/68°C. Cool at room temperature until 100°F/38°C, then store in a refrigerator for up to 1 week. This can also be frozen and held up to 2 to 3 weeks.

macaroni and cheese loaf

MAKES 17 LB/7.71 KG

Cure Mix

2 tsp/10 mL Insta
Cure No. 1

3¼ oz/92 g kosher salt

¾ oz/21 g dextrose

Spice Blend

½ oz/14 g ground
white pepper

¼ oz/7 g Colman's
dry mustard

½ oz/14 g onion powder

1 tsp/5 mL ground ginger

1½ tsp/7.50 mL
ground mace

2 lb 8 oz/1.13 kg boneless
beef, cleaned, cut into
1-in/3-cm cubes

2 lb 8 oz/1.13 kg boneless
pork, cleaned and cut
in 1-in/3 cm cubes

4 lb/1.81 kg pork, 50/50
(jowl fat or pork bellies),
cut in 1-in/3-cm cubes

3 lb/1.36 kg crushed ice

5¾ oz/177 g nonfat dry milk

1 lb/454 g raw
elbow macaroni

2 lb/907 g Cheddar or
any high melting cheese,
small dice (see Note)

1. Combine all the ingredients for the cure mix. In a separate mixing bowl, combine the ingredients for the spice blend. Toss the cubed beef and pork with the cure mix and spice blend. Place in resealable plastic bags and semifreeze.

2. Progressively grind the beef and pork from the coarse plate (⅜ in/9 mm) through the fine plate (⅛ in/3 mm) into a mixing bowl over an ice bath. Reserve under refrigeration.

3. Progressively grind the 50/50 mixture from the coarse plate (⅜ in/9 mm) through the fine plate (⅛ in/3 mm) into a mixing bowl over an ice bath. Reserve under refrigeration.

4. Transfer the ground meat to a Stephan cutter. Place the ice on top of the ground meat. Process until the mixture reaches a temperature of 30°F/−1°C.

5. Continue processing until the temperature reaches 40°F/4°C.

6. Add the fat and process until the temperature reaches 45°F/7°C.

7. Add the nonfat dry milk and process until the temperature reaches 58°F/14°C.

8. Make a taste tester and adjust the seasoning as needed.

9. Add the macaroni and cheese to the emulsion and mix well. The emulsion should be held over an ice bath while mixing in the garnish.

10. Place the mixture into well-greased loaf pans or 2- to 3-lb/907- to 1360-g mold, smoothing over the top. Let the loaves cure covered overnight.

11. Bake covered in a 350°F/177°C conventional oven in a hot-water bath to an internal temperature of 155°F/68°C. Cool at room temperature until 100°F/38°C, then store in the refrigerator for up to 1 week. This can also be frozen and held up to 2 to 3 weeks.

Note: A high melting cheese can be specified and purchased from a purveyor.

From left to right, top to bottom: mortadella, Bierschinken, Black and Green Olive Loaf, Macaroni and Cheese Loaf, Tongue loaf

smoked chicken and roasted fennel terrine

MAKES ONE 2 LB/907 G GUTTER MOLD TERRINE

3 medium fennel bulbs, tops trimmed

3 boneless, skinless, chicken breasts

1 qt/1.92 L Poultry Brine (page 117)

2 cups/480 mL vegetable or fennel stock

1 gelatin sheet, bloomed and wrung out

¼ cup/60 mL chopped fennel fronds

1 cup/240 mL Pickled Red Onion (page 322), drained

Kosher salt, as needed

Ground black pepper, as needed

Garnish

8 micro breakfast radishes

2 tbsp/30 mL Fennel Oil (recipe follows)

¼ cup/60 mL chopped flat-leaf parsley

Ground black pepper, as needed

1. Wrap the fennel bulbs in foil and roast for 1 hour at 350°F/177°C, until the fennel is tender through center. Cool to room temperature and cut into medium dice. Reserve.

2. Place the chicken breasts in brine; make sure they are submerged in the brine for 6 to 10 hours. Rinse in hot water and dry well. Hot-smoke the chicken to an internal temperature of 165°F/74°C. (See Chapter 6 for full information on smoking.) Do not overcook. Cool the chicken breasts to 40°F/4°C internal temp. Slice the chicken breasts lengthwise into ¼-in/3-mm slices.

3. Fill a 3-qt/3-L sauce pot with water and fit a stainless-steel mixing bowl over the top. Pour the stock into the bowl. Warm the stock to 80°F/27°C.

4. Add the gelatin to the stock and let it sit for 5 to 10 minutes. Heat to 110°F/43°C and let cool to 90°F/32°C. Add the fennel fronds to the stock.

5. Place the fennel, chicken, and onion in separate stainless-steel mixing bowls. Season each separately with salt and pepper as needed.

6. Add enough of the gelatin mixture to each bowl to cover the ingredients.

7. Spray a terrine mold with vegaline spray. Line the mold with plastic wrap, leaving an overhang evenly on all sides.

8. Assemble the terrine by placing a layer of chicken on the bottom of the mold just overlapping slightly. Spoon some pickled onion on top of the chicken and pour a little of the gelatin mixture on top, just enough to cover the onion. Add another layer of chicken; you might have to trim the chicken breast to fit just inside the terrine mold evenly. Cover with the gelatin mixture. Spoon some of the diced fennel on top of the chicken.

9. Alternate layers in the same order until the terrine mold is filled. The top layer should be chicken. Make sure there is some liquid just to cover but not too much. Fold over the liner to cover. Let the terrine cool for about 20 minutes.

10. Place a press plate (Plexiglas that is just shorter and narrower than the mold itself) on top and weight with a 1-lb/454-g weight. Secure the weight so that it lays flat and even on top. Refrigerate overnight.

11. Unmold the terrine and rewrap it tightly with new plastic wrap. Refrigerate for up to 2 to 3 days.

Presentation idea: To serve, cut into ¼-in/6-mm slices. Place a couple slices of terrine on the plate. Place a few breakfast radish micro greens on the plate next to the terrine. Add some fennel oil in a nice fashion, like drops or a smear of the sauce on the plate; for example, place some sauce down, then take the back of the spoon and drag it through the sauce. Sprinkle with some chopped parsley and fresh ground pepper.

fennel oil

MAKES 1 CUP/240 ML

½ cup/120 mL fennel fronds, packed

½ cup/120 mL spinach leaves

½ cup/120 mL flat-leaf parsley

½ cup/120 mL extra-virgin olive oil

¾ cup/180 mL grapeseed oil

1. Blanch the fennel fronds, spinach, and parsley in simmering water for about 30 seconds.

2. Shock and drain on paper towels. Chop coarsely and squeeze out any excess liquid.

3. Purée in a blender with the olive and grapeseed oils. Refrigerate for 1 day.

4. Strain through a fine-mesh sieve, but make sure you have some of the body of the fennel go through the sieve. Place into a container to hold. You do not need to line the fine strainer. Refrigerate and decant into a tightly covered container. Cover and refrigerate until needed. This will hold for about 1 week.

chilled emincé of chicken and vegetables

MAKES ONE 2 LB/ 907 G TERRINE

8 chicken legs, whole

7 cups/1.68 L chicken stock

2 parsley sprigs

1 tarragon sprig

21 chive sprigs

Garnish

3 oz/85 g carrots, sliced ⅛ in/3 mm thick, blanched

4 oz/113 g zucchini, outer part only, small dice, blanched

3 oz/85 g chanterelle mushrooms, cut into quarters, sautéed

Butter, as needed

1 tsp/5 mL green peppercorns, drained

1 tbsp/15 mL chopped fresh parsley

1½ tsp/7.50 mL chopped fresh tarragon

1 tsp/5 mL kosher salt

¼ tsp/1.25 mL ground black pepper

1 tbsp/15 mL lemon juice

1. In a stockpot, combine the chicken, 1½ qt/1.44 L of the stock, and the parsley, tarragon, and chives. Simmer the chicken legs slowly until very tender.

2. Meanwhile, blanch the garnish vegetables individually in the remaining stock. Sauté the mushrooms in a little butter. Remove and cool the vegetables to room temperature; reserve. Add the stock to the chicken legs.

3. When the chicken legs are very tender, remove them from the stock and let cool until you can handle them.

4. Degrease the stock and strain if necessary. Reduce the stock to 1½ cups/ 360 mL to make sure that the gelatin is sliceable strength. Test, and if it is not, then fortify with gelatin (refer to "Gelatin for Aspic Gelée" on page 280).

5. Remove and discard the skin, bones, and any fat from the cooled chicken legs. Break up the meat into large pieces.

6. Combine the chicken meat, blanched vegetables, mushrooms, green peppercorns, parsley, tarragon, salt, pepper, lemon juice, and reduced stock. Mix well, check the seasonings, and adjust the seasoning if needed.

7. Spray the terrine mold with vegaline spray or oil. Line a terrine mold with plastic wrap, leaving an overhang. Pack the chicken mixture into the mold. Make sure that there is ample liquid mixed in with the chicken and vegetables. Fold over the liner to cover.

8. Refrigerate the mold for 15 to 30 minutes. Apply a press plate and a 1-lb/454-g weight and press overnight under refrigeration. (The plate or Plexiglas should be narrower and shorter than the terrine mold.)

9. The terrine is now ready to slice and serve, or wrap and refrigerate for up to 1 week.

Presentation idea: Arrange slices of the terrine on a plate of greens and serve with Cajun-Style Lime and Mustard Seed Dressing (page 292).

créole beef daube

Vegetable oil, as needed

1 lb 4 oz/567 g lean
boneless beef, cut into
1-in/3-cm cubes

1 lb 4 oz/567 g lean
boneless veal, cut into
1-in/3-cm cubes

1 bay leaf

3 or 4 parsley stems

1 thyme sprig

2 qt/960 mL brown stock

Garnish

2 oz/57 g yellow
onions, thinly sliced

4 oz/113 g carrots,
thinly sliced, blanched

2 garlic cloves, minced

Vegetable oil, as needed

½ tsp/2.50 mL cayenne

½ tsp/2.50 mL ground
black pepper

1 tsp/5 mL kosher salt

1. Heat a small amount of oil in a pan over medium-high heat. Add the beef and veal and brown the meat on all sides.

2. Wrap the bay leaf, parsley, and thyme in cheesecloth and tie with butcher's twine to make a sachet. Combine the meat, stock, and sachet in a small stockpot. Simmer, covered, until the meat is very tender.

3. Remove the meat from the stock. Cut the meat into small pieces and reserve in a mixing bowl.

4. Strain and degrease the stock. Reduce the stock to 1½ cups/360 mL. Check the gelatin strength (by chilling it completely to be set up) and fortify if necessary (see page 280).

5. Sauté the garnish ingredients in a small amount of oil until the onion is slightly softened.

6. Combine the sautéed vegetables and reduced stock with the meat.

7. Season with the cayenne, pepper, and salt. Taste and adjust the seasoning as needed.

8. Spray the terrine mold with vegaline spray, then line a terrine mold with plastic wrap, leaving an overhang. Pack the meat mixture into the lined mold. Fold over the liner to cover and press the top flat with a press plate. Refrigerate overnight.

9. Carefully unmold and remove the plastic wrap from the finished terrine. Slice and serve with vinaigrette, or rewrap and refrigerate for up to 2 weeks.

tête pressée (rolled pressed pig's head)

MAKES 1 ROLL

1 pig's head, ears and brain removed, cut in half

3 gal/11.52 L Pork and Beef Brine (page 115)

3 lb/1.36 kg mirepoix, diced 2 to 3 in/5 to 8 cm

2 bay leaves

½ tsp/2.50 mL black peppercorns

½ tsp/2.50 mL thyme

2 gal/7.68 L chicken stock

4 oz/113 g shallots or yellow onions, minced

4 oz/113 g parsley, chopped

Oil, as needed

Ground nutmeg, as needed

Ground white pepper, as needed

1. Place the pig's head in a deep plastic or stainless-steel container and add enough brine to cover it. Use a plate or plastic wrap to keep it completely submerged. Brine under refrigeration for 3 days.

2. Drain the head and rinse off the brine with warm water to melt the salt.

3. Place the pig's head in a small stockpot. Add the mirepoix, bay leaves, peppercorns, and thyme. Cover with chicken stock and bring to a simmer.

4. Simmer until the meat is tender, 2½ to 3 hours (you will be able to poke your finger through the skin when it is ready).

5. Meanwhile, sauté the shallots and parsley in oil until the shallots become translucent to develop the aroma and the sweet flavor of the onions. Remove from the heat and set aside to cool.

6. Remove the head and discard the bones, eyes, and eardrums. Peel the pork tongue. Strain the stock, return it to a clean container, and keep it hot.

7. Place half of the head, skin side down, on a 24 by 30-in/61 by 76-cm rectangle of wet cheesecloth. Sprinkle the meat with nutmeg and white pepper. Spread the shallot mixture evenly over the entire surface.

8. Place the second half of the head on top of the first half, skin side up.

9. Roll the head tightly in cheesecloth and secure with butcher's twine. Place the head back into the hot stock. If the stock is not hot, then reheat the stock. Cover and refrigerate overnight.

10. For servicing, remove the rolled head from the stock, unwrap the cheesecloth, and scrape the excess gelatin from the head.

11. Slice thinly and serve with sliced red onions and a mustard vinaigrette. The head may be held for up to 1 week in the stock under refrigeration.

Tête Pressée

head cheese

1 pig's head, ears and brain removed, cut in half

4 pig's feet, cut in half lengthwise

1 lb 8 oz/680 g boneless pork butt, cleaned

2 gal/7.68 L Pork and Beef Brine (page 115)

3 gal/11.52 L unsalted bouillon or clear, flavorful broth

1 bouquet garni, including ½ tsp/2.50 mL crushed black peppercorns

1 oignon piqué

2 medium carrots, peeled

7 oz/198 g pimientos, drained, diced small

One 10-oz/284-g jar gherkins, drained, diced small

Champagne vinegar, as needed

Kosher salt, as needed

Ground white pepper, as needed

1. Place the pig's head, pig's feet, and pork butt in a deep plastic or stainless-steel container and add enough brine to cover. Use a plate or plastic wrap to keep them completely submerged. Brine under refrigeration for 2 days.

2. Drain and rinse the meats. Place them in a stockpot with enough bouillon to cover. Add the bouquet garni, oignon piqué, and carrots. Bring to a boil, then lower to a simmer. Simmer the meat until tender, 2½ to 3 hours (you will be able to poke your finger through the skin when it is ready).

3. Remove the bouquet garni, onion, and carrots. Drain the meat and reserve the stock. Cool the meat enough to be able to handle it. Peel the tongue. Discard the eyes and eardrums. Discard the skin from the head and feet. Pick as much meat as possible from the bones; discard the bones. Trim away excess fat—in the old days, they used all the fat; now some fat needs to be there but other fat is trimmed away—and discard. The pork butt gets picked over as well, so it is broken up into small pieces.

4. Place the picked-over meat in a 2-in/5-cm hotel pan lined with plastic wrap. Press with another hotel pan with a 2- to 3-lb/907- to 1360-g weight on top. Reserve overnight under refrigeration.

5. Degrease the stock and cool it until it congeals. Determine if the stock is of sliceable strength and adjust as needed for sliceable strength (see "Gelatin for Aspic Gelée" on page 280). Heat the liquid to 110°F/43°C over a water bath. Taste and adjust the seasoning if needed. The stock should be slightly overseasoned so that it will taste good when cold.

6. On the next day, dice the meat into ½-in/1-cm cubes. Add the pimientos and gherkins and season with a little Champagne vinegar, salt, and white pepper.

7. Bring the stock to a temperature of 70° to 75°F/21° to 24°C and adjust the seasoning if necessary.

8. Spray the terrine mold with vegaline spray. Line the terrine mold with plastic wrap with an overhang of ½ in/1 cm on all sides. Place the meat mixture in a 3-lb/1.36-kg rectangular mold. Pour the stock over the mixture, making sure that the liquid surrounds the mixture and covers the top completely.

9. Tap the mold a little to get rid of any air pockets. Cool completely. Fold the plastic overhangs over and place in the refrigerator overnight to set.

10. Slice and serve immediately with a shallot-mustard vinaigrette or store under refrigeration for up to 1 week, although it is recommended that the head cheese be eaten fresh.

sulze head cheese

1 pig's head, ears and brain removed, cut in half

2 gal/7.68 L Pork and Beef Brine (page 115)

1 lb/454 g mirepoix, diced

1 *oignon piqué*

2 bay leaves

½ tsp/2.50 mL black peppercorns

½ tsp/2.50 mL fresh thyme

3 gal/11.52 L unsalted bouillon or clear, flavorful broth

4 oz/113 g pimientos, diced

4 oz/113 g dill pickles, diced

1½ oz/43 g fresh parsley, chopped

Kosher salt, as needed

Ground black pepper, as needed

Ground nutmeg, as needed

Champagne or white wine vinegar, as needed

1. Place the pig's head in a deep plastic or stainless-steel container and add enough brine to cover. Use a plate or plastic wrap to keep it completely submerged. Brine under refrigeration for 4 days.

2. Remove and rinse off the brine. Place the pig's head in a small stockpot. Add the mirepoix, oignon piqué, bay leaves, peppercorns, and thyme. Cover with the bouillon and bring to a simmer. Simmer until the meat is tender, 2½ to 3 hours (you will be able to poke your finger through the skin when it is ready).

3. Remove the head and discard the bones, eyes, eardrums, and skin. Strain and reserve the broth. Cut the fat into small pieces and the meat into medium pieces.

4. In a mixing bowl, combine the fat, meat, pimientos, pickles, parsley, salt, pepper, and nutmeg; toss well.

5. Degrease the stock, determine if the stock is of sliceable strength, and adjust as needed for sliceable strength (see "Gelatin for Aspic Gelée," on page 280). Add vinegar as needed.

6. Place the mixture into a lined terrine mold. Fill the molds with stock until the liquid covers the meat mixture. Refrigerate to set overnight. The head cheese may be held for up to 1 week under refrigeration.

sausages

chapter eight

Sausages are defined as chopped or ground meat that has been blended with spices and other seasonings and usually stuffed in natural or manufactured casing. Sausages were developed for one reason: to preserve meat. Extending the life of meat was most important because it gave people a way to hold the meat through the wintertime for sustainability.

The origin of meat processing has been lost over time, but it probably began when mankind learned that salt was an effective preservative. Sausage making evolved as an effort to economize and preserve meat that could not be consumed fresh at slaughter. In sausage making, most parts of the animal carcass are used while still maintaining quality standards.

Early sausage makers found that a wide range of raw ingredients could be used to make a savory product. In those days, the primary ingredients of sausage were the parts of the animal carcasses that could not be used in other ways. Today many prime parts are used in the production of sausages; however, the less tender cuts of an animal, organ meats, and even blood can be made delicious when ground, spiced, and placed in a casing.

The procedure of stuffing meat into casings today remains very similar to that used in the past, but sausage recipes have been greatly refined and sausage making has become a highly respected culinary art. Good sausage makers are as discriminating about what goes into sausage as winemakers are about selecting grapes. From this early sausage making has evolved a craft in which chefs seek out the best ingredients available in the market for their purpose and are not just using leftovers. Chefs have gone searching for rare breeds of pork known for their marbleized meat and good amount of fat for use in sausage and forcemeat production.

sausage-making basics

The word *sausage* comes from the Latin word *salsus*, which means "salted" or "preserved." This process was necessary for people to allow their meat products to keep longer. Sausage making became a crucial method for using the ground or chopped scraps and trim that were left over after the slaughter of an animal too large to consume in one or two meals. Trimmings were always enclosed in the intestines, appendix, or bladder of the slaughtered animal. The manner in which these trimmings were enclosed became distinct by region, and developed into a culinary art form. Sausages became known by the names of the towns where they originated. For instance, bologna comes from a city in the Emilia-Romagna province of northern Italy with the same name.

In some parts of the world, especially in colder climates, sausages survive during the winter without refrigeration, allowing people to eat them regularly during the bleak months. The processes of smoking and drying sausages allowed people living in warmer climates the opportunity to have sausage available year-round, without the need for continuous cooling.

MAKING HEALTHIER CHARCUTERIE PRODUCTS

Modern forcemeat production has taken a drastic change from the classical processes we saw with the gratin, straight, and country methods for forcemeat preparation, where the forcemeats had a ratio of 1 to 1 for fat to meat. The forcemeats were rich, flavorful, and filling, but were made with quite a bit of fat. At the present time, these terrines are made with a ratio of 2 to 1 meat to fat. Then there was the mousseline forcemeat, easily made in a hot kitchen, especially when dealing with fish forcemeats, for stuffings. In mousseline-style forcemeats, you would use one type of meat, usually a lean white meat or a fish, and egg or egg white to help bind, and cream as the fat. The mousseline forcemeats are popular in the hot kitchen because they are able to be prepared quickly, take on the flavor of products added to them, and are not nearly as filling when eaten. Now we are searching for new ideas to make these items lighter, contain less fat, and have greater flavors.

HEALTHY SAUSAGE PREPARATION IDEAS

The process of reducing fat while still having the mouthfeel of having fat is the challenge at hand when choosing to make healthier and less fatty sausages. The process of taking protein, adding salt, grinding it through the coarse plates of the meat grinders, and letting it sit for a few hours or overnight allows us to extract more binding power from the protein. We can then add any variety of seasonings and finish the grinding process. We add a lot of fresh herbs and a fair amount of garnish to achieve the specific bind and flavor that is desired. Another way to substitute fat in sausages is to replace the fat with cooked rice, cooked potato, tofu, or Plum Powder. These items give the mouth the full flavor sensation that we miss when we are not using fat or when we are keeping the actual fat content to a minimum in our products. Plum Powder, in particular, acts to retain water and lends a nice mouthfeel while deterring bacterial growth. To use Plum Powder, do not exceed 4 percent of the total weight, and dissolve the powder first in distilled water before adding it to the mixture.

There are many ways of creating low-fat sausages using an emulsion technique. One such method involves using chicken or turkey as a base, adding ice, puréeing the mixture in a food processor, adding nonfat milk powder, and puréeing the mixture again. This process gives you a creamy and smooth forcemeat that can be used in a sausage. Adding flavorful substances, such as sun-dried tomatoes, mozzarella cheese, or basil, can create a flavorful sausage that can be frozen for shipping, but needs to be utilized immediately after being heated and cannot be held in a chauffer. The longer this sausage is kept heated, the tougher it will get.

Sausage making has turned to extracting the protein from meat and adding more liquids to the product, thus almost eliminating the fat from the sausage while still keeping a flavor true to the product. When using this process, however, you have to compensate for the lack of fat by using herbs, spices, and seasonings in order to create a flavorful product.

A perfect example of this would be the Chicken Sausage with Mushrooms and Asiago (page 246) my friend Henry Rapp developed for use at The Culinary Institute of America. Henry takes cubed chicken, adds salt and seasonings, mixes well, and then grinds it through a ¼-inch grinder plate. He makes an emulsion by puréeing the chicken in a food processor with ice, then adds nonfat dry milk powder to it and further emulsifies until the mixture reaches 52°F/13°C. He then folds in the roasted products that have been ground through the ⅛-inch grinder plate to the emulsion, mixing well by hand. He stuffs the casings and poaches the product. The product is then ready to be used. The amount of seasonings and roasted items being used in this particular recipe helps to provide flavor and mouthfeel in place of the fat that would normally be in a regular sausage recipe.

USDA classification of sausages

SAUSAGE CLASS	MADE FROM	CURE	SMOKING	STORAGE	COOKING REQUIRED	EXAMPLES
Fresh sausage	Fresh uncured and uncooked meat	Uncured	Unsmoked	Keep refrigerated	Cook thoroughly before serving	Breakfast, Italian
Uncooked smoked sausage	Fresh meat	Cured with nitrates/nitrites	Cold-smoked; air-dried	Keep refrigerated	Cook before serving	Chorizo, andouille
Cooked sausage	Fresh meat	Cured or uncured	Unsmoked, cooked by poaching	Keep refrigerated	Ready to eat	Liverwurst, bratwurst
Cooked, smoked sausage	Fresh meat	Cured with nitrites	Hot-smoked	Keep refrigerated	Fully cooked, ready-to-eat; Reheat by poaching, grilling, or sautéing	Frankfurters, knockwurst
Dry and semi-dry sausage	Fresh meat	Cured and fermented through addition of lactic acid culture (Fermento*) or a starter culture; drying and fermenting under controlled temperature and humidity	Smoked or unsmoked	May be kept unrefrigerated; the lower pH levels preserve the sausage and give it a tangy flavor	Ready to eat	Cooked salami, summer sausage
Dry sausage	Fresh meat	Cured with nitrates and a starter culture; drying and fermenting under controlled temperature and humidity	Usually unsmoked	May be kept unrefrigerated	Ready to eat raw	Hard salami, pepperoni
Cooked meat specialties (sausage-type preparations)	Fresh meat	Cured with nitrite, not in casings (molded or shaped)	Unsmoked; may contain smoked product	Keep refrigerated	Fully cooked, ready to eat	Leberkäse, pâtés, terrines, olive loaf

*Fermento is a brand name for a dairy-based controlled fermentation product. It is a lactic acid–producing bacteria culture and should only be used in semidry fermented products. It is recommended at levels between 1 and 6 percent, with 3 percent of total weight. being a general starting level. More than 6 percent of total weight will cause sausages to break down and become mushy. Fermento also controls (lowers) pH and adds a tangy flavor.

Cultures, from left to right:
Fermento, lactobacillus, malolactic
culture

sausage ingredients

The finished product is only as good as the ingredients it contains. Meat should be fresh and high quality, have the proper lean-to-fat ratio, and have good binding qualities. The meat should be clean and not contaminated with bacteria or other microorganisms. Spices and seasonings should be selected and combined in proper amounts. The meats and seasonings must complement each other to create a satisfying product.

There are four main ingredients in sausage making. How and in what order they are used will make a difference in the final outcome of the product you are making.

meat

Any type of fresh meat, poultry, or seafood can be used. It should always be carefully trimmed and cut into ½- to 1-in/1- to 3-cm cubes. When trimming meat, you need to make sure you are cleaning all the sinew and fat away from the meat. You want the meat to be clean. The meat is cubed into pieces so that it can fit in the body of the grinder and can be cut easily in the grinder. Add the proper amount of fat afterward. During processing, the meat should be kept very cold.

The size of the grind will help determine the finished texture of the sausage. Finely ground meat will have a smoother, firmer texture; coarsely ground meat will have a chunky, crumbly texture.

fat

Fat adds moisture and flavor to a recipe. Lean meats need to have fat added to the recipe. Too little fat makes a dry product. But fat can be replaced with moisture-holding ingredients such as cooked rice (see "Panadas," page 152). Fat content cannot exceed 30 percent of the total weight; most sausage recipes contain about 25 to 30 percent fat by weight.

Pork jowl and fatback are preferred over kidney or internal fat. Fatback is always cleaned of the skin and cubed into ½- to 1-in/1- to 3-cm pieces. Jowl fat is cleaned of

Sausage components, clockwise from top left: cubed meat, jowl fat, ice water, salt and pepper, cubed fatback

the skin and the glands are trimmed from the meat. Do not use poultry fat, which is too soft, or lamb fat, which is too hard and has a strong flavor.

water

FSIS regulations permit manufacturers of fresh sausage to add water up to 3 percent of the total product weight. Cooked sausage manufacturers are allowed to vary the amount of added water according to the amount of fat. The maximum fat content is limited to 30 percent, and the amount of fat and water combined is limited to 40 percent. So the manufacturers can increase water to substitute for reduced fat. Water dissolves cure and flavorings, as well as adding moisture; ice is often substituted for water, which also helps to keep the product cold while processing. Wine and stock can also be used.

salt

Salt preserves product, enhances flavors, and solubilizes the meat protein in order to improve the binding properties of the mixture. It preserves by dehydrating bacteria and can help in preventing trichinae parasites from developing if enough salt is there for a long enough time. In addition, salt draws moisture from dry-cured, air-dried products, further limiting the environment for the growth of pathogens. Of course, salt is well known as a flavor enhancer. Finally, salt assists in protein extraction (solubilization) in basic-grind and emulsion-method sausage products to improve binding and texture.

other sausage ingredients

seasonings

The seasonings used are sometimes what distinguish one sausage product from another; think of hot versus sweet Italian sausage. "Seasonings" is another general term that refers to any substance that is used to impart flavor to the food product. Some examples of common spices and seasonings include allspice, peppers, cardamom, caraway, coriander, cumin, garlic, sage, mustard, nutmeg, paprika, rosemary, thyme, and turmeric. "Spices" are defined as any aromatic vegetable substance that is intended to contribute flavoring in food. The active aromatic or pungent properties of spices that contribute the most to the flavoring effect are mostly present in the volatile oils, resins, or aleoresins of the spice.

Flavorings are substances that are extracted from a food (such as fruits, herbs, roots, or meats and seafood) that are also intended to contribute flavoring instead of nutritional substance. Smoked items should be cured with Insta Cure No. 1, or another of its commercial versions. Seasonings have to be added by taste.

Sweeteners counteract the bitterness in liver products. Dextrose counteracts the harshness of salt. It is an ideal nutrient for lactic acid culture in fermented sausage, and aids in the fermentation of salami-type products. It also has hygroscopic qualities, which means it increases the sausage's ability to retain water. If you want to make a substitution, remember that 1 oz/28 g of dextrose is the equivalent of ⅔ oz/21 g of granulated sugar. Dextrose and other sweeteners help stabilize the pink color of the product when used with Insta Cure No. 1. Curing agents such as nitrite or nitrates have been used in sausage formulation, originally as a contaminant present in salts and later added intentionally in the form of saltpeter. Nitrite has antioxidant properties and improves the taste and color of the sausage. Nitrates prevent the growth of bacteria, such as *Clostridium botulinum* bacteria, which cause botulism. Some sweeteners also function as binders.

garnish

Garnish is optional and should complement the other items in the sausage. Examples include cubed fat and pistachios in mortadella, and ham or tongue added to make variations of bologna (page 257).

permissible additives

secondary binders

Binders and extenders have a number of uses in a sausage formulation. Manufacturers use extenders such as dry milk powder, cereal flours, and soy protein as a lower-cost method to increase the overall yield of the formulation, to get a better bind, and to achieve a particular slicing quality, as well as to add flavor characteristics. A sausage can include up to 3.5 percent of these substances.

NONFAT DRY MILK absorbs as much as 50 percent of its weight and helps prevent shrinkage. It has a slight but pleasing taste.

SODIUM CASEINATE is nonfat dry milk with the calcium removed; it also absorbs up to half its weight. It has a 90-percent protein content, and is primarily used to bind, hold moisture, and prevent water purge during packaging and storage.

SODIUM PHOSPHATE improves binding and makes the emulsion creamier, as well as giving a better product yield. It raises the pH of meat, and has hygroscopic (moisture-retaining) properties. The water-binding property of the meat is improved using phosphates; they also act as antioxidants and stabilize the flavor and color of the product. Phosphates also help increase the shelf life of a product. The maximum amount of phosphates approved for sausage products is limited to 0.5 percent of the finished product weight.

SOY PROTEIN, SOY CONCENTRATE, AND SOY PROTEIN ISOLATE are secondary binders that improve binding. Soy protein isolate can absorb as much as 95 percent of its weight.

Left to right, top to bottom: soy protein isolate, nonfat dry milk, sodium phosphate, sugar, dextrose, salt, Insta Cure No. 1, Insta Cure No. 2

sodium erythorbate

This is similar to sodium ascorbic acid, an expensive chemical that slows down nitrite reaction to produce a greater yield and helps the product develop and retain better color. It is an antioxidative agent required in commercial bacon production to prevent nitrites turning into nitrosamines during the cooking process.

nitrites and nitrates

These preservatives have purposely been tinted pink to avoid confusion with salt in the kitchen. For a full discussion of nitrites and nitrates used in sausages, see Chapter 5.

TINTED CURE MIX (TCM/INSTA CURE NO. 1/PRAGUE POWDER I)

- Contains: sodium chloride (salt) 94 percent, sodium nitrite 6 percent

- 4 oz/113 g TCM needed to cure 100 lb/45.36 kg of sausage meat to prevent botulism. TCM develops and stabilizes the pink "cured color" in the lean muscle tissue of meat. It also inhibits the growth of a number of food-poisoning and spoilage organisms, in particular the *Clostridium botulinum* organism. TCM contributes to the characteristic flavor of cured meats.

- Retards lipid fat oxidation, also known as rancidity, in product, preventing stale taste.

INSTA CURE NO. 2/PRAGUE POWDER II

- Contains: salt (sodium chloride) 94 percent, sodium nitrite ($\frac{1}{2}$ percent), sodium nitrate ($5\frac{1}{2}$ percent). It helps develop a pink color in meats and is normally used to produce dry and dry-fermented products.

SALTPETER (POTASSIUM NITRATE)

- Use limitedly after 1975 by USDA.

- Saltpeter is not allowed in the production of smoked or cooked meat or sausages. This restriction is primarily related to the fact that the exact level of residual nitrites in products treated with potassium nitrate is hard to determine in advance.

For thousands of years man has been eating meat cured with salt. The reddening effect on meats was first mentioned during the latter part of the Roman Empire. Nitrate was probably present in the crude form of salt that was used: in many cases it was the result of evaporated sea water. In the early 1900s it was discovered that salt did not produce the red color but that sodium and potassium nitrates present in impure salt did. They also discovered that sodium nitrate was converted into sodium nitrite by bacteria found in meat and then into nitric oxide. The amount of color change is dependent on the amount of myoglobin present in meat (the more myoglobin, the darker reddish pink the cured color). Chicken has the lowest myoglobin content, whereas beef has the highest content. Seafood contains no myoglobin.

More important than color enhancement, nitrites have been the only acceptable substance to prevent botulism in cured and smoked products, even though more than 700 substances have been tested as possible replacements. For more information on nitrites, see page 75.

As a result of these tests, there is stricter control of the use of nitrite in food processing. Less nitrite is used to cure meats, and residual nitrites must be less than 200 ppm (parts per million) in finished processed meats. Today bacon contains erythorbate or some other vitamin C compound to prevent nitrosamine formation. Also, nitrite cannot be premixed with paprika and pepper in spice blends; they are packaged separately and should be mixed and then used right away.

casings

Casings may be natural (derived from animal sources) or artificial (manufactured from collagen, plastic, paper, or wood pulp); they may be edible or nonedible. They come in many different sizes and shapes, which can be part of what distinguishes one sausage product from another. Their use can be to merely contain the sausage, or they can also add flavor to the finished product.

Natural casings used for fresh sausage are washed, scraped, and treated, graded for size and condition, then salted, packaged, and shipped in brine or propylene glycol (for preservation) to the sausage manufacturer.

Synthetic casings are made from a variety of food-grade materials; some are edible and some are not. Synthetic casings are often the choice for consistency of product.

natural casings

Natural casings are derived from animals, and are used in their natural shape and form. They are cleaned, sanitized, and packed in salt (slush pack) or brine. There are several types of natural casings. The casings you most typically see are dry casings. These are packed in salt, and have been preflushed and pretubed, which means they are placed on a thin plastic tube that you pull off after placing it on a nozzle.

One of the advantages to using natural casings is that they are traditional in appearance and texture. Furthermore, they cook easily and are tolerant to treatments.

- Natural casings readily permit deep smoke penetration.

- Natural casings have excellent characteristics of elasticity and tensile strength, to allow for high-efficiency production and expansion during filling.

- Natural casings protect the fine flavor of sausage, without contributing any conflicting flavoring of their own.

- Sausage in natural casing has that special "snap" and tender "bite" that's like no man-made product and is highly demanded by today's knowledgeable consumers.

- Sausage in natural casings stays tender and juicy.

However, this type of casing also has disadvantages. They are not uniform, not all the same size, nor all the same width. Some are more fragile than others. Moreover, these usually cost more than manufactured casings.

sheep casings

There are three sizes of sheep casings. These casings are made from the small intestine, and are approximately $\frac{5}{8}$ to 1 in/1.50 to 3 cm in diameter, about the size of your thumb. These are bought in a unit of measure called a hank (300 ft/91 m) and are normally used for foods like breakfast links, frankfurters, Swiss bratwurst, and beer sticks. Swiss bratwurst might use the larger size of the sheep casing. To stuff, you'll need 4 ft/1.22 m per 1 lb/454 g of product.

Sheep casings come in two grades: Grade A has no holes and is great for emulsions; Grade B has some holes and is good for coarse-ground sausages.

hog casings

These casings are also made from the small intestine but from the hog. The casing is approximately 1 to $1\frac{1}{2}$ in/3 to 4 cm in diameter and fits over three fingertips. They are also bought in a hank (300 ft/91 m). These casings are generally used for Italian sausage, knockwurst, and pork sausage (rope sausage), as well as fresh German bratwurst. You need 2 ft/61 cm of casing per 1 lb/454 g of product.

hog middles (chitterlings)

They are bought as a set (27 ft/8.24 m, $2\frac{1}{4}$ in/55 to 60 mm in diameter) and are used in traditional sausages like sopressata, mettwurst, and black pudding.

hog bung casings

Hog bung is one of the casings typically used for larger sausages. The size is 2 in/5 cm and up, while the length is approximately 4 ft/1.2 m.

Natural casings, from left to right: sheep, hog, beef middle, beef round, beef bung

beef round

Made from the small intestine of the cow, these casings are approximately $1^3/_{16}$ to $1^7/_8$ in/3.5 to 4.6 cm in diameter, and fit over three extended fingers. Unlike the other casings mentioned so far, these casings are generally bought in a unit of measure called a set (100 ft/30.5 m). They are most commonly used for kielbasa, ring liverwurst, and blood sausage. You need 15 in/38 cm of casing per 1 lb/454 g of product.

beef middles

These casings are different from the others in that they are made from the cow's large intestine, and are approximately $1^3/_4$ to $2^1/_2$ in/4.5 to 6.5 cm or more in diameter, and fit over four extended fingers. Beef middles are bought in a unit of measure called a set, which in this case is 57 ft/17.37 m. These casings are most commonly used for salamis and summer sausages. You need 9 in/23 cm of casing per 1 lb/454 g of product.

beef bung

Made from the appendix, this casing is 4 to 8 in/10 to 20 cm in diameter, and fits over a whole arm. Unlike most casings, it's bought by the piece. This casing is commonly used for mortadella, bologna, and capacolla. It can hold 18 to 35 lb/8.16 to 15.88 kg of product.

artificial casings

Artificial casings are impermeable fibrous casings that are treated with an internal moisture barrier of plastic wrap. They offer the advantage of a gas and moisture barrier while maintaining the appearance of an uncoated fibrous casing. Sausages made with artificial casings have a longer shelf life, decreased product moisture loss, and increased microbiological protection.

These casings can be water cooked or steam cooked, which provides a more efficient heat transfer than typical smokehouse processes. Also, for smaller processors, the capital investment for water tanks, necessary for water or steam cooking, is dramatically lower than smokehouses.

Use of the RSD reduces a need for flexibility of the casing. If overstuffed, the sausage will expand during cooking, but the casing must have the capacity to follow and stretch, An overstuffed/overstretched casing could expand too much and then burst or cause peeling problems.

edible collagen casings

Edible collagen casings are made from the corium layer of the cattle hide. The raw material is treated and extruded as a tube. Edible collagen casings make a strong argument against natural casings: They have uniformity, tenderness, stuffing performance, and easier production planning. Edible casings are made to fulfill customized needs.

The bite of edible collagen casings is influenced by drying and smoking. Processing the sausage in these ways will result in toughness. Thus, the right addition of relative humidity helps to produce a tender bite.

Prior to using, collagen casings (except for those with a small diameter size) are to be soaked or flushed for 20 to 30 minutes in warm water (78°F/26°C) with 10 to 15 percent salt concentration. This will improve the elasticity and "machinability" of the casings.

nonedible artificial casings

These are shaped and formed to specification. They are normally used by commercial producers, and are usually some sort of plastic or cloth, though there are many other materials that can be used. They may be spice lined. They are usually removed before packaging, as in the case of hot dogs.

CELLULOSE SAUSAGE CASING

These casings are manufactured from a straight-chain polysaccharide found as the primary component of wood and also from straw and cotton. These casings are nonedible and are to be peeled off before eating.

Fibrous cellulose casings are formed by adding regenerated cellulose fibers to allow for increased water vapor and smoke permeability. These casings are to be soaked for 15 to 30 minutes before they are stuffed to improve flexibility, which allows them to be stuffed to their proper diameter. The consistent uniformity of size makes the fibrous casing ideal for all types of sliced sausage products, including bologna, cooked salami, and other smoked cold-cut meat products.

SKINLESS CASINGS

Skinless casings are the most widely used artificial casings. They are called skinless casings because the casing is peeled off from the sausage prior to packaging. The casing is used to give sausages uniformity of size and weight and is additionally needed to help develop a meaty sausage skin.

The casing is made of cotton or wood pulp fibers, which are transformed by a chemical process into a viscose solution. The viscose is then extruded into the shape of a tube. Further chemical processing steps result in a regenerated cellulose casing—an artificial sausage casing of regenerated cellulose adapted to be shirred and stuffed with meat, produced by annularly extruding viscose into a tubular product having a dried wall thickness of less than about 0.90 mm, regenerating and coagulating the tubular product for sufficient time and conditions to retard the rate of viscose regeneration to coagulation to form a casing product, wherein the casing has a wall thickness less than about 0.90 mm and has a skin cross-sectional area wall structure in which the skin comprises at least 20 percent of the cross-sectional area of the casing wall, said casing having a plasticizer content of less than 14 percent based on the weight of the casing.

Skinless casings are shirred and ready to stuff. No premoisturizing is required before stuffing. The casing does not have to be soaked first.

Skinless casings are available as standard or with a peeling agent to increase the peelability, if required. The peeling agents commonly used are called RP and EP.

NONEDIBLE COLLAGEN CASINGS

Collagen casings are made as straight (middles) and curved (rounds) casings. These casings are considered to be inedible because of the thicker wall, which is hard to chew.

They are made stronger so that they have good machinability and can be stuffed tight. Nonedible collagen casings are also made in different manners for applications like dry sausage, semidry sausage, and cooked sausage. For dry and cooked sausage they are used in large quantities, especially for mold-coated, fermented, and dry sausages. Nonedible collagen casings should be presoaked in a 10 to 15 percent brine solution to have the best possible stuffing performance. These casings are still used in Eastern European markets. In Western Europe, these casings allow the mold to form on the outside and some will be treated so the mold forms easier. These casings have a natural look, good smoke acceptance, and high permeability.

FIBROUS CASINGS

Fibrous casings are manufactured using the viscose process: wood cellulose is solubilized and treated, so viscose is formed. The viscose is then used to impregnate into a special filament paper as it is being formed into a tube. This coated tube moves into a bath, which regenerates the original cellulose.

Fibrous casings are the toughest casings produced, and they are used where maximum uniformity of the finished product diameter, be it sausage or smoked meat, is desired. The uniformity of product stuffed in these casings makes them ideal for slicing for prepackaging.

Fibrous casings are made by forming a tube from a specific grade of paper, impregnating the paper with cellulose, and sealing the seam with viscose. Fibrous casings are advanced because of their strength, uniformity, machinability, and technological performance.

The advantages of using fibrous casings are:

- Excellent size uniformity, giving uniform product and increased yields
- Consistent casing color due to a controlled dyeing process
- Availability of a wide range of colors
- Can be printed, clipped, string tied, cut, and shirred
- Nonrefrigerated storage
- Permeability to smoke and moisture
- Strength

Fibrous casings need to be soaked before stuffing. They can also be purchased premoisturized and ready to stuff.

IMPERMEABLE FIBROUS CASINGS

Impermeable fibrous casings are available with inside or outside moisture barrier coating. Additional to the moisture barrier the casings have a different appearance from the final product. The moisture barrier does not allow moisture to enter the sausage or if outside does not allow it to leave the casing. The distinction between regular and impermeable fibrous casings is based on the application and the type of sausage.

INSIDE-COATED CASINGS

These casings develop a consistent pressure on the sausage product during cooking because of the uncoated cellulose surface on the outside. Depending on the mix, this helps to prevent gel separation to a certain extent. After processing, the sausage needs to be cooled by showering. This is because the cellulose surface on the outside needs to be relaxed by water to avoid breakage. The casing has a dull appearance.

OUTSIDE-COATED CASINGS

These casings have the moisture barrier on the outside. The casings are used for products that do not release much moisture during cooking because no gel forms under the surface. These casings need less showering after cooking because they do not need to be relaxed.

PLASTIC CASING

Plastic casings are mostly used for cooked sausage, liver sausage, blood sausage, and cooked-in-ham products. This means items like ham or ham-style products are cooked inside the plastic casing. The plastic casings are advanced because of the barrier functions. They are multilayered for a high barrier to moisture and oxygen to maximize shelf life. The variety of plastic casings is large because of requirements, extrusion technology, and the different plastic raw materials. These are used for products that require the use of pressure stuffers and are possibly made into large sizes.

SPICE-LINED CASINGS

These are plastic casings with a coarse spice mixture coating the inside of the casing. Once the sausage is cooked and the casing removed, the spices will remain on the outside of the sausage.

PROTEIN-LINED CASINGS

A protein coating on the inside of these casings gives them the ability to cling to the meat as it is shrinking. Soak 20 to 30 minutes before using.

LAMINATED CASINGS

There are dry and semidry versions of these casings. They are used for their uniform size and embedded strings. Laminates are engineering materials made from layers of fibrous reinforcement, such as cotton cloth, paper, or woven glass cloth, which are bonded together with high-quality plastic resins. The layers are pressed together under high pressure and the resin is baked until it becomes solid, fusing the material into a tough, strong, and dense material.

NOVELTY CASINGS

Novelty casings are sewn natural, fibrous, or collagen casings that are made into various shapes, whether they are animals, sports items, beer bottles, or something else.

Synthetic casings are made from a variety of food-grade materials, some edible and some not, and may be colored, lined with herbs, or may impart a particular flavor to the sausage.

preparing casings

unpacking casings bought in hanks

Handle hanks of casings carefully so as not to tangle the individual casings.

1. Carefully unwind a hank out onto a table in serpentine fashion (lay out from one side of the table to the other, so all the casing fits on the table).

2. Untie the ring from one end of the hank and carefully untangle one strand of casing at a time. Do not pull the casings too hard or they may knot.

3. Wind each strand around four fingers and seal by wrapping an end around the bundle and tucking it in.

4. Store in a pan, covered with salt, in the refrigerator until needed.

preparing casing bought in hanks

Larger nonedible casings are secured with a metal clip called (hog rings); they are applied with pliers made for the rings to crimp the ends tightly, sealing the meat in. This is used instead of string. To prepare the casings,

1. Weigh the product to be stuffed.

2. Measure the proper amount of casings.

3. Reconstitute in warm water.

4. Place casing on stuffer. Fill casing, then pinch and tie or pinch and twist.

preparing casings bought in sets

1. Weigh the product to be stuffed.

2. Measure the proper amount of casing.

3. Cut the casing to the desired length, usually stated in the recipe.

4. Reconstitute in warm water (100°F/38°C), change the water, and repeat the process.

5. Flush the inside of the casing with clean lukewarm water; repeat the process.

6. Tie one end of the casing in a bubble knot.

7. Moisten the correct size nozzle of the sausage stuffer with water and apply the casing to the nozzle.

8. Stuff, then tie end with a bubble knot.

preparing beef bung

1. Weigh the product to be stuffed.

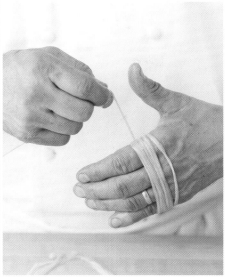

Lay out the casings and remove any knots before forming them into smaller bundles.

Natural casings should be rewound from their original groups to make smaller bundles that are easier to handle and store.

Rewound casings should be packed in salt and refrigerated until needed.

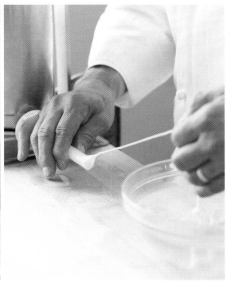

To prepare casings for use, flush them with water to remove all residual salt and impurities.

Fit the casings onto the end of the feeder tube of the sausage stuffer, keeping the nozzle lubricated with water to prevent the casing from sticking and tearing.

THE ART OF CHARCUTERIE

2. Use either a whole or half bung.

3. Reconstitute in warm water (100°F/38°C), change the water, and repeat the process.

4. Flush the inside of the casing with clean lukewarm water; repeat the process.

5. If you cut the beef bung in two, tie one end of each cut piece closed using a bubble knot.

6. Moisten the correct size nozzle with water and apply the casing.

7. Stuff. Tie end using bubble knot.

CASING NOTES

- Natural casings are available through most meat purveyors.
- The larger the casing, the thicker the walls.
- The larger the casing, the longer it takes to reconstitute.
- When packed in salt, shelf life is one year or more.
- When you dry and smoke the sausage, it dries the casing and makes it harder.
- Moisture and heat soften the casing as you process it.
- You need to condition a casing to accept smoke; get the casing to be tacky and follow the process for smoking. It cannot be too wet or it will turn dull gold in appearance. (When the pellicle forms, it becomes a little tacky so the smoke can adhere to it.)
- The size and type of casing used depend on what sausage product is made.

sausage making: grinding and mixing

The basic grind procedure for sausage making is as follows:

1. SANITIZE AND CHILL EQUIPMENT.
   - Helps keep products cold
   - Helps prevent fat smear
   - Helps prevent bacterial growth

2. WEIGH THE MEAT AND FAT.
   - Usually 70 percent lean, 30 percent fat
   - Follow the proportion given in the recipe

3. WEIGH THE SEASONINGS.
   - Mix in with the meat
   - Mix now for better distribution
   - Salt starts to solubilize proteins

4. REFRIGERATE OR PARTIALLY FREEZE.
   - Cold meat grinds better than warm
   - Cold meat has less elasticity
   - Semifrozen is ideal

5. ASSEMBLE THE GRINDER.

6. GRIND THE MEAT INTO A CHILLED CONTAINER.
   - Do not force meat into the grinder
   - Problems are caused by:
     - *Improper grinder assembly*
     - *Dull grinder knife*
     - *Meat or equipment too warm*

7. ADD ICE OR COLD LIQUID.
   - Usually 1 lb/454 g per 10 lb/4.54 kg of meat
   - Replenishes moisture lost in processing
   - Helps to disperse seasonings
   - Helps to solubilize proteins

8. MIX.
   - Mix on speed #1 for 1 minute
   - Mix on speed #2 for 15 to 30 seconds, until sticky
   - Overmixing will cause loss of
     - *Texture*
     - *Grain definition*

9. TASTE A SAMPLE.
   - Poach a taste tester wrapped in plastic wrap in 170°F/77°C water
   - Seasoning is easier to fix before stuffing

10. STUFF.
   - Into reconstituted casings
   - Shape into patties or logs and wrap in caul fat or plastic wrap
   - Place into molds

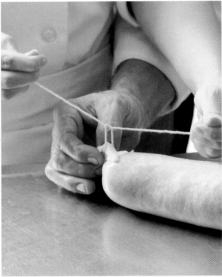

To properly tie a bubble knot, secure the casing at one end with a simple knot, then fold the overhanging casing back over the knot and secure it in place with another knot.

Remove any air bubbles trapped inside the casing with a teasing needle.

Larger sausages should be secured with a second bubble knot.

All sausages should be properly labeled and dated for monitoring during the aging process.

Steps of the aging process, from left to right: fresh stuffed, 3 weeks, 6 weeks

emulsion forcemeats

In reference to meat, emulsification is a homogeneous blending of ground or chopped meats, fat, and ice into a uniform suspension. In forcemeat and sausage preparation, salt acts as the primary emulsifying agent. Sometimes additives are used to stabilize the emulsion, bind excess water, and have stabilizers or phosphates mix properly. Water in the form of ice is used to keep the temperature down and prevent fat separation.

A typical emulsion forcemeat will always contain five parts meat, four parts fat, and three parts ice, by weight, hence the name 5/4/3.

method for emulsified-type sausage

Chill the meat if possible between the grinding and chopping steps to compensate for heat added by grinding.

1. Sanitize and chill all metal equipment that will touch the meat and fat. Temperature control is important.

2. Trim and weigh the meat(s) and fat.

3. Cut the meat(s) into 1-in/3-cm cubes; chill or partially freeze.

4. Cut the fat into 1-in/3-cm cubes; chill or partially freeze.

5. Grind the fat with the fine plate; chill.

6. Mix the salt, TCM (if using; not all emulsified sausages require TCM), dextrose (if using), and other seasonings with the meat; grind through the fine plate.

7. Place the meat in a Stephan cutter or other suitable food chopper. Add ice.

8. Process the meat and ice until the mixture reaches a temperature of 30°F/1°C or lower. Continue processing until the temperature rises to 40°F/4°C.

9. At 40°F/4°C, add fat and continue processing until the temperature is between 45° and 50°F/7° and 10°C.

10. Add nonfat dry milk and continue processing until the temperature is 58°F/14°C.

11. Cook a taste tester, check the binding and the flavor, adjust the seasoning if necessary.

12. Process into the desired sausage product.

stuffing the casing

The following method describes the procedure for filling sausage casings using a sausage-stuffing machine.

1. **ASSEMBLE AND FILL THE SAUSAGE STUFFER PROPERLY.** Keep the nozzle of your stuffer as well as the work table lubricated with a bit of water as you work to prevent the casing from sticking and tearing. Be sure that all parts of the sausage stuffer that will come in contact with the forcemeat are clean and chilled. Fill the stuffer with the sausage meat, tamping it down well to remove any pockets.

2. **PRESS THE SAUSAGE INTO THE PREPARED CASING.** Gather the open end of the casing over the nozzle of the sausage stuffer. Press the sausage into the casing (if you are using a hand stuffer or piping the sausage into the casing, slide the open end over the nozzle of the hand stuffer or over the tip of the piping bag). Support the casing as the forcemeat is expressed through the nozzle and into the casing.

3. **TWIST OR TIE THE SAUSAGE INTO THE APPROPRIATE SHAPE.** If the sausage is to be made into links, use either of the following methods: Press the casing into links at the desired intervals and then twist the link in alternating directions for each link, or tie the casing with twine at the desired intervals. Larger sausages should be secured with a bubble knot (see page 222), to allow the sausage to expand as it cooks. After the sausage has been formed into links, loops, or other shapes, pierce the casing with a teasing needle, sausage maker's knife, or similar tool to allow the air bubbles to escape (see page 222).

finishing and storing sausages

After being prepared (that is stuffed, cooked if needed, cooled, then packaged in containers, wrapped or sealed, weighed, and labeled), fresh sausages should be stored under refrigeration and used as soon as possible. They may also be wrapped well and frozen for 2 to 3 months. Sausages such as fresh kielbasa, Italian sausage with roasted peppers, Italian hot sausage, breakfast sausage, and liverwurst need to be poached and can be cold-smoked afterwards. Blood sausage is another example of a product that would need to be poached and then cooled before storage. Frankfurters are an example of a product that would need to be hot-smoked to temperature and then cooled completely before storing. Chorizo sausage requires cold-smoking and then drying before it is ready to be held for serving or sale. Chorizo must then be cooked before consuming. Salami and other raw products have three basic maturation stages: curing, incubation, and drying/ripening. Each stage requires different temperatures and relative humidity for its environment.

curing stage
When you add the curing salts to the meat, the curing stage has begun. At this point, along with the salt, seasonings are added to the meat and fat. Chill the product well or allow it to become semifrozen, grind it, and then allow the forcemeat to cure for at least 2 days (24 to 48 hours) to ensure the safety of the product. After the curing stage is complete, stuff the forcemeat into the proper casings.

incubation stage
The next stage is the incubation stage. The sausage must be kept in a dark controlled environment with a relative humidity of 75 to 85 percent and an ambient temperature of 70°F/21°C for another 24 to 48 hours.

drying/ripening stage

The drying/ripening process is the final phase. Again, the sausage is kept in a cool, dry environment with a relative humidity of 50° to 60°F/10° to 16°C. This phase can take up to 8 months. During this time the sausage may lose up to 50 percent of its weight due to water loss and mold may build up on the casings; but not to worry—this is a natural and expected part of the process.

smoking sausages

Sausage is smoked and heated in order to pasteurize it and extend its shelf life, as well as to impart a smoky flavor and improve its appearance. Smoking and heating also fix the color and cause protein to move to the surface of the sausage so it will hold its shape when the casing is removed. See Chapter 6 for more information on smoking.

Let the sausage dry to form pellicle. To form a pellicle, use a refrigerator with a lot of air movement; 60 to 70 percent humidity is good. Smoke at 120°F/49°C for 1 hour, then at 130°F/66°C for 2 hours more, and finally at 165°F/77°C for 2 hours or until an internal temperature of 155°F/68°C is reached. Remove the sausage from the smokehouse and spray it with warm water for 15 to 30 seconds. Follow this with a cold shower or dip it in a slush tank—a tank or a container that contains some water and plenty of ice—until the internal temperature reaches 100°F/38°C. Let it dry for 1 to 2 hours, then place it in a cooler.

poaching sausages

Poached sausage, sometimes called cold cuts, is prepared by the same method as other raw sausages. The difference is that after filling the casings, the sausages are poached in warm water. Sometimes the sausage, such as French garlic sausage, mortadella, and bratwurst, is smoked before being poached. This gives them a better color and aroma.

After stuffing the ground ingredients into the casings, place the sausage in a pan of warm water. Heat the water to 160° to 170°F/71° to 77°C and hold it at that temperature until the sausage reaches an internal temperature of 155°F/68°C. An instant-read thermometer is essential for obtaining the proper temperature. The water should not boil, as this will ruin the product.

The sausages are then placed into a slush tank to cool down to 100°F/38°C. After taking the sausages out of the ice water, hang them on sausage sticks to dry.

drying sausages

dry and semidry sausages

Dry sausages may or may not be characterized by a bacterial fermentation. When fermented, the intentional encouragement of lactic-acid bacteria growth is useful as a meat preservative as well as producing the typical tangy flavor. The ingredients are mixed with spices and curing materials, stuffed into casings, and put through a carefully controlled, long, continuous air-drying process.

Dry sausages require more production time than other types of sausages, which results in a concentrated form of meat. Medium-dry sausage is about 70 percent of its "green" weight when sold. "Green weight" is the weight of the raw article before the addition of added substances or before cooking. Less dry and fully dried sausages range from 60 to 80 percent of the original weight at completion. The temperature is usually around 50° to 60°F/10° to 16°C, and the humidity is around 70 percent.

Dry sausages include:

- Frizzes (similar to pepperoni but not smoked)

- Pepperoni (not cooked but air-dried)

Dry sausage assortment

- Lola or Lolita and Lyons sausage (mildly seasoned pork with garlic)

- Genoa salami (Italian, usually made from pork but may have a small amount of beef; it is moistened with wine or grape juice and seasoned with garlic)

Semidry sausages are usually heated in the smokehouse to cook the product fully and partially dry it. Semidry sausages are semisoft sausages with good keeping qualities because of their lactic-acid fermentation. "Summer sausage" (another word for cervelat) is the general classification for mildly seasoned, smoked, semidry sausages like Lebanon bologna.

fermented sausages

Fermented sausages such as summer sausage, Landjäger, dry-cured Genoa salami, and California spicy sopressata are typically made from beef or pork, water, salt, curing agents, and sugar. Often a starter culture is added to the mixture (especially for semi-dry sausage) to increase the amount of friendly bacteria that will carry out the fermentation process in the meat. It is imperative to use pork that is labeled certified, to be certain that it is trichinosis-free (see the table on "Certifying Pork via Freezing" on page 63). The certified pork is used to ensure that there is no trichinosis in the pork.

alternate periods of freezing at temperatures indicated

MAXIMUM INTERNAL TEMPERATURE	MINIMUM INTERNAL TEMPERATURE	TIME
32°F/0°C	18°F/−8°C	106 hours
41°F/5°C	21°F/−6°C	82 hours
50°F/10°C	23°F/−5°C	63 hours
59°F/15°C	26°F/−3°C	48 hours
68°F/20°C	29°F/−2°C	35 hours
77°F/25°C	32°F/0°C	22 hours
86°F/30°C	35°F/2°C	8 hours
95°F/35°C	37°C/3°C	½ hour

During the production of fermented sausage, it is important to inhibit or eliminate the growth of bacteria that can cause spoilage. While they age, keep the sausages in a climate-controlled environment. The sausages will become firm during the aging process due to the lactic acid. When you incubate the sausage, you are providing the environment for the bacteria to produce given the temperature and time. Here is when you develop the tangy flavor we associate with fermented sausage.

common types of sausage

SAUSAGE	DESCRIPTION	CLASSIFICATION	CASING USED
ANDOUILLE	Pork, spicy, cured, semidry. Medium texture	Smoked, uncooked	Sheep casing
BLOOD SAUSAGE	Contains blood, spices, pork jowl, finely ground meat, sometimes cooked rice or other grain. National varieties include French (*boudin noir*), German (*blutwurst*), Italian (*sanguinaccio*), Polish (*kiszka*), Spanish (*morcilla*)	Cooked	Hog and beef middle
BOCKWURST	Contains veal, pork, milk, chives, parsley. Has a fine texture	Fresh, cooked	Sheep casing
BOLOGNA	Contains cured beef and pork, finely ground with spices	Cooked, smoked	Beef middle or beef bung
BRATWURST	Contains pork or pork and veal, seasoned, finely emulsified or fresh cooked, or medium-grind textures. First cured, then smoked	Smoked	Hog casing
BRAUNSCHWEIGER	Contains liver, meat, smoked meats, all finely ground. One of many varieties of liverwurst	Cooked	Beef middle or beef bung
BREAKFAST	Contains seasoned pork, fine to medium grind. Commonly found in links or patties. Has many seasoning variations	Fresh	Sheep casing
CERVELAT	Contains pork, or beef and pork, all medium to coarse grind. Mildly seasoned, cured, then smoked. One of many varieties of summer sausage	Semidry	Beef or hog middle
CHIPOLATA	Contains pork or pork and veal. Mildly seasoned. A very fine emulsion, giving it a mousse-like texture. Made in cocktail-size link	Cooked	Sheep casing
CHORIZO	Contains coarse-textured pork. Highly spiced. Cured, then smoked. Has many regional and national varieties: Mexican, Colombian, Portuguese, Spanish	Smoked, uncooked	Hog casing
FRANKFURTERS, HOT DOGS, WIENERS	Usually contains beef and pork or all beef, now chicken or turkey. May be cured, smoked, or cooked. A fine emulsified texture. Well seasoned. Many variations of seasonings and sizes	Cooked, smoked	Sheep casing
FRENCH GARLIC	Contains cured pork, fat, and spices. Has a predominant garlic flavor. Can be cooked or smoked. Many regional varieties: *saucisse de Lyon, saucisson à l'ail*; also called *Lyonerwurst, Jagdwurst*	Cooked, smoked	Beef middle

228   SAUSAGES

common types of sausage

HEAD CHEESE, SOUSE	Contains diced cooked pork head meat in concentrated jellied stock, flavored with vinegar, garnished with pickles, pimentos, parsley. Can be cooked or cured	Cooked meat specialty	No casing
ITALIAN	Contains coarsely ground pork. Hot Italian sausage is highly seasoned; sweet Italian sausage is mildly seasoned	Fresh	Hog casing
KIELBASA, POLISH SAUSAGE, KALBASSI, COLBASI	Contains pork or pork and beef. Has a fine, emulsified, or medium texture	Cooked, smoked or uncooked, cured	Beef round
KNOCKWURST	Contains beef and pork or all beef, seasoned similar to frankfurters. Can be cured, smoked, or cooked. Has a fine emulsified texture	Cooked, smoked	Hog casing
LANDJÄGER	Contains pork and beef. Has a medium texture. Usually cured and dried A flattened shape. Many varieties. Name means "land soldier": was a carry-along sausage	Semidry	Sheep or hog casing
LEBERKÄSE, BAVARIAN LOAF	Contains a bologna mix, beef and pork, sometimes veal. Can be baked in a loaf pan	Cooked meat specialty	No casing; loaf pan or mold
LIVERWURST	Contains liver, other fresh or smoked meats. Finely ground. *Hildesheimer* is the most famous kind	Cooked	Beef middle or beef bung
MORTADELLA	Contains finely emulsified pork, garnish of diced fat, and pistachios. Many variations. An Italian specialty sausage	Cooked	Beef middle or beef bung (cap)
SALAMI	Contains pork or pork and beef, which is cured. Highly seasoned with fermented flavor. Medium texture. It is air-dried. There are many varieties of this sausage	Dry, fermented	Beef bung cap or artificial
SCRAPPLE	Contains cornmeal and ground pork cooked prior to stuffing. Made into loaves or bricks	Cooked meat specialty	No casing: loaf pan or mold
TUSCAN	Contains coarsely ground pork. Seasoned with cheese and tomatoes	Fresh or cooked	Hog casing
WEISSWURST	Contains pork and veal. Mildly seasoned. Has a fine emulsified texture. A white sausage similar to bockwurst	Cooked	Sheep or hog casing

breakfast sausage

MAKES 9 LB/4.08 KG

8 lb/3.63 kg boneless pork butt, 75/25, cleaned, cut into 1-in/3-cm cubes

2¼ oz/64 g kosher salt

½ oz/14 g ground white pepper

¼ oz/7 g poultry seasoning

12 oz/340 g ice-cold water

16 ft/5 m prepared sheep casings, or as needed (optional)

1. In a mixing bowl, combine the pork, salt, pepper, and poultry seasoning.

2. Grind the meat once through the ³/₁₆-in/5-mm plate into a mixing bowl over an ice bath.

3. Transfer the meat to a mixer with a paddle attachment. Add the water and mix on speed #1 for 1 minute, then mix on speed #2 until the meat is sticky, 15 to 30 seconds.

4. Make a taste tester and adjust the seasoning if necessary.

5. To make bulk sausage, place 1 lb/454 g of sausage meat on plastic wrap, roll it up, twist the ends of the plastic wrap tightly, and tuck the ends under. The diameter of the finished sausage roll should be 2½ in/6 cm.

6. For link sausages, place the mixture into a sausage stuffer, making sure there are no air pockets. Stuff into the prepared casings. Measure, pinch, and twist into 5-in/13-cm lengths. Cut the sausages apart at the twists.

7. The sausages may be stored under refrigeration for up to 1 week and can be frozen for up to 1 month.

breakfast sausage with applesauce

MAKES 12 LB/5.44 KG

8 lb/3.63 kg boneless pork butt, cleaned, cut into 1-in/3-cm cubes

2¼ lb/64 g pork fatback, cut into 1-in/3-cm cubes

1 cup/240 mL onion flakes, toasted

2 oz/57 g kosher salt

½ oz/14 g poultry seasoning

⅓ oz/9 g ground white pepper

1 lb 7 oz/652 g unsweetened applesauce, chilled

Fresh white bread crumbs, as needed

Bacon fat, as needed

1. In a mixing bowl, combine the pork butt, fatback, onion flakes, salt, poultry seasoning, and pepper.

2. Progressively grind the mixture from the coarse plate (³⁄₈ in/9 mm) through the fine plate (¹⁄₈ in/3 mm) into a mixing bowl over an ice bath.

3. Transfer the mixture to a mixer with a paddle attachment. Add the applesauce and mix on speed #1 for 1 minute, then mix on speed #2 until the meat is sticky, 15 to 30 seconds.

4. Make a taste tester and adjust the seasoning if necessary.

5. Divide into 2-oz/57-g portions and form into patties ½ in/1 cm thick.

6. Coat with fresh bread crumbs and pan fry in bacon fat.

7. The sausages may be stored under refrigeration for up to 1 week and can be frozen for up to 1 month.

Note: To make bulk sausage, place 1 lb/454 g of sausage meat on plastic wrap, roll it up, twist the ends of the plastic wrap tightly, and tuck the ends under. The diameter of the finished sausage roll should be 2½ in/6 cm.

Variations: For link sausages, place the mixture into a sausage stuffer, making sure there are no air pockets. Stuff into the prepared casings. Measure, pinch, and twist into 5-in/13-cm lengths. Cut the sausages apart at the twists.

When making sausage patties, a wrapping of caul fat keeps the patties' shape, then melts away during cooking.

Italian Sausage with Roasted Peppers

italian sausage with roasted peppers

MAKES 5 LB 8 OZ/2.50 KG

5 lb/2.27 kg boneless pork butt, 75/25, cleaned, cut into 1-in/3-cm cubes

1½ oz/43 g kosher salt

¾ oz/21 g coarsely ground black pepper

¾ oz/21 g fennel seeds

½ oz/14 g dextrose

¼ oz/7 g sweet Spanish paprika

8 oz/227 g ice-cold water

GARNISH

1 lb/454 g red bell peppers

1 lb/454 g green bell peppers

8 oz/227 g Spanish onions, diced

Olive oil, as needed

4 tsp/20 mL chopped fresh basil

7 to 8 ft/ 2.13 to 2.44 m prepared hog casings, or as needed

1. In a mixing bowl, combine the pork butt, salt, pepper, fennel seeds, dextrose, and paprika. Place the mixture in resealable plastic bags, press out all the air, and partially freeze.

2. Grind the meat once through the coarse plate (³⁄₈ in/9 mm) into a mixing bowl over an ice bath.

3. Transfer the ground meat to a mixer with a paddle attachment. Add the water and mix on speed #1 for 1 minute, then mix on speed #2 until the meat is sticky, 15 to 30 seconds. Transfer to a clean storage container, cover, and refrigerate.

4. Roast the red and green peppers over an open flame until tender. Wrap the peppers in plastic wrap and cool to room temperature. Peel the peppers, discard the seeds, and cut in ¹⁄₂-in/1-cm dice. Reserve under refrigeration.

5. Sauté the onions in oil over high heat to brown them slightly, making sure they are cooked until they are transparent. Cool and reserve with the peppers.

6. Fold the peppers, onions, and basil into the meat mixture by hand so that the peppers and onions don't break up, but the mixture needs to be mixed very well.

7. Make a taste tester and adjust the seasoning as needed.

8. Place the mixture into a sausage stuffer, making sure there are no air pockets. Stuff into the prepared casings. Measure, pinch, and twist into 5-in/13-cm lengths.

9. Refrigerate the sausages for about 30 minutes.

10. Cut the sausages apart at the twists.

11. The sausages may be stored under refrigeration for up to 1 week and can be frozen up to 1 month.

hot italian sausage

MAKES 11 LB/4.99 KG

10 lb/4.54 kg boneless
pork butt, 75/25, cleaned,
cut into 1-in/3-cm cubes

3 oz/85 g kosher salt

1¼ oz/35 g red
pepper flakes

1¼ oz/35 g
granulated sugar

1 oz/28 g dextrose

¾ oz/21 g fennel seeds

¾ oz/21 g hot
Spanish paprika

¾ oz/21 g sweet
Hungarian paprika

½ oz/14 g ground coriander

½ oz/14 g coarsely
ground black pepper

⅛ oz/3.50 g cayenne

2 cups/480 mL
ice-cold water

12 to 14 ft/3.66 to
4.27 m prepared hog
casings, or as needed

1. In a mixing bowl, combine the pork butt, salt, pepper flakes, sugar, dextrose, fennel seeds, paprikas, coriander, black pepper, and cayenne.

2. Place in resealable plastic bags, press out all the air, and chill the mixture thoroughly or partially freeze.

3. Grind the meat once through the coarse plate (⅜ in/9 mm) into a mixing bowl over an ice bath.

4. Transfer the ground meat to a mixer with a paddle attachment. Add the water and mix on speed #1 for 1 minute, then mix on speed #2 until the meat is sticky, 15 to 30 seconds.

5. Make a taste tester and adjust the seasoning if necessary.

6. Place the mixture into a sausage stuffer, making sure there are no air pockets. Stuff into the prepared casings. Measure, pinch, and twist into 5-in/13-cm lengths. Cut the sausages apart at the twists.

7. The sausages may be stored under refrigeration for up to 1 week and can be frozen for up to 1 month.

fresh kielbasa

MAKES 10 LB/4.54 KG

10 lb/4.54 kg boneless pork butt, 70/30, cleaned, cut into 1-in/3-cm cubes

3 tbsp/45 mL kosher salt

2 tbsp/30 mL yellow mustard seeds, crushed

2½ tsp/12.5 mL ground black pepper

1½ tsp/7.5 mL ground allspice

1 tsp/5 mL garlic powder

1 tsp/5 mL marjoram

½ tsp/2.5 mL celery salt

3 cups/720 mL ice-cold water

12 to 13 ft/ 3.66 to 4.00 m prepared beef round casings, or as needed

1. In a mixing bowl, combine the pork, salt, mustard seeds, pepper, allspice, garlic powder, marjoram, and celery salt. Place in resealable plastic bags, press out all the air, and partially freeze.

2. Grind the pork through the medium plate (¼ in/6 mm) into a mixing bowl over an ice bath.

3. Transfer the mixture to a mixer with a paddle attachment and add the water. Mix on speed #1 for 1 minute, then mix on speed #2 until the meat is sticky, 15 to 30 seconds.

4. Cut the beef round casings into 18- to 20-in/46- to 51-cm lengths. Tie a bubble knot at one end of each casing, making sure you have extra string left to tie the ends together when stuffed.

5. Place the mixture into a sausage stuffer, making sure there are no air pockets. Stuff into the prepared casings and prick all air bubbles before tying a bubble knot in the open end to seal the sausage. Tie the two ends together to form a circle.

6. The sausage may be poached, grilled, or sautéed to an internal temperature of 150°F/66°C. Store under refrigeration.

kielbasa krakowska

Krakowska is made from fresh ham. Hams are boned and the lean meat is kept separate.

MAKES 15 LB/6.80 KG

10 lb/4.54 kg boneless fresh ham, cleaned

3 lb/1.36 kg 1 tsp/5 mL pork butt, cleaned, cut into 1-in/3-cm cubes

2 lb/907 g pork jowl fat, cleaned

7 tbsp/105 mL kosher salt

2 tsp/10 mL Insta Cure No. 1

2 tbsp/30 mL dextrose

2 oz/57 g garlic powder

1½ tsp/7.50 mL ground white pepper

1 tsp/5 mL ground coriander

2 tbsp/30 mL dry mustard

½ tsp/2.50 mL dried marjoram

1 qt/960 mL ice-cold water

8 to 10 ft/ 2.44 to 3 m prepared beef middle casings, or as needed

1. Cut 5 lb/2.27 kg of the ham into 1-in/3-cm cubes. Reserve under refrigeration.

2. Cut the remaining 5 lb/2.27 kg ham into ½- to ¾-in/1- to 2-cm cubes. Reserve under refrigeration.

3. Combine the pork butt, larger ham pieces, and jowl fat. Mix well.

4. Add the salt, Insta Cure, dextrose, garlic powder, pepper, coriander, mustard, and marjoram. Place the meat in a freezer until semifrozen.

5. Progressively grind the meat mixture from the coarse plate (⅜ in/9 mm) through the fine plate (⅛ in/3 mm) into a mixing bowl over an ice bath.

6. Transfer the ground meat to a mixer with a paddle attachment. Add the water and remaining cubed ham, and mix on speed #1 for 1 minute, then mix on speed #2 until the meat is sticky, 15 to 30 seconds.

7. Make a taste tester and adjust the seasoning if necessary.

8. Cut beef middle casings into 24-in/61-cm lengths and tie a bubble knot at the end of each one.

9. Place the mixture into a sausage stuffer, making sure there are no air pockets. Stuff into the prepared casings (should be stuffed until it is fairly firm) and prick all the air bubbles before tying a bubble knot to seal, leaving enough string to make a loop at each end so that the sausages can be hung from the hanging sticks.

10. Hang in a cooler overnight to air-dry and form a pellicle.

11. Hot-smoke at 120°F/49°C for about 1 hour. Use medium smoke and your choice of wood.

12. Apply a medium smoke and increase the smoke temperature to 130°F/54°C for about 1 hour.

13. Increase the smokehouse temperature to 160°F/71°C and maintain a medium smoke. Keep the sausages in the smokehouse until they reach an internal temperature of 152°F/67°C.

14. When the sausages are cooked, shock in an ice-water bath. Cool the sausages to about 110°F/43°C.

15. Remove the sausages from the water and wipe dry. Hang the sausages in the cooler overnight.

16. The sausages are now ready to eat or may be stored under refrigeration for up to 1 week and can be frozen for up to 1 month.

southwest green chile sausage

MAKES 10 LB/4.54 KG (ABOUT EIGHTY 2-OZ/57-G PATTIES)

8 lb/3.63 kg boneless pork butt, cleaned, cut into 1-in/3-cm cubes

2 lb/907 g pork belly, skinned, cut into 1-in/3-cm cubes

1 oz/28 g ground white pepper

3 oz/85 g kosher salt

2 tbsp/30 mL dried oregano

2 tsp/10 mL chopped fresh basil

2 tsp/10 mL Tabasco sauce

4 tsp/20 mL ground cumin

4 oz/113 g chili powder

2 lb 8 oz/1.13 kg green chiles, seeded and chopped

1 cup/240 mL ice-cold water

Cornmeal for dredging, as needed

Oil, as needed

1. In a mixing bowl, combine the cubed pork butt and belly, the pepper, salt, oregano, basil, Tabasco sauce, cumin, chili powder, and chiles. Mix well.

2. Transfer the meat mixture to resealable plastic bags, press out all the air, and partially freeze.

3. Grind the mixture through the coarse plate (³⁄₈ in/9 mm), then through a ³⁄₁₆-in/5-mm plate into a mixing bowl set over an ice bath.

4. Transfer the mixture to a mixer with a paddle attachment and add the water. Mix on speed #1 for 1 minute, then mix on speed #2 until the mixture is sticky, 15 to 30 seconds.

5. Make a taste tester and adjust the seasoning if needed.

6. Form the meat into patties and dredge them in cornmeal.

7. Fry the patties in oil until golden brown. Finish in a 350°F/177°C conventional oven to an internal temperature of 155°F/68°C.

8. The raw forcemeat may be stored under refrigeration for up to 4 days, or up to 1 week when cooked, and can be frozen for up to 1 month.

Blood Sausage

blood sausage

MAKES 10 LB/4.54 KG

5 lb/2.27 kg pork jowl fat, cleaned

2 lb/1.13 kg beef (or pork) tongue

2 lb/1.13 kg pork skin

1 lb/454 g tripe

1 lb 8 oz/680 g cooked barley

6 tbsp/90 mL kosher salt

3 tbsp/45 mL onion powder

3½ tsp/17.50 mL coarsely ground black pepper

1¼ tsp/6.25 mL dried marjoram

4 tsp/20 mL ground allspice

2 cups/480 mL pork blood

2 tsp/10 mL Insta Cure No. 1

7 to 8 ft/2.13 to 2.44 m prepared beef middle casings

1. In a stockpot, simmer the pork jowls, tongue, pork skin, and tripe in salted water to cover until tender, at least 2 hours. Cool the meats in the liquid.

2. Drain the meats. Peel the tongue and cut the meats into 1-in/3-cm cubes. Chill until the product is semifrozen.

3. Grind the meats through a $^3/_{16}$-in/5-mm plate into a mixing bowl over an ice bath.

4. Transfer the meats to a mixer with a paddle attachment and add the cooked barley, salt, onion powder, pepper, marjoram, allspice, blood, and Insta Cure. Mix well.

5. Cut the beef middle casings into 18-in/46-cm lengths and tie a bubble knot at the end of each one.

6. Place the mixture into a sausage stuffer, making sure there are no air pockets. Stuff into the prepared casings (should be stuffed fairly firm) and prick all the air bubbles before tying a bubble knot to seal, leaving enough string to make a loop at each end so that the sausages can be hung from the sausage sticks.

7. Hang in a cooler overnight to air-dry and form a pellicle.

8. Poach the sausages in 160°F/71°C water to an internal temperature of 152°F/67°C.

9. Remove the sausages from the water and shower them with cool water or place in an ice-water bath until the internal temperature is reduced to 110°F/43°C.

10. Hold the sausages under refrigeration for at least 24 hours before using.

11. The sausages may be stored under refrigeration for up to 1 week or frozen up to 1 month.

tuscan sausage

10 lb/4.54 kg boneless pork butt, 80/20, cleaned, cut into 1-in/3-cm cubes

2 oz/57 g kosher salt

4½ tsp/22.50 mL ground black pepper

4 tsp/20 mL minced garlic

4 oz/113 g mozzarella, cubed

1¼ cups/300 mL sun-dried tomatoes, drained

5 tbsp/75 mL fresh basil, washed and chopped

2 cups/480 mL port wine

8 ft/ 2.44 m prepared hog casings, or as needed

1. Grind the meat through the coarse plate (³⁄₈ in/9 mm) into a mixing bowl set over an ice bath.

2. Add the salt, pepper, garlic, mozzarella, tomatoes, and basil and mix well. Transfer the mixture to resealable plastic bags, press out all the air, and partially freeze.

3. Grind the mixture through a ³⁄₁₆-in/5-mm plate into a mixing bowl set over an ice bath.

4. Transfer the mixture to a mixer with a paddle attachment. Add the port and mix on speed #1 for 1 minute, then mix on speed #2 until the meat is sticky, 15 to 30 seconds.

5. Make a taste tester and adjust the seasoning if necessary.

6. Place the mixture into a sausage stuffer, making sure there are no air pockets. Stuff into the prepared casings. Measure, pinch, and twist into 4-in/10-cm lengths and tie with string.

7. Chill the sausages overnight at 39°F/3°C to allow the flavors to blend.

8. Gently poach the sausages in 160° to 170°F/71° to 77°C salted water to an internal temperature of 150°F/66°C.

9. The raw forcemeat may be stored under refrigeration for up to 4 days. After they are cooked, the sausages can be frozen for up to 1 month.

spicy lamb sausage

MAKES 10 LB/4.54 KG (ABOUT THIRTY-TWO 5-IN/13-CM LINKS)

7 lb/3.18 kg boneless lamb shoulder, cleaned of fat and sinew, cut into 1-in/3-cm cubes

2 lb/907 g pork jowl fat, cleaned, cut into 1-in/3-cm cubes

1 lb/454 g pancetta, cut into 1-in/3-cm cubes

1½ oz/43 g minced garlic

5 oz/142 g minced shallots

3¼ oz/92 g kosher salt

1 tsp/5 mL Insta Cure No. 1

1 oz/28 g honey

⅛ oz/3.5 g ground black pepper

1¾ tsp/8.75 mL crushed red pepper flakes

1¾ tsp/8.75 mL hot Spanish paprika

2 tsp/10 mL ground coriander

1 bunch thyme leaves, coarsely minced

½ cup/120 mL chopped flat-leaf parsley

¼ bunch rosemary, coarsely chopped

1 cup/240 mL ice-cold chicken stock

24 ft/7.32 m prepared hog casings, or as needed

1. In a mixing bowl, combine the lamb meat, jowl fat, and pancetta. Mix in the garlic, shallots, salt, Insta Cure, honey, black pepper, red pepper, paprika, coriander, thyme, parsley, and rosemary. Transfer the mixture to plastic storage bags and place in a freezer until semifrozen.

2. Grind the mixture through the medium plate (¼ in/6 mm) into a mixing bowl set over an ice bath.

3. Transfer the mixture to a mixer with a paddle attachment and mix on speed #1 for 1 minute, gradually adding the chicken stock. Mix on speed #2 until the mixture is sticky, 15 to 30 seconds.

4. Make a taste tester and adjust the seasoning as necessary.

5. Place the mixture into a sausage stuffer, making sure there are no air pockets. Stuff into the prepared casings. Measure, pinch, and twist into 5-in/13-cm links. Cut apart at the twists.

6. The sausages may be stored under refrigeration for up to 4 days and can be frozen for up to 1 month.

lamb and pine nut sausage

MAKES 6 LB/2.72 KG (ABOUT THIRTY-TWO 3-OZ/85-G PATTIES)

5 lb/2.27 kg boneless lamb shoulder, cleaned of fat and sinew, cut into 1-in/3-cm cubes

12 oz/340 g boneless pork, 80/20, cleaned, cut into 1-in/3-cm cubes

2 tsp/10 mL ground white pepper

2 garlic cloves, mashed

1½ oz/42 g kosher salt

2 tsp/10 mL dried thyme

2 tsp/10 mL dried oregano

6 oz/170 g pine nuts, toasted

½ cup/120 mL red wine, chilled

¼ cup/60 mL ice-cold water

Fresh white bread crumbs, as needed

Oil, as needed

1. In a mixing bowl, combine the lamb and pork with the pepper, garlic, salt, thyme, oregano, and pine nuts; mix well. Transfer the mixture to plastic storage bags and place in a freezer until semifrozen.

2. Progressively grind the meat mixture from the coarse plate (³⁄₈ in/9 mm) through the fine plate (¹⁄₈ in/3 mm) into a mixing bowl over an ice bath.

3. Transfer the mixture to a mixer with a paddle attachment and add the wine and water. Mix on speed #1 for 1 minute, then on speed #2 until the mixture is sticky, 15 to 30 seconds.

4. Make a taste tester and adjust the seasoning if needed.

5. Form the meat into patties. Dredge the patties in bread crumbs and fry in oil until golden brown. Finish the patties by baking them in a 350°F/177°C conventional oven to an internal temperature of 155°F/68°C.

6. The raw mixture can be refrigerated for 3 to 4 days. This mixture can also be frozen for up to 1 week after the patties are cooked.

morteau sausage

3 lb 12 oz/1.70 kg boneless pork, lean, cut into 1-in/3-cm cubes

1 lb 4 oz/567 g boneless fowl meat (such as poultry or older hen), skinless, cut into 1-in/3-cm cubes

¼ oz/7 g Insta Cure No. 1

1½ oz/43 g kosher salt

¼ oz/7 g ground black pepper

Pinch of ground cumin

Pinch of ground nutmeg

1 oz/28 g shallot, finely chopped

⅓ oz/9 g garlic, finely chopped

1 cup/240 mL dry white wine

2 oz/57 g nonfat dry milk

3 to 4 ft/91 to 122 cm prepared hog casings, or as needed

1. In a mixing bowl, combine the pork and fowl with the Insta Cure and salt. Add the pepper, cumin, and nutmeg; mix well. Transfer to resealable plastic bags and partially freeze.

2. Grind the meat through the medium plate (¼ in/6 mm) into a mixing bowl set over an ice bath. Reserve under refrigeration.

3. Simmer the shallot and garlic in the white wine with the lid on for 3 to 4 minutes to infuse the flavor. Cool the mixture. Strain and squeeze the shallot mixture through cheesecloth into a bowl, making sure to squeeze all the wine and juices out. Discard the shallot and garlic.

4. Combine the nonfat dry milk with the reserved wine and add to the ground meat.

5. Transfer the mixture to a mixer with a paddle attachment and mix on speed #1 for 1 minute, then on speed #2 until the mixture is sticky, 15 to 30 seconds.

6. Make a taste tester and adjust the seasoning if needed.

7. Place the mixture into a sausage stuffer, making sure there are no air pockets. Stuff into the prepared casings. Measure, pinch, and twist into 4-in/10-cm lengths and tie with string.

8. Hang the sausages on sausage sticks, and dry under refrigeration for 12 hours to air-dry and form a pellicle.

9. Cold-smoke the sausages for 12 to 14 hours. Morteau is traditionally smoked over pine.

10. The sausages may be stored under refrigeration for up to 4 weeks and can be frozen for up to 2 months.

buffalo wing–style sausages

MAKES 6 LB 8 OZ/2.95 KG (ABOUT FIFTY-TWO 2-IN/5-CM LINKS)

5 lb/2.27 kg chicken, all thigh meat or ½ breast/½ thigh, boneless, skinless

1 lb 8 oz/680 g pork fatback

2 oz/57 g kosher salt

½ oz/14 g black pepper

5 tsp/25 mL cayenne

½ cup/120 mL ice-cold water

2 tbsp/30 mL hot sauce, preferably Frank's

13 to 14 ft/3.96 to 4.27 m prepared sheep casings, or as needed

1. Cut the chicken and fatback into 1-in/3 cm cubes. In a mixing bowl, combine the meat and fat with the salt, pepper, and cayenne pepper. Transfer mixture to plastic storage bags and semifreeze.

2. Grind the meat mixture through the medium plate (¼ in/6 mm) into a mixing bowl over an ice bath.

3. Transfer the mixture to a mixer with a paddle attachment and add the water and hot sauce,. Mix on speed #1 for 1 minute, then on speed #2 until sticky, 15 to 30 seconds.

4. Make a taste tester and adjust seasoning if necessary.

5. Place the mixture into a sausage stuffer, making sure there are no air pockets. Stuff into the prepared casings. Measure, pinch, and twist into 2-in/5-cm lengths and tie with string.

6. Poach the sausages in 160° to 170°F/71° to 77°C salted water to an internal temperature of 150°F/66°C.

7. Shock the sausages in an ice water bath until they drop to an internal temperature of 50°F/10°C.

8. The sausages may be stored under refrigeration for up to 1 week; however, they are best used fresh as soon as you make them.

weisswurst (munich sausage)

MAKES 12 LB 8 OZ/5.67 KG (APPROXIMATELY SIXTY 4-IN/10-CM SAUSAGES)

4 lb/1.81 kg pork jowl fat, cleaned

1 lb 8 oz/680 g boneless, skinless chicken breast, cut into 1-in/3-cm cubes (see Note)

1 lb 8 oz/680 g boneless chicken thigh, cut into 1-in/3-cm cubes

2 lb/907 g boneless pork butt, very lean, cut into 1-in/3-cm cubes

3 oz/85 g kosher salt

2 oz/57 g dextrose

1 lb/454 g pork skins

1 cup/240 mL sliced yellow onions

Butter, as needed

3 lb/1.36 kg crushed ice

1 tbsp/15 mL finely ground white pepper

2 tsp/10 mL ground nutmeg

½ tsp/2.50 mL ground mace

6 oz/170 g nonfat dry milk

1 tsp/5 mL finely grated lemon zest

10 ft/3 m prepared hog casings, or as needed

Milk, as needed

3 bay leaves

1 *oignon piqué*

1. Cube the jowl fat and freeze. In a mixing bowl, combine the chicken and the pork butt. Mix in the salt and dextrose. Transfer the meat to resealable plastic bags and partially freeze.

2. Place the pork skins in a pot and cover with cold water. Bring to a boil and cook until tender, about 2 to 3 hours. Drain, shock, and cube, then set aside. Sauté the onions in butter for 4 to 5 minutes until translucent and aromatic. Chill and reserve.

3. Grind the meat through the medium plate (¼ in/6 mm) into a mixing bowl set over an ice bath. Reserve under refrigeration.

4. Grind the jowl fat through the fine plate (⅛ in/3 mm) into a mixing bowl set over an ice bath. Reserve under refrigeration.

5. Transfer the ground lean meat to a Stephan cutter. Add the ice, pepper, nutmeg, and mace. Process until the mixture reaches a temperature of 30°F/−1°C. Continue processing until the temperature rises to 40°F/4°C.

6. Add the jowl fat and process until the temperature reaches 50°F/10°C.

7. Add the nonfat dry milk, pork skins, onions, and the lemon zest and process until the temperature reaches 58°F/14°C.

8. Make a taste tester and adjust the seasoning as needed.

9. Place the mixture into a sausage stuffer, making sure there are no air pockets. Stuff into the prepared casings. Measure, pinch, and twist into 5-in/13-cm lengths and tie with twine.

10. Hang the sausages on sausage sticks overnight under refrigeration.

11. Poach the sausages in enough milk to cover with the bay leaves and oignon piqué at 160° to 165°F/71° to 74°C to an internal temperature of 165°F/74°C.

12. Chill the sausages in an ice-water bath to 100°F/38°C. Drain and dry them.

13. Pan fry the sausages in butter to finish.

14. The sausages may be stored raw under refrigeration for up to 4 days and up to 1 week after being cooked. They can also be frozen for up to 2 weeks.

Note: Veal, pork, and/or rabbit work very well with this recipe instead of chicken.

chicken sausage with mushrooms and asiago

MAKES 12 LB/5.44 KG (APPROXIMATELY SIXTY 4½-IN/11-CM LINKS)

8 lb/3.63 kg boneless, skinless chicken, ½ breast/½ thigh meat, cubed

2¾ oz/78 g kosher salt

2 pinches of cayenne

¼ cup/60 mL white wine

6 tbsp/90 mL lemon juice

2 lb/907 g crushed ice

10 oz/284 g nonfat dry milk

2 cups/481 mL heavy cream

VEGETABLE GARNISH

1 qt/960 mL cremini mushrooms, stems trimmed, washed, dried, roasted

10 oz/284 g Asiago, cut into 1-in/3-cm pieces

1 red bell pepper, sliced into 1-in/3-cm strips

1 green bell pepper, sliced into 1-in/3-cm strips

4 small yellow onions, roasted

½ medium zucchini

1 carrot, peeled, cut into 1-in/3-cm pieces

2 oz/57 g green beans, trimmed, blanched

½ cup/120 mL fresh basil

15 ft/4.57 m prepared hog casings, or as needed

1. In a mixing bowl, combine the chicken with the salt and cayenne. Transfer the mixture to plastic storage bags and semifreeze.

2. Grind the chicken through the medium plate (¼ in/6 mm) into a mixing bowl over an ice bath.

3. Add the wine and lemon juice to the ground chicken.

4. Transfer the ground meat to a Stephan cutter. Add the ice. Process until the mixture reaches a temperature of 30°F/−1°C. Continue processing until the temperature rises to 45°F/7°C.

5. Add the nonfat dry milk and process until the temperature reaches 52°F/12°C.

6. Stir in the heavy cream, making sure it is incorporated well. Transfer to a mixing bowl and reserve under refrigeration.

7. Grind the vegetable garnish ingredients through the fine plate (⅛ in/3 mm) into a mixing bowl over an ice bath. Gently fold the vegetable mixture into the meat mixture.

8. Make a taste tester and adjust the seasoning as needed.

9. Place the mixture into a sausage stuffer, making sure there are no air pockets. Stuff into the prepared casings. Measure, pinch, and twist into 4½-in/11-cm lengths and tie with string.

10. Poach the sausages in 170°F/77°C salted water to an internal temperature of 150°F/66°C.

11. Shock in an ice-water bath until the sausages drop to 50°F/10°C internal temperature. Drain and dry.

12. The sausages may be stored under refrigeration for up to 1 week. Freezing is not recommended.

Note: When reheating chicken sausages, it is important to reheat them slowly due to the lack of fat in the sausages.

duck and foie gras sausage

MAKES 4 LB/1.81 KG (APPROXIMATELY FORTY-FIVE 2-IN/5-CM LINKS)

1 lb/454 g boneless, skinless duck thigh or leg meat, free of sinew from leg meat

12 oz/340 g boneless, skinless chicken thigh or leg meat

3 oz/936 g kosher salt

¼ tsp/1.25 mL ground white pepper

12 oz/340 g foie gras, B grade

2 oz/57 g minced shallots

Butter, as needed

1 tsp/5 mL Insta Cure No. 1

2 tbsp/30 mL brandy

2 egg whites

2 to 2½ cups/480 to 600 mL heavy cream

1 oz/28 g chopped truffles

1 bunch chives, minced

1 bunch chervil, coarsely chopped

30 ft/9.14 m prepared sheep casings, or as needed

1. Cut the duck and chicken into ½-in/1-cm cubes. Add the salt and pepper and mix well. Chill well or semifreeze.

2. Grind the meat through the medium plate (¼ in/6 mm) into a mixing bowl over an ice bath. Reserve under refrigeration.

3. Dice the foie gras into rough ¼-in/6-mm cubes, making sure the foie gras is deveined. Reserve under refrigeration.

4. Sweat the shallots in butter until tender. Cool.

5. In a mixing bowl, combine the ground duck and chicken with the shallots, Insta Cure, and brandy. Transfer to a food processor (R-6 with a metal base) and pulse until smooth. Add the egg whites and mix until smooth.

6. Add the foie gras and process for 1 second, then begin to add the heavy cream slowly until the cream is totally worked into the mixture. (Be careful that this mixture does not get heated up too much by the friction created by the blade.)

7. Fold the truffles, chives, and chervil into the forcemeat, mixing well.

8. Make a taste tester and adjust the seasoning if needed.

9. Place the forcemeat into a sausage stuffer, making sure there are no air pockets. Stuff into the prepared casings. Measure, pinch, and twist into 2-in/5-cm lengths and tie with string.

10. Poach the sausages in 165°F/74°C salted water until just firm to the touch. Drain and cool.

11. These can be used immediately or can be refrigerated for 3 to 4 days.

Presentation idea: The sausages may be finished by poaching, sautéing, or grilling.

duck sausage with fresh sage and roasted garlic

MAKES 5 LB/2.27 KG (APPROXIMATELY FORTY-FIVE 2-IN/5-CM LINKS)

3 lb/1.36 kg duck meat (legs preferred), skinned, boned, sinew removed

1 lb/454 g pork jowl fat, cleaned

⅓ cup/80 mL finely chopped sage

3 tbsp/45 mL finely minced roasted garlic

1½ oz/43 g kosher salt

⅓ oz/9.33 g coarsely ground black pepper

½ cup/120 mL ice-cold water

½ cup/120 mL red wine, chilled

8 to 10 ft/2.44 to 3.05 m prepared sheep casings or as needed

1. Cut the duck meat and pork fat into ½-in/1-cm pieces.

2. In a mixing bowl, combine the sage, garlic, salt, pepper, water, and wine with the meat and fat and mix well. Place in a resealable plastic bag, press out all the air, and refrigerate for 8 to 10 hours or overnight.

3. Place in the freezer until partially frozen.

4. Grind the mixture through the medium plate (¼ in/6 mm) into a mixing bowl over an ice bath; mix lightly.

5. Grind through the fine plate (⅛ in/3 mm) into a mixing bowl over an ice bath and mix well.

6. Make a taste tester and adjust the seasoning if needed.

7. Place the mixture into a sausage stuffer, making sure there are no air pockets. Stuff into the prepared casings. Measure, pinch, and twist 2-in/5-cm lengths and tie with twine.

8. The sausages may be stored under refrigeration for up to 1 week and can be frozen for up to 2 weeks.

Presentation idea: The sausages may be pan fried in a heavy skillet or roasted in an oven to finish them off.

smoked turkey and dried apple sausage

3 lb 8 oz/1.59 kg boneless, skinless turkey thigh meat, cut into 1-in/3-cm cubes

1 lb 8 oz/680 g pork belly, skinned, cut into 1-in/3-cm cubes

2½ oz/71 g kosher salt

⅕ oz/5.60 g Insta Cure No. 1

2 oz/57 g granulated sugar

½ oz/14 g ground black pepper

2 bunches thyme, coarsely chopped

2 bunches sage, coarsely chopped

6 garlic cloves, minced

4 oz/113 g minced shallots

1 tsp/5 mL vegetable oil

3 oz/85 g dried apples

Chicken stock, as needed

1 cup/240 mL apple cider, chilled

22 ft/6.71 m prepared sheep casings, or as needed

1. In a mixing bowl, combine the turkey meat and pork belly with the salt, Insta Cure, sugar, pepper, thyme, and sage. Cover and reserve under refrigeration.

2. Sweat the garlic and shallots in a small amount of oil until tender. Drain off the excess fat and cool. Add the garlic and shallots to the meat. Place into plastic storage bags, press the air out, and place the mixture in the freezer until semifrozen.

3. Grind the meat through the medium plate (¼ in/6 mm) into a mixing bowl set over an ice bath. Reserve half of the ground meat under refrigeration and grind the remaining meat through the fine plate (⅛ in/3 mm) or pulse in a food processor until a smooth paste is made. Combine both meats and reserve under refrigeration.

4. Simmer the apples in enough stock to cover. Cook gently until the apples become tender, about 5 to 10 minutes Drain well, dry, and cool. Reserve and cool ¾ cup/180 mL of the stock.

5. Once cooled, cut the apples into rough small dice and add to the forcemeat.

6. Transfer the forcemeat to a mixer fitted with a paddle attachment, and mix on speed #1 for 1 minute, gradually adding the apple cider. Mix on speed #2 until the mixture is sticky, 15 to 30 seconds.

7. Make a taste tester and adjust the seasoning as necessary. The reserved stock may be added to adjust the consistency.

8. Place the mixture into a sausage stuffer, making sure there are no air pockets. Stuff into the prepared casings. Measure, pinch, and twist into 5-in/13-cm links and tie.

9. Hang the sausages on a sausage stick in a refrigerator overnight to air-dry and form a pellicle.

10. Cold-smoke at below 80°F/27°C for 1½ hours with medium smoke from hickory.

11. Raw sausages may be stored under refrigeration for 3 to 4 days; cooked sausages keep for up to 1 week.

Presentation idea: The sausage may be poached, grilled, or sautéed to a finished internal temperature of 165°F/74°C.

smoked pheasant sausage with wild rice

MAKES 11 LB/4.99 KG, APPROXIMATELY FORTY 5-IN/13-CM LINKS

7 lb/3.18 kg boneless, skinless pheasant, cut into 1-in/3-cm cubes

2 lb 8 oz/1.13 kg pork fatback, cut into 1-in/3-cm cubes

3 oz/85 g kosher salt

½ oz/14 g ground white pepper

1 tbsp/15 mL onion powder

1 tbsp/15 mL Insta Cure No. 1

1 oz/28 g granulated sugar

½ oz/14 g poultry seasoning

1½ cups/360 mL ice-cold water or stock

1 cup/240 mL wild rice, cooked, cooled

12 to 14 ft/3.66 to 4.27 m prepared sheep casings, or as needed

1. In a mixing bowl, combine the pheasant and fatback. Add the salt, pepper, onion powder, Insta Cure, sugar, and poultry seasoning and mix well. Place in resealable plastic bags, press out all the air, and partially freeze the meat.

2. Progressively grind the meat from the medium plate ($^{1}/_{4}$ in/6 mm) through the fine plate ($^{1}/_{8}$ in/3 mm) into a mixing bowl set over an ice bath.

3. Transfer the mixture to a mixer fitted with a paddle attachment. Add the water and wild rice and mix on speed #1 for 1 minute, then mix on speed #2 until meat is sticky, 15 to 30 seconds.

4. Make a taste tester and adjust seasoning if needed.

5. Place the mixture into a sausage stuffer, making sure there are no air pockets. Stuff into the prepared casings. Measure, pinch, and twist into 5-in/13-cm lengths and tie with thin string.

6. Place the sausage on sausage sticks, and hang in the refrigerator overnight to air-dry and form a pellicle.

7. Cold-smoke for 1 to 2 hours with medium smoke from hickory and under 80°F/27°C, keeping items cool.

8. The sausage may be held under refrigeration for 3 to 4 days or it may be cooked and served immediately.

Presentation ideas: The sausages may be grilled, sautéed, or finished in an oven to an internal temperature of 150°F/66°C.

The sausages may be served with lentils or on biscuits.

chicken sausage with plums and ginger

MAKES 7 LB/3.18 KG (APPROXIMATELY THIRTY 4½-IN/11-CM LINKS)

6 lb/2.72 kg boneless, skinless chicken thigh or leg meat

3 oz/85 g kosher salt

¼ oz/7 g ground black pepper

¼ oz/7 g cilantro, destemmed

12 Italian plums, pitted, diced small

6 tbsp/90 mL minced ginger

3 tbsp/45 mL sesame seeds

Juice from 6 limes

3 oz/90 mL rice vinegar

1 oz/28 g honey

½ cup/120 mL sake

1 lb 8 oz/680 g crushed ice

8 oz/227 g nonfat dry milk

7 to 8 ft/2.52 to 2.88 m prepared hog casings, or as needed

1. Cut the chicken meat into 1-in/3-cm cubes; combine with salt, pepper, and cilantro. Place the mixture in a plastic storage bag, press all air out, and semifreeze.

2. Grind the meat through the fine plate (⅛ in/3 mm) into a mixing bowl over an ice bath. Reserve under refrigeration.

3. Wrap the plums in foil and roast in a conventional oven at 350°F/177°C to an internal temperature of 170°F/77°C. Cool to room temperature.

4. Sweat the ginger over medium-low heat until soft, about 3 to 4 minutes. Cool to room temperature.

5. Gently fold the ginger and plums into the ground chicken. Add the sesame seeds, lime juice, vinegar, and honey. Mix to incorporate. Add the sake and mix well.

6. Transfer the mixture to a Stephan cutter. Add the ice. Process until the mixture reaches a temperature of 30°F/−1°C. Continue processing until the mixture's temperature rises to 45°F/7°C.

7. Add the nonfat dry milk and process until the temperature reaches 52°F/12°C.

8. Make a taste tester and adjust the seasoning as needed.

9. Place the mixture into a sausage stuffer, making sure there are no air pockets. Stuff into the prepared casings. Measure, pinch, and twist into 4½-in/11-cm lengths and tie with twine.

10. Poach in 160° to 170°F/71° to 77°C salted water to an internal temperature of 150°F/66°C.

11. Shock in an ice-water bath until the sausage drops to an internal temperature of 50°F/10°C.

12. The sausages may be stored under refrigeration for up to 1 week. Freezing is not recommended.

Note: When reheating chicken sausages, it is important to reheat them slowly due to the lack of fat in the sausages.

veal and mushroom sausage

3 lb 8 oz/1.59 kg lean veal, cut into 1-in/3-cm cubes

1¾ oz/50 g kosher salt

⅜ oz/10.50 g dextrose

½ oz/14 g ground white pepper

⅛ oz/3.50 g ground dried thyme

⅛ oz/3.50 g poultry seasoning

1 lb/454 g pork jowl fat, cleaned, cut into 1-in/3-cm cubes

1 lb 8 oz/680 g crushed ice

3 oz/85 g nonfat dry milk

VEGETABLE GARNISH

4 oz/113 g carrots, cut into brunoise

4 oz/113 g celery, cut into brunoise

8 oz/227 g yellow onions, finely minced

1 tbsp/15 mL vegetable oil

1 lb/454 g button or chanterelle mushrooms, diced small

½ cup/120 mL white wine

1 tbsp/15 mL chopped fresh parsley

12 ft/3.66 m prepared sheep casings, or as needed

1. In a mixing bowl, combine the veal with the salt, dextrose, pepper, thyme, and poultry seasoning. Transfer the veal to resealable plastic bags, press out all the air, and semifreeze. Freeze the jowl fat.

2. Progressively grind the veal from the coarse plate (⅜ in/9 mm) through the fine plate (⅛ in/3 mm) into a mixing bowl set over an ice bath. Reserve under refrigeration.

3. Progressively grind the jowl fat from the coarse plate (⅜ in/9 mm) through the fine plate (⅛ in/3 mm) into another mixing bowl set over an ice bath.

4. Transfer the ground veal to a Stephan cutter. Add the ice. Process until the mixture reaches a temperature of 30°F/−1°C. Continue processing until the temperature rises to 40°F/4°C.

5. Add the ground fat and process until the temperature reaches 45°F/10°C.

6. Add the nonfat dry milk and process until the temperature reaches 58°F/14°C. Transfer to a storage container, cover, and reserve under refrigeration.

7. Sauté the carrots, celery, and onions in oil until slightly cooked or until they become soft. Add the mushrooms and sauté. When the mushrooms release water, add the wine. Reduce until almost dry (no moisture present). Remove from the pan and chill.

8. Add the chilled vegetable garnish and chopped parsley to the forcemeat.

9. Transfer the forcemeat to a mixer fitted with a paddle attachment and mix until incorporated. Mix on speed #1 for about 2 to 3 minutes.

10. Make a taste tester and adjust the seasoning as needed.

11. Place the forcemeat into a sausage stuffer, making sure there are no air pockets. Stuff into the prepared casings. Measure, pinch, and twist into 2- or 4-in/5- or 10-cm lengths and tie with twine.

12. Poach the sausages in 160°F/71°C salted water to an internal temperature of 155°F/68°C.

13. Shock the sausages immediately in an ice-water bath until cooled all the way through.

14. The sausages may be stored under refrigeration for up to 2 weeks and can be frozen for up to 2 weeks

Presentation idea: To prepare the sausages, reheat them in hot water and finish by grilling or sautéing them.

german bratwurst

MAKES 5 LB 8 OZ/2.50 KG (APPROXIMATELY TWENTY TO TWENTY-FIVE 5-IN/13-CM LINKS)

4 lb/1.81 kg pork butt, cleaned, cut into 1-in/3-cm cubes

1 lb/454 g pork belly, skinned, cut into 1-in/3-cm cubes

2 oz/57 g Bratwurst Seasoning Mix (page 37)

1 cup/240 mL ice-cold water

6 to 7 ft/1.83 to 2.52 m prepared hog casings

1. In a mixing bowl, combine the pork butt and pork belly with the bratwurst seasoning. Place in a resealable plastic bag, press out all the air, and partially freeze.

2. Progressively grind the meat from the coarse plate (³/₈ in/9 mm) through the fine plate (¹/₈ in/3 mm) into a mixing bowl over an ice bath.

3. Transfer the mixture to a mixer with a paddle attachment. Add the water. Mix on speed #1 for 1 minute, then mix on speed #2 until the meat is sticky, 15 to 30 seconds.

4. Place the mixture into a sausage stuffer, making sure there are no air pockets. Stuff into the prepared casings. Measure, pinch, and twist into 5-in/13-cm lengths and tie with thin string.

5. Poach the sausage in 165°F/74°C water to an internal temperature of 155°F/68°C.

6. Shock the sausage in an ice-water bath until the sausage drops to a 65° to 70°F/18° to 21°C internal temperature.

7. The sausages can be stored in a refrigerator for up to 1 week and can be frozen for 2 to 3 weeks.

Note: Use sheep casings to make smaller bratwurst. Measure, pinch, and twist into 4-in/10-cm lengths and tie with thin string.

Variations

Smoked Bratwurst: Add 1 tsp/5 mL Insta Cure No. 1 with the bratwurst seasoning. After stuffing and tying, hang in the cooler overnight to air-dry and form a pellicle, then cold-smoke the meat for about 2 hours. Cold-smoke below 70°F/21°C with hickory or wood of your choice. Follow the storage instructions in step 7.

liverwurst

MAKES 11 LB/4.99 KG

1 lb 8 oz/680 g pork skins

2 lb/907 g beef tripe

5 lb/2.27 kg pork liver

1 lb 8 oz/680 g pork jowl fat, cleaned

2 lb/907 g boneless pork butt, cleaned

2 kaiser rolls (12 oz/340 g)

5½ tbsp/82.50 mL kosher salt

8 tsp/40 mL onion powder

2 tbsp/30 mL dextrose

2 tsp/10 mL Insta Cure No. 1

1½ tbsp/22.50 mL ground white pepper

1½ tsp/7.50 mL fresh chopped sage

1½ tsp/7.50 mL, fresh chopped marjoram

1 tsp/5 mL ground nutmeg

¼ tsp/1.25 mL ground ginger

7 to 8 ft/2.13 to 2.44 m prepared beef middle casings, or as needed (see Note)

1. In a large stockpot, simmer the pork skins covered in lightly salted water for 2 hours. Add the liver, jowl fat, and pork butt and cook for 1 hour, until tender.

2. Cool the meats to room temperature in the liquid. Drain and reserve the cooking liquid.

3. Weigh the pork skins to make sure that they have not lost weight from the cooking process. It may be necessary to add a small amount of the stock to bring them back up to the green weight of 1 lb 8 oz/680 g. Chill the product until semifrozen.

4. Cut the meats into 1-in/3-cm cubes. Grind through the $^3/_{16}$-in/5-mm plate into a mixing bowl over an ice bath. Reserve under refrigeration.

5. Soak the rolls in some of the cooking liquid for 5 to 10 minutes, until they become saturated with the juice.

6. Drain the rolls and add to the ground meat mixture. Add the salt, onion powder, dextrose, Insta Cure, pepper, sage, marjoram, nutmeg, and ginger and mix well until the spices are evenly distributed.

7. Grind the mixture through the fine plate ($^1/_8$ in/3 mm) into a mixing bowl set over an ice bath.

8. Transfer the mixture to a mixer with a paddle attachment. Mix on speed #1 for 1 minute, then speed #2 until the mixture is tacky, 15 to 30 seconds.

9. Cut the beef middle casings into 12- to 16-in/30- to 41-cm lengths. Tie one end of each piece with a bubble knot.

10. Place the mixture into a sausage stuffer, making sure there are no air pockets. Stuff the prepared casings firmly and prick all the air bubbles before tying a bubble knot to seal them.

11. Poach the liverwurst in 170°F/77°C water; allow the temperature to drop to 160°F/71°C and hold at that temp. Cook the liverwurst to an internal temperature of 150° to 152°F/66° to 67°C, 1 to 1½ hours.

12. Transfer the liverwurst to an ice-water bath, adding enough ice to chill the liverwurst as quickly as possible, for at least 45 minutes. Remove the liverwurst from the water bath and let it dry at room temperature. Transfer the liverwurst to a refrigerator to chill overnight wrapped.

13. The liverwurst may be stored under refrigeration for up to 1 week or frozen for about 2 to 3 weeks.

Note: Sewed synthetic casings may be used in place of beef middle casings if desired.

kassler liverwurst

MAKES 8 LB/3.63 KG

3 lb/1.36 kg boneless pork butt, cleaned, cut into 1-in/3-cm cubes

2 lb 8 oz/1.13 kg pork liver, cut into 1-in/3-cm cubes

1 lb/454 g pork jowl fat, cleaned, cut into 1-in/3-cm cubes

2 oz/57 g onion, minced

½ oz/14 g kosher salt

1 tsp/5 mL ground white pepper

1 tsp/5 mL Pâté Spice Mix No. 1 (page 35)

¼ oz/7 g Insta Cure No. 1

6 oz/170 g potato starch

½ cup/120 mL white wine

6 medium eggs

GARNISH

8 oz/227 g boiled ham, diced small

½ cup/120 mL pistachio nuts, shelled, blanched, cut in half

5 ft/1.52 m prepared beef middle casings, or as needed

1. Semifreeze the pork butt, then grind it through the coarse plate (³⁄₈ in/9 mm) of a meat grinder into a mixing bowl over an ice bath. Reserve under refrigeration.

2. Semifreeze the liver, then grind the liver and the ground pork butt from the medium plate (¼ in/6 mm) through the fine plate (⅛ in/3 mm) into another mixing bowl over an ice bath. Reserve under refrigeration.

3. Freeze the jowl fat, then grind it through the fine plate (⅛ in/3 mm) into a third mixing bowl over an ice bath.

4. Combine the ground meats and fat and transfer to a mixer with a paddle attachment. Add the onion, salt, pepper, pâté spice mix, Insta Cure, potato starch, wine, and eggs and mix on speed #1 for 1 minute. Mix on speed #2 until well mixed, 15 to 30 seconds.

5. Make a taste tester and adjust the seasoning as needed.

6. Add the ham and the pistachios; fold in well.

7. Cut the beef middle casings into 12-in/30-cm lengths and tie with heavy string at one end using a bubble knot.

8. Place the mixture into a sausage stuffer, making sure there are no air pockets. Stuff the prepared casings and prick all the air bubbles before tying a bubble knot with string to seal them.

9. Poach the liverwurst in 170°F/77°C salted water to an internal temperature of 155°F/68°C.

10. Shock in an ice-water bath until cold.

11. Dip the liverwurst in hot water and dry the outside with paper towels to remove the fat.

12. Hang the liverwurst in the refrigerator at around 40°F/4°C to air-dry and form a pellicle.

13. Cold-smoke under 70°F/21°C, using hickory or any hard wood of your choice, for 2 to 4 hours or until desired color.

14. The liverwurst may be stored under refrigeration for up to 1 week and can be frozen up to 2 to 3 weeks.

basic bologna

MAKES 12 LB 8 OZ/5.67 KG

2 lb/907 g beef plate, clean, trimmed, and cut into 1-in/3-cm cubes

2 lb/907 g cleaned pork jowl fat, skinned, cut into 1-in/3-cm cubes

CURE MIX

3¼ oz/92 g kosher salt

2 tsp/10 mL Insta Cure No. 1

¾ oz/21 g dextrose

SEASONINGS

½ oz/14 g ground white pepper

2 tsp/10 mL caraway seeds, ground

2 tsp/10 mL ground nutmeg

1½ oz/43 g onion powder

5 lb/2.50 kg lean boneless beef, cut into 1-in/3-cm cubes (or a combination of pork, veal, and/or beef)

3 lb/1.36 kg crushed ice

5½ oz/156 g nonfat dry milk

10 ft/3.05 m prepared beef middle casings, or as needed

1. Trim the beef plate and cut into 1-in/3-cm cubes. Place in the freezer until partially frozen.

2. Skin and clean the jowl fat and cut into 1-in/3-cm cubes. Place in the freezer until partially frozen.

3. In a small mixing bowl, combine the ingredients for the cure mix. In another bowl, combine the seasonings.

4. In a mixing bowl, combine the lean beef with the cure mix and seasonings. Place in resealable plastic bags, press out all the air, and partially freeze.

5. Progressively grind the lean beef from the coarse plate (⅜ in/9 mm) through the fine plate (⅛ in/3 mm) into a mixing bowl over an ice bath. Reserve under refrigeration.

6. Progressively grind the beef plate and the jowl fat from the coarse plate (⅜ in/9 mm) through the fine plate (⅛ in/3 mm) into a mixing bowl over an ice bath. Reserve under refrigeration.

7. Transfer the ground lean meat to a Stephan cutter. Add the ice. Process until the mixture reaches a temperature of 30°F/−1°C. Continue processing until the temperature rises to 40°F/4°C.

8. Add the beef plate and process until the temperature reaches 50°F/10°C.

9. Add the nonfat dry milk and process until the temperature reaches 58°F/14°C.

10. Make a taste tester and adjust the seasoning as needed.

11. Cut the beef middle casings into 16-in/41-cm lengths and tie a bubble knot at one end of each piece.

12. Place the mixture into a sausage stuffer, making sure there are no air pockets. Stuff the prepared casings and prick all the air bubbles before tying a bubble knot to seal them.

13. Hang the bologna on sausage sticks in the refrigerator and air-dry overnight to form a pellicle.

14. Hot-smoke the bologna at 160°F/71°C using medium smoke from hickory, or hard wood of your choice, until they turn a reddish color, 30 minutes to 1 hour.

15. Poach the bologna in 160° to 170°F/71° to 77°C water to an internal temperature of 155°F/68°C.

16. Shock in an ice-water bath until the bologna drops to an internal temperature of 60°F/16°C. Blot dry and store in the refrigerator. Do not freeze.

Note: If desired, the bologna may instead be cold-smoked, using hickory or any hard wood of your choice, for 3 hours at 70° to 100°F/21° to 38°C before poaching.

If bulk bologna is preferred, you can use a beef bung casing instead.

Variations:

To each fully prepared basic recipe, before stuffing into casings fold in 4 lb/1.81 kg of one of the following garnish ingredients:

Ham Bologna: Cured pork, cut in ¾- to 1-in/2- to 3-cm cubes

Amish Bologna: Cured, cooked, and diced pig head meat, cut in ¾-in/2-cm cubes

Tongue Bologna: Cured, cooked beef tongue, cut in ¾- to 1-in/2- to 3-cm cubes

turkey frankfurters

MAKES 12 LB 8 OZ/5.67 KG (APPROXIMATELY FORTY TO FORTY-FIVE 4-IN/10-CM LINKS)

CURE MIX

3¼ oz/92 g kosher salt

2 tsp/10 mL Insta Cure No. 1

¾ oz/21 g dextrose

SEASONINGS

¼ oz/7 g ground white pepper

¼ oz/7 g ground coriander

¼ oz/7 g ground nutmeg

½ oz/14 g onion powder

½ tsp/2.50 mL garlic powder

5 lb/2.27 kg boneless, skinless, lean turkey breast or thigh meat, cut into 1-in/3-cm cubes

4 lb/1.81 kg pork jowl fat, cleaned, cut into 1-in/3-cm cubes, partially frozen

3 lb/1.36 kg crushed ice

5½ oz/156 g nonfat dry milk

18 to 20 ft/5.49 to 6.10 m prepared sheep casings, or as needed

1. In a small mixing bowl, combine the cure mix ingredients. In a separate small bowl, combine the seasonings.

2. In a mixing bowl, combine the turkey with the cure mix and seasonings. Place in resealable plastic bags, press out all the air, and chill the turkey thoroughly or partially freeze. Place the jowl fat in resealable plastic bags, press out all the air, and chill the jowl fat until thoroughly frozen.

3. Progressively grind the turkey from the coarse plate (³⁄₈ in/9 mm) through the fine plate (¹⁄₈ in/3 mm) into a mixing bowl over an ice bath. Reserve under refrigeration.

4. Progressively grind the jowl fat from the coarse plate (³⁄₈ in/9 mm) through the fine plate (¹⁄₈ in/3 mm) into a mixing bowl over an ice bath. Reserve under refrigeration.

5. Transfer the ground turkey to a Stephan cutter. Add the ice. Process until the mixture reaches a temperature of 30°F/−1°C. Continue processing until the temperature rises to 40°F/4°C.

6. Add the jowl fat and process until the temperature reaches 50°F/10°C.

7. Add the nonfat dry milk and process until the temperature reaches 58°F/14°C.

8. Make a taste tester and adjust the seasoning as needed.

9. Place the mixture into a sausage stuffer, making sure there are no air pockets. Stuff into the prepared casings. Measure, pinch, and twist into 6-in/15-cm lengths and tie with thin string.

10. Hang the frankfurters on sausage sticks in the refrigerator overnight to air-dry and form a pellicle.

11. Hot-smoke the frankfurters, using hickory or any hard wood of your choice, in a preheated smokehouse at 120°F/49°C for about 1 hour. Apply a medium smoke and increase the smoke temperature to 130°F/54°C for about 1 hour. Then increase the smokehouse temperature to 160°F/71°C and apply a medium smoke again to obtain the desired color.

12. Poach them in 170°F/77°C water to an internal temperature of 155°F/68°C.

13. Shock in an ice-water bath until the frankfurters' internal temperature drops to 60°F/16°C.

14. The frankfurters may be stored for 1 to 2 weeks under refrigeration or can be frozen for 2 to 3 weeks until needed.

Variation: After the frankfurters have air-dried in the refrigerator overnight, cold-smoke them, using hickory or any hard wood of your choice, at less than 80°F/27°C until the desired color is achieved, 1 to 1½ hours. Follow the instructions for poaching and shocking.

wisconsin-style smoked cheddar and jalapeño sausage

MAKES 14 LB/6.35 KG (APPROXIMATELY FORTY TO FORTY-FIVE 6-IN/15-CM LINKS)

2 lb 12 oz/1.25 kg boneless beef shoulder, 80/20, cleaned, cut into 1-in/3-cm cubes

5 lb 8 oz/2.50 kg pork butt, 80/20, cleaned, cut into 1-in/3-cm cubes

2 lb 12 oz/1.25 kg pork belly, 50/50, skinned, cut into 1-in/3-cm cubes

4⅓ oz/122.36 g kosher salt

½ oz/12.43 g Insta Cure No. 1

½ oz/12.43 g sodium tripolyphosphate

2 cups/480 mL cold water

1 lb/454 g crushed ice

4⅓ oz/122.36 g light corn syrup

¾ oz/24.80 g dextrose

⅔ oz/16.26 g ground black pepper

¼ oz/6.12 g Colman's dry mustard

⅛ oz/3.10 g garlic powder

0.03 oz/0.78 g ground ginger

Pinch oz/2.71 g sodium erythorbate

1. Place all of the cubed meat in the freezer and leave until partially frozen.

2. Grind the beef shoulder through a coarse plate into a mixing bowl set over an ice bath. Reserve under refrigeration.

3. Grind the pork butt through a coarse plate into another mixing bowl set over an ice bath. Reserve under refrigeration.

4. Grind the pork belly through a coarse plate into a third mixing bowl set over an ice bath. Reserve under refrigeration.

5. Combine the ground beef and pork butt. Transfer to a mixer with a paddle attachment. Start mixing on speed #1. Add the salt and Insta Cure and continue mixing for 1 minute on speed #1.

6. Dissolve the sodium tripolyphosphate in the water. Add half of the water to the meat. Add the pork belly, the ice, corn syrup, dextrose, pepper, mustard, garlic powder, ginger, sodium erythorbate, and ground jalapeños. Mix for 5 minutes on speed #1. Chill the mixture until semifrozen.

7. Regrind the mixture through a ³/₁₆-in/5-mm plate into a mixing bowl set over an ice bath. Reserve under refrigeration.

8. Rehydrate the whole jalapeños for 5 minutes in enough water to soften. Drain off and discard any excess water. Transfer the mixture to a mixer with a paddle attachment. Add the Cheddar cheese and rehydrated jalapeños and the other half of the water-phosphate mixture. Mix for 2 minutes on speed #1.

9. Place the mixture into a sausage stuffer, making sure there are no air pockets. Stuff into the prepared casings. Measure, pinch, and twist into 6-in/15-cm lengths, and tie with twine.

0.10 oz/2.85 g ground
dried jalapeños or
jalapeño powder

0.60 oz/17 g dehydrated or
fresh jalapeños, deseeded,
dried, and cut in half

2 lb/907 g Cheddar
cheese, shredded

8 ft/2.44 m hog casings,
or as needed

10. Hang the sausages on sausage sticks in the refrigerator overnight to air-dry and form a pellicle.

11. Hot-smoke the sausages using a hard wood, like hickory, at 120°F/49°C for 2 hours, then 130°F/54°C for 2 hours, and finally at 185°F/85°C to an internal temperature of 155°F/68°C.

12. Shock the sausage in ice-water until an internal temperature of 60°F/16°C is reached, then hang them on sausage sticks to air-dry.

13. The sausages may be stored under refrigeration for up to 4 days or can be frozen for 2 to 3 weeks.

wisconsin-style smoked wild rice sausage

MAKES 14 LB/6.35 KG (APPROXIMATELY FORTY-FIVE TO FIFTY 4-INCH LINKS)

2 lb 12 oz/1.25 kg boneless beef shoulder, 80/20, cleaned, cut into 1-in/3-cm cubes

5 lb 8 oz/2.50 kg pork butt, 80/20, boneless, cut into 1-in/3-cm cubes

2 lb 12 oz/1.25 kg pork belly, 50/50, skinned, cut into 1-in/3-cm cubes

4⅓ oz/122.36 g kosher salt

½ oz/12.43 g Insta Cure No. 1

½ oz/12.43 g sodium tripolyphosphate

2 cups/480 mL water

1 lb/454 g crushed ice

4⅓ oz/122.36 g light corn syrup

¾ oz/24.80 g dextrose

⅔ oz/19.10 g ground black pepper

¼ oz/6.12 g Colman's dry mustard

⅛ oz/3.10 g garlic powder

Pinch oz/0.78 g ground ginger

0.096 oz/2.71 g sodium erythorbate

⅛ oz/2.84 g onion powder

1 lb 2 oz/511 g wild rice, cooked, cooled

7 to 8 ft/2.13 to 2.44 m prepared hog casings, or as needed

1. Place all of the cubed meat in the freezer until partially frozen.

2. Separately grind the pork butt, beef, and pork belly through a coarse plate into separate mixing bowls set over an ice bath. Reserve under refrigeration.

3. Combine the ground beef and pork butt. Transfer to a mixer with a paddle attachment. Start mixing on speed #1. Add the salt and Insta Cure and continue mixing for 1 minute on speed #1.

4. Dissolve the sodium tripolyphosphate in half of the water. Then add the other half of the water to the meat. Add the ground pork belly, ice, corn syrup, dextrose, pepper, mustard, garlic powder, ginger, and sodium erythorbate. Mix for 5 minutes on speed #1. Chill the mixture until partially frozen.

5. Regrind the mixture through a ³⁄₁₆-in/5-mm plate into a mixing bowl set over an ice bath.

6. Transfer the mixture to a mixer with a paddle attachment. Add the other half of water with the phosphate, the onion powder, and rice, and mix for 2 minutes on speed #1. Mix well, make a taste tester, and adjust the seasonings if needed.

7. Place the mixture into a sausage stuffer, making sure there are no air pockets. Stuff into the prepared casings. Measure, pinch, and twist into 6-in/15-cm lengths and tie with twine.

8. Hang the sausages on sausage sticks in the refrigerator overnight to air-dry and form a pellicle.

9. Hot-smoke the sausages using a hard wood like hickory at a medium smoke intensity at 120°F/49°C for 2 hours, then at 130°F/54°C for 2 hours, and finally at 185°F/85°C, to an internal temperature of 155°F/68°C.

10. Shock the sausage in an ice-water bath until an internal temperature of 60°F/16°C is reached, then on sausage sticks to air-dry.

11. The sausages may be stored under refrigeration for up to 4 days or frozen for 2 to 3 weeks.

dried chorizo

8 lb/3.63 kg boneless pork butt, cleaned, certified, cut into ½- to 1-in/1- to 3-cm cubes (see Notes)

2 lb/907 g boneless pork, 50/50, cleaned, certified, cut into ½- to 1-in/1- to 3-cm cubes (see Notes)

7 tbsp/105 mL kosher salt

1 cup/240 mL distilled white vinegar

4 tbsp/60 mL smoked Spanish paprika

3 tbsp/45 mL cayenne

3 tbsp/45 mL granulated garlic

3 tbsp/45 mL fresh chopped oregano

2 tsp/10 mL coarsely ground black pepper

2 tsp/10 mL Insta Cure No. 2

3 tbsp/45 mL light corn syrup solids

1½ cups/360 mL Fermento

1 cup/240 mL ice-cold water

10 ft/3.05 m prepared hog casings, or as needed

1. Place the pork butt and 50/50 pork into resealable plastic bags (5 lb/2.27 kg per bag), press out all the air, and partially freeze.

2. Grind the meat and fat through the coarse plate (³/₈ in/9 mm) into a mixing bowl over an ice bath.

3. Transfer the ground meats to a mixer with a paddle attachment. Add the salt, vinegar, paprika, cayenne, granulated garlic, oregano, pepper, Insta Cure, corn syrup solids, Fermento, and water and mix well.

4. Transfer the meat to a clean storage container and pack it very well to avoid air pockets. Place plastic wrap directly on top of the meat and cover with a lid. Cure the meat in the refrigerator overnight at 38°F/3°C.

5. Grind the meat through the medium plate (¼ in/6 mm) into a mixing bowl over an ice bath.

6. Place the mixture into a sausage stuffer, making sure there are no air pockets. Stuff into the prepared casings. Measure, pinch, and twist every 8 in/20 cm, and tie with twine.

7. Place the sausage on sausage sticks, leaving about 1 in/3 cm or so between links as you hang to ferment, Allow the sausage to ferment for 3 days at 70° to 75°F/21° to 24°C with a relative humidity of 70 to 80 percent.

8. Space the sausages 3 to 4 in/8 to 10 cm apart and dry for 15 days at 50° to 55°F/10 to 13°C and a relative humidity of 60 to 70 percent.

9. The chorizo may be stored under refrigeration for up to 3 weeks or frozen for up to 1 month.

Notes: Like other dry, uncooked sausages in this book, this recipe requires that certified pork be used. See the table on "Certifying Pork via Freezing" on page 63.

Chorizo can be made using a combination of any lean cut of pork plus jowl fat or skinned pork belly, or 100 percent pork butt.

Chorizo in tortillas with salsa

spanish chorizo

MAKES 9 LB/4.08 KG (APPROXIMATELY THIRTY-TWO TO
THIRTY-SIX 5-IN/13-CM LINKS)

SEASONING MIX

½ cup/120 mL
cream sherry

2 tbsp/30 mL kosher salt

1 cup/240 mL
smoked paprika

1½ tsp/7.50 mL
Insta Cure No. 2

2 tsp/10 mL dextrose

2 tsp/10 mL
granulated garlic

2 tsp/10 mL coarsely
ground black pepper

2 lb/907 g boneless
pork butt, certified,
70/30, cut into 1-in/3-
cm cubes (see Notes)

5 lb/2.27 kg boneless pork
butt, certified, cleaned
of fat and sinew, cut
into 1-in/3-cm cubes

2 lb/907 g pork belly
or jowl fat, 50/50, cut
into 1-in/3-cm cubes

7 ft/2.13 m prepared hog
casings, or as needed

1. In a small mixing bowl, combine the ingredients for the seasoning mix.

2. In a large mixing bowl, combine the cubed pork butts with half of the seasoning mix. In another bowl, combine the 50/50 pork with the remaining seasoning mix. Transfer each meat to resealable plastic bags, press out all the air, and refrigerate overnight.

3. Semifreeze the pork butt and 50/50 pork.

4. Grind the pork butt through the coarse plate (³⁄₈ in/9 mm) into a mixing bowl set over an ice bath. Reserve under refrigeration.

5. Grind the 50/50 pork through the medium plate (¼ in/6 mm) into a mixing bowl over an ice bath.

6. Combine the ground pork butt and the 50/50 pork and transfer to a mixer fitted with a paddle attachment. Mix on speed #1 for 1 minute, then on speed #2 until the mixture is sticky, 15 to 30 seconds.

7. Make a taste tester and adjust the seasoning if needed.

8. Place the mixture into a sausage stuffer, making sure there are no air pockets. Stuff into the prepared casings. Measure, pinch, and twist into 5-in/13-cm lengths, and tie with twine.

9. Hang the sausages on sausage sticks in the refrigerator overnight to air-dry and form a pellicle.

Option 1, Cold-Smoke: Cold-smoke the sausages at 70°F/21°C or less, using hickory or any hard wood of your choice, for 12 to 14 hours. Air-dry for 12 hours at 60° to 70°F/16° to 21°C with a relative humidity of 60 to 70 percent. The sausages may be stored under refrigeration for up to 2 weeks.

Option 2, Cold-Smoke: Cold-smoke the sausages 70°F/21°C or less, using hickory or any hard wood of your choice, for 2 hours after letting the meat hang at 77°F/ 25°C for 48 hours.

(continued)

Option 3, Dry-Cure: Dry-cure the sausages at 50°F/10°C and 75 percent relative humidity until the sausages lose 25 percent of their weight, 10 to 15 days. Remove any mold that forms with a rag dipped in a vinegar-water solution. The sausages may be stored under refrigeration for up to 3 weeks.

Notes: This sausage is commonly used in paellas and to flavor other dishes.

Like other dry, uncooked sausages in this book, this recipe requires that certified pork be used. See the table on "Certifying Pork via Freezing" on page 63.

Although it is most often cooked, this sausage can be eaten raw as an appetizer or as bar food.

calabrese salami

MAKES 11 LB/4.99 KG

6 lb/2.72 kg boneless pork butt, certified, cleaned, cut into 1-in/3-cm cubes (see Note)

2 lb/907 g pork fatback, certified, cut into 1-in/3-cm cubes

2 lb/907 g pork belly, certified, skinned, cut into 1-in/3-cm cubes

3½ tbsp/52.50 mL kosher salt

2½ tbsp/37.50 mL glucose

3 tbsp/45 mL red pepper flakes

2 tsp/10 mL Insta Cure No. 2

1 tbsp/45 mL ground white pepper

2 tsp/10 mL anise seed

½ tsp/2.50 mL ascorbic acid

¼ tsp/1.25 mL F-LC SafePro starter culture

2 tbsp/30 mL distilled water

1 cup/240 mL sweet vermouth

12 ft/3.66 m prepared hog casings, or as needed

1. In a large mixing bowl, mix the pork butt, fatback, and pork belly. Transfer to resealable plastic bags, press out all the air, and place in the freezer until partially frozen.

2. Grind the pork mixture through the coarse plate (⅜ in/9 mm) into a mixing bowl over an ice bath.

3. Mix in the salt, glucose, red pepper flakes, Insta Cure, white pepper, anise seed, and ascorbic acid. Dissolve the starter culture in the distilled water and add to the meat mixture. Add the vermouth to the meat.

4. Transfer the mixture to a mixer fitted with a paddle attachment. Mix on speed #1 for 1 minute, then speed #2 until the mixture is sticky, 15 to 30 seconds.

5. Cut the hog casings into 24-in/61-cm lengths and tie a bubble knot at one end of each one.

6. Stuff the prepared casings and prick all of the air bubbles before tying a bubble knot to seal them. Pinch and tie each salami in the middle. Weigh the salamis to get the green weight.

7. Hang the salamis in the refrigerator at around 38° to 40°F/3° to 4°C to dry for 3 hours.

8. Place the salamis in an area at 75° to 80°F/24° to 27°C at about 80 percent relative humidity for about 24 hours.

9. Let the temperature drop to about 70°F/21°C and hold for the next 6 hours at 70°F/21°C.

10. Hold the salamis in an area at 60°F/16°C with about 70 percent relative humidity, until they lose about 30 percent of their green weight, about 6 weeks. A white mold should grow on the salamis during this time. This is beneficial and preserves the salamis while making it hard for other bacteria to grow. Check on the salamis toward the end of the 6 weeks to make sure that the casings do not harden. If the casings start to harden, adjust the moisture/humidity as needed, increasing the humidity so the casings do not dry too fast.

Note: Like other dry, uncooked sausages in this book, this recipe requires that certified pork be used. See the table on "Certifying Pork via Freezing" on page 63.

dry-cured genoa salami

MAKES 10 LB/4.54 KG

7 lb/3.18 kg boneless lean pork, cleaned, certified, cut into 1-in/3-cm cubes (see Notes)

1 lb 8 oz/680 kg boneless pork, 50/50, certified, cut into 1-in/3-cm cubes

1 lb 8 oz/680 kg pork fatback, certified, cut into 1-in/3-cm cubes

7 tbsp/105 mL kosher salt

3 tbsp/45 mL light corn syrup solids

1 tbsp/15 mL black peppercorns

1 tbsp/15 mL ground white pepper

1 tbsp/15 mL garlic powder

4 tsp/20 mL yellow mustard seeds

2 tbsp/30 mL hot paprika

1 tbsp/15 mL anise seeds, crushed

⅓ cup/80 mL dry white wine, preferably Italian

2 tsp/10 mL Insta Cure No. 2

2 tbsp/30 mL light corn syrup

Starter culture (see Notes), as needed

Distilled water, as needed

½ tsp/2.50 mL sodium erythorbate

½ cup/120 mL ice-cold grappa

1 prepared hog bung (20 in/51 cm; see Notes)

1. Combine the lean pork, 50/50 pork, and fatback. Place in resealable plastic bags, press out all the air, and partially freeze.

2. Grind the meat through a ¾-in/2-cm plate into a mixing bowl over an ice bath.

3. Transfer the mixture to a mixer with a paddle attachment. Add the salt, corn syrup solids, black peppercorns, white pepper, garlic powder, mustard seeds, paprika, anise seeds, wine, Insta Cure, and corn syrup. Mix on speed #1 for 1 minute, then on speed #2 until the mixture is sticky, 15 to 30 seconds.

4. Place the mixture not more than 6 in/15 cm high into plastic containers and pack tightly to get rid of any air pockets. Place plastic wrap directly on top of the meat and cover tightly with a lid. Place in a cooler at 38°F/3°C for 48 hours.

5. Transfer the meat mixture to a mixing bowl. Measure the correct amount of starter culture according to package specifications. Dissolve the starter culture in enough distilled water to obtain a slurry consistency. Dissolve the sodium erythorbate in the grappa. Add the starter culture and sodium erythorbate to the meat mixture and mix well. Make a taste tester and adjust the seasoning if necessary.

6. Tie a bubble knot at one end of the hog bung. Stuff the prepared hog bung firmly with the salami mixture. Prick all the air bubbles before tying a bubble knot to seal the bung. Place the hog bung in a net for better handling.

7. Hang the salami to cure at 70° to 75°F/21° to 24°C with a relative humidity of 70 to 80 percent for 48 hours.

8. After the 48 hours, hang the salami in a cooler at 45° to 55°F/7° to 13°C with a relative humidity of 75 percent for 70 to 80 days.

9. The salami may be stored under refrigeration for up to 3 weeks or it may be frozen for up to 1 month for later use.

Notes: Like other dry, uncooked sausages in this book, this recipe requires that certified pork be used. See the table on "Certifying Pork via Freezing" on page 63.

Different commercial starters may use different amounts; follow the package specifications. In place of the hog bung, you can use protein-lined casings or cloth casings.

Variation: When using hog bungs, after stuffing the salamis, place them in a brine at a 50-degree salinometer reading at a temperature of 34 to 38° F/1° to 3°C for 1 or 2 days. After removing the salami from the brine, place it into simmering water for 3 seconds. This process will help to remove all of the excess fat and will open the pores of the hog bung, which in turn promotes the drying of the salami.

california spicy sopressata

MAKES APPROXIMATELY 6 LB/2.72 KG (APPROXIMATELY SIX 1-LB/454-G SAUSAGES)

3 lb 12 oz/1.70 kg boneless pork butt, certified, cleaned, cut into ½- to 1-in/1- to 3-cm cubes (see Note)

1 lb 4 oz/567 g boneless pork, 50/50, certified, cleaned, cut into ½- to 1-in/1- to 3-cm cubes

1 tsp/5 mL Insta Cure No. 2

2¼ oz/64 g Kosher salt

2 tbsp/30 mL light corn syrup

8 oz/227 g pork fatback, small dice, frozen, ground through ¼-in/6-mm plate and reserved for garnish

2 tsp/10 mL very coarsely ground black pepper

1 tbsp/15 mL red pepper flakes, crushed medium fine

1 tsp/5 mL garlic powder

1 tbsp/15 mL hot paprika

1 tsp/5 mL cayenne

½ cup/120 mL ice-cold grappa

2 tsp/10 mL anise seeds, crushed

20 ft/6.10 m prepared beef round casings, or as needed

1. In a mixing bowl, combine the pork butt and the 50/50 pork, with the Insta Cure, salt, and corn syrup. Pack in resealable plastic bags, press out all the air, and freeze until partially frozen.

2. Place the fatback in a plastic bag, freeze, and grind through a ¼-in/6-mm plate. Reserve under refrigeration.

3. Grind the mixture twice through the medium plate (¼ in/6 mm) into a mixing bowl over an ice bath. Reserve half under refrigeration and grind the other half through the fine plate (⅛ in/3 mm) into a mixing bowl over an ice bath.

4. Combine all the ground meats in a mixer with a paddle attachment. Add the fatback, the black pepper, red pepper, garlic powder, paprika, cayenne, grappa, and anise seeds and mix on speed #1 for 1 minute, then on speed #2 until the mixture is sticky, 15 to 30 seconds.

5. Make a taste tester and adjust the seasoning if necessary.

6. Cut the beef round casings into 8-in/10-cm lengths and tie a bubble knot at one end of each piece.

7. Place the mixture into a sausage stuffer, making sure there are no air pockets. Stuff the prepared casings and prick all the air bubbles before tying a bubble knot to seal them. Weigh the sopressata to get the green weights and record the weights.

8. Hang the sopressata for 4 days in a 50°F/10°C environment with low humidity and a lot of air movement.

9. Hang in a refrigerator until firm, about 4 weeks. The sopressata is ready when it has lost 20 to 25 percent of its green weight.

10. The sopressata may be stored for up to 3 weeks under refrigeration.

Note: Like other dry, uncooked sausages in this book, this recipe requires that certified pork be used. See the table on "Certifying Pork via Freezing" on page 63.

kabanosy

5 lb/2.27 kg boneless pork butt, cleaned, cut into 1-in/3-cm cubes

1 lb/454 g pork belly, skinned, cut into 1-in/3-cm cubes

5 tbsp/75 mL kosher salt

2 tsp/10 mL Insta Cure No. 1

3 tbsp/45 mL dextrose

4 lb/1.81 kg boneless fresh ham, cleaned, cut into 1-in/3-cm cubes

4 tsp/20 mL ground black pepper

2 garlic cloves, mashed

1¼ tsp/6.25 mL ground nutmeg

2 tsp/10 mL caraway seeds, ground

20 ft/6.10 m prepared sheep casings (.85 in/22 mm), or as needed

1. In a mixing bowl, combine the pork butt and pork belly with 2½ tbsp/37.50 mL of the salt, 1 tsp/5 mL of the Insta Cure, and 1½ tbsp/22.50 mL of the dextrose; mix well. Transfer to a resealable plastic bag, press out all the air, and place in the freezer until partially frozen.

2. In another mixing bowl, combine the fresh ham with the remaining salt, Insta Cure, and dextrose; mix well. Transfer to a resealable plastic bag, press out all the air, and place in the freezer until partially frozen.

3. Grind the pork butt and pork belly through a ³⁄₁₆-in/5-mm plate into a mixing bowl over an ice bath. Reserve under refrigeration.

4. Grind the fresh ham through the fine plate (⅛ in/3 mm) into a separate mixing bowl over an ice bath.

5. Transfer the ground meats to a mixer with a paddle attachment. Add the pepper, garlic, nutmeg, and caraway and mix on speed #1 for 1 minute, then on speed #2 until the mixture is sticky, 15 to 30 seconds.

6. Make a taste tester and adjust the seasoning as needed.

7. Place the mixture into a sausage stuffer, making sure there are no air pockets. Stuff into the prepared casings. Measure, pinch, and twist into 24-in/61-cm lengths and tie with twine. Weigh the links to get the green weight and record the weights.

8. Place the links on sausage sticks and hang overnight at 39°F/4°C to air-dry and form a pellicle.

9. Cold-smoke the kabanosy, using hickory wood and a medium-smoke intensity for 3 hours.

10. Hot-smoke the kabanosy using hard wood like hickory and a medium-smoke intensity at 120°F/49°C for 1 hour, then at 130°F/54°C for 1 hour more.

11. Finish hot-smoking the kabanosy at 185°F/85°C to an internal temperature of 155°F68°C. The kabanosy should have a dark brown color.

12. Remove the links from the smokehouse and cure for 7 days at 65°F/18°C and about 70 percent humidity until they reach 55 percent of their green weight.

13. The kabanosy may be stored under refrigeration for up to 2 weeks and can be frozen for about 2 to 3 weeks.

landjäger

7 lb 8 oz/3.41 kg boneless beef shoulder, cleaned, cut into 1-in/3-cm cubes

5 lb/2.27 kg boneless lean pork, certified, cleaned, cut into 1-in/3-cm cubes (see Note)

½ oz/14 g Insta Cure No. 2

1½ tsp/7.50 mL garlic powder

5 oz/142 g ice-cold water

2 tsp/10 mL ground caraway seeds

1 oz/28 g dextrose

4½ oz/128 g kosher salt

3 oz/85 g Fermento

¾ tsp/3.75 mL finely ground black pepper

8 to 10 ft/2.44 to 3.05 m prepared hog casings, or as needed

1. In a mixing bowl, combine the beef, pork, and Insta Cure. Place in resealable plastic bags, press out all the air, and partially freeze.

2. Progressively grind the meats from the coarse plate (³/₈ in/9 mm) through the fine plate (¹/₈ in/3 mm) into a mixing bowl over an ice bath.

3. Transfer the ground meats to a mixer with a paddle attachment and add the garlic powder, water, caraway, dextrose, salt, Fermento, and pepper. Mix on speed #1 until the meat feels sticky, about 1 minute.

4. Make a taste tester and adjust the seasoning as needed.

5. Place the mixture into a sausage stuffer, making sure there are no air pockets. Stuff into the prepared casings and press the sausages in a landjäger mold.

6. Place the mold on a plastic sheet tray. Cover the mold with plastic wrap and weight the sausages by setting two wooden cutting boards on top of the press. Remove the sausages from the mold and place in a refrigerator at 38° to 40°F/3° to 4°C for 2 to 4 days, so they will hold their square shape.

7. Cold-smoke the sausages at 70°F/21°C or less, using hickory or a hard wood of your choice, for 12 to 24 hours.

8. Dry at 65°F/18°C with a relative humidity of 60 percent for 3 to 4 days, until the desired firmness is reached.

9. The sausage may be stored for up to 2 weeks under refrigeration or can be frozen for 1 to 2 months.

Note: Like other dry, uncooked sausages in this book, this recipe requires that certified pork be used. See the table on "Certifying Pork via Freezing" on page 63.

cotechino

8 oz/227 g pork skin, cut into ¼ by ¾-in/6 mm by 2-cm strips

1 vanilla bean, split

¾ cup/180 mL white wine

5 garlic cloves, minced

¼ tsp/1.25 mL ground allspice

8 bay leaves

4 lb 8 oz/2.04 kg boneless pork butt, lean, cleaned, cut into 1-in/3-cm cubes

¼ cup/60 mL kosher salt

1½ tsp/7.50 mL ground black pepper

1 lb 8 oz/680 g pork jowl fat, cleaned, cut into 2-in/5-cm cubes

0.26 oz/7.28 g Insta Cure No. 1

1½ tsp/7.50 mL black peppercorns

4 ft/1.22 m prepared beef middle casings

1. Boil the skin with the vanilla bean in water to cover until the skin is tender, about 2 hours.

2. Drain the skin. Remove and discard the vanilla bean. While hot, toss the skin with the wine, garlic, allspice, and bay leaves. Cool to room temperature.

3. Season the pork butt with the salt and ground pepper. Transfer the pork butt to resealable plastic bags and place in a freezer until semifrozen.

4. Grind the pork butt through a medium plate (¼ in/6 mm) into a mixing bowl over an ice bath. Reserve under refrigeration.

5. Transfer the jowl fat to resealable plastic bags and place in a freezer until semifrozen. Grind the jowl fat through a medium plate (¼ in/6 mm) into another mixing bowl over an ice bath. Reserve under refrigeration.

6. Remove the bay leaves and then grind the cold pork skin through the fine plate (⅛ in/3 mm) into a third mixing bowl over an ice bath.

7. In a mixing bowl over an ice bath, combine the ground pork butt, pork skin, pork fat, Insta Cure, and peppercorns and mix well.

8. Make a taste tester and adjust the seasoning if necessary.

9. Cut the casings into 12-in/30-cm lengths. Tie each piece at one end with a bubble knot. Place the mixture into a sausage stuffer, making sure there are no air pockets. Stuff into the casings and prick all the air bubbles before tying a bubble knot to seal them.

10. Weigh the cotechino to get their green weight and record the weights.

11. Hang to dry in an area at 60°F/16°C at 60 to 75 percent relative humidity for 4 to 6 weeks. The cotechino is ready when it has lost 10 to 15 percent of its green weight.

12. Poach the cotechino in 160° to 170°F/71° to 77°C water for 1 hour to an internal temperature of 155°F/68°C, then cool in an ice-water bath to an internal temperature of 60°F/16°C.

13. The sausages may be stored for up to 1 week under refrigeration or can be frozen for 2 to 3 weeks.

Variation

Zambone: To make this traditional Italian charcuterie item, cure 1 boned trotter each under refrigeration in a solution of 2 lb/907 g salt, 1 lb/454 g granulated sugar, and 1 gal/3.84 L water for 24 hours. Drain and rinse the trotters and stuff with the cotechino mixture. Braise or cold-smoke. If cold-smoking, do so for about 2 hours on medium-high smoke, using a hard wood like hickory. Finish with another cooking method. Zambone may be served hot or cold.

condiments

{ chapter nine

We will look at condiments used in charcuterie to complement and bring out the flavors of the product.

Back to front, left to right: Spiced Watermelon Rind (page 328), Fresh-Pack Dill Pickles (page 319), Pickled Seckel Pears (page 323), Pickle Relish (page 304), Zesty Cranberry Ketchup (page 315), Sweet Pickle Chips (page 330), Apple and Banana Chutney (page 311), Sweet Mixed-Pickle Chow Chow (page 329), Mustard Horseradish Sauce (page 296), Pickled Red Onion (page 322), Mango, Papaya, Orange, and Lime Salsa (page 316).

Saucemaking is an art. A good sauce can change an ordinary dish into something extraordinary. . . . Sauce can run the gamut, from the classical French Mother sauces that can often require many hours of preparation with expensive ingredients, to simple preparations that take only a few minutes to incorporate together. —BONEWERKS CULINARTÉ

When I look back on my time as saucier in Le Chantilly restaurant in New York City, I remember the sauces required hours to develop the rich sheen and transparency they possessed and the flavor they brought to the plates they were to enhance.

The use of sauces has changed dramatically during the past fifteen years. We have been influenced by various cuisines, cultures, and nutritional data in a way that has shaped a new outlook on the food industry. The old sauces, though rich in flavor and texture, are being replaced by lighter, highly flavored glazes and sauces that are used more as final seasoning agents than anything else. Newer ways of making these sauces might seem simple, but you need a good grasp of the basic sauce making to bring your ingredients together to create a complete plate.

There are myriad cold sauces you may be familiar with that remind me of the sauces I made as a saucier. The first that comes to mind is a Cumberland sauce, which accompanies terrines, pâtés, and galantines. There are also mayonnaise-based sauces such as sauce gribiche, sauce rémoulade, sauce verte, and—of course—tartar sauce, which we associate with New England and fried foods. There are vinaigrette-based sauces like mignonette sauce, which is used for oysters.

cold sauces

Cold sauces should bring flavor, moisture, sheen, and visual interest to the plate.

TYPES OF COLD SAUCES

Coulis and purées

Emulsions

Coating sauces

Dairy-based sauces

Contemporary sauces

Note: Parts of this chapter are based on material from Escoffier's *Le Guide Culinaire* (London, Heinemann, 1986); *The Sauce Bible: A Guide to the Saucier's Craft* by David Paul Larousse (Wiley, 1993); *Condiments: The Art of Buying, Making, and Using Mustards, Oils, Vinegars, Chutneys, Relishes, Sauces, Savory Jellies, and More*, by Kathy Gunst (G. P. Putnam, 1984); *and Sauces: Classical and Contemporary Sauce Making* by James Peterson (Wiley, 2008).

coulis and purées

The classic definition of a coulis, according to Escoffier in *Le Guide Culinaire*, is the "well reduced, highly concentrated essential flavors of a food, in either purée or liquid form." The word *purée* is frequently used interchangeably with coulis. In the modern cold kitchen, coulis are made by puréeing raw or cooked fruits or vegetables to a sauce-like consistency. They are usually thickened by the pulp of the main ingredient, or sometimes by reduction. The texture of these sauces can range from very light and smooth to coarse. They have a slightly thicker and grainier texture than a refined or roux-thickened sauce. They may be served as is, or may be adjusted by adding stocks, wines, infusions, oils, or cream.

Coulis and purées may begin to weep a clear liquid as they sit. To prevent this, bring the sauce to a simmer and add a small amount of diluted arrowroot or cornstarch. This is a helpful practice whenever advanced plating is required, as might be the case for a banquet or reception.

emulsions

Vinaigrettes and mayonnaise are two emulsions made by combining ingredients that would not otherwise blend into a homogenous mixture. In order to understand how these sauces are prepared, we will first discuss what an emulsion is and how it is formed. An emulsion consists of two phases: the dispersed phase and the continuous phase. When making vinaigrette, for example, the dispersed phase is the oil, meaning that the oil has broken up into very small droplets by either shaking or mixing the sauce. Each oil droplet is suspended throughout the continuous phase—in this case the vinegar.

temporary emulsions

Temporary emulsions, such as vinaigrettes, form quickly and require only the mechanical action of whipping, shaking, or stirring. They are not stable and will break apart into their components when left to sit for a while.

semipermanent emulsions

To make an emulsion stable enough to keep the oil in suspension, additional ingredients known as emulsifiers are necessary. Emulsifiers used in cold sauces such as vinaigrettes include egg yolks, mustard, roasted garlic, fruit or vegetable purées, and glace de viande. A small addition of any of these can change a temporary emulsion into a semipermanent emulsion in which the texture is creamier and the emulsion will hold together for a longer period of time.

permanent emulsions

Stable permanent emulsions such as mayonnaise are made by very carefully controlling the rate at which the oil is added to the sauce. Egg yolks provide both the liquid that holds the oil droplets in suspension and a special emulsifier known as lecithin. The oil is added very gradually at first so that the droplets can be made extremely fine.

The more oil that is added to the yolks, the thicker the sauce will become. If the oil is added too rapidly early on, the emulsion cannot start to form properly. Also, if the emulsion becomes too thick early in the mixing process, the full amount of oil cannot be added; the sauce then needs to be thinned with a little water or an acid such as vinegar or lemon juice.

In Europe, mayonnaise is used more often as a sauce or an ingredient in sauces such as sauce Chantilly, sauce verte, aïoli, or rouille.

coating sauces

Although coating sauces are not as popular as they once were, they still have applications for the garde manger. They can be used to coat canapés and other hors d'oeuvres, to prepare platters for display and service, and to coat timbales and other appetizers. Chaud-froids were classically made by adding gelatin to a warm sauce such as demi-glace, béchamel, or velouté. Mayonnaise mixed with aspic was used next; the combination of sour cream and aspic is more common nowadays.

gelées

Clear coating sauces, known as aspic gelée or simply aspics, are made by clarifying stocks, juices, or essences and fortifying them with enough gelatin to achieve the desired strength. After making the aspic, temper the mixture by stirring it constantly with a rubber spatula over an ice bath to cool it to the proper temperature. Once it just begins to thicken, ladle or pour the aspic over the desired application.

Aspics are made by adding gelatin to clarified stocks or juices to achieve the strength desired for the chosen application.

Give slices of the finished product a glossy sheen by sealing with aspic solution before serving.

Different applications will call for different strengths of gelée. In this case, mousse-strength gelée is being used.

Aspic gelée is one of the more versatile coating sauces used in garde manger. It is also utilized frequently to seal an edible item, such as pâté en croûte, both after it is baked to fill in the air gaps and after it is sliced.

To check the gelatin strength, place the aspic in the refrigerator and allow it to set up until it is completely firm. That is, it should be cold and firm when you press your finger against the aspic. The more resistance when you press it, the stronger the gelatin strength and the firmer the hold. Use the chart for gelatin strength to determine what strength the aspic is, then determine the difference from the strength aspic you need. For example, suppose you need mousse-strength aspic, but you have delicate. Take the difference in the gelatin amount and weigh the gelatin; take your aspic that has been heated to room temperature. Sprinkle (rain) gelatin over the liquid, let bloom (absorb the water) for 5 to 10 minutes, and then heat on a water bath to 110°F/43°C. Now it is ready to use.

gelatin for aspic gelée

GEL STRENGTH	AMOUNT PER GALLON	AMOUNT PER PINT	POSSIBLE USES
Delicate gel	2 oz/57 g	¼ oz/7 g	When slicing is not required; individual portion of meat, vegetable, or fish bound by gelatin; jellied consommés
Coating gel	4 oz/113 g	½ oz/14 g	Edible chaud-froid; coating individual items
Sliceable gel	6 to 8 oz/170 to 227 g	1 oz/28 g	When product is to be sliced; filling pâté en croûte, head cheese
Firm gel	10 to 12 oz/ 284 to 340 g	1¼ to 1½ oz/ 35 to 43 g	Coating platters with underlayment for food show or competition
Mousse-strength gel	16 oz/454 g	2 oz/57 g	When product must retain shape after unmolding

dairy-based sauces

Dairy-based sauces are used as salad dressings or dips. They are easy to blend, and are made from natural bases: soft cheeses such as fraîche, quark, mascarpone, and cream cheese; cultured milks such as sour cream, crème fraîche, or buttermilk; heavy cream; or low- or reduced-fat versions of ricotta, sour cream, or cottage cheese. These dressing are generally white or ivory, so they can take on a pastel color from purées or coulis of herbs, fruits, or vegetables. The finished sauce is always opaque in appearance.

Chaud-froid with sealed-in garnishes

Chaud-froid made with demi-glace

Typical additions to dairy-based sauces are cheeses (especially blue cheese, Parmesan, and feta), fresh lemon, black pepper, and minced or puréed herbs. Diced, minced, or grated vegetables, pickles, capers, and olives add texture as well as flavor. Creamy sauces can be prepared in a range of textures, from a relatively stiff sauce to serve as a dip or spread to a pourable sauce that easily dresses a green salad. For a light, almost mousse-like texture, whipped cream can be folded into the sauce at the last moment.

contemporary sauces

Contemporary sauces are based on fresh, high-quality ingredients that are usually lighter, less caloric, and more nutritious. They are sometimes called simple or independent sauces because they are prepared independently of the foods they accompany. They derive none of their character from the preparation itself. These sauces may actually be simple, or complex.

ketchup

When it comes to hamburgers or French fries, nothing can beat the classic condiment we now know as ketchup. Today, when you ask someone what ketchup is, they will point you to the tomato-based sauce that is found on every diner counter and in virtually every household refrigerator in America. In reality, thought, the number of varieties of ketchup is enormous. But it is only over the past hundred years or so that "ketchup" has come to mean just this one sauce. To give you an idea, an old American cookbook included ketchups made from cucumbers, cranberries, onions, grapes, lemons, and apples, along with combinations like tomatoes and red wine or cucumbers and black pepper.

Although there is some disagreement about exactly where it came from, everyone agrees that what we now call ketchup originated somewhere in Asia as a salty fish-based sauce. If you try to trace it by linguistics, however, you can't get too precise; you have your choice of ketsiap from China, kechap from Malaysia, or ketjap from Indonesia.

Ketchup arrived in Europe sometime in the seventeenth century. However, since fish brine was not a common ingredient there, European versions of this condiment were based on vinegar and spices and contained a wide range of ingredients in place of the standard tomato we think of today. Making ketchup out of something was thought of primarily as a way of preserving that product, and home cooks and chefs alike made ketchups of everything from mushrooms to walnuts to horseradish root.

salsa

Salsas are combinations of more or less finely chopped vegetables and sometimes fruit. They may be raw (salsa cruda) or cooked, and are seasoned and flavored in many different ways, but usually contain hot peppers, coriander leaves (cilantro), lime juice, and tomatoes. The ingredients, instead of being puréed or infused into a liquid, are allowed to retain their texture and individuality within the mixture. Salsas are usually bright colored and have a direct and refreshing flavor. Because of this, the more traditional salsas are excellent with grilled and highly flavored foods. They can be surprisingly complex in flavor, and balance the dishes they are served with.

oils, vinegars, reductions, foams, and juice extractions

Good-quality oils and vinegars can be infused with spices, aromatics, herbs, and fruits or vegetables to create products with many applications. They work well as condiments, added in a drizzle or as droplets to lend a bit of intense flavor and color to a plated dish. They also are excellent to use as a dressing for vegetables, pastas, grains, or fruits. And, of course, they are well suited to use as part of vinaigrettes and other dressings for a special effect.

The oils and vinegars used may be of many varieties or infused with other food products such as herbs or garlic.)

METHODS FOR INFUSING OILS AND VINEGARS

Method 1: **WARM INFUSION:** Heat the oil or vinegar very gently over low heat with flavoring ingredients such as citrus zest or spices, just until the aroma is apparent. Let the liquid steep off of the heat with the flavoring ingredients until cool, then pour into storage bottles or containers. You may opt to strain the liquid for a clearer final product, or leave the flavoring ingredients in for more intensity. It is recommended to use damp cheesecloth when straining flavored vinegars.

Method 2: **STEEPING:** Place the herbs or other aromatics in a glass or plastic bottle. Heat the oil or vinegar briefly, just until warm. Pour the liquid over the aromatics, and let it rest until the desired flavor is achieved. You may wish to add fresh aromatics after the liquid has steeped for several days to give an even more intense flavor.

Method 3: **PURÉEING:** Purée raw, blanched, or fully cooked vegetables, herbs, or fruits. Bring the purée to a simmer, reducing if necessary to concentrate the flavors. Add the oil or vinegar and transfer to a storage container. You may leave the mixture as is and use it as you would a purée, or you may strain it to remove the fiber and pulp.

Method 4: **COLD INFUSION:** Combine room-temperature oil or vinegar with ground spices and transfer to a storage container. Let the mixture settle until the liquid is clear and the spices have settled in the bottom of the container. Carefully decant the liquid into a clean container once the desired flavor is reached.

Note: When you introduce fresh or raw ingredients to an oil or vinegar, you run the risk of food-borne illness if the finished product is not carefully stored. Although commercially prepared versions of flavored oils and vinegars are shelf stable, you should keep yours refrigerated, especially if you have used raw garlic or shallots, as those ingredients may be carrying *Clostridium botulinum* and the liquid provides the anaerobic environment necessary for its growth. Use them within a few days to be sure that they will have the best flavor and color.

FLAVORED OILS

Flavored oils have been made for centuries by cooks in the Mediterranean when they placed sprigs of herbs in jars of olive oil and used the infused oils for salads, to baste roasting meats, and as condiments for grilled fish. Recently, chefs have become much more interested in infused oils. By blanching and puréeing a wide variety of herbs and vegetables, chefs have created full-flavored, highly colored oils that can be emulsified with other ingredients in vinaigrettes or simply dribbled over foods as sauces themselves. Flavored oils can be prepared from a variety of spices and from concentrated vegetable juice as well. Although no less rich than butter, these oils contain no cholesterol and have a brightness of color and flavor that enhances a dish much more than butter.

VINEGARS

Like oil, vinegar can be used as a condiment by itself. It can be sprinkled over grilled or sautéed fish instead of a sauce or lemon juice. Malt vinegar is often used on fried fish. Vinegar and oil can be sprinkled on grilled dishes. You could also use aged vinegars like authentic balsamic or aged sherry vinegar, where just a few drops are placed on the items. Fruit-flavored vinegars are used as sauce for main items on a plate. Herbs such as basil, tarragon, thyme, rosemary, oregano, marjoram, savory, and lavender, and blends such as herbes de Provence are being used to flavor the vinegars, much as herbs are being used to flavor oils.

REDUCTIONS

Liquid is simmered separately and stirred constantly to evaporate excess quantity (such as water), thus reducing the volume of the liquid into a thicker consistency, providing a more intense flavor. The resulting liquid is strained and then used as a base for sauces, soups, and stews. Gravies, meat sauces, wine sauces, and fruit sauces are all examples of reduction sauces that are used to enhance the flavor of foods being served.

Cook the reduction sauce until evaporation decreases the sauce to half its beginning volume, turning down the heat to medium, being careful not to reduce the sauce too much, which would result in a somewhat dull-tasting sauce with less aroma. Some sauces require additional thickening, so it may be wise to add a little cornstarch or flour to assist with the consistency if necessary. Also, butter, extra-virgin olive oil, or cream can be added to provide a thicker or more flavorful sauce.

FOAMS

Foams consist of natural flavors, such as fruit juices, mixed with a gelling or stabilizing agent such as agar or lecithin, and either whipped with a handheld immersion blender or extruded through a whipped cream canister equipped with N_2O cartridges. Foams have been described as "airy," with the flavor taking precedence over the substance it is suspended in. Foams allow cooks to integrate new flavors without changing the physical composition of a dish.

JUICE EXTRACTIONS

Juice extractions provide the sauce maker with a variety of ways to enhance a sauce, dressing, or marinade's nutritional profile, flavor, and color. One of the simplest applications involves thickening the juice and using it as the primary sauce. You can also use the juice as a poaching liquid, which can impart flavor and color to many different vegetables and proteins. Beet juice is an example of an extraction used to naturally add color to other foods, such as pickled turnips or eggs. There are many different juice combinations you can create to achieve interesting flavors and aromas, or to intensify flavors already in a dish. You can also use the juice by itself as a dish: fresh vegetable juices as beverages on menus are always appreciated.

The best way to obtain fresh juice is through mechanical juice extractors that use sharp knives and centrifugal forces. Always use fully ripened fruits and vegetables, and thoroughly wash and/or scrub the fruit or vegetable before putting it through the extractor. Some juices should be simmered very gently to allow to self-clarify.

Freshly extracted juices spoil very quickly and loses their original flavor rapidly. They should be protected from high temperatures and light to avoid loss of nutrients and flavor. Keep them covered at all times; sealed jars work very well to extend the shelf life of extractions. They may also be frozen, protected well from air and freezer burn.

relish

Relish is a cooked, pickled, and chopped vegetable or fruit that is typically used as a condiment.

A relish may be as simple as a mound of sliced cucumbers or radishes, or as complex as a curried onion relish, cooked in a pickle or brine, highly seasoned, and garnished with dried fruits. Relishes are served cold to act as a foil to hot or spicy foods, or to liven up dishes that need some extra kick. Relishes consist of mixed chopped vegetables or fruits and spices, with or without mustard. They may be sweet and sour. Usually the vegetables have been pickled or preserved; better results are obtained by the use of salt-stock vegetables (see page 287) than by fresh.

A good relish has an attractive color and appetizing appearance; most relishes are crisp, fairly uniform pieces of vegetables with a very small amount of liquid. The relish is moist but not watery.

chutney

Chutney is similar in consistency to jelly, salsa, or relish and is used as a sweet-and-sour condiment. Usually made fresh, chutney contains fruit and sugar to give it a sweet taste, and almost all chutney contains vinegar and perhaps onions to give it a corresponding sour flavor. The ingredients are mixed together and then simmered slowly. While chutney is primarily sweet-and-sour, there can also be many variations of spices, often giving it a hot and spicy flavor.

Like jams and jellies, chutney can be chunky or smooth. In India, spicy chutney is usually served with curry and often with cold meats and vegetables. Sweet chutney is a pleasant addition to bread or crackers and cheese and can serve as a snack or small meal.

Some of the more popular ingredients for chutney, in addition to mangos, are limes, apples, peaches, plums, apricots, tomatoes, lemons, and even coconuts. Additional spices may include cloves, garlic, cilantro, mustard, cinnamon, ginger, cayenne, jalapeños, tamarind, and mint. Chutney is so diverse that it can be made with only a few of these ingredients or several, to make a variety of flavors and styles.

Chutney is usually eaten fresh in its native India. In the United States and Britain, offering chutney as a condiment is becoming nearly as popular as offering jam, relish, and even ketchup. Chutney can be served at a formal dinner as a condiment for a fancy meal or at a casual picnic with tortilla chips or crackers. Whatever the occasion, chutney is a tasty, sweet-and-sour treat that is sure to please.

compote

Originally from Eastern Europe, compotes are made by cooking fruits or vegetables in a flavorful liquid, often in syrup. For the garde manger, savory compotes can be used to accompany galantines or pâtés in much the same way that a chutney is used.

pickles

While we tend to think of cucumbers when we think of pickles, many other vegetables and fruits can be pickled. Cabbage is pickled with salt to become sauerkraut; apples, pears, peaches, and watermelon rind are pickled with flavored vinegar brines.

Pickling cucumbers and other vegetables should be processed as soon after harvesting as possible, preferably within 24 hours.

Choose fresh, good-quality fruits and vegetables free of blemishes and uniform in size. Imperfect and irregular fruits and vegetables can be cut up for relish after pickling. Fruit may be slightly underripe. Wash all fruits and vegetables gently but thoroughly to remove dirt and grit, which could start bacterial action.

Cider vinegar can be substituted for distilled white vinegar, although its deeper color may cause a slight darkening of foods.

Use only fresh whole spices for full flavor unless a recipe specifies ground spices. Old spices may give a dusty flavor to pickles.

Use water that is free of minerals as much as possible.

Use pure granulated salt rather than ordinary table salt when brining pickles.

curing pickles

The traditional way to make cucumber pickles is by curing them in a salt-and-water solution until the raw cucumbers have been transformed into translucent pickle. This takes 6 to 8 weeks. The "salt stock" is then drained and the surplus salt in the cucumbers is withdrawn by soaking or light cooking. Next, vinegar, spices, sugar, and other seasonings are added, depending on the type of pickles desired.

Sauerkraut is pickled with salt alone and allowed to ferment. Other vegetables and fruits are pickled in vinegar solutions, often with salt, sugar, and other seasonings.

applejack-brandied cherry coulis

MAKES 3 CUPS/720 ML

1 lb 8 oz/680 g sweet cherries, pitted

¼ cup/60 mL applejack brandy

3 tbsp/45 mL minced shallots

1 tbsp/15 mL cider vinegar

1 tbsp/15 mL brown sugar

4 bay leaves

½ tsp/2.50 mL Worcestershire sauce

¼ tsp/1.25 mL kosher salt

1. Combine all of the ingredients in a 2-qt/2-L sauce pot.

2. Simmer covered over low heat for 15 minutes, stirring occasionally.

3. Uncover and simmer until the liquid is almost dry, 5 to 10 minutes.

4. Remove from the heat and cool to room temperature.

5. Remove the bay leaves. Purée in a blender, then pass through a tamis or sieve. Transfer to a clean storage container and refrigerate.

6. Store under refrigeration for up to 2 weeks or freeze for later use.

orange marmalade and jalapeño sauce

MAKES 1 CUP/240 ML

12 oz/340 g orange marmalade

¼ cup/60 mL ruby port wine

1 tbsp/15 mL lemon juice

1 tsp/5 mL minced jalapeño

½ tsp/2.50 mL chili powder

¼ tsp/1.25 mL ground cumin

¼ tsp/1.25 mL soy sauce

Combine all the ingredients in a 1-qt/1-L saucepan. Simmer on low heat for about 10 minutes. Remove from the heat and cool to room temperature. Transfer to a clean storage container, cover, and refrigerate until needed.

fresh plum and horseradish coulis

MAKES 2 CUPS/480 ML

2 cloves

2 allspice berries

2 bay leaves

1 lb/454 g plums, pitted, cut into ½-in/1-cm chunks

½ tsp/2.50 mL finely minced garlic

2 tbsp/30 mL chopped shallot

¼ cup/60 mL red wine

1 tbsp/15 mL grated horseradish

1 tsp/5 mL lemon juice

⅛ tsp/0.625 mL kosher salt

1. Wrap the cloves, allspice, and bay leaves in cheesecloth and tie with string to make a sachet. Place the sachet in a small saucepan.

2. Add the plums, garlic, shallot, wine, horseradish, lemon juice, and salt, and mix to combine. Cover and simmer for 15 minutes.

3. Remove from the heat and cool to room temperature. When the mixture is lukewarm, remove the sachet. Purée in a blender until smooth.

4. Adjust the seasoning and cool completely. Store covered under refrigeration until needed.

adobo sauce

8 garlic cloves, unpeeled

2 oz/57 g dried ancho chiles, stemmed, seeded

1½ oz/43 g dried New Mexico chiles, stemmed, seeded

Boiling water, as needed

10 black peppercorns

2 bay leaves, crushed

1 cinnamon stick, ½ in/1 cm long

⅛ tsp/0.625 mL cumin seeds

3 fl oz/90 mL cider vinegar

¼ cup/60 mL water

¼ cup/60 mL chocolate sauce

2 tsp/10 mL kosher salt

½ tsp/2.50 mL dried oregano

½ tsp/2.50 mL dried thyme

1. Roast the garlic cloves on a griddle or heavy skillet over medium heat, turning frequently, until blackened in spots and very soft, about 15 minutes. Set aside to cool.

2. Peel the cloves and rough-chop. Set aside.

3. While the garlic is roasting, tear the chiles into flat pieces and toast them a few at a time on a griddle or heavy skillet. Use a metal spatula to press them firmly against the hot surface for a few seconds until they blister, crackle, and change color, then flip them over and press them flat to toast the other side.

4. Place the chiles in a small mixing bowl and cover them with boiling water. Cover the chiles with a plate to keep them submerged. Soak the chiles for 30 minutes.

5. Drain the chiles and tear them into smaller pieces. Set aside.

6. With a mortar and pestle or in a spice grinder, grind the peppercorns, bay leaves, cinnamon, and cumin.

7. In a blender, combine the garlic, chiles, and spice mixture. Add the vinegar, water, chocolate sauce, salt, oregano, and thyme. Pulse until the mixture reduces to a paste. Continue pulsing, scraping the sides of the blender with a rubber spatula, and stirring the mixture until smooth. Add additional water if it is absolutely necessary.

8. Strain the paste through a medium-mesh sieve into a nonreactive container with a tight-fitting lid. Cover and refrigerate until needed.

cinnamon-rum applesauce

MAKES 1 QT/960 ML

8 medium apples, peeled, cut into 1-in/3-cm chunks

½ cup/120 mL light brown sugar

1 tsp/5 mL ground cinnamon

½ tsp/2.50 mL kosher salt

1½ tbsp/22.50 mL lemon juice

¼ cup/60 mL white wine

¼ cup/60 mL dark rum

¾ cup/180 mL hazelnuts, toasted, peeled, and coarsely chopped

½ cup/120 mL dried currants

1. In a medium sauce pot, combine the apples, sugar, cinnamon, salt, lemon juice, and wine. Add 3 tbsp/45 mL of the rum and ¼ cup/60 mL of the hazelnuts. Cover and simmer over low heat for 45 minutes.

2. Remove from the heat and cool the mixture slightly. Run through the fine screen of a food mill.

3. Add the remaining 1 tbsp/15 mL rum, ½ cup/120 mL chopped hazelnuts, and the currants.

4. Mix and adjust the seasoning. Transfer to a clean storage container, cover, and refrigerate until needed.

cajun-style lime and mustard-seed dressing

MAKES 2½ CUPS/600 ML

2 to 4 tbsp/30 to 60 mL lime juice

2 tsp/10 mL grated lime zest

1½ cups/360 mL mayonnaise

2 tbsp/30 mL minced green onions, green and white parts

2 tbsp/30 mL minced red pepper

½ cup/120 mL milk

2 tbsp/30 mL yellow mustard seeds, toasted

1 tbsp/15 mL Creole mustard

1½ tsp/7.50 mL kosher salt

1 tbsp/15 mL brown sugar

1 tbsp/15 mL minced fresh oregano or basil

Whisk all the ingredients together in a stainless-steel bowl until well incorporated. Transfer to a clean storage container, cover, and refrigerate until needed.

vinaigrette dressing

MAKES 1 QT/960 ML

½ cup/120 mL
cider vinegar

½ cup/120 mL water or
stock, like vegetable

1 to 2 oz/28 to 57 g
Dijon mustard

½ tsp/2.50 mL kosher salt

⅛ tsp/0.625 mL ground
white pepper

1 tbsp/15 mL chopped
fresh parsley

1½ tsp/7.50 mL
chopped chives

1½ tsp/7.50 mL chopped
fresh tarragon

3 cups/720 mL salad oil

Whisk together the vinegar, water, mustard, salt, pepper, parsley, chives, and tarragon. Gradually whisk in the oil. Adjust the seasoning if needed. Transfer to a clean storage container, cover, and refrigerate until needed.

Presentation idea: Serve with head cheese and jellied meat products.

fresh horseradish

MAKES 1 CUP/240 ML

1 cup/240 mL grated
horseradish, packed

¼ cup/60 mL distilled
white vinegar

1½ tbsp/22.50 mL
kosher salt

Combine all ingredients thoroughly. Transfer to a clean storage container, cover, and refrigerate until needed.

herbed horseradish sauce

½ cup/120 mL heavy cream

⅔ cup/160 mL mayonnaise

3 tbsp/45 mL grated
fresh horseradish

1½ tsp/7.50 mL Dijon mustard

1½ tsp/7.50 mL chopped
fresh parsley

1½ tsp/7.50 mL chopped
fresh tarragon

1½ tsp/7.50 mL chopped
fresh chervil

1½ tsp/7.50 mL chopped
fresh chives

½ tsp/2.50 mL kosher salt

½ tsp/2.50 mL ground
white pepper

1. In a stainless-steel mixing bowl, whip the cream to soft peaks.

2. In a separate mixing bowl, combine the remaining ingredients and mix well.

3. Fold in the whipped cream. Transfer to a clean storage container, cover, and refrigerate until needed.

apple and horseradish cream

1 cup/240 mL coarsely grated peeled Granny Smith apple

1 tsp/5 mL lemon juice

¼ cup/60 mL prepared horseradish

2 tbsp/30 mL minced shallot, blanched

¼ cup/60 mL mayonnaise

½ tsp/2.50 mL kosher salt

1 tsp/5 mL granulated sugar

1 cup/240 mL heavy cream

1. Combine the grated apple and lemon juice. Mix well.

2. Add the horseradish, shallot, mayonnaise, salt, and sugar. Mix gently.

3. Whip the cream to stiff peaks. Fold into the apple mixture.

4. Transfer to a clean storage container, cover, and refrigerate until needed.

mustard horseradish sauce

MAKES 2½ CUPS/600 ML

2 cups/480 mL mayonnaise

½ cup/120 mL
Dijon mustard

3 tbsp/45 mL fresh or
prepared horseradish

2 tbsp/30 mL lemon juice

Tabasco sauce, as needed

Kosher salt, as needed

Combine all ingredients thoroughly. Adjust the seasoning as needed. Transfer to a clean storage container, cover, and refrigerate until needed.

cranberry horseradish cream

MAKES 1 QT/960 ML

3 cloves

1 bay leaf

1 cinnamon stick,
about 3 in/8 cm

8 oz/227 g cranberries

¼ cup/60 mL honey

1½ tbsp/22.50 mL
brown sugar

⅓ cup/80 mL dry sherry

2 tbsp/30 mL
prepared horseradish

½ cup/120 mL mayonnaise

¼ cup/60 mL heavy cream

1. Wrap the cloves, bay leaf, and cinnamon in cheesecloth and tie with string to make a sachet.

2. In a saucepan, combine the sachet, cranberries, honey, sugar, and sherry. Simmer for 15 to 20 minutes.

3. Remove from the heat. Remove the sachet. In a blender, purée the cranberry mixture. Transfer to a mixing bowl and cool to room temperature.

4. Fold the horseradish, mayonnaise, and whipped cream into the cranberry mixture. Adjust seasoning. Transfer to a clean storage container, cover, and refrigerate until needed.

cranberry–green peppercorn mayonnaise

MAKES 2 CUPS/600 ML

2 bay leaves

1 cinnamon stick, about 3 in/8 cm

2 cloves

½ cup/120 mL cranberries

3 tbsp/45 mL white wine

⅓ cup/80 mL honey

1½ tbsp/22.50 mL green peppercorns, chopped

1 cup/240 mL mayonnaise

1. Wrap the bay leaves, cinnamon, and cloves in cheesecloth and tie with string to make a sachet. In a saucepan, combine the sachet, cranberries, wine, and honey.

2. Cover and simmer for 20 minutes.

3. Remove from the heat and cool to room temperature.

4. Remove the sachet. Transfer to a cutting board and coarsely chop the mixture. Transfer to a mixing bowl.

5. Add the peppercorns and mayonnaise. Adjust the seasoning as needed. Transfer to a clean storage container, cover, and refrigerate until needed.

dill and mustard sauce

MAKES 1 CUP/240 ML

4 tsp/20 mL Colman's dry mustard

4 tsp/20 mL Dijon mustard

5 tbsp/75 mL granulated sugar

½ tsp/2.50 mL kosher salt

2 tbsp/30 mL olive oil

¼ tsp/1.25 mL lemon juice

1 tbsp/15 mL white wine vinegar

½ cup/120 mL sour cream

2 tbsp/30 mL chopped fresh dill

1. In a mixing bowl, whisk together the mustards, sugar, and salt. Whisk in the oil, lemon juice, and vinegar alternating.

2. Stir slowly until blended, then whisk vigorously to fully incorporate the ingredients.

3. Fold in the sour cream and dill. Transfer to a clean storage container, cover, and refrigerate until needed.

Presentation idea: Serve with cold fish and shellfish.

crème fraîche and red-onion dill sauce

MAKES 1½ CUPS/600 ML

10 oz/284 g crème fraîche

¼ cup/60 mL minced
red onion

1 tbsp/15 mL chopped
fresh dill

1 tsp/5 mL ground
white pepper

1 tbsp/15 mL
Worcestershire sauce

1 tsp/5 mL granulated sugar

½ tsp/2.50 mL Tabasco sauce

1 garlic clove, minced

Combine all ingredients thoroughly. Transfer to a clean storage container, cover, and refrigerate until needed.

mascarpone sauce

4 garlic cloves

1½ tsp/7.50 mL kosher salt

1 lb/454 g mascarpone cheese

¼ cup/60 mL milk

¼ cup/60 mL Creole mustard

2 tbsp/30 mL chopped fresh oregano

1 tbsp/15 mL honey

1 tbsp/45 mL chopped fresh basil

2 tsp/10 mL distilled white vinegar

1 tsp/5 mL lemon juice

½ tsp/2.50 mL ground black pepper

Mash the garlic with the salt to form a paste. In a stainless-steel mixing bowl, thoroughly combine the garlic paste with the remaining ingredients. Adjust the seasoning as needed. Transfer to a clean storage container, cover, and refrigerate until needed.

Presentation idea: Serve with beef carpaccio.

curried peanut sauce

½ cup/240 mL raw peanuts, shelled, blanched

1½ tbsp/22.50 mL curry powder

1 tbsp/15 mL butter

2 medium shallots, finely minced

1 garlic clove, minced

1 cup/240 mL mayonnaise

¼ cup/60 mL milk

2 tsp/10 mL lemon juice

½ tsp/2.50 mL Tabasco sauce

1. Toast the peanuts and curry in the butter until brown. Add the shallots and garlic and sweat for about 3 minutes.

2. Remove from the heat and rough-chop.

3. In a mixing bowl, combine the peanut mixture and the remaining ingredients. Transfer to a clean storage container, cover, and refrigerate until needed.

cumberland sauce

MAKES 3 CUPS/720 ML

¼ oz/7 g orange zest, finely julienned

¼ oz/7 g lemon zest, finely julienned

Juice from 2 medium juicing oranges

6 tbsp/90 mL lemon juice

¼ oz/7 g minced shallot

Boiling water, as needed

2 cups/480 mL currant jelly

1 cup/240 mL port wine

2 tsp/10 mL Colman's dry mustard

½ tsp/2.50 mL kosher salt

Small pinch of cayenne

Small pinch of ground ginger

1. Prepare the zests before juicing the fruits.

2. Blanch the zests and shallot by placing them in boiling water. Allow the water to return to a boil and drain immediately.

3. In a saucepan, combine all the ingredients and bring to a simmer. Simmer for 10 minutes. Remove from the heat and cool. Transfer to a clean storage container, cover, and refrigerate until needed.

Presentation idea: Serve with pâtés and terrines.

cold tarragon sauce

1 garlic clove, finely minced

¼ tsp/1.25 mL chopped shallots

¼ cup/60 mL white wine

¼ cup/60 mL chicken stock

⅓ cup/80 mL chopped fresh tarragon leaves

1 tbsp/15 mL honey

1 tbsp/15 mL white wine or tarragon vinegar

½ tsp/2.50 mL ground black pepper

½ tsp/2.50 mL kosher salt

1 tsp/5 mL soy sauce

½ cup/120 mL heavy cream

1. Combine the garlic, shallot, white wine, and chicken stock in a small sauce pot. Cover and simmer for 5 minutes.

2. Uncover and reduce by half. Strain and reserve the liquid.

3. Combine the tarragon leaves, honey, vinegar, pepper, salt, and soy sauce in a stainless-steel mixing bowl. Add the reserved liquid and mix thoroughly.

4. Whip the cream to soft peaks and fold into the tarragon mixture.

5. Transfer to a clean storage container, cover, and refrigerate until needed.

garlic and walnut sauce

MAKES 1²/₃ CUPS/400 ML

1 cup/240 mL mayonnaise

⅓ cup/80 mL walnuts,
toasted, chopped

2 tbsp/30 mL olive oil

1 tbsp/15 mL
balsamic vinegar

1 tbsp/15 mL chopped
fresh oregano

1 tsp/5 mL
Worcestershire sauce

3 garlic cloves, minced

½ tsp/2.50 mL ground
black pepper

Combine all the ingredients in a stainless-steel mixing bowl. Adjust the seasoning. Transfer to a clean storage container, cover, and refrigerate until needed.

pickle relish

2 cups/480 mL peeled, thinly sliced European cucumbers

½ medium yellow onion, thinly sliced

1½ tsp/7.50 mL kosher salt

⅓ cup/80 mL distilled white vinegar

½ cup/120 mL granulated sugar

1. Combine the cucumbers and onion in a nonreactive mixing bowl. Sprinkle with the salt. Cover and let stand for 2 to 3 hours under refrigeration.

2. Drain and rinse well.

3. In a small sauce pot, combine the vinegar and sugar. Bring to a simmer, remove from the heat, and cool to room temperature.

4. Pour the cooled vinegar mixture over the cucumbers and onions. Mix thoroughly.

5. Transfer to a clean storage container, cover, and refrigerate until needed. If desired, this may be frozen; the vegetables will be crisp and crunchy when thawed.

new england rhubarb relish

MAKES 3 CUPS/720 ML

½ garlic clove

1½ tsp/7.50 mL ground cinnamon

1½ tsp/7.50 mL minced ginger

1½ tsp/7.50 mL pickling spice

1 qt/960 mL sliced rhubarb, in 1½-in/4-cm pieces

2 cups/480 mL thinly sliced white onions

2 cups/480 mL brown sugar

½ cup/120 mL cider vinegar

1 tsp/5 mL kosher salt

1. Wrap the garlic, cinnamon, ginger, and pickling spice in cheesecloth and tie with string to make a sachet.

2. In a sauce pot, combine the rhubarb, sachet, onions, sugar, vinegar, and salt. Simmer over low heat until the rhubarb is tender but not falling apart, 10 to 15 minutes.

3. Remove from the heat. Remove the sachet. Cool and transfer to a clean storage container. Cover and refrigerate for up to 2 weeks.

savory autumn relish

10 medium green tomatoes (2 lb /907 g)

1½ medium green bell peppers

1½ medium red bell peppers

1½ celery stalks

1½ large yellow onions

¼ medium head green cabbage

½ European cucumber, peeled

2 cups/1 pt roughly chopped plum tomatoes

¼ cup/60 mL kosher salt

3 cups/720 mL white wine vinegar

½ tsp/2.50 mL sweet or hot paprika

½ tsp/2.50 mL Colman's dry mustard

2 cups/480 mL brown sugar

1. Rough-chop the green tomatoes, green and red peppers, celery, onions, cabbage, and cucumber. Layer the plum tomatoes and other vegetables in a stainless-steel mixing bowl and sprinkle with the salt. Cover and let stand overnight under refrigeration.

2. Drain and press out the liquid.

3. In a sauce pot, combine the vinegar, paprika, mustard, and sugar. Add the well-drained vegetables and boil gently for 1 hour, or until the vegetables are transparent.

4. Cool and transfer to a clean storage container with a tight-fitting lid. Cover and refrigerate for up to 2 weeks.

sweet mango relish with raisins

MAKES 3 TO 4 CUPS/720 TO 960 ML

3 cups/720 mL peeled, pitted green mangoes,

1 large yellow onion

3 medium red peppers, seeded

1 jalapeño or Fresno chile pepper

1½ tsp/7.50 mL kosher salt

1½ tsp/7.50 mL white mustard seeds

1½ tsp/7.50 mL celery seeds

2 cups/480 mL granulated sugar

½ cup/120 mL distilled white vinegar

½ cinnamon stick

1 cup/240 mL raisins

1. Place the mangos in a nonreactive sauce pot.

2. Chop the onion and peppers in the food processor.

3. Add the onion mixture, salt, mustard seeds, celery seeds, sugar, vinegar, cinnamon, and raisins to the mangos. Bring to a boil and simmer for 10 minutes.

4. Remove from the heat and cool to room temperature. Let stand overnight under refrigeration.

5. Return the sauce pot to the heat and cook the relish until slightly thickened, 10 to 15 minutes.

6. Cool and transfer to a clean storage container. Cover and refrigerate for up to 2 weeks.

tropical relish

2 qt/1.92 mL peeled,
seeded guavas,

12 oz/340 g raisins

½ garlic clove

8 oz/227 g
preserved ginger

2 tbsp/30 mL white
mustard seeds

½ tsp/2.50 mL dried
Thai bird chiles

1 cup/240 mL distilled
white vinegar

2½ cups/600 mL
granulated sugar

⅛ tsp/0.625 mL
celery seeds

⅛ tsp/0.625 mL kosher salt

1. In a food processor, combine and chop the guavas, raisins, garlic, ginger, mustard seeds, and chiles. Transfer to a nonreactive sauce pot and add the vinegar, sugar, celery seeds, and salt.

2. Boil for 30 minutes. Remove from the heat and cool to room temperature. Cover and let stand overnight under refrigeration.

3. If the relish is too thick, reheat it and add more vinegar to thin it out. Let cool again.

4. Transfer to clean storage containers. Cover and refrigerate for about 2 weeks to develop the flavor before using.

plain chutney

MAKES 4 TO 5 CUPS/960 ML TO 1.20 L

12 oz/340 g brown sugar

1¼ cups/300 mL
cider vinegar

3 medium apples,
such as Granny Smith,
peeled, diced small

8 oz/227 g dates,
pitted, diced small

4 jalapeños, seeded,
diced small

8 oz/227 g currants

4 oz/113 g preserved
ginger, diced

1 tsp/5 mL grated ginger

8 oz/227 g dark raisins

8 oz/227 g orange and
lemon peels, diced small

1 tbsp/15 mL ground
cinnamon

2 tbsp/30 mL kosher salt

1½ tsp/7.50 mL
ground allspice

2 oz/57 g onion,
ground to a paste

½ oz/14 g garlic,
ground to a paste

1. In a sauce pot, combine the sugar and vinegar and boil for 30 minutes.

2. Add the remaining ingredients and simmer until thick, 10 to 15 minutes.

3. Cool and transfer to a clean storage container. Cover and refrigerate for up to 2 weeks.

dried-fruit chutney

MAKES 4 TO 5 CUPS 960 ML TO 1.20 L

4 oz/113 g dried apples

4 oz/113 g dried peaches

4 oz/113 g dried apricots

4 oz/113 g seedless raisins

4 oz/113 g dates, pitted

1 garlic clove,
finely chopped

1¼ cups/300 mL
distilled white vinegar

8 oz/227 g
granulated sugar

1½ tsp/7.50 mL
ground allspice

1½ tsp/7.50 mL kosher salt

Pinch of cayenne

1. Soak the apples, peaches, and apricots overnight in water to cover.

2. Drain and reserve the liquid. Cut the fruit into small dice.

3. Combine the apples and reserved liquid in a sauce pot. Stew for 3 to 5 minutes. Add the peaches and apricots and stew for an additional 5 to 10 minutes, until the fruits have become soft.

4. Rough-chop the raisins and dates in a food processor. Add the garlic and rough chop.

5. Add the raisin mixture, vinegar, sugar, allspice, salt, and cayenne to the sauce pot and cook for 30 minutes, until the chutney is thick and soft, stirring frequently so that the mixture will not stick to the bottom.

6. Cool and transfer to clean storage containers. Cover and refrigerate for up to 2 weeks.

apple and banana chutney

1 lb/454 g apples, such as Granny Smith, peeled, cored

6 oz/170 g yellow onions

4 oz/113 g raisins

9 bananas

1 cup/240 mL distilled white vinegar

1 oz/28 g kosher salt

1 cup/240 mL granulated sugar

½ tsp/2.50 mL ground cinnamon

¼ tsp/1.25 mL cardamom pods

½ tsp/2.50 mL ground ginger

½ oz/14 g curry powder

1. Finely chop the apples and onions. Cut the raisins in half. Peel the bananas and slice into disks ¼ to ½ in/6 mm to 1 cm thick.

2. In a sauce pot, combine the vinegar, salt, sugar, cinnamon, cardamom, ginger, and curry powder. Bring to a boil. Add the fruit.

3. Simmer gently for 2 hours, stirring frequently to prevent the bananas from burning. When the mixture becomes thick and the fruit is tender, remove from the heat.

4. Cool and transfer to a clean storage container. Cover and refrigerate for up to 2 weeks.

corky's southwest-style BBQ sauce

MAKES 2 CUPS/480 ML

4 tbsp/60 mL butter

1 cup/240 mL diced yellow onions

1 tbsp/15 mL minced garlic

2 tbsp/30 mL diced jalapeño chiles

2 tbsp/30 mL chili powder

½ cup/120 mL strong brewed coffee

½ cup/120 mL Worcestershire sauce

½ cup/120 mL ketchup

¼ cup/60 mL cider vinegar

¼ cup/60 mL brown sugar

1 tbsp/15 mL cornstarch

¼ cup/60 mL water

1. Melt the butter in a large saucepan. Add the onion and sweat until tender.

2. Add the garlic and chile. Continue to cook for 2 to 3 minutes.

3. Stir in the chili powder and cook over moderate heat until the flavor of the chili powder is developed, 2 to 3 more minutes.

4. Add the coffee, Worcestershire sauce, ketchup, vinegar, and sugar. Simmer for about 45 minutes.

5. Whisk the cornstarch with the water until smooth.

6. Stir the slurry into the sauce to adjust the thickness. Bring the sauce back to a boil before cooling.

7. Transfer to a clean storage container, cover, and refrigerate for up to 1 week.

tomato ketchup

MAKES 1 QT/960 ML

6 lb/2.72 kg plum tomatoes

1½ large yellow onions, diced small

1 medium red bell pepper, seeded, diced small

¼ garlic clove

1 cinnamon stick (1½ in/4 cm long)

½ tsp/2.50 mL black peppercorns

½ tsp/2.50 mL allspice berries

1½ tsp/7.50 mL cloves

½ dried chile

½ tsp/2.50 mL celery seeds

½ cup/120 mL light brown sugar, packed

¾ cup/180 mL distilled white vinegar

¾ tbsp/11.25 mL kosher salt

1½ tsp/7.50 mL sweet paprika

1½ tsp/7.50 mL Colman's dry mustard

1. Peel and rough-chop the tomatoes.

2. In a nonreactive, sauce pot, combine the tomatoes, onions, bell pepper, and garlic. Cook slowly until the vegetables become soft, 15 to 20 minutes.

3. Strain through a fine-mesh sieve and transfer to a clean sauce pot. Simmer over low heat for about 30 minutes.

4. Wrap the cinnamon, peppercorns, allspice, cloves, chile, and celery seeds in cheesecloth and tie with string to make a sachet. Add the sachet, sugar, vinegar, salt, paprika, and mustard to the sauce pot. Simmer for 3 to 4 hours, until very thick, stirring frequently.

5. Remove from the heat and discard the sachet. Strain through a fine-mesh sieve.

6. Cool and transfer to plastic storage containers with tight-fitting lids. Cover and refrigerate for up to 2 weeks.

papaya ketchup

¼ cup/60 mL vegetable oil

2 oz/57 g yellow onion, diced small

½ medium red pepper, diced small

½ medium green pepper, diced small

1 tsp/5 mL minced garlic

1 tsp/5 mL ground allspice

1 tsp/5 mL curry powder

1 tsp/5 mL ground cumin

1 papaya, (17.9 oz/507.4 g), peeled, seeded, diced medium

½ cup/120 mL pineapple juice

¼ cup/60 mL distilled white vinegar

1 tbsp/15 mL molasses

1½ tbsp/22.50 mL lemon juice

¾ tbsp/11.25 mL kosher salt

¼ tsp/1.25 mL ground black pepper

1. Heat the oil in a sauté pan over medium heat until hot, but not smoking.

2. Sauté the onion, stirring frequently, until the onion becomes translucent and begin to char slightly, 5 to 7 minutes.

3. Add the bell peppers and cook 2 minutes, stirring frequently.

4. Add the garlic, allspice, curry, and cumin and cook an additional 2 minutes, stirring constantly. The mixture will be quite dry at this point.

5. Add the papaya, pineapple juice, vinegar, and molasses. Mix well and bring to a boil.

6. Reduce heat to low; simmer until the mixture is slightly thinner than tomato ketchup, 20 to 25 minutes. Remove from the heat and cool. (The mixture will thicken more as it cools.)

7. Add the lemon juice, salt, and pepper. Adjust seasoning as needed. Transfer to a clean storage container, cover, and refrigerate for up to 2 weeks.

peach ketchup

MAKES 4 TO 5 CUPS/960 ML TO 1.20 L

3 lb 8 oz/1.59 kg tomatoes, peeled, chopped

4 medium peaches (6.155 oz/174.6 g ea), peeled, pitted, chopped

1 lb/454 g brown sugar

1 cup/240 mL distilled white or cider vinegar

¼ oz/7 g ground cloves

¼ oz/7 g ground cinnamon

1. In a sauce pot, simmer the tomatoes and peaches for 20 to 25 minutes.

2. Strain into a clean sauce pot. Add the sugar, vinegar, cloves, and cinnamon and boil for 2 hours.

3. Cool and transfer to clean storage containers. Cover and refrigerate for up to 2 weeks.

zesty cranberry ketchup

MAKES 4½ CUPS/1.08 L

2 lb 8 oz/1.13 kg cranberries

8 oz/227 g yellow onions, chopped

1½ cups/360 mL water

3 cups/720 mL granulated sugar

1½ cups/360 mL white vinegar

1 tsp/3.75 mL ground cloves

1½ tsp/7.50 mL ground cinnamon

1½ tbsp/22.50 mL lemon juice

1½ tsp/7.50 mL ground black pepper

1½ tsp/7.50 mL ground allspice

1½ tsp/7.50 mL kosher salt

1. In a sauce pot, cook the cranberries and onions in the water until tender, 20 to 25 minutes.

2. Strain through a fine-mesh sieve into a clean sauce pot. Add the sugar, vinegar, cloves, cinnamon, lemon juice, pepper, allspice, and salt and boil until thick, about 2 hours. Remove from heat and cool.

3. Transfer to a clean storage container. Cover and refrigerate for up to 2 weeks.

mango, papaya, orange, and lime salsa

MAKES 2 CUPS/480 ML

2 medium oranges
(7 oz/198 g)

1 medium mango (19.82
oz/561.9 g), peeled,
seeded, diced small

1 medium Hawaiian papaya
(17.9 oz 507.4 g), peeled,
seeded, diced small

2 oz/57 g red onion cut
into ⅓-in/1-cm cubes

2 oz/57 g red pepper cut
into ⅓-in/1-cm cubes

1½ to 2 tbsp/22.50 to 30 mL
lime juice

2 tbsp/30 mL cilantro,
cut into chiffonade

2 tbsp/30 mL mint,
cut into chiffonade

1½ tbsp/22.50 mL toasted
ground New Mexico chiles

½ tsp/2.50 mL
ground cumin

½ tsp/2.50 mL ground
black pepper

Salt, as needed

Grate the orange zest. Make suprêmes from the oranges. In a nonreactive mixing bowl, combine and mix the suprêmes with the remaining ingredients. Adjust the seasoning. Serve immediately or transfer to a clean storage container, cover, and refrigerate until needed.

green chile salsa

MAKES 2 QT/1.92 L

8 oz/227 g yellow onions, diced small

1 tbsp/15 mL minced garlic

2 tbsp/30 mL olive oil

6 green onions, green and white parts, chopped

One 29-oz/822-g can tomato purée

One 28-oz/794-g can mild green chiles

½ cup/120 mL distilled white vinegar

3 tbsp/45 mL chopped cilantro

3 tbsp/45 mL granulated sugar

2 to 4 tbsp/30 to 60 mL lime juice

1 tbsp/15 mL minced jalapeño

1 tbsp/15 mL mild chili powder

1 tbsp/15 mL Worcestershire sauce

2 tsp/10 mL cumin seeds, toasted, crushed

1. In a sautoir, sweat the onions and garlic in the oil over medium-high heat until lightly tender.

2. Stir in the green onions. Remove from the heat. Let cool slightly.

3. Add the remaining ingredients and mix well. Adjust the seasoning. Serve immediately or transfer to a clean storage container, cover, and refrigerate until needed.

corn salsa

2 lb/907 g tomato concassé

2 lb/907 g corn kernels, preferably fresh

1 medium yellow onion, diced small

⅓ cup/80 mL cider vinegar

2 tbsp/30 mL chopped cilantro

2 tbsp/30 mL tomato paste

2 tsp/10 mL chopped fresh oregano

2 garlic cloves, minced

1 jalapeño, seeded, diced

Salt, as needed

1. In a sautoir, combine the tomato concassé, corn, onion, vinegar, cilantro, tomato paste, oregano, and garlic. Bring to a simmer and simmer over low heat for about 10 minutes.

2. Add the jalapeño and simmer for 10 to 15 minutes.

3. Reduce the liquid to a syrupy consistency, about 5 minutes. Remove from the heat and let cool. Season with salt as needed. Serve immediately or transfer to a clean storage container, cover, and refrigerate until needed.

beet sauce

10 medium red beets, peeled

½ tsp/2.50 mL kosher salt

¼ tsp/1.25 mL ground black pepper

4 tsp/20 mL rice vinegar

6 tbsp/90 mL unsalted butter

1. Using a juicer, juice enough beets to make 4 cups/960 mL liquid (see Note).

2. Pour the beet juice into a sauce pot and slowly reduce by half, skimming away the foam as it forms. Season as needed with salt and pepper.

3. Add the rice wine vinegar and simmer for 1 to 2 minutes.

4. Mount the beet sauce with butter just before use.

Note: The juice can be kept for 3 or 4 days in the refrigerator, or frozen for later use.

fresh-pack dill pickles

MAKES 50 LB/22.68 KG

45 to 50 lb/20.41 to 22.68 kg
Kirby pickling cucumbers

6¾ cups/1.62 L pure
granulated Kosher salt

6 gal/23.04 L cool water

1 gal 2 cups/4.32 L
distilled white vinegar

6¾ qt/6.48 L water

¾ cup/180 mL
granulated sugar

1 cup/240 mL mixed
pickling spices, divided
into 2 sachets

4 garlic heads,
divided into 2 sachets

3 bunches dill heads,
green or dry, divided
into 2 sachets
or
1 cup/240 mL dill seed,
divided into 2 sachets

21 dried Thai bird chile,
divided into 2 sachets

1. Wash the cucumbers thoroughly. Rinse and drain the cucumbers. In a large plastic bucket or tub, cover them with a brine made of 4½ cups/1.08 L salt and 6 gal/23.14 L cool water. Let stand overnight under refrigeration. Make sure to keep the cucumbers submerged in brine.

2. Rinse and drain the cucumbers.

3. In a large stockpot, combine the vinegar, 6¾ qt/6.48 L water, the remaining 2¼ cups/540 mL salt, and sugar. Bring to a boil and keep hot.

4. Wrap the pickling spices, garlic heads, dill heads green or dry, or dill seeds and chiles in cheesecloth and tie with string to make sachets.

5. Pack half of the cucumbers to within ½ in/1 cm of the top of a 5-gal/19.20-L tub. Cover with hot pickling liquid and top with one sachet. Fill a second tub with the remaining cucumbers, pickling liquid, and sachet.

6. Cover the tubs with tight-fitting lids.

7. Let the pickles rest for 3 weeks under refrigeration. Remove the sachets and hold for another use.

little pickled apples

MAKES 2 QT/1.92 L

1 tbsp/15 mL
allspice berries

1 tbsp/15 mL cloves

1 cinnamon stick
(3 in/8 cm)

2 cups/480 mL
cider vinegar

2 cups/480 mL white
wine vinegar

2 lb/907 g brown sugar

6 lb/2.72 kg crab apples
or small tart apples

1. Wrap the allspice, cloves, and cinnamon stick in cheesecloth and tie with string to make a sachet. In a sauce pot, bring the vinegars, sugar, and sachet to a boil. Continue simmering for 15 minutes, skimming as necessary.

2. Trim the blossom ends of the apples. Wash the apples and add them to the sauce pot.

3. Simmer over low heat until the apples are tender, about 30 to 40 minutes. Remove the apples using a slotted spoon.

4. Transfer the apples to clean storage containers.

5. Reduce the cooking liquid until it forms a thick syrup. Pour the syrup over the apples.

6. Cover the containers with tight-fitting lids and refrigerate. The apples may be refrigerated for up to 2 weeks or frozen for 1 to 2 months if desired.

Note: If the apples are cored, cut the cooking time by a third or about 10 minutes so that the apples will not lose their shape.

pickled lady apples

MAKES 6 CUPS/1.44 L

3 cinnamon sticks
(3 in/8 cm ea)

16 cloves

1 lb 8 oz/680 g
granulated sugar

1 cup/240 mL cider vinegar

3 lb/1.36 kg lady apples

1. Wrap the cinnamon sticks and cloves in cheesecloth and tie with string to make a sachet.

2. In a sauce pot, bring the sugar, vinegar, and sachet to a boil. Boil for 10 minutes.

3. Steam the apples over the boiling liquid until tender, about 40 minutes. Transfer the apples to clean storage containers.

4. Pour the hot syrup over the apples. Cover the containers with tight-fitting lids and refrigerate. The apples may be refrigerated for up to 2 weeks.

Note: Check the apples to make sure they are not bruised. The apples should be left whole and unpeeled.

pickled red onion

1 small red onion,
cut into julienne

½ cup/120 mL water

½ cup/120 mL white
wine vinegar

¼ cup/60 mL
granulated sugar

1 tbsp/15 mL kosher salt

1 tsp/5 mL yellow
mustard seeds

1 tsp/5 mL black peppercorns

1 tsp/5 mL chopped ginger

1 clove

1. In a sauce pot, combine all of the ingredients and simmer for 10 minutes, until the sugar and salt have dissolved.

2. Remove from the heat and let steep for 20 minutes.

3. Cool to room temperature and transfer to clean storage containers. Cover and refrigerate for up to 2 weeks.

pickled seckel pears

4 cups/960 mL
granulated sugar

1 qt/960 mL distilled
white vinegar

1½ cups/360 mL water

2 cinnamon sticks
(4 in/10 cm long)

1 tbsp/15 mL cloves

3¼ tsp/16.25 mL
allspice berries

2 tsp/10 mL yellow
mustard seeds

1 dried Thai bird chile

4 lb/1.81 kg Seckel pears

1 gal/3.84 L cold water

3 tbsp/45 mL kosher salt

3 tbsp/45 mL distilled
white vinegar

4 cinnamon sticks
(2 in/5 cm long)

1. In a sauce pot, combine the sugar, vinegar, water, and the larger cinnamon sticks. Wrap the cloves, allspice, mustard seeds, and chile in cheesecloth and tie with string to make a sachet. Add the sachet to the sauce pot and simmer, covered, for about 30 minutes.

2. Wash and peel the pears. Remove the blossom ends, leaving the stems on.

3. Combine the cold water, salt, and vinegar in a large container. Hold the pears in the container while the cooking liquid simmers. Drain the pears before use.

4. When the syrup has simmered for 30 minutes, drain and add the pears. Cover with a clean towel or cloth to ensure proper poaching. Continue simmering for 20 to 25 minutes.

5. Remove the pears with a slotted spoon and transfer them to storage containers.

6. Add 1 small cinnamon stick to each container, then cover the pears with boiling syrup to within ½ in/1 cm of the top. Cover with tight-fitting lids and refrigerate for up to 2 weeks.

sauerkraut

The Pennsylvania Dutch are credited with introducing sauerkraut to the United States. Its health-giving properties have been recognized for 200 years. For this recipe, choose large, firm, well-ripened heads of cabbage. Let the cabbage stand at room temperature for a day to wilt. The wilting causes the leaves to become less brittle. The cabbage is less likely to break during cutting when it is wilted.

MAKES 16 QT/15.36 L

50 lb/22.68 kg large heads green cabbage

2 cups/480 mL kosher salt

1. Trim the outer leaves of the cabbages. Wash the cabbages. With a large knife, cut the heads into halves or quarters.

2. Remove the cores. Cut the cabbages using an electric slicer. The blade should be set to about the thickness of a dime. (The setting may be varied, depending upon individual preference, for a finer or coarser cut.)

3. Mix the salt and cabbage in a large mixing bowl or stainless-steel pan. Let the salted cabbage stand for 3 to 5 minutes.

4. Pack the cabbage into stone jars, crocks, or plastic pickle buckets. If these are unavailable, a deep plastic container may be used instead.

5. Press the cabbage into the container until the juices comes to the surface.

6. Cover the cabbage with a clean cheesecloth or plastic cover and then with a cover that fits inside the container. (The cover is very important and should be of a size that fits snugly inside the container.)

7. Place a weight on top of the cover so that the juices come up to the bottom of the cover, but not over it.

8. Place the cabbage at a room temperature of 68° to 72°F/20° to 22°C. This temperature is recommended so that the cabbage can ferment. The cabbage will be ready after 5 to 6 weeks. If it is kept at 75° to 80°F/24° to 27°C, the fermentation will take place faster, and should be ready in about 2 weeks.

9. During this time, check the sauerkraut often. If the juice level is too high, place a lighter weight on the cover, or if there is not enough juice, use a heavier weight.

10. Every few days, skim the scum off the surface of the brine and change and replace the cheesecloth, if using. When the sauerkraut is finished, it can be packed in 1-gallon zippered bags, and stored under refrigeration.

Notes: Packing is often the cause of unnecessary bruising and tearing and can result in a softening of the sauerkraut. Let the cabbage stand at room temperature, and when you are placing the sauerkraut in the barrel, try not to bruise it by pushing down too much.

If you allow the cabbage to stand for a few minutes after salting, you should have enough brine so that the cabbage can easily be packed by hand.

Common indications of spoilage are off-flavors, off-odors, soft texture, and undesirable color (the sauerkraut turns pink). Softness in sauerkraut may be caused by insufficient salt, uneven distribution of salt, air pockets from improper packing, or too high an ambient temperature during fermentation. You can slow the fermentation or speed the process by placing it in a warmer environment or by a colder place.

Growth of certain types of yeasts on the surface of the sauerkraut, due to excess salt or uneven distribution of salt, causes the sauerkraut to turn pink. It will also turn pink if it has been improperly covered or weighted during the fermentation process. Clear off the top part and the remainder should be fine.

sauerkraut salad

MAKES 3 CUPS/720 ML

2 cups/480 mL
prepared sauerkraut

1 medium yellow
onion, diced small

1 medium Granny Smith
apple (9 oz/255 g),
coarsely grated

2 dill pickles (8 oz/227 g),
diced small

½ cup/120 mL
grated carrots

3 tbsp/45 mL olive oil

2 tbsp/30 mL chopped
fresh parsley

1 tsp/5 mL caraway seeds

Salt, as needed

Ground black pepper,
as needed

Granulated sugar,
as needed

Drain the sauerkraut slightly. Combine all ingredients thoroughly. Adjust the seasoning if needed. Serve immediately or transfer to a clean storage container, cover, and refrigerate.

spiced pears

MAKES 3 TO 4 CUPS/720 TO 960 ML

1 lb 12 oz/794 g pears (7 or 8 ea)

¾ cup/180 mL plus 1 tbsp/45 mL distilled white vinegar

2½ cups/600 mL water

1¼ cups/300 mL granulated sugar

1 tbsp/15 mL lemon juice

1-in/3-cm piece ginger, peeled

1 tbsp/15 mL cloves

3½ cinnamon sticks (3 in/8 cm long)

1. Wash, peel, and core the pears. Cut them into wedges. Mix the 1 tbsp/45 mL vinegar and ½ cup/120 mL of the water. Add the pears to the vinegar-water solution to prevent browning.

2. In a sauce pot, combine the remaining 2 cups/480 mL water, the ¾ cup/180 mL vinegar, the sugar, and lemon juice. Bring to a boil.

3. Wrap the ginger, cloves, and cinnamon in cheesecloth and tie with string to make a sachet. Drain the pears. Add the pears and sachet to the sauce pot. Cover and simmer for 5 minutes, or until tender.

4. Remove the sachet. Using a slotted spoon, remove the pears from the cooking liquid and transfer them to clean storage containers. Add cooking liquid to within 1 in/3 cm of the top of the containers.

5. Cover with tight-fitting lids and refrigerate. (The pears are best when left to sit and develop flavor for 1 week.)

spiced watermelon rind

MAKES 2 QT/1.92 L

3 lb/1.36 kg watermelon rind (see Notes)

5 cups/1.20 L water

2 tbsp/30 mL kosher salt

4 cups/1.20 L granulated sugar

2 cups/480 mL plus 1 tbsp cider vinegar

1 tbsp/15 mL cloves

3¼ tsp/16.25 mL allspice berries

1 tbsp/15 mL coarsely chopped cinnamon stick

1 lemon, sliced

1. Remove all of the green skin from the rind and cut the rind in large dice (see Notes). Place in a nonreactive container.

2. Cover the watermelon rind with 4 cups/960 mL of the water. Add the salt, cover, and let the rind sit overnight.

3. Drain the rind. In a sauce pot, combine the rind and enough water to cover. Cook the rind, covered, over low heat until tender, about 2 hours.

4. Meanwhile, in another sauce pot, combine the sugar, vinegar, and remaining 1 cup/240 mL water. Wrap the cloves, allspice, cinnamon, and lemon slices in cheesecloth and tie with string to make a sachet. Add the sachet to the sugar-vinegar mixture. Boil for 5 minutes.

5. Drain the watermelon rind and add it to the vinegar mixture. Cook until the rind is transparent, 45 minutes to 1 hour.

6. Remove the sachet. Cool and transfer the rind to clean storage containers. Pour the cooking liquid over the rind. Cover and refrigerate for up to 4 weeks. The spiced rind may be eaten by itself or served in salads.

Notes: Watermelons with thick rind make the best pickles.

For a fancier look, the watermelon rind can be cut into various shapes, such as diamonds, by hand or with small cookie cutters.

sweet mixed-pickle chow chow

1 medium head cauliflower

1 medium green bell pepper

1 medium red bell pepper

12 oz/340 g medium yellow onions

1¼ cups/300 mL distilled white vinegar

¾ cup/180 mL water

¾ cup/180 mL granulated sugar

1½ tbsp/22.50 mL kosher salt

1½ tsp/7.50 mL yellow mustard seeds

1½ tsp/7.50 mL celery seeds

1½ tsp/7.50 mL turmeric

1. Wash the cauliflower and break it down into small florets.

2. Cook the florets in boiling water for 5 minutes. Drain the florets. Cut the peppers into ¼-in/6-mm strips. Peel and quarter the onions. Set the vegetables aside.

3. In a sauce pot, combine the vinegar, water, sugar, salt, mustard and celery seeds, and turmeric. Cover and bring to a boil.

4. Add the vegetables to the sauce pot and boil, uncovered, for 2 minutes.

5. Cool and transfer the vegetables to clean storage containers, packing the vegetables to about ⅛ in/3 mm from the top.

6. Pour the vinegar mixture over the vegetables. Cover and refrigerate until needed.

sweet pickle chips

3 lb/1.36 kg Kirby or
regular cucumbers

5½ cups/1.32 L
cider vinegar

1½ tsp/7.50 mL kosher salt

¾ tbsp/11.25 mL yellow
mustard seeds

3 cups/720 mL
granulated sugar

¾ cup/180 mL distilled
white vinegar

½ tsp/2.50 mL celery seeds

½ tsp/2.50 mL
whole allspice

½ tsp/2.50 mL turmeric

1. Wash the cucumbers thoroughly. Slice the cucumbers into ¼-in/6-mm slices.

2. Combine the cucumbers with the cider vinegar, salt, mustard seeds, and ¼ cup/60 mL of the sugar in a sauce pot. Simmer, covered, for 10 minutes. Drain the cucumbers and discard the liquid.

3. Bring the remaining 2¾ cups/660 mL sugar, the white vinegar, celery seeds, allspice, and turmeric to a boil, making sure the sugar is dissolved. Lower to a simmer. While the vinegar mixture is simmering, transfer the cucumbers to clean storage containers and fill to within ⅛ in/3 mm from the top. Pour enough of the vinegar mixture over the cucumbers to cover.

4. Cover with tight-fitting lids and refrigerate until needed.

apple and fennel salad

MAKES 2 CUPS/480 ML

1 cup/240 mL shaved
fennel bulb

3 medium red
apples (8 oz/227 g),
unpeeled, julienned

2 tbsp/30 mL lemon juice

1 tbsp/15 mL
extra-virgin olive oil

Salt, as needed

Ground pepper, as needed

Combine the fennel, apples, lemon juice, and olive oil. Adjust the seasoning as needed. Serve immediately or transfer to a clean storage container, cover, and refrigerate until needed.

fennel purée

MAKES ½ CUP/120 ML

½ cup/120 mL chopped
fennel fronds

¼ cup/60 mL chopped
fennel bulb

¼ cup/60 mL
extra-virgin olive oil

3 tbsp/45 mL cold water

2 tsp/10 mL lemon juice

½ tsp/2.50 mL
minced garlic

Salt, as needed

Ground pepper, as needed

Purée the fennel fronds and bulb, oil, water, lemon juice, and garlic together in a blender. Strain through a fine-mesh sieve into a clean storage container and season. Cover and refrigerate until needed.

resources

The following are some Web sites that may be of use when learning about charcuterie:

http://en.wikipedia.org/wiki/Charcuterie

http://www.fsis.usda.gov/fact_Sheets/Sausage_and_Food_Safety/index.asp

http://www.jlindquist.net/generalmicro/324sausage.html

http://www.nysaes.cornell.edu/necfe/pubs/pdf/FactSheets/FS_FermentedSausages.pdf

suggested resources

books

Hugh Fearnley-Whittingstall. *The River Cottage Meat Book*. 2007.

Jane Grigson. *The Art of Charcuterie*. Alfred A Knopf, 1968.

John Kinsella and David T. Harvey. *The Professional Charcuterie*. John Wiley & Sons, Inc., 1996.

Rytek Kutas. *Great Sausage Recipes and Meat Curing*. The Sausage Maker, Inc., 1999.

Meat Evaluation Handbook. www.meatsscience.org.

The Meat We Eat. www.amazon.com.

Lue & Ed Parks. *The Smoked-Foods Cookbook*. Stackpole Books, 1992.

Michael Ruhlman & Brian Polcyn. *Charcuterie*. W. W. Norton & Company Ltd., 2005.

web sites
government

UNITED STATES DEPARTMENT OF AGRICULTURE www.usda.gov

INTERNATIONAL MEAT & POULTRY HACCP ALLIANCE www.haccpalliance.org

PARTNERSHIP FOR FOOD SAFETY EDUCATION www.fightbac.org

IOWA STATE UNIVERSITY www.extension.iastate.edu/foodsafety

associations

AMERICAN MEAT SCIENCE ASSOCIATION www.meatscience.org

NATIONAL PORK BOARD www.porkboard.org

equipment and supplies

SARATOGA FOOD SPECIALTIES BArmstrong@saratogaafs.com

ALKAR tombetley@alkar.com

COZZINI, INC. Ggrady@cozzini.com

KOCH EQUIPMENT Willy.Nunez@kochequipment.com

WORLD PAC INTERNATIONAL U.S.A. world_pac_conv@hotmail.com

POLY-CLIP SYSTEM CORPORATION MarkP@polyclip-usa.com

CHR HANSEN www.chr-hansen.com

LANCE INDUSTRIES

conversion tables

weights

To calculate weight, use following:

> 1 ounce = 28.35 grams
>
> 1 pound = 453.59 grams

Round to the nearest gram (ending in 5 or 0), or to two decimal points for kilograms

U.S. UNIT	METRIC EQUIVALENTS	U.S. UNIT	METRIC EQUIVALENTS
½ ounce	14	11 ounces	312
¾ ounce	21.26	12 ounces (¾ lb)	340
1 ounce	28.35	13 ounces	369
1½ ounces	43	14 ounces	397
1¾ ounces	49.61	15 ounces	425
2 ounces	57	16 ounces (1 lb)	454
2½ ounces	70	1 lb	454
3 ounces	85	1 lb 1 oz	482
3½ ounces	100	1 lb 2 oz	510
4 ounces (¼ lb)	114	1 lb 3 oz	540
4½ ounces	128	1¼ lb (1 lb 4 oz)	567
5 ounces	142	1 lb 5 oz	595
6 ounces	170	1 lb 6 oz	624
7 ounces	198	1 lb 7 oz	652
8 ounces	227	1½ lb (1 lb 8 oz)	680
9 ounces	255	1 lb 9 oz	709
10 ounces	284	1 lb 10 oz	734
10½ ounces	300	1 lb 11 oz	765

U.S. UNIT	METRIC EQUIVALENTS
1¾ lb (1 lb 12 oz) (28 oz)	794
1 lb 13 oz	822
1 lb 14 oz	851
1 lb 15 oz	879
2 lb	908
2¼ lb	1.02 kg
2½ lb	1.14 kg
2¾ lb	1.25 kg
3 lb	1.36 kg
3¼ lb	1.47 kg
3¼ lb (3 lb 8 oz)	1.59 kg
3¾ lb (3 lb 12 oz)	1.70 kg
4 lb	1.81 kg
4¼ lb (4 lb 4 oz)	1.93 kg
4½ lb (4 lb 8 oz)	2.04 kg
4¾ lb	2.15 kg
5 lb	2.27 kg

U.S. UNIT	METRIC EQUIVALENTS
5½ lb	2.50 kg
6 lb	2.27 kg
7 lb	3.18 kg
7½ lb	3.40 kg
8 lb	3.63 kg
9 lb	4.08 kg
10 lb	4.54 kg
11 lb	4.98 kg
12 lb	5.44 kg
13 lb	5.90 kg
13½ lb	6.12 kg
14 lb	6.35 kg
15 lb	6.80 kg
16 lb	7.25 kg
20 lb	9.07 kg
21 lb	9.52 kg
25 lb	11.34 kg

volumes

1 tablespoon = 14.8 milliliters
1 cup (8 fl oz) = 237 milliliters

U.S. VOLUME MEASURE	CONVERSION OPTIONS (IN ORDER OF PREFERENCE)	METRIC EQUIVALENT
¼ teaspoon		1 mL
½ teaspoon		2 mL
¾ teaspoon		3 mL
1 teaspoon		5 mL
½ fl oz	1 tablespoon	15 mL
1 fl oz	2 tablespoons 1/8 cup	30 mL
1½ fl oz	3 tablespoons	45 mL
2 fl oz	¼ cup 4 tablespoons	60 mL
22/3 fl oz	1/3 cup 51/3 tablespoons	80 mL
3 fl oz	6 tablespoons	90 mL
4 fl oz	½ cup 8 tablespoons ¼ pint	120 mL
5 fl oz	1 cup plus 2 tablespoons 10 tablespoons	150 mL
6 fl oz	¾ cup 12 tablespoons	180 mL
7 fl oz	¾ cup plus 2 tablespoons 14 tablespoons	200 mL
8 fl oz	1 cup ½ pint 16 tablespoons	240 mL
10½ fl oz	1 cup plus 5 tablespoons 21 tablespoons	300 mL
11 fl oz	1 cup plus 5 tablespoons	325 mL

U.S. VOLUME MEASURE	CONVERSION OPTIONS (IN ORDER OF PREFERENCE)	METRIC EQUIVALENT
12 fl oz	1½ cups ¾ pint	360 mL
13 fl oz	1½ cups plus 2 tablespoons	385 mL
14 fl oz	1¾ cups	415 mL
15 fl oz		445 mL
16 fl oz	2 cups 1 pint	480 mL
20 fl oz	2½ cups 1¼ pints	600 mL
22 fl oz	2¾ cups	660 mL
24 fl oz	3 cups 1½ pints	720 mL
26 fl oz		780 mL
28 fl oz	3½ cups 1¾ pints	840 mL
32 fl oz	4 cups 1 quart	.95 L (1L)
36 fl oz	4½ cups 1 quart plus 4 oz	
40 fl oz	5 cups 2½ pints	1.2 L
48 fl oz	6 cups 3 pints 1½ quarts	1.41 L (1.4L)
64 fl oz	2 quarts 8 cups ½ gallon	1.89 L (2L)

volumes (continued)

U.S. VOLUME MEASURE	CONVERSION OPTIONS (IN ORDER OF PREFERENCE)	METRIC EQUIVALENT
96 fl oz	3 quarts 12 cups	2.8 L
112 fl oz	7 pints 14 cups 3½ quarts	3.3 L
128 fl oz	1 gallon 4 quarts 8 pints 16 cups	3.75 L
160 fl oz	5 quarts 1¼ gallons 10 pints 20 cups	4.75 L
192 fl oz	6 quarts 1½ gallons 12 pints	5.75 L
224 fl oz	7 quarts 1¾ gallons 14 pints	6.65 L
256 fl oz	2 gallons 8 quarts	7.5 L
288 fl oz	9 quarts 2¼ gallons	8.5 L
320 fl oz	10 quarts 2½ gallons	9.5 L
11 quarts	2¾ gallons	10.5 L
12 quarts	3 gallons	11.36 L
4 gallons		15 L
5 gallons		18.75 L
6 gallons		22.5 L

temperature

To convert from Fahrenheit:

$$°F - 32 \times 5 / 9$$

TEMPERATURES	F°	C°
FREEZING	32	0
	40	4
	100	38
	105	40
	110	43
	115	46
	120	49
	125	52
	130	55
	135	58
	140	60
	145	63
	150	65
	160	70
	165	73
	170	75
	175	80
	180	82
	185	85
	190	88
	195	90
	200	95

temperature (continued)

TEMPERATURES	F°	C°
BOILING	212	100
	220	105
	225	107
SYRUP	230 234	110 112
FUDGE SOFT BALL	234 238 240	112 114 115
CARAMEL FIRM BALL	244 248	118 120
DIVINITY HARD BALL	250 260 266	121 125 130
BUTTERSCOTCH SOFT CRACK	270 275 290	132 135 143
BRITTLE HARD CRACK	300 310	150 155
BARLEY SUGAR (SUGAR MELTS CLEAR)	320	160
	324	162
	325	165
	330	166
	335	168
CARAMEL (MELTED SUGAR TURNS BROWN)	338	170
	340	171
	350	175
	360	180

CONVERSION TABLES

TEMPERATURES	F°	C°
	365	182
	370	185
	375	190
	380	195
	390	200
	400	205
	425	220
	450	230
	475	245
	500	260
	575	275
	600	315

table of final/resting temps

FRESH BEEF, VEAL, AND LAMB

Rare	135°F / 58°C	interior appearance shiny
Medium rare	145°F / 63°C	
Medium	160°F/70°C	
Well done	170°F/75°C	
FRESH PORK		meat opaque throughout
Medium	160°F/70°C	slight give, juices with faint blush
Well done	170°F/75°C	slight give, juices clear
HAM		
Fresh ham	160°F/71°C	see pork
Precooked (to reheat)	140°F/60°C	meat already fully cooked
POULTRY		
Whole birds (chicken, turkey, duck, goose)	180°F/82°C	leg easy to move in socket, juices with only blush
Poultry breasts	170°F/75°C	meat opaque, firm throughout
Poultry thighs, legs, wings	180°F/82°C	meat releases from bone
Stuffing (cooked alone or in bird)	165°F/74°C	
GROUND MEAT AND MEAT MIXTURES		
Turkey, chicken	165°F/74°C	opaque throughout, juices clear
Beef, veal, lamb, pork	160°F/71°C	opaque, may have blush of red, juices opaque, no red some (lean white)
SEAFOOD		
Fish	145°F/63°C or until opaque	still moist, separates easily into segments
Shrimp, lobster, crab		shells turn red, flesh becomes pearly opaque
Scallops		turn milky white or opaque and firm
Clams, mussels, oysters		shells open

sodium content of commonly used salts

	BRAND	TEASPOON MEASUREMENT	WEIGHT MEASUREMENT	MILLIGRAMS OF SODIUM	INGREDIENTS
Kosher Salts	Diamond Crystal	¼ teaspoon	.7 grams	280 mg	Salt
	Morton	¼ teaspoon	1.2 grams	480 mg	Salt, yellow prussiate of soda (a water-soluble, anti-caking agent)
	North American Salt Company	¼ teaspoon	1.2 grams	480 mg	Salt
Sea Salts	Lima French Atlantic	¼ teaspoon	1 gram	330 mg	Salt
	La Baleine (fine crystals)	¼ teaspoon	1.5 grams	580 mg	Sea salt, magnesium oxide (an anti-caking agent)
Table Salt	Morton table salt	¼ teaspoon	1.5 grams	590 mg	Salt, calcium silicate (dextrose and potassium iodide are also added to Morton iodized salt)

glossary

a

ACID: A substance having a sour or sharp flavor. A substance's degree of acidity is measured on the pH scale; acids have a pH of less than 7. Most foods are somewhat acidic. Foods generally referred to as "acids" include citrus juice, vinegar, and wine. See also *alkali*.

AEROBIC BACTERIA: Bacteria that require the presence of oxygen to function.

AIR-DRYING: Exposing meats and sausages to proper temperature and humidity conditions to change both flavor and texture for consumption or further processing. Times and temperatures will vary depending on the type of meat or sausage.

ALBUMEN: The white of an egg; also the major protein in egg whites (also spelled albumin); used in dry form in some cold food preparations.

ALKALI: A substance that tests at higher than 7 on the pH scale. Alkalis are sometimes described as having a slightly soapy flavor. Olives and baking soda are some of the few alkaline foods. See also *acid*.

ALLUMETTE: Vegetables, potatoes, or other items cut into pieces the size and shape of matchsticks; ⅛ in by ⅛ in by 1 to 2 in/3 by 3 mm by 3 to 5 cm is the standard measure for the cut.

ANAEROBIC BACTERIA: Bacteria that do not require oxygen to function.

ANDOUILLE: A spicy pork sausage that is French in origin but now is more often associated with Cajun cooking. There are hundreds of variations of this regional specialty.

ASPIC: A clear jelly made from clarified stock (or occasionally from fruit or vegetable juices) thickened with gelatin. Used to coat foods, or cubed and used as a garnish.

ASCORBIC ACID: Otherwise known as vitamin C and its conjugate salt, sodium ascorbate, it acts as an antioxidant, by which it prevents the oxidation of fats and proteins and, in turn, prevents spoiling.

b

BACTERIA: Microscopic organisms. Some have beneficial properties, while others can cause food-borne illnesses when contaminated foods are ingested.

BARD: To cover an item with thin slices, sheets, or strips of fat, such as bacon or fatback, to baste it during roasting. The fat is usually tied on with butcher's twine.

BASTE: To moisten food during cooking with pan drippings, sauce, or other liquid. Basting prevents food from drying out, improves color, and adds flavor.

BINDER: An ingredient or appareil used to thicken a sauce or hold together a mixture of ingredients.

BLANCH: To cook an item briefly in boiling water or hot fat before finishing or storing it. This sets the color and can make the skin easier to remove.

BLOOD SAUSAGE: Also called black pudding or blood pudding, a sausage where the main ingredient is liquid blood.

BLOOM: To soften gelatin in lukewarm liquid before use. Also, to allow casing on smoked sausage to darken at room temperature after smoking.

BOUQUET GARNI(FR.): A small bundle of herbs tied with string that is used to flavor stocks, braises, and other preparations. Usually contains bay leaf, parsley, thyme, and possibly other aromatics, such as leek and celery stalk.

BRINE PUMP: Tool used for injecting a brine into meat for a more uniform distribution. A brine pump consists of a plunger, cylinder, strainer, hose, and needle. Brine pumps come in different volume-size pieces.

BUBBLE KNOT: Also called a triple knot. Used to tie beef round, middle, and bung casings. A piece of casing is caught between the first two knots, and a third knot is used to lock the previous knots in place. A length of string is often left at the end for hanging.

BULK SAUSAGE: Sausage that is not contained in a casing. Sausages commonly found in bulk include breakfast sausage and Italian sausages meant to be used in pizzas or other dishes. Generally, only fresh sausage is packaged bulk.

(BEEF) BUNG CAP: Beef appendix, typically used for larger sausages such as bologna and mortadella. Generally, 2 to 2½ ft/61 to 76 cm long with a diameter of about 4 to 6 in/10 to 15 cm, a beef bung can hold from 10 to 20 lb/4.54 to 9.07 kg of sausage.

C

CARAMELIZATION: The process of browning sugar in the presence of heat. The temperature range in which sugar begins to caramelize is approximately 320° to 360°F/160° to 182°C.

CASING: A synthetic or natural membrane (usually pig, beef, or sheep intestines) used to enclose sausage forcemeat.

CAUL FAT: A fatty membrane from a pig or sheep that lines the stomach and resembles fine netting; used to bard roasts and pâtés and to encase sausage forcemeat.

CELLULOSE: A complex carbohydrate; the main structural component of plant cells.

CHARCUTERIE (FR.): The preparation of pork and other meat items, such as hams, terrines, sausages, pâtés, and other forcemeats that are usually preserved in some manner, such as smoking, brining, and curing.

CHAUD-FROID (FR.): Literally, "hot-cold." A sauce that is prepared hot but served cold as part of a buffet display, usually as a decorative coating for meats, poultry, or seafood; classically made from béchamel, cream, or aspic.

CHIPOLATA: A small, spicy sausage usually made from pork or veal and stuffed into a sheep casing.

CHITTERLINGS: Hog middle intestines.

CLARIFIED BUTTER: Butter from which the milk solids and water have been removed, leaving pure butterfat. Has a higher smoking point than whole butter but less butter flavor. Also known as ghee.

COAGULATION: The curdling or clumping of protein usually due to the application of heat or acid.

COLD SMOKING: Used to give smoked flavor to products without cooking them

COLLAGEN: A fibrous protein found in the connective tissue of animals that is used to make sausage casings as well as glue and gelatin. Breaks down into gelatin when cooked in a moist environment for an extended period of time.

COLLAGEN CASING: Casings made from collagen that is usually obtained from animal hides. Collagen casings are easy to use and store and have the advantage of being uniform and consistent.

COUNTRY-STYLE: A forcemeat that is coarse in texture, usually made from pork, pork fat, liver, and various garnishes.

CROSS CONTAMINATION: The transference of disease-causing elements from one source to another through physical contact.

CURE: To preserve a food by salting. Also, the ingredients used to cure an item.

CURING SALT: A mixture of 94 percent table salt (sodium chloride) and 6 percent sodium nitrite used to preserve meats. Also known as tinted curing mixture, or TCM. Curing salt is distinguished by its pink color.

CURRY: A mixture of spices used primarily in Indian cuisine; may include turmeric, coriander, cumin, cayenne or other chiles, cardamom, cinnamon, clove, fennel, fenugreek, ginger, and garlic. Also, a dish seasoned with curry.

d

DRY CURE: A combination of salts and spices used usually before smoking to process meats and forcemeats.

e

EMULSION: A mixture of two or more liquids, one of which is a fat or oil and the other of which is water-based, so that tiny globules of one are suspended in the other. This may involve the use of stabilizers, such as egg or mustard. Emulsions may be temporary, permanent, or semipermanent.

EP/EDIBLE PORTION: The weight of an item after trimming and preparation (as opposed to the purchased weight, or AP).

ERYTHORBIC ACID AND SODIUM ERYTHORBATE: Stereoisomers of ascorbic acid and sodium ascorbate. These are more commonly used than ascorbic acid.

f

FACULTATIVE BACTERIA: Bacteria that can survive both with and without oxygen.

FARCE: Forcemeat or stuffing (*farci* means "stuffed").

FAT: One of the basic nutrients used by the body to provide energy. Fats also provide flavor in food and give a feeling of fullness.

FERMENTATION: The breakdown of carbohydrates into carbon dioxide gas and alcohol, usually through the action of yeast on sugar.

FERMENTO: A commonly used brand of dairy-based fermentation product for semi-dry fermented sausages, used to lower pH and give a tangy flavor.

FINES HERBES: A mixture of fresh herbs, usually equal parts by volume of parsley, chervil, tarragon, and chives.

FOIE GRAS: The fattened liver of a force-fed duck or goose.

FOOD-BORNE ILLNESS: An illness in humans caused by the consumption of an adulterated food product. For a food-borne illness outbreak to be considered official, it must involve two or more people who have eaten the same food and it must be confirmed by health officials.

FORCEMEAT: A mixture of chopped or ground meat or seafood and other ingredients used for pâté, sausages, and other preparations.

g

GARDE MANGER: Cold kitchen chef or station; the position responsible for cold food preparations, including pâtés.

GARNISH: An edible decoration or accompaniment to a dish.

GELATIN: A protein-based substance found in animal bones and connective tissue. When dissolved in hot liquid and then cooled, it can be used as a thickener and stabilizer.

GELATINIZATION: A phase in the process of thickening a liquid with starch in which starch molecules swell to form a network that traps water molecules.

GRATINÉ (FR.): A forcemeat in which some portion of the dominant meat is seared and cooled before grinding

GRAVLAX: Raw salmon cured with salt, sugar, and fresh dill. A regional dish of Scandinavian origin.

GRINDER: A machine used to grind meat, ranging from small hand-operated models to large-capacity motor-driven models. Meat or other foods are fed through a hopper into the grinder where the worm or auger pushes them into a blade. The blade cuts and forces the item through different-size grinder plates. Care should be taken to keep the machine as clean as possible to lessen the chances of cross contamination when using.

GRINDER PLATES: Used to determine the texture of the ground meat, plates come in varying sizes, from as small as $^1/_8$ in/3 mm for fine-textured ground meat to as large as $^3/_8$ in/9 mm, used mostly to create garnishes for emulsion sausages.

GROSSE PIÈCE (FR.): Literally, "large piece." The main part of a pâté or terrine that is left unsliced and serves as a focal point for a platter or other display.

h

HANGING STICKS: Hanging sticks are stainless metal sticks that are used for smoking and drying sausages. Hanging sticks may be used to suspend other items in the smoker as well.

HEAD CHEESE: A jellied meat product typically made from diced boiled pork head meat held together by the natural gelatin contained in the reduced stock left over from boiling the head. Garnished with pickles, pimientos, and parsley and flavored with vinegar.

HOCK: The lowest part of an animal's leg, could be considered the ankle, usually for pork (i.e., ham hock).

HOG CASINGS: Casings are made from the small and middle hog intestine (as well as the beef bung). Used for countless sausages, hog casings range in diameter size from $1^1/_4$ to $1^1/_3$ in/32 to 35 mm (used for bratwurst and Italian sausage) to $1^1/_2$ to $1^2/_3$ in/38 to 42 mm (used for Polish sausage and pepperoni). The type of hog casing used will depend on the intended application.

HOT SMOKING: A technique used when a fully cooked smoked item is desired. Both cured and uncured items can be hot smoked. Smoking temperature and time will depend on the product.

HYGIENE: Conditions and practices followed to maintain health, including sanitation and personal cleanliness.

HYDROMETER AND HYDROMETER JAR (SALIMETER): The hydrometer is an item that measures the density of a liquid.

INFUSION: Steeping an aromatic or other item in liquid to extract its flavor. Also, the liquid resulting from this process.

INSTANT-READ THERMOMETER: A thermometer used to measure the internal temperature of foods. The stem is inserted in the food, producing an instant temperature readout.

j

JUS (FR.): Juice. *Jus de viande* is meat juice. Meat served au jus is served with its own juice.

k

KOSHER: Prepared in accordance with Jewish dietary laws.

KOSHER SALT: Pure, refined rock salt often preferred for pickling because it does not contain magnesium carbonate and thus it does not cloud brine solutions. (Also known as coarse salt or pickling salt.)

l

LARD: Rendered pork fat used for pastry and frying. Also the process of inserting strips of fat or seasonings into meat before roasting or braising to add flavor and succulence.

LARDON (FR.): A strip of pork fat, used for larding; may be seasoned.

LINKS: Particular segments of sausage created when a filled casing is twisted or tied off at intervals.

LOOPED SAUSAGE: Also known as ring-tied sausages; kielbasa is an example of these longer sausages. Also refers to sausage made in beef round casings.

MAILLARD REACTION: A complex browning reaction that results in the distinctive flavor and color of foods that do not contain much sugar, including roasted meats. The reaction, which involves carbohydrates and amino acids, is named after the French scientist who first discovered it. There are low-temperature and high-temperature Maillard reactions; high temperature starts at 310°F/154°C.

MANDOLINE: A slicing device of stainless steel with carbon-steel blades. The blades may be adjusted to cut items into various cuts and thicknesses.

MARBLING: The intramuscular fat found in meat that makes the meat tender and juicy when cooked.

MESOPHILIC: A term used to describe bacteria that thrive within the middle-range temperatures—between 60°F and 100°F/16°C to 43°C.

MISE EN PLACE: Literally, "put in place." The preparation and assembly of ingredients, pans, utensils, and plates or serving pieces needed for a particular dish or service period.

MPR: Moisture to protein ratio.

O

OFFAL: Variety meats including head meat, tail, and feet as well as organs such as brains, heart, kidneys, lights (or lungs), sweetbreads, tripe, and tongue.

ORGAN MEAT: Meat from an organ, rather than the muscle tissue, of an animal.

P

PANADA: An appareil based on starch (such as flour or crumbs) moistened with a liquid; used as a binder.

PARCHMENT: Heat-resistant paper used to line baking pans, cook items en papillote, construct pastry cones, and cover items during shallow poaching.

PARCOOK: To partially cook an item before storing or finishing by another method; may be the same as blanching.

PÂTE (FR.): Pastry or noodle dough.

PÂTÉ (FR.): A rich forcemeat of meat, game, poultry, seafood, and/or vegetables, baked in pastry or in a mold or dish.

PÂTÉ DE CAMPAGNE: Country-style pâté, with a coarse texture.

PÂTÉ EN CROÛTE: Pâté baked in a pastry crust.

PELLICLE: A sticky "skin" that forms on the outside of produce, salmon, sausage, or meats through air drying and helps smoke particles adhere to the food, resulting in a better, more evenly smoked product.

PH SCALE: A scale with values from 0 to 14 representing degree of acidity. A measurement of 7 is neutral, 0 is most acidic, and 14 is most alkaline. Chemically, pH measures the concentration/activity of the element hydrogen.

PICKLING SPICE: A mixture of herbs and spices used to season pickles; often includes dill seed, coriander seed, cinnamon stick, peppercorns, and bay leaves.

PINCÉ (FR.): To caramelize an item by sautéing; usually refers to a tomato product.

PROSCUITTO: A dry-cured ham. True proscuitto comes from Parma, Italy, although variations can be found throughout the world.

q

QUENELLE (FR.): A light, poached dumpling based on a forcemeat (usually chicken, veal, seafood, or game) bound with eggs that is typically shaped into an oval.

r

REDUCE: To decrease the volume of a liquid by simmering or boiling; used to provide a thicker consistency and/or concentrated flavors and color.

REDUCTION: The product that results when a liquid is reduced.

REFRESH: To plunge an item into, or run under, cold water after blanching to prevent further cooking. Also referred to as shocking.

RENDER: To melt fat and clarify the drippings for use in sautéing or pan frying.

s

SACHET D'ÉPICES: Literally, "bag of spices." Aromatic ingredients, encased in cheesecloth that are used to flavor stocks and other liquids. A standard sachet contains parsley stems, cracked peppercorns, dried thyme, a bay leaf, and sometimes garlic.

SALÉ (FR.): Salted or pickled.

SALT COD: Codfish that has been salted and dried to preserve it. Also referred to as baccalà or bacalao.

SALTPETER: Potassium nitrate. Formerly used to preserve meat. It is a component of curing salt; it gives certain cured meats their characteristic pink color. Not used commercially since 1975 because its residual amounts are not consistent.

SANITATION: The practice of preparation and distribution of food in a clean environment by healthy food workers.

SANITIZE: To kill pathogenic organisms by chemicals and/or moist heat.

SCALD: To heat a liquid, usually milk or cream, to just below the boiling point. May also refer to blanching fruits and vegetables.

SCORE: To cut the surface of an item at regular intervals to allow it to cook or cure evenly.

SEA SALT: Salt produced by evaporating sea water. Available as refined or unrefined, crystallized or ground. Also called *sel gris,* French for "gray salt."

SILVERSKIN: The tough, connective tissue that surrounds certain muscles.

SLURRY: Starch (flour, cornstarch, or arrowroot) dispersed in cold liquid to prevent it from forming lumps when added to hot liquid as a thickener.

SMEARING: A fault in sausages; if sausage is processed at too high a temperature, fat will soften and become smeared throughout the sausage. Smeared fat has a tendency to leak out of the sausage and leave it dry.

SMOKE ROASTING: Roasting over wood or chips in an oven to add a smoky flavor. A method for roasting foods in which items are placed on a rack in a pan containing wood chips that smolder and emit smoke when the pan is placed on the range top or in the oven.

SMOKING: Any of several methods for preserving and flavoring foods by exposing them to smoke. Methods include cold smoking (in which smoked items are not fully cooked), hot smoking (in which the items are cooked), and smoke roasting.

SMOKING POINT: The temperature at which a fat begins to smoke when heated.

SODIUM: An alkaline metal element necessary in small quantities for human nutrition; one of the components of most salts used in cooking.

SODIUM NITRATE: Used in curing meat products that are not going to be heated by cooking, smoking, or canning.

STRAIGHT FORCEMEAT: A forcemeat combining pork and pork fat with another meat, made by grinding the mixture together.

SWEETBREADS: The thymus glands of young animals, usually calves but possibly lambs. Usually sold in pairs of lobes.

t

TABLE SALT: Refined, granulated rock salt. May be fortified with iodine and treated with magnesium carbonate to prevent clumping.

TCM/TINTED CURING MIX: See *Curing salt*.

TEMPER: To heat gently and gradually. May refer to the process of incorporating hot liquid into a liaison to gradually raise its temperature. May also refer to the proper method for melting chocolate.

TENDERLOIN: A cut of tender expensive meat from the loin or hind quarter, usually beef or pork.

TERRINE: A loaf of forcemeat, similar to a pâté but cooked in a covered mold in a bain-marie. Also, the mold used to cook such items, usually a loaf shape made of ceramic.

THERMOPHILIC: Heat-loving; describes bacteria that thrive within the temperature range of 110°F to 171°F/43°C to 77°C.

TOMALLEY: Lobster liver, which is olive green in color and turns red when cooked or heated.

TOTAL UTILIZATION: The principle advocating the use of as much of a product as possible to reduce waste and increase profits.

TRICHINELLA SPIRALIS: A spiral-shaped parasitic worm that invades the intestines and muscle tissue; transmitted primarily through infected pork that has not been cooked sufficiently.

TRICHINOSIS: The disease transmitted by *Trichinella spiralis*.

TRIPE: The edible stomach lining of a cow or other ruminant. Honeycomb tripe comes from the second stomach and has a honeycomb-like texture.

TRUSS: To tie up meat or poultry with string before cooking it to give it a compact shape for more even cooking and better appearance.

V

VARIETY MEAT: Meat from a part of an animal other than the muscle; for example, organs.

VENISON: Originally meat from large game animals; now specifically refers to deer meat.

VERTICAL CHOPPING MACHINE (VCM): A machine similar to a blender that has rotating blades used to grind, whip, emulsify, or blend foods.

VINAIGRETTE (FR.): A cold sauce of oil and vinegar, usually with various flavorings; it is a temporary emulsion sauce. The standard proportion is three parts oil to one part vinegar.

W

WHITE MIREPOIX: Mirepoix that does not include carrots and may include chopped mushrooms or mushroom trimmings and parsnips; used for pale or white sauces and stocks.

Y

YEAST: Microscopic fungus whose metabolic processes are responsible for fermentation; used for leavening bread and in making cheese, beer, and wine.

YOGURT: Milk cultured with bacteria to give it a slightly thick consistency and sour flavor.

Z

ZEST: The thin, brightly colored outer part of citrus rind. It contains volatile oils, making it ideal for use as a flavoring.

subject index

Page numbers in *italics* indicate photographs or illustrations.

a

Acetic acid, 69, 127
Acid hydrolysis, 26
Acidity, 10–11, 59, 69, 73, 225.
    See also pH
Acids
    ascorbic (*See* Ascorbic acid)
    citric, 29, 30, 31, 32
    erythorbic, 30, 31, 75, 211
    lactic (*See* Lactic acid)
    ortophosphoric, 33
    produced by smoke, 127
    pyrophosphoric, 33
    role in marinades, 83, 84, 85
Actin, 42, 46
Additives, 28–33, 73, 209–11
Agar, 285
Age of animal, 43, 47
Aging process of meat, 11, *222*, 227
Aitchbone, 105
Alcohol
    to aid pellicle formation, 129
    bound to fatty acids to create fat, 44
    bourbon to store truffles, 22
    in brines, 80
    to eliminate heat from pepper, 18
    in forcemeats, 151
    See also Wine
Aleoresins, 208

Alkalinity, 10–11, 33. *See also* pH
Allergens and allergic reactions, 63, 67
Allspice, 22, 28, 208
Anaerobic environment, 56, 61
Andouille, 206, 228
Anise seed, 22, 23, 28
Antioxidants, 29, 30, 31, 32, 127, 209
Appendix. *See* Bung
Appetizers, coating sauces for, 279
Arrowroot, 278
Ascorbic acid (vitamin C)
    about, 30, 31, 32
    to prevent formation of nitrosamines,
        29, 75, 211
Aspic, 173, *279*, 279–80
aw. *See* Water activity

b

Back fat cut, *49*
Bacon
    about, 87
    Canadian, 87
    to line terrine mold, 150
    meat-to-dry cure ratio, 90
    meat-to-nitrate/nitrite ratio, 29
    and nitrosamines, 75, 211
    products which use, 27
    woods used for smoking, 90, 92, 93,
        137
Bacon comb, 14
Bacteria
    beneficial, 56–57 (*See also* Lactic acid,

bacterial cultures which produce)
breakdown of nitrates by, 29
color- and flavor-forming, 69
in sausage, 59–62
in seafood, 51
temperature danger zone, 56, 61,
127, 130
See also specific bacteria
Bactoferm F-LC, 34
Bactoferm T-SPX, 34
Barbecue, 133
Basil, 21, 23, 28, 72
Bavarian loaf, 206, 229
Bay (laurel) leaves, 21, 28, 80, 137
Beef
braised, 28, 173
casings (*See under* Casings)
corned, 28, 82, 87
cuts, *48*
ground, 28
sausage, 19, 27, 28
woods used for smoking, 137, 139,
140, 256, 257
Beet powder, 75
Belly cut, *49*
Benzoate, 65
Berbere, 86
Binders
for forcemeats, 149, 150, *151*, 151–
52, 164, 205
gelatin, 46
hydrocolloids, 76
for pastes, 87
for sauces, 278
for sausages, 209–10
sodium caseinate, 30, 32, 209
sodium phosphate, 32
soy protein, soy concentrate, and soy
protein isolate, 33, 210
for terrines, 173
of water for cures or brines, 76
See also Emulsifiers
Blades, 2, *3*, 7, *7*, 8
Bleeding out, 42

Blenders, 15, 86, 285
Blood, 42, 228. *See also* Hemoglobin
Bockwurst, 228
Bologna
about, 204, 228
casings, 213, 214, 228
emulsification of fat in, 46
garnish used in, 209
Lebanon, 227
spices and herbs used in, 19, 26
Boston butt cut, *49*
Bottom sirloin cut, *48*
Botulism. *See Clostridium botulinum*
Bouquet garni, 20
Bratwurst, 27, 206, 212, 225, 228
Braunschweiger, 23, 27, 228
Bread, as binder for forcemeats, *151*,
152
Breast cut, *48*, *49*
Brine
about, 79–80
for fish, 114
function of specific ingredients in, 72
measurement of liquid density, 10
for pork and beef, 115, 122, 268
for poultry, 117, 121
for scallops or shrimp, 116
Brining process
about, 14, 72, 79
fish, prior to hot-smoking, 136
gray spots, 82–83
procedure, 79–82, 136
spoilage, 83, 325
Brisket, 28, *48*, 82, 87, 137
Browning, 27, 44
Bucket, skin, 14
Buffer solutions and sachets, 11
Bung
beef, 213, *213*, 218, 220, 228, 229
hog, 212, *213*, 228, 229
Butt cut, *49*
Buttermilk, 83, 85

C

Calcium, 42, 51, 85
Calibration, 11, 68
Capacolla, 110, 213
Caraway seed, 22, 28, 208
Carbohydrates, 42, 43, 45
Carbon bonds, 44
Carbonyls, 127
Carcass. *See* Slaughter
Cardamom, 23, 208
Carotenoids, 50
Cartilage, 52, 67
Casein, 30
Casings
  artificial, 211, 213–17, *217*
  hardened from improper humidity, 11
  hog rings and casing clips to seal,
    9–10, 218
  natural, *213*
    about, 211–12
    beef bung, 213, *213*, 218, 220, 228,
      229
    beef round, 110
    hog bung, *213*, 228, 229
    inspection, 66
  novel-shaped, 217, *217*
  preparation, 214, 215, 217, 218, *219*,
    220
  release of air by teasing needle, 15,
    222, 224
  skin, for galantines, 169
  storage and transport, 14, 66
  substitutions, 268
  types, 211–17, *212*, *217*, 228–29
Cattle
  Appendix. (*See* Bung, beef)
  carcass breakdown and cuts, *48*

hide, collagen in, 214
  intestines (*See under* Casings
CDC. *See* Centers for Disease Control
  and Prevention
Celery juice, 75
Celery seed, 21, 28
Cellulose, 214, 215
Centers for Disease Control and
  Prevention (CDC), 60
Cervelat. *See* Sausages, summer
Ceviche, 84
Charcuterie, ix, 40, 57
Chaud-froid, 279, 280, *281, 282*
Cheese, 137, 229, 280, 283
Cheesecloth, 169, *170, 171*
Cherries, 153, 175
Chervil, 28
Chicken
  brining times, 82
  fat, 208
  low myoglobin content, 75, 211
  smoked, 130, 137
  terrine, 172
Chiles, 80
Chili powder, 20
Chimney, *184*
Chipolata, 228
Chitterlings, 212, 228
Chives, 23
Chopper, buffalo, 6, *6*
Chorizo, 130, 206, 224, 228
Chuck cut, *48, 49*
Chutney, 286–87
Cilantro, 19
Cinnamon, 28, 137
Citric acid, 29, 30, 31, 32
Clams, 137
Cleanliness
  garments, 67
  grinding equipment, 2, 7, 56, 67
  hands, 56, 67
  ice box and ice scoop, 66
  pH meter probe, 11
  sanitize all surfaces, 56, 59, 136

Curing process (*continued*)

   See also Brining; Dry curing process

Curing tub, 14

Curry paste, 86

Curry powder, 28

Cuts of meat and carcass breakdown, 48, *48–49*

Cutters, 6, *6*, 8, *9*, 223

d

Dairy products, 83, 85, 280, 283

Dehydrator, 139, 141

Demi-glace, 279, *282*

Density of a liquid, measurement, 10

Dextrose, *24, 210*

   about, 24, 32, 209

   to aid in browning, 27

   conversions, 74, 209

   metabolization by beneficial bacteria, 73

   relative sweetness, 74

Die/plate assembly, 2, *3*, 7, *7*, *8*, *152*

Diet of animal, 44, 50, 51, 87

Diglyceride, 83

Dill, 28

Dill seed, 28

Documentation

   smoking procedure for fish, 138

   standard operating procedures chart, 67

   temperature readings during smoking, 136

   written procedure for sanitation of equipment, 67

Dry-cured meats

   common, 87

   Insta Cure No. 2 for, 75

meat-to-dry cure ratio, 90

meat-to-nitrate/nitrite ratio, 29

sausage, 225–27, *226*

Dry curing process

   about, 58, 77, 204, 225–26

   to control trichinae, 63

   gravlax-style, 78

   procedure, 34, 77–79

   role of acidity, 69

   sausages, 225–27

Duck, 133

e

E. coli. See Escherichia coli

Eggs, 150, 151, *151*, 205, 278–79

Elastin, 43

Emulsification process, 46, 76, 223

Emulsifiers

   for fat, 30, 31

   made creamier with sodium phosphate, 32

   mustard, 23, 278

   salt, 32, 223

   for vinaigrette and mayonnaise, 83, 278–79

   See also Binders

Emulsions

   for meat

     and binding by mustard, 18, 26

     chicken-ice-milk powder for sausage, 205

     5/4/3 or 543, 8, 149, 155, 223

   for sauces, 278–79

Enzymes, 42, 52, 69, 85, 173

Epimysium, 47

Equilibrium relative humidity (ERH), 12–13

Equipment
    commonly used, 14–15
    grinders (*See* Grinding equipment)
    importance of cleanliness, 2, 7, 56, 67
    juice extractor, 286
    maintenance, 68
    measurement instruments, 10–13
    pastry bag, *177, 183*
    poissonier, *171*
    resources, 333
    for rubs, 86
    stuffing, 9–10, 218 (*See also* Stuffer,
        sausage)
ERH. *See* Equilibrium relative humidity
Erythorbic acid (erythorbate), 30, 31,
    75, 211
Escherichia coli, 58, 60
Ethanol, 69
Ethnic foods, 76
Extractions, juice, 285–86
Extractor, juice, 286

f

Fat
    ascorbic acid to prevent oxidation, 30
    caul, 150, 221, *231*
    chicken, 208, 246
    fatback
        about, 150, 164
        to line terrine mold, *177–78*
        in sausage, 40, 208, *208*
    in forcemeats, 150, 151, 155, 164, 223
    as a garnish, 209
    intramuscular, 47
    jowl, 40, 63, 151, 164, 207–8, *208*
    lamb, 208
    leaf (kidney), 104, 207

    meat-to-fat ratio, 40, 149, 151, 205, 220
    percent in lean red meat, 41
    percent in muscle, 45
    percent in sausage, 164, 207
    pork belly to provide, 40
    saturated and unsaturated, 43–44, 51
    in sausage, 40, 207–8
    separation of globules (*See*
        Emulsification process; Emulsifiers)
    substitutions, 205, 207
    vegetable, 44
Fatty acids, 43–44, 51
FDA. *See* U.S. Food and Drug
    Administration
Fennel seed, 20, 23, 27, 28
Fermentation
    of carbohydrates, 69, 225
    encouraged by dextrose, 24, 32
    fatty acids affect temperature of, 44
    in sauerkraut production, 325
    in sausage production, 225, 227
    temperatures, 34
Fermento, 34, 206
Fibril, 41
Fibrous casings, 214, 215–16, 217
Fig, 85
Fines herbes, 21
First in–first out system, 67
Fish
    blackened, 86
    brining and kippering procedure, 79
    dry cure times, 79
    farmed, 51
    fin, 51–52, 53
    gravad, 65
    muscle, 47, 50, 52
    nutrients, 51
    pathogens in, 51, 64–65
    salmonids, 50 (*See also* Salmon; Trout)
    smoking procedures, 133, 136, 137
    See also specific fish
5/4/3 or 543 emulsion, 8, 149, 155,
    223
Five-spice powder, 72

Flank cut, *48*
Flavor enhancers
  in brine, 81
  hydrocolloids, 76
  Insta Cure No. 1, 210
  rubs and pastes, 86, 87
  salt, 32
  smoke, 127, 130, 133
Flavor of meat
  chemical sources, 44
  creation of flavor profile, 76
  ethnic flavor profiles, 76
  palatability, factors which affect, 47
  stability, 31, 44
  "tang" of sausage, 27, 225, 227
Flavors *vs.* flavorings, 208
Flour, 152, 285
Foams, 285
Food processor, 8
Food safety
  allergens and allergic reactions, 63, 67
  biological hazards (*See specific microorganisms*)
  chilled equipment and meat
    during brining, 79, 80, 83
    forcemeat, 164, 167
    during grinding, 2, *3, 5,* 7
    sausage, 208, 220, 221
    temperature, 56, 67, 150
  cover all items, 56
  creosote production and cancer, 135
  cross contamination (*See* Cross contamination)
  do not reuse marinade, 84
  importance of proper refrigeration, 13, 56
  inspections, 40
  nitrites and cancer, 29, 31, 75, 211
  parasites, 62–63
  prevention of microorganisms (*See* Microorganisms, prevention of growth)
  seafood, 51, 52, 138
  smoking process, 128, 135, 136, 225

  use gloves, 56
  wash hands, 56, 67, 136
  wood selection for hot-smoking, 135
Food Safety and Inspection Service (FSIS), 66, 208, 332
Foot cut, *49*
Forcemeat
  binders, 149, *151,* 151–52
  causes of bad, 150
  cooking procedure, 154, *154*
  country-style or campagne, 149, 155, *156, 158*
  emulsification in, 46, 223
  four basic components, 150
  garnishes, 151, 153, *153,* 155
  gratin-style, 149, 155, *163, 172*
  healthier, 149, 205
  mousseline-style, 149, 150, 155, *165–66,* 205
  preparations and styles, 149, 155
  progressive grinding, 152, *152*
  recipe development, 154–55
  seafood, 130
  straight-style, 149, 155, *160–61*
Foreign materials in meat, 67, 68
Foreshank cut, *48, 49*
Formaldehyde, 127
Frankfurters, hot dogs, and wieners
  about, 228
  additives used in, 25–26, 31
  casings, 212, 228
  hot-smoking used for, 224
  spices and herbs used in, 19, 23, 25
  USDA classification, 206
Freezing, 63, 227, 286
Frizzes, 226
Fructose, 43, 73, 74
Fruit
  in chutneys, 286
  enzymes in, 85
  as a garnish, 153, 175
  juice (*See* Juices, fruit)
  in oil or vinegar infusions, 284, 285
  pickled, 287

purée as an emulsifier, 278
in sauces, 280, 283
See also specific fruits
FSIS. *See* Food Safety and Inspection Service
Fungi. *See* Molds; Truffles; Yeasts

g

Galactose, 74
Galantines, 151, 169
Game meat, 137
Garde manger, ix, 149, 280, 287
Garlic
  about, 19–20
  as an emulsifier, 278
  in cures or brines, 72, 80
  in forcemeats, 151
  in jellied and pressed meats, 174
  in marinades, 84
  in pastes, 87
  products which use, 25, 26, 27
  in sausage, 208, 225, 227
  and sense of taste, 26
  used as smoking fuel, 137
Garnish
  in forcemeats, 151, 153, *153*, 155
  inlay or lay-in, 153, *153*
  in jellied and pressed meats, 173
  in sausage, 209
  sealed-in, *281*
GDL. *See* Glucono delta lactone
Gelatin
  as an additive, 46, 76
  in aspic gelées, *279*, 279–80
  formation during sausage production, 216
  in jellied meats, 173, 174

in terrines, 173
Gelation process, 46, 76, 173, 280, 285
Gelées, *279*, 279–80, *281*, *282*
Ginger, 20, 28, 85
Glace de viande, 278
Glaze, 19, 27, 28, 72
Glucono delta lactone (GDL), 31
Glucose, 43, 73
Glycerol, 44, 57
Glycogen, 50
Goose, 171
Gratin. *See* Forcemeat, gratin-style
Gravlax-style cure, 78
Gray spots, with brining, 82–83
"Green" weight, 226
Grinding equipment
  do not overload, 2
  meat grinder, *3*, *5*, 7, *7*, *8*
  safe operation, 2
  spice grinder, 15, 86
Grinding process
  chilled equipment and meat
    about, 2, *3*, *5*, 7
    forcemeat, 164, 167
    sausage, 208, 220, 221
    temperature, 56, 150
  mise en place, *4*, *158*, *160*, *163*, *166*
  mix to distribute fat and lean
    components, *3*
  progressive, 152, *152*
  safety considerations, 2
Gums, 76

h

HACCP procedure, 126
Ham
  bone-in, 78, 82

Ham (*continued*)
  boneless, 82
  country-cured, 69
  dry-cured, 87, 133, 150
  in forcemeats, 150, 153
  as a garnish, 209
  molded, 87
  Parma, 87
  prosciutto, 87
  Smithfield, 87, 133
  smoked, 87, 133, 137
  spices and herbs used in, 28
Hank, 212, 218
Head cheese, 229, 280
Health department, local, 126
Healthier style of eating
  context, ix
  forcemeat, 149, 205
  frankfurters, 25
  omega-3 fatty acids, 51
  sausage, 205
  seafood, 50–51
  terrines and pâtés, 172–73, 205
  unsaturated fat, 44, 51
  use of less salt, 126
Heart, 42, 47
Hemoglobin, 42, 50
Hepatitis A virus, 64–65
Herbs. *See* Spices, herbs, and seasonings
Historical background
  brining, 79
  charcuterie, ix
  dry curing, 77
  forcemeats and terrines, 149
  galantines, 169
  ketchup, 283
  salt curing, 74, 219
  sauerkraut, 324
  sausage, 204
Hock cut, *49*
Hog
  breeds with good marbling, 204
  carcass breakdown and cuts, *48*

casings from, 212, *213*, 228, 229
  peanuts in diet, 87
Hog ring, 9–10, 218
Honey, *24*, 74, 77, 80
Hot dogs. *See* Frankfurters, hot dogs,
  and wieners
Hot sauce, 84
HRI (hotel, restaurant, and institution)
  cuts, 48
Humidity, 11, 12–13, 14, 58, 225
Hydrocolloids, 76
Hydrogen and hydrogenation, 11, 44
Hydrometer and hydrometer jar, 10

i

Ice, 164, 171, 208, 221, 223
Ice box and ice scoop, 66
Infusions, 284, 285
Ingredient list, on label, 67
Injection, 58, 72, 81
Inspections, 40, 66–67, 68, 171
Insta Cure No. 1 (Tinted Cure Mix)
  about, 29, 32, 75
  in sausage, 208, 209, 210
  use in cold-smoking, 129
Insta Cure No. 2, 29, 75, 210, *210*
Instruments, measurement, 10–13
Intestines. *See* Casings, natural
Iodine, 51
Iron, 41, 45
Irradiation, 63
Isoelectric point, 46

j

Jaggery, 24, *24*
Jasmine, 135, 137
Jellied meats, 173–74
Jerky, 58, 139
Jowl
    cut, *49*
    fat, 40, 63, 151, 164, 207–8, *208*
Juice extractions, 285–86
Juices
    fruit
        to bind pastes, 87
        in brine, 80
        grape, in sausage, 227
        lemon, 31
        in marinades, 83, 84, 85
        vegetable, 75
Juniper berry, 22

k

Kalbassi, 229
Kale, 175
Ketchup, 283
Kidneys, 19, 27, 28
Kielbasa and Polish sausage
    about, 229
    casings, 213, 229
    hot-smoking used for, 133
    poaching with cold-smoking used for,
       224
    spices and herbs used in, 21, 23, 26

Kippering, 79
Kitchen safety, 2. *See also* Food safety
Kiwi, 85
Knife, sausage maker's, 224
Knockwurst, 206, 212, 229
Knot, bubble, 220, *222*, 224
Kocuria, 69
Kosher, 73
Kramlich, W. E., 14

l

Labels, 67, *222*
Lactic acid
    bacterial cultures which produce, 69,
       73, 206, 209
    "tang" from, 27, 225, 227
Lactobacillus, 69, 73, 225
Lactones, 44
Lactose, 43, 74
Lamb
    cuts, *48*
    fat, 208
    spices and herbs used in, 19, 27, 28
    woods used for smoking, 137
Laminates, in casings, 217
Landjäger, 229
Lay-in, *153*
Leberkäse, 206, 229
Lecithin, 285
Leg cut, *48*, *49*, 105
Lemon, 28, 86, 137, 283
Lemon juice, 31
Lipid oxidation, 44, 127, 210
Lipids, 43. *See also* Fat
Listeria monocytogenes, 61–62, 65
Listeriosis. See *Listeria monocytogenes*

by sucrose, 24

by white mycelium, 69

temperature danger zone, 56, 61, 127, 130

and water activity, 13, 57–58

See also Bacteria; Molds; Parasites; Viruses; Yeasts

Middles (straight casings)

beef, 213, *213*, 228, 229

collagen casing, 215

hog, 212, 228

Milk, nonfat dry, 27, 32, 205, 209, *210*

Mint, 28, 86, 137

Mise en place, *4, 158, 160, 163, 166*

Miso, 72

Mitochondria, 41, 42

Mixers, 8–9, *9*

Moisture. *See* Water

Moisture/Protein Ratio (MPR), 58

Molasses, 24, *24*, 80

Molds (hollow forms), *148*, 149, 174, 229, 271

Molds (microorganisms)

breakdown of nitrates by, 29

on casings, 66, 215, 267

and food safety (*See* Temperature danger zone)

in sausage, 63

white mycelium, 69

Monoglyceride, 83

Monosaccharides, 43

Mortadella, *193*, 209, 213, 225, 229

Mortar and pestle, 15, 86

Mousseline. *See* Forcemeat, mousseline-style

Mouthfeel, 149, 150, 205

MPR. *See* Moisture/Protein Ratio

Muscle

cardiac, 42, 47

composition, 42–44

contraction, 42

fish, 47, 50, 52

myoglobin in (*See* Color of meat, role of myoglobin)

organization, 40, 47

percent of total body weight, 41

slow, 50

smooth, 42, 47

structure, 41–42

types, 41, 42

Muscle fiber, 41–42, 47, 50

Muscle sheath, 47

Mushrooms. *See* Truffles

Mussels, 137

Mustard

about, 18

products which use, 25, 26, 28

in sausage, 208

tarragon in, 21

Mustard seed, 23, 28

Mycelium, white, 69

Myocammata, 47, 50

Myofibrillar protein, 41–42, 45

Myoglobin

breakdown by nitric oxide, 28, 30, 31, 210

and meat color (*See* Color of meat, role of myoglobin)

Myosepta, 52

Myosin, 42, 46, 151, 164

Myotomes, 47, 50, 52

n

Neck cut, *49*

Needle, 14. *See also* Teasing needle

Nicholson, William, 10

Nitrates

decomposition and health effects, 28–29, 30, 66

pink colorant added to, 210

prevention of botulism by, 30, 61, 209

Nitrates (*continued*)

    role in sausage, 66, 209

    from vegetable products, 75

    See also Potassium nitrate; Sodium nitrate

Nitric oxide, 28, 30, 31, 74, 210

Nitrites

    and cancer, 75, 211

    decomposition and health effects, 28–29, 30, 31, 66

    to develop flavor and pink color, 72, 209

    function in cures or brines, 72, 74–75

    pink colorant added to, 210

    prevention of botulism by, 61, 72, 75

    residual, with use of potassium nitrate, 210

    See also Potassium nitrite; Sodium nitrite

Nitrogen dioxide, 65

Nitrosamine, 29, 31, 75, 211

Nitrous acid, 30

Nitrous oxide, 285

Norwalk virus, 64–65

Nozzle sizes, *8*

Nutmeg

    about, 18, 23

    products which use, 23, 26, 27, 28

    in sausage, 208

    and sense of taste, 26

    used as smoking fuel, 137

Nuts. *See* Peanuts; Pistachios

O

Oils

    to bind pastes, 87

    botulism in, 61, 284

    flavored, 21, 61, 284, 285

    in marinades, 83, 84

    in sauces, 278–79

    volatile, in spices and herbs, 208

Omega-3 fatty acids, 51

Onion

    about, 22

    in brines, 80

    in forcemeats, 151

    in jellied and pressed meats, 174

    in pastes, 87

    products which use, 22, 26, 27

Oregano, 21, 23, 28, 137

Ortophosphoric acid, 33

Osmosis, 73

Overhauling, 77

Oxidation, 30. *See also* Lipid oxidation

Oxtails, 173

Oxygen, 42, 44, 45, 50, 136

Oxymyoglobin, 45

P

Packaging

    contamination, 57, 59

    metal in recycled cardboard, 68

    pâté de foie gras, 171

    sausage, 57, 59

    smoked fish, 138

    vacuum-packed foods, 62, 138

Palm sugar, 24, *24*

Panada, *158, 160, 163*

    about, 152

    cream in, 150

    maximum percentage used in product, 155

Papain, 85

Papaya, 85

Paprika
    about, 18, 23
    as a colorant, 18, 27
    and nitrosamine formation, 75, 211
    products which use, 23, 27
    in sausage, 208
Parasites, 51, 62–63, 208
Parsley, 20, 23, 28
Paste, 87
Pastrami, 87
Pâte à choux, 152
Pâté de foie gras, 171–72
Pâté en croûte, 171, 280
Pâtés, 151, 171–73, 206, 280
Pathogens. *See* Microorganisms
Peanuts, 87, 133, 135, 137
Pectin, 57
Pediococcus, 69
Peeling agents, for casing, 215
Pellicle
    formation, 127, *128*, 129, 133, 225
    smoke adherence to, 220
Pepper
    alcohol to eliminate heat, 18
    avoid preground, 86
    black, 18, 23, 26, 27
    cayenne, 23
    and nitrosamine formation, 75, 211
    red, 18, 26, 27
    in sausage, 208
    white, 18, 23, 27
Peppercorns, 23, 27, 28, 80, 86
Pepperoni, 20, 22, 58, 206, 226
Perimysium, 47
Pesto, 21
pH
    to control *Clostridium*, 65
    decrease by lactic acid bacteria, 69, 206
    definition, 11
    elevation with alkaline phosphate salts, 33
    marinade, 85
    and water retention, 46

    See also Acidity; Alkalinity
Phenolic compounds, 127
pH meter, 10–11
Phosphates
    about, 31, 32
    in cures or brines, 76, 81
    increase in water retention due to, 31, 45
    in lipids, 43
    and solubility of protein, 31, 46
    See also Sodium acid pyrophosphate; Sodium phosphate; Sodium tripolyphosphate
Phospholipids, 43
Pickles, 287
Pickling solution, 72, 123, 287
Pickling spices, 22, 80, 287
Picnic cut, *49*
Pigments. *See* Carotenoids; Memyoglobin; Myoglobin; Oxymyoglobin
Pineapple, 85
Piping bag, 224
Pistachios, 153, 175, 180, 209
Plastic
    casings, 216–17
    wrap
        for galantine, 169, *170, 171*
        to line terrine mold, 150, *177–78*
        saran for sausage casing, 213
Plate, of a grinder, *3, 7, 8, 152*
    maintenance, 7
    procedure, 2, 7
Plate, press, *178*
Plate cut, *48*
Pliers, hog ring, 10, 218
Plum Powder, 205
Poaching liquid, 21, 245, 286
Poaching process, 225
Polish sausage. *See* Kielbasa and Polish sausage
Polysaccharides, 43
Polysorbate-80, 83

Pork
  certified
    dry uncooked sausages, 267, 268,
      269, 271
    fermented sausages, 227, 263, 266
    labeling, 227
    via freezing, 63, 227
  cuts, *48*
  parasites, 59, 62–63
  spices and herbs used in, 19, 27, 28
  woods used for smoking, 137, 253
Pork belly, 40, 78
Pork butt, 82, 87
Pork fatback, 150, 151, 164, *177–78*,
  180
Pork loin, 82
Potassium nitrate (saltpeter)
  about, 30, 32, 210–11
  acceptable maximum level, 66
  to preserve meat, 29, 30, 209
Potassium nitrite, 66
Potassium sorbate, 63
Potatoes, 76, 152, 205
Poultry, 130, 133, 137. *See also* Chicken;
  Duck; Turkey
Prague powder, 32, 75, 210. *See also*
  Insta Cure No. 1; Insta Cure No. 2
Preservatives. *See* Microorganisms,
  prevention of growth
Pressed meats, 173
Press plate, *178*
Primal cuts, 48, *48–49*
Propylene glycol, 211
Propylparaben, 63
Prosciutto, 87, 150
Proteases, 42, 85
Protein
  about, 42–43
  ascorbic acid to prevent oxidation, 30
  coagulated, 130
  degradation process and nitrosamine
    formation, 29
  denatured, 85, 130
  during emulsification process, 46
  as food source, 41
  during gelation, 46
  hydrolyzed, 26
  in milk, 30
  in mustard, 18
  percent in lean red meat, 41
  percent in muscle, 45
  percent in mustard, 18
  protein-lined casings, 217
  solubilization (extraction), 31, 46,
    208, 221
  soy, 33, 76, 210
  structure, 40, 46, 85
  types, 41, 42
Pudding, black, 212
Pumping process for brine, 14, 80–81, *82*
Purées, 278
Pyrophosphoric acid, 33

r

Rack cut, *48, 49*
Ragoût, ix
Rancidity. *See* Lipid oxidation
Rapp, Henry, 205
Recommended stuffing diameter (RSD),
  214
Record keeping. *See* Documentation
Reductions, 278, 285
Refrigeration, 13–14, 56, 59. *See also*
  Freezing
Regional cuisine, 204
Regulations
  fat, maximum percentage, 164
  nitrate, maximum level, 66
  nitrite, maximum level, 66, 75, 211
  pork cooking standards, 62–63, 130
  poultry cooking standards, 130

Relative humidity, 11, 58, 225
Relish, 286
Rempah, 86
Resins, 208, 217
Resources, 332–33
Rib cut, *48*
Rice, 152, 205, 207
Rigor mortis, 42
Rings, hog, 9–10, 218
Robot Coupe food processor, 8
Rosemary
    in cures or brines, 72
    decrease in lipid oxidation due to, 44
    in marinades, 84
    products which use, 28
    in sausage, 208
    used as smoking fuel, 137
Round cut, *48*
Rounds (curved casings), 110, 213, *213*, 215, 229
RSD. *See* Recommended stuffing diameter
Rubs, 72, 86–87

S

Saddles, 48, *48–49*
Safety considerations. *See* Food safety; Kitchen safety
Saffron, 28
Sage
    about, 20
    in marinades, 84
    products which use, 20, 23, 27, 28
    in sausage, 208
Salami
    about, 229
    casings, 213, 229

    cotto (cooked), 23, 27, 214
    Genoa, 227
    hard, 206
    Italian, 69
    production, 224
    USDA classification, 206
Salimeter, 10
Salmon, 79, 130, 136, 137
Salmonella enteritidis, 59
Salsa, 283–84
Salt, *210*
    about, 32
    alkaline phosphate, 33
    as an emulsifier, 32, 223
    to bind forcemeat, 164
    in brines, 72–73, 79, 81
    concentration used, 32
    to control microorganisms
        about, 208
        Clostridium, 57
        in forcemeat, 164
        historical background, 204
        parasites, 32, 63
        Salmonella, 59
    corns (pellets), 77
    curing, 57, 72–73, 77, 208, 210
    garlic, 20
    harshness decreased with dextrose, 32, 209
    increase in lipid oxidation due to, 44
    increase in water retention due to, 45, 57
    kosher, 73
    in pickling solution, 287
    in sausage, 208, *208*
    smoked, 93
    sweetener-to-salt ratio in dry cure, 78
    table, 73
    types used in cures or brines, 73
    unrefined, 73
    water as dispersing medium, 33
    See also specific salts
Saltpeter. *See* Potassium nitrate
Sanitation, 54–69

t

Teasing needle, 15, *222*, 224

Temperature danger zone, 56, 61, 127, 130

Tenderizers, 81, 83, 84, 85, 87

Tenderloin cut, *48*

Tendon, 42

Terrines
  examples, *172*
  fat for lining, 150
  healthier, 172–73, 205
  molds, *148*, 149
  spices and herbs used in, 21, 22, 23
  USDA classification, 206

Tester, taste, 154, *154*, 221, 223

Tetrasodium pyrophosphate, 33

Texture
  of casings, 212, 214
  of meat
    additives which enhance, 30
    carbohydrates and firmness, 43
    crustaceans and cooking technique, 52
    effects of emulsification of fat, 46
    and fatty acid composition, 44
    forcemeat, 150, *160, 163, 166*
    mushy, 85, 206
    tenderizers, 81, 83, 84, 85, 87
    and type of muscle, 47
    and water retention, 45
  of sauce, 278

Thermocouple, 12, 58

Thermometer, 11–12

Thickeners, 30, 285

Thyme, 21, 28, 72, 208

Tinted Cure Mix (TCM), 29, 32, 75, 210. *See also* Insta Cure No. 1

Tofu, 205

Tongue
  in galantines, 180
  as a garnish, 153, 209
  in loaves, *193*
  spices and herbs used in, 19, 27, 28

Traiteur, ix

Trichinella spiralis, 59, 62–63, 208, 227

Trichinosis. *See Trichinella spiralis*

Triglycerides, 43

Tripe, ix, 19, 27, 28

Tripier, ix

Tropomysin, 42

Trout, 79

Truffles, 22, 153, 171, 180

Tub, brine, 14

Tumbler, 15, 72

Turbinado sugar, 24, *24*

Turkey, *81*, 82, 133, 137, 259

Turmeric, 208

Twine, *222*, 224

u

U.S. Code of Federal Regulations, 62–63. *See also* Regulations

U.S. Department of Agriculture (USDA)
  nitrate/nitrite regulation, 29, 66
  saltpeter regulation, 32, 210
  sausage classification, 206
  web site, 332
  See also U.S. Code of Federal Regulations

U.S. Food and Drug Administration (FDA), 25, 29

USDA. *See* U.S. Department of Agriculture

V

Vacuum packing, 62
Veal, 19, 27, 28
Vegetables
    beet juice, 75, 286
    celery juice, 75
    in chutneys, 286
    in oil or vinegar infusions, 284, 285
    pickled, 287
    purée as an emulsifier, 278
    in relishes, 286
    in sauces, 280, 283, 284, 285, 286
    starches from, 76
    terrine, 173, 175
    woods used for smoking, 137
    See also specific vegetables
Vibrio cholerae, 64–65
Vibrio parahaemolyticus, 64–65
Vibrio vulnificus, 64–65
Vinaigrettes, 278
Vinegars, 83, 84, 85, 284, 285
Viruses, 51, 57, 64–65
Viscose process, 215
Vitamin C. *See* Ascorbic acid

W

Water
    additives to bind, 57, 76
    in brines, 76, 268
    contaminated, 64
    function in meat products, 33
    to lubricate sausage-stuffing table, 9,
        223
    in marinades, 85
    Moisture/Protein Ratio, 58
    percent in lean red meat, 41
    percent in muscle, 45
    percent lost during curing, 90, 97,
        104, 225–26
    removal from meat
        by acidity, 69
        by nitrates/nitrites, 28, 30
        purge (water cooked out), 31
        by salt, 72, 73, 164, 208
        by smoking, 125, 130
    retention in meat
        about, 45–46
        increase by corn syrup, 25
        increase by higher pH, 46
        increase by phosphates, 31, 33, 45,
            81
        increase by salt, 45
        increase by starch, 76
        water weight regulations, 208
    in sausages, 208, *208*
    for sausages during and after
        smoking, 14–15
    to store pH probe, 11
    to store wet-bulb thermometer, 12
    vapor pressure, 12
    weight of one pint, 155
    See also Ice
Water activity (aw), 12, 13, 57–58, 65
Water movement meter, 12–13
Water Phase Salt (WPS), 65, 136
Waxes, 43
Web sites, 332–33
Weisswurt, 23, 229
Wet cure process. *See* Brining process
Wieners. *See* Frankfurters, hot dogs, and
    wieners
Wine
    to bind pastes, 87
    in forcemeats, 151

recipe index

Page numbers in *italic* indicate photographs.

a

Adobo Sauce, 290
Alcohol. *See* Wine; *specific liquors*
Allspice, in Blood Sausage, *238*, 239
Amish Bologna (variation), 257
Anise seeds, in Spicy Duck Capacolla, 110
Appetizers, Spanish Chorizo, *264*, 265–66
Apple(s)
    and Banana Chutney, *276*, 311
    and Fennel Salad, 331
    and Horseradish Cream, 295
    Lady, Pickled, 321
    Little Pickled, 320
    in Plain Chutney, 309
    Sausage, Smoked Turkey and Dried, 249
Applejack-Brandied Cherry Coulis, 288
Applesauce
    Breakfast Sausage with, 231, *231*
    Cinnamon-Rum, 291
Asiago, Chicken Sausage with Mushrooms and
    about, 205
    recipe, 246
Asian-Style Rub, 88

b

Bacon
    Dry-Rub Barbecued, 93
    Duck Breast, 98
    Maple-Cured, 92
    recipe, 90, *91*
Balsamic Herbal Marinade, 112
Banana, Chutney, Apple and, *276*, 311
Barley, in Blood Sausage, *238*, 239
Basic Bologna, 256–57
Basil
    in Balsamic Herbal Marinade, 112
    in Italian Sausage with Roasted Peppers, *232*, 233
    Marinade, 113
    in Tuscan Sausage, 240
Bavarian Loaf, 189
Bay leaves
    in Cotechino, 272–73
    in Dry-Cured Pancetta, 94, *95*
Beef (meat)
    Basic Bologna, 256–57
    brined, spiced, smoked (*See* Pastrami)
    Daube, Créole, 197
Beef bottom round, Corned Beef (variation), 120
Beef brisket
    Corned Beef, 120
    Pastrami, *118*, 119
Beef eye round, Bresaola, 96

C

Tête Pressée (Rolled Pressed Pig's Head),
     198, *199*
Tomato
     in Corn Salsa, 318
     Ketchup, 313
     in Peach Ketchup, 315
     in Tuscan Sausage, 240
Tripe
     in Blood Sausage, *238, 239*
     in Liverwurst, 254
Tropical Relish, 308
Trout, Smoked Dry-Cured Fish (variation), 142
Turkey
     Frankfurters, 258–59
     Pâté de Campagne (variation), 181
     Smoked, and Dried Apple Sausage, 249
Tuscan Sausage, 240

V

Vanilla bean, in Cotechino, 272–73
Veal
     in Créole Beef Daube, 197
     and Mushroom Sausage, 252–53
     Weisswurst (variation), 245
Vegetables
     in Chicken Sausage with Mushrooms and
          Asiago
          about, 205
          recipe, 246
     Chilled Emincé of Chicken and, *172,* 196
     garnish, in Veal and Mushroom Sausage,
          252–53
     Savory Autumn Relish, 306
     Sweet Mixed Pickle Chow Chow, *276,* 326
     See also specific vegetables
Venison
     Jerky (variation), 139

Jerky, Dry-Cured (variation), 141
Vermouth
     in Calabrese Salami, 267
     in Maple Brine for Poultry, 117
Vinaigrette Dressing, 293
Vinegar
     in Balsamic Herbal Marinade, 112
     in Vinaigrette Dressing, 293

W

Walnut Sauce, Garlic and, 303
Watermelon Rind, Spiced, *276,* 328
Weisswurst (Munich Sausage), 245
Whitefish, Smoked Dry-Cured Fish, 142
Wieners. *See* Frankfurters
Wild rice
     Sausage, Wisconsin-Style Smoked, 262
     Smoked Pheasant Sausage with, 250
Wine
     in Cotechino, 272–73
     in Honey-Brined Duck, 121
     in Lamb and Pine Nut Sausage, 242
     in Tuscan Sausage, 240
Wisconsin-Style Smoked Cheddar and
     Jalapeño Sausage, 260–61
Wisconsin-Style Smoked Wild Rice Sausage,
     262

Z

Zambone (variation), 273
Zesty Cranberry Ketchup, *276,* 315